Counseling Children and Adolescents in Schools

We dedicate this text to two groups
of students with whom we have been privileged to work.

First, to the elementary, middle, and high school students who attend school
each day despite obstacles and challenges. Their determination and resolve to
overcome those challenges and fulfill their dreams continues to inspire us.

And, to the courageous school counselors-in-training
and school psychologists-in-training who have embraced excellence.
We are humbled by your accomplishments. It is you who will continue
to shape the future of our professions and become the champions
who advocate on behalf of your students.

Counseling Children and Adolescents in Schools

Robyn S. Hess
University of Northern Colorado

∎

Sandy Magnuson
*Retired Counselor Educator and
Elementary School Counselor*

∎

Linda Beeler
Capella University

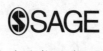

Los Angeles | London | New Delhi
Singapore | Washington DC

Los Angeles | London | New Delhi
Singapore | Washington DC

FOR INFORMATION:

SAGE Publications, Inc.
2455 Teller Road
Thousand Oaks, California 91320
E-mail: order@sagepub.com

SAGE Publications Ltd.
1 Oliver's Yard
55 City Road
London EC1Y 1SP
United Kingdom

SAGE Publications India Pvt. Ltd.
B 1/I 1 Mohan Cooperative Industrial Area
Mathura Road, New Delhi 110 044
India

SAGE Publications Asia-Pacific Pte. Ltd.
33 Pekin Street #02-01
Far East Square
Singapore 048763

Acquisitions Editor: Kassie Graves
Editorial Assistant: Courtney Munz
Production Editor: Karen Wiley
Copy Editor: Mark Bast
Typesetter: C&M Digitals (P) Ltd.
Proofreader: Annie Lubinsky
Indexer: Molly Hall
Cover Designer: Katie Winters
Marketing Manager: Katie Winter
Permissions Editor: Adele Hutchinson

Printed in the United States of America

Library of Congress Cataloging-in-Publication Data

Hess, Robyn.

Counseling children and adolescents in schools / Robyn Hess, Sandy Magnuson, Linda Beeler.

p. cm.
Includes bibliographical references and index.

ISBN 978-1-4129-9087-5 (pbk.)

1. Educational counseling. 2. Counseling in elementary education. 3. Counseling in secondary education. 4. Action research in education.
I. Magnuson, Sandy. II. Beeler, Linda. III. Title.

LB1027.5.H48 2012
371.4'22—dc23   2011033240

This book is printed on acid-free paper.

11 12 13 14 15 10 9 8 7 6 5 4 3 2 1

Contents

Preface

As is likely the case for many textbook authors, our desire to write this text grew from our frustration in finding "just the right book" for our counseling field experience courses. There are so many issues to cover in any type of field experience, especially in a school setting. Do we focus on the basic skills, or do we need to help our students operate from a theoretical orientation from the beginning? How do we help students generalize their skills to the school setting? With the current emphasis on evidence-based practice, should we only teach manualized therapies? How do we help our students navigate the complexities of the school system?

Given these many questions, we returned to our basic beliefs. No matter one's theoretical orientation, we believe the counseling relationship is the basis for effective helping be it consulting with a parent, sitting with an adolescent who has lost a loved one, or helping a child who is struggling with homework completion. Basic skills facilitate the development of this relationship and also assist in the collaboration and team building that is a part of school-based practitioners' roles. We have operated from this premise in our work in the schools and have communicated this belief to the hundreds of students that we have taught over the years. One of the key aspects of building a relationship is getting to know the other person; therefore we offer the following brief introductions.

I (R.S.H.) originally trained as a counselor but then switched to the field of school psychology where I earned my doctorate. I wanted to be able to intervene with younger populations because I recognized that many of the difficulties experienced by adult populations could have been prevented with appropriate, early services. As a school psychologist, I have worked with all levels of students, from preschool to high school, and am particularly partial to young adolescents. I love the ways that these youth struggle to find themselves by exploring different possibilities around who and what they will be. My theoretical orientation is cognitive-behavioral, although I believe that the foundation of any therapeutic interaction is the relationship. Although I enjoy counseling and see it as an important tool for the schools, more and more I am drawn to systemic interventions as there is no way to meet the needs of all students by only working with one at a time. I have taught the counseling practicum since 2004.

I (S.M.) obtained my master's degree in elementary school counseling. My primary experience related to play therapy; however, my first counseling position was at a private women's college where I was a counselor in residence. After one year as a K–12 school counselor, I began advanced training in couples and family therapy. Several years later, I saw the synergistic value of the two areas of specialization when I designed and implemented a comprehensive school counseling program at an elementary laboratory school that was affiliated with a counselor education program at a regional university. Although my primary theoretical preferences follow Alfred Adler and Murray Bowen, I am committed to the work and essential philosophy of Carl Rogers. Because I have retired, let me say I have taught practicum and advanced practicum many times!

I (L.B.) have worked mostly with at-risk adolescents, in one form or another, my entire career. Whether as a teacher, a community mental health worker, a school-based intervention specialist, or a licensed school counselor, the joy and challenge of the work has inspired me. I am a true believer in the power of the therapeutic relationship and have witnessed firsthand the astonishment adolescents express when they feel like someone finally "gets it." In a school setting, the work I do necessitates and fits well with a brief solution-focused approach. However, I always rely on my person-centered approach to build the relationship first. Carl Rogers believed, as do I, that people naturally grow toward self-actualization if the core therapeutic conditions are present. I have been teaching school counseling pre-practicum, practicum, and internship for the last two years and enjoy it tremendously.

We developed this text and an accompanying *Practice and Application Guide* to allow instructors the greatest level of flexibility in using these materials. Early on, we recognized that training programs had many different ways for organizing the presentation of this material. Some offered a course in basic skills separate from the school-based practicum, while others incorporated this material directly into that initial practicum. The accompanying guide is designed to assist the pre-service professional in learning and/or reviewing the microskills of counseling as applied to children and adolescents. We end each chapter with different types of activities to facilitate reflection, additional resources, and extended learning opportunities.

We have organized the text into four distinct sections. The first section sets the stage for helping the school-based professional learn the broad context of the school setting and how to adapt one's skills to work within the overlapping systems of the school, family, and community. Additionally, we present an overview of child and adolescent development. In Section II, we focus on the most common therapeutic orientations used in the schools. We start this section with two case illustrations that present typical issues experienced by an elementary-aged male and a female student who is in high school. Using these cases as a foundation, we present the application of different theoretical models and strategies. We have emphasized Adlerian theory, cognitive-behavioral therapy, solution-focused therapy, and reality therapy because these models represent a short-term, structured approach that is well suited for use with children and adolescents in school settings. In Section III, we discuss ways to move theory into practice by providing information on different techniques and modalities that can be incorporated into the counseling relationship (e.g., play, art, games). Use of group models allows student clients to learn from one another and is an efficient and effective method of service delivery. It is also in this section that we have included a chapter on responding to crisis as that has become an all too common role for the school-based professional.

We had two intentions in mind when we developed Sections II and III. The first was to provide pre-service professionals with a clearer understanding of how to apply the theory and techniques of commonly used models. The second was to help them consider how they might need to modify these counseling strategies and theories when working with children of different ages and how development plays a role in their therapeutic interventions.

The decision regarding which theories to present was not an easy one. We looked for ones that were generally brief, well suited to younger populations, empirically supported, and most commonly used in school settings. Our intention was not to dismiss the use of other therapeutic interventions with children, only to deepen the presentation of the selected theories. We view the most therapeutic approach as one that incorporates the presenting issue, age of the client, and the context. Because these components vary widely, we contend that it is important that individuals be prepared in more than one theoretical orientation or modality.

In the final section of this book, we turn our attention to family, school, and community systems. It is our belief that children and adolescents are best understood within the contexts in which they live and learn. We review legal and ethical issues of school-based practice and provide strategies for developing mental health teams that meet the broadest needs as well as those of special populations. In these final chapters, we describe how the different mental health providers within schools and communities can work together through consultation and collaboration to create a continuum of care for students and their families. Additionally, we discuss strategies for evaluating the effectiveness of those services.

One unique feature of this text is that it is written with school counselors and school psychologists in mind. As colleagues, we (S.M. and R.S.H.) frequently discussed the ways that our three fields were both similar and different. Ultimately, we decided that the specific discipline of the school-based practitioner was not as important as the effectiveness of the services provided. Professionals with specialized training in mental health are needed now more than ever to help children and their families to cope with the stress in their lives, to overcome mental health difficulties, and to attain the highest level of competence in their interpersonal interactions.

We recognize that school social workers are also school-based professional helpers and introduce their role in Chapters 1 and 14. However, we have not included them in our vignettes or case studies. Since we were not trained from that perspective, we were hesitant to speak for this group. Members in each of these disciplines may hold differing perspectives on their roles and methods for intervening, but each fills a critical role in schools. It is our hope that we have written an inclusive text that helps pre-service professionals who are preparing to become school-based helpers to improve their practice with children, adolescents, and their families, as well as to learn and value the different ways that they can work together to create a network of services.

Acknowledgments

Throughout our process of writing *Counseling Children and Adolescents in Schools*, we have valued the support and encouragement of many individuals. Kassie Graves and Courtney Munz have consistently, cheerfully, and promptly responded to the many tedious questions we asked. Mark Bast meticulously copyedited the text and patiently guided us through our roles in the final production processes. We also acknowledge the tenacity of colleagues across the country who reviewed drafts of the document and shared insightful, practical, and useful suggestions: Natasha K. Segool at the University of Hartford, Bridget Roberts-Pittman at Indiana State University, Michelle M. Perfect at the University of Arizona, Linda Caterino at Arizona State University, Kathy DeOrnellas at Texas Woman's University, Wanda L. Staley at Morehead State University, Paul Jantz at Idaho State University, Darren E. Dobrinski at Minot State University, Patricia Robey at Governers State University, and Brett Zyromski at Southern Illinois State University. Additionally, our thanks go to Kathy Sanchez, Kenya Jones-Brown, Rachael Leavitt, and Liana Smith, graduate students at the University of Northern Colorado. Their creativity and knowledge of technology helped immensely as we entered the home stretch.

Robyn: I would like to thank the many students who have inspired me to write this book in the first place. Your questions, concerns, and experiences related to school-based practice helped me to recognize the need for this text. My coauthors, Linda and Sandy, helped to make this project fun with their unfailing positive attitudes and their ability to help me bridge the fields of school psychology and school counseling. Since the beginning of this project, Sandy has been an ongoing source of support who helped me find my voice as a writer. Finally, I would like to express my deep love and appreciation to Dr. Robert Walch.

Sandy: My contributions to *Counseling Children and Adolescents in Schools* were significantly influenced by four extraordinary counselor educators: Dr. Bill Rippee and Dr. Shirley Hendricks who taught at Southwest Missouri State University (now Missouri Southern University), Dr. Allen Wilcoxon who continues to teach at the University of Alabama, and Dr. Ken Norem who is also my life partner. You shaped my career as a counselor, professor, supervisor, and author through your instruction, example, and encouragement. You became and remain my personal and professional mentors, and I can't thank you enough. And, thanks to Robyn and Linda. I am looking forward to reading what you write next!

Linda: I would like to recognize the many students with whom I have worked. They have challenged and taught me and have proven over and over again that most kids just need to know that someone "gets" them. I would like to thank K. G. Campanella-Green for her tutelage in "all things crisis." That coupled with many years serving on the St. Vrain Valley School District Trauma Response teams prepared me to contribute to the chapter on crisis response. I am honored and humbled to be a part of this *Counseling Children and Adolescents in Schools* project and would like to express my gratitude to Robyn and Sandy for inviting me to join their team. Finally, to Dr. B. V. Andrews, thank you for your unwavering support and for being the one who "gets" me.

SECTION I

Introduction to Section I

It is easier to build strong children than to repair broken men.

Frederick Douglass

This first section focuses on using the skills you have learned in your previous counseling classes and applying them to a school setting. In order to do so, you must first understand the broad context of schools and the role of support services in the schools. A second foundational piece is to better understand children's development and the ways that counseling skills must be modified to meet the needs of your youngest students. As a school-based helper, you will be an important person in the lives of children. The relationship you build provides a healthy model for students who encounter difficult issues in their school or home settings. To build this relationship, you must be able to utilize basic skills that facilitate the development of this relationship and allow a young person to trust the change process. In order to use your skills effectively, you must be able to phrase your comments in a way that can be understood by an eight-year-old or that is meaningful to a 17-year-old. The process begins with building a working relationship and continues to the point when a student is ready to conclude the relationship and use his or her new skills independently.

This text was designed to accompany your school-based field experience. We wrote this first section, and other chapters in this book, assuming that you have had coursework in human development, counseling theories, and legal and ethical issues prior to your enrollment in this class. Although we will present information on each of these topics, detailed coverage of these components is beyond the scope of this text. Instead, we place our emphasis on modification of counseling strategies and theories when working with children of different ages and consideration of development in selecting therapeutic interventions.

One of the ways to frame this section is to consider a "typical day" in the life of a school-based professional. One of the joys *and* the frustrations of the school setting is that every day is different; there is no typical day. On the plus side, it is challenging, fun, and rarely boring. On the down side, some days there are just too many things to do; although you have worked tirelessly all day, it is difficult to point to any one thing that you accomplished. The following excerpts reflect a "typical day" for an elementary school counselor, a secondary school counselor, and a school psychologist. They are presented to provide you a beginning context for understanding your role in the school setting. They also highlight some of the similarities and differences between elementary and secondary practice as well as between the different disciplines.

Typical Day for an Elementary School Counselor (S.M.)

The worst-case scenario was often when I arrived at work with a relatively unscheduled day. On these days, I casually sat at my desk to sip coffee and thoughtfully respond to e-mail. I often returned to my office later in the day to find the e-mail I started at 7:30 a.m. on the monitor, waiting to be finished, or waiting to have the send button pushed. Here are my notes from one day:

7:40:   Check in/Check out students are knocking on the door. While I'm getting their daily agreements prepared, several girls arrive at the door. "Miss Sandy, we need to talk to you." Their faces tell me it is serious.

          Serious indeed. Another fifth-grade student has told them she was planning to commit suicide.

8:00:   I consult with the school nurse, who is always an essential confidant. We decide I should call the student's mother. She does not answer the phone. I persist in calling. When I reach her, she seems to dismiss my concern. "She's just trying to get attention." I send an e-mail to the administration.

9:28:   I grab my materials for a 9:30 lesson.

10:00:   As I walk back to my office, a teacher stops me in the hall. "Sandy, Teddy's behavior is getting worse. You have to do something."

10:45: I pick up a child for individual counseling. I leave the sand tray assembled and put it on the tall cabinet. While I am trying to capture the intense session in my notes, the phone rings. "Sandy, can you come to the office?"

11:45: The girls' lunch group members arrive, and I quickly clean the table.

12:30: I discuss the morning situation with the administrator and begin making phone calls to gather more information. I call the parents of one of the reporting students and request permission to share information that was given to me. "If it's okay with Joan, it's okay with me." I find Joan and request her permission.

12:55: Oh, no! I forgot my 12:45 check on a first grade student who is doing Check in/Check out.

1:00: I walk into a classroom to facilitate their weekly class meeting.

1:30: I return to my office. Oh my! Messages. E-mails.

1:55: I pick up a child for individual counseling. While I'm in the hall, a child asks, "Miss Sandy, when are you going to come get me?"

2:40: I barely make it to a class. What am I doing today? Oh yes. Telling a story. Enthusiasm, Sandy.

3:15: Check in/Check out kids are waiting for me when I return. "Can I figure out my own score?" (My thought: I can do it so much faster!)

3:35: The phone rings. It is a call from Joan's mother. She has more information.

"Sorry, guys. You'll have to go now. I need to take this call."

"We'll be quiet."

"It's one that is private. Night! See you tomorrow morning!"

Typical Day for a Secondary School Counselor (L.B.)

Arrive at school by 7:00 a.m.

A parent is waiting in the office to speak to me about his student's calculus teacher, asking for a schedule change.

As I unlock my office and turn on the computer to look at the requested change, I see a note taped to my door. The note is from a student pleading for me to come get

(Continued)

(Continued)

her out of first period (before she dresses out for PE) because she really needs to talk to me about our last session, during which we discussed "cutting."

The phone rings, and I let it go to voice mail.

The bell rings, and my computer is finally up and running. I speak to the parent about the difficulties of changing a schedule this late in the semester, and note that the requested change would throw off the entire schedule, because his son is taking several courses (like AP physics or Shakespeare) that are only offered once during the day.

The phone rings again, and I let it go to voice mail.

The assistant principal, with a student beside her, leans into my office and asks if I could please speak to this ninth-grade student about her poor attendance.

The phone rings, and I let it go to voice mail.

After talking with the student for 20 minutes and determining that she and her family need some additional resources, I walk the student to her class. This is the only way to ensure she actually arrives there!

I stop by the gym to see if the student who left the note on my door is in class. She is, but she refuses to speak with me because I had not gotten her before she dressed out. I tell her I'll check in with her later.

I stop by the room of the calculus teacher and let her know I have, at the parent's request, switched a student out of her class. She is upset and informs me that she had already spoken to the student and the parent about ways to make the rest of the semester manageable and successful.

As I return to my office, I ask a few students who are hanging out in the halls for their passes allowing them to be out of class. They do not have passes, so I escort them to class.

I check my e-mail and begin to read some of the 20+ messages that have come in since I left at 5:00 p.m. the day before. I have three minutes before the Student Study Team meeting and need to check my inbox for the still-missing evaluation forms from teachers, which we will discuss at the meeting.

The phone rings, and I let it go to voice mail.

After collecting the forms from the printer, I run to my meeting. We discuss four students and determine what things can be done to help these students become more successful at school. These plans range from additional follow-up with teachers, to securing a Release of Information from parents to speak with their student's therapist, to forming a group from which this student could benefit. I return to my office and begin to follow up on these tasks.

The phone rings, and I pick it up. The parent on the line is very angry. She states that she has called seven times and left messages and is wondering why no one has bothered to call her back.

The bell rings, and first period is over. Only three more to go!

Typical Day for a School Psychologist (R.S.H.)

The day starts with an early morning staffing to determine whether a child will qualify for special education services. Although his mother wants him to get help, the idea of her son needing special help makes her tearful. I check with her about her concerns and whether she would like to have the meeting on another day. She puts on a brave face and asks that we continue. After close to two hours, the meeting comes to a conclusion, and the parent seems to feel better about the services her son will receive.

I look at the tasks that I have planned for the day. I need to complete a couple of observations, I would like to get started testing a student, and today is the day I have my social skills group with five students from the intensive learning support. In the afternoon, I have a problem-solving team meeting, and I need to review a student's data in order to be ready for the meeting. Because my morning meeting ran longer than usual, I have only 15 minutes to get down to the kindergarten room to observe the new student. His teacher is worried because he is aggressive with other students, and he becomes extremely angry whenever he perceives something to be unfair or that another child has slighted him. During the few minutes of watching him, it is clear that he is very bright and very angry. He is able to answer all of the questions that the teacher asks the class, although he shouts out the answer rather than raising his hand. When seated in a group activity, he and a neighboring child exchange barbs about the quality of each other's drawing. Although I don't see an angry explosion, it is clear that I need more information about this student and make a note to myself to call his mother, to connect with the school psychologist at his old school, and to review his cumulative file.

(Continued)

(Continued)

Off to the first-grade room to follow up on another student who has been having behavioral outbursts and is now on a behavior plan. He appears to be having a good morning. After spending a few minutes in the room, it becomes clear that the behavior plan is not being implemented. I set an appointment with the first-grade teacher during her planning period in the afternoon to see whether we can modify the plan so that she can use it more easily.

Back in my office, I receive a phone call from a worried parent who states that her son was acting strangely last night and that she is worried about him. She wonders if I can talk to him to see if something is bothering him. I decide that the best time to talk to him will be in about a half hour, when the fifth-grade literacy block ends. In the meantime, I'll try to return some e-mails, make a few phone calls, and figure out a new plan for the rest of my day since I have added more to my to-do list.

CHAPTER 1

What Is So Special About Counseling in the Schools?

Learning Objectives

- Understand some of the distinctive features of providing counseling services in the schools
- Identify the position of your professional organization toward the practice of counseling in the schools, as well as the different school-based helpers who provide this service
- Develop an understanding of the role of counseling within the broad context of service delivery in the schools

Your first school-based field experience is likely to be different from any other course you have had thus far in your academic career. Not only will you continue to advance your skills in counseling, but you will be asked to do so in a dynamic, challenging school environment. In order to be successful, you will need to use your cognitive skills to conceptualize, categorize, and memorize new information and apply it to this unique setting, while engaging in the more personal and emotional levels of processing that are a critical component of practicum and internship.

THE CONTEXT OF SCHOOL

Schools are dynamic, complex, challenging, and fun. As a school-based professional helper, your role will be to advocate for children and to help create learning environments that are safe, caring, and supportive. Conversely, the adults with whom you will work (i.e., teachers, principals, and parents) are facing greater challenges because of limited resources and the push for greater achievement. Sometimes the drive for academic achievement seems to take precedence over the social and emotional needs of children. In this type of climate, those who provide support services and advocate for the emotional needs of students may feel as if their area of expertise is given a backseat to academic goals. In fact, these contrasting priorities create an underlying tension; therefore, it is helpful to consider the broader context in which you will practice. In the following chapter, we provide more detailed information on the general nature of school-based counseling. We discuss how it fits within a tiered model of service delivery to promote positive youth resiliency and address the mental health needs of students.

On any given day in the school setting, you will have the opportunity to positively impact hundreds of lives. To those of you who are just beginning your careers, this statement is energizing, powerful, and—frightening. It communicates the seriousness of the role of a school-based helper, and it implies a high level of responsibility. Fortunately, you are not expected to carry out every program and intervention on your own. You will have the chance to work with a talented team of professionals (e.g., teachers, administrators, and other mental health staff) to enact prevention and intervention programming that makes a difference in students' lives. As we introduce and discuss the various school-based helpers throughout this text, it is important that we begin with a consideration of our terminology.

A WORD ABOUT WORDS

We have a novel task in attempting to write a book about counseling for preservice professionals who are studying to be school counselors, school psychologists, or perhaps school social workers. The mental health needs of children are so great, and the important contributions made by representatives of each of these fields are unique. Thus, an important goal in writing this book was to highlight the similarities, the differences, and the many ways that those who address the social, emotional, and behavioral needs of students can work together and with others to create seamless systems of support for children, adolescents, and families.

One of our greatest challenges was deciding on a term to address our readers that would be inclusive of individuals in the different professional tracks but would not be such a mouthful that no one would ever use it. Although we liked the term *school-based professional helper*, throughout the text we have sometimes shortened it to *professional, school-based professional, professional helper*, or some other variation. Additionally, we sometimes simply refer to the specific discipline (e.g., school psychologist). We also realized that the term *students* could refer to individuals in K–12 settings or to our readers, who are students in graduate school. To avoid such confusion, we use the term *students* when we are referring to K–12 students overall. We use the term *student client* when referring to a student with whom a professional helper is actively working versus other students in the school. Finally, we address our audience of graduate students as *pre-service professionals.*

As we were writing, we found that we used different words for similar concepts. From a school psychology perspective, *psychoeducational group* would be the term used to refer to any group that focuses on teaching skills (e.g., social skills, problem solving) to a group of students. The same activity might be considered a curriculum activity from a school counseling perspective. Due to the different histories and emphases in our respective fields, we have developed unique terminology for similar activities. We have used these terms broadly and interchangeably, with clear description, to provide clarity and recognition of the different disciplines. Another important clarification is needed in relation to "counseling." We provide a working definition for this term and describe its application in a school setting.

School-Based Counseling Versus Psychotherapy

There are many terms to define the act of helping an individual overcome barriers and maximize growth (e.g., *counseling, coaching, helping*). Additionally, the names for the individuals who provide these services (e.g., *counselor, psychotherapist, helper*) and the recipients of these services (e.g., *student, client, helpee*) vary based on theoretical models, definitions of counseling, and context (e.g., school, clinic). Some make a firm distinction between the practices of counseling and psychotherapy (Nystul, 2003), while others suggest that this distinction may be superficial because both use similar techniques and have similar goals (Thompson & Henderson, 2007).

School-based professionals typically provide counseling rather than psychotherapy. Generally speaking, counseling is a short-term service delivered to individuals or groups to increase their adaptive functioning. Therefore, school-based professionals most often focus on helping student clients function more effectively in the classroom and with their peers. Counseling is also considered to be a helping process that is delivered to individuals who are basically healthy but require support to address a variety of developmental or situational difficulties. The American Counseling Association (2010b) has recently adopted the following definition for *counseling*: "Counseling is a professional relationship that empowers diverse individuals, families, and groups to accomplish mental health, wellness, education, and careers." An illustration of a counseling intervention that meets this definition is when a school counselor helps a student client who is struggling in her peer relationships to find solutions to reduce the conflict. A school psychologist might visit with a young student who is tearful and apparently having a rough day to explore his concerns and support him in learning strategies to manage his frustration.

Conversely, psychotherapy tends to be a longer-term service. The issues or concerns that an individual presents are more serious and may reflect pathology (e.g., depression, suicidal ideation, eating disorder) (Hughes & Theodore, 2009). A broader definition proposed by Weiner and Bornstein (2009) described the unique contribution of psychotherapy as the "intentional effort of therapists to communicate their understanding of a patient's difficulties and help him or her share in this understanding" (p. 3). Therefore, both counseling and psychotherapy clearly involve a personal relationship with an individual or group with the goal of positive change (Hughes & Theodore, 2009). Neither of these approaches should be confused with the generic term *therapy*, which refers to any sort of treatment (e.g., speech therapy) or cure. Further, counseling and psychotherapy are not behavior modification programs, environmental modifications, or psychopharmacology, although these might be elements of broad-based interventions (Weiner & Bornstein, 2009).

With school-based services, it is important to address those issues that are relevant to the context of a student's academic, career, or social-emotional functioning within the school. This distinction does not mean that school-based professionals never work with students who have a diagnosable disorder. It just means that their focus is one of support rather than treatment. For example, a student may have a serious disorder (e.g., generalized anxiety disorder) but still be seen by a school-based professional who works with the student on strategies to manage her anxiety while she is at school in order to achieve her academic goals. Ideally, this student is also working with a private therapist to resolve her anxiety disorder. Here again, the school-based professional can play an important role by providing the family with referrals to local therapists (if the student does not already have one), by staying in close contact with the therapist, by reinforcing the student's use of newly learned coping strategies, and by consulting with the student's teachers as appropriate. In Chapter 14 we outline additional strategies that school-based professionals can use to coordinate support plans and help teachers understand students' needs so they can implement accommodations that will help facilitate success.

Some school-based professionals object to the use of terms such as *client*, *mental health*, or *therapeutic interventions* because they suggest a clinical approach rather than one from the field of counseling. Although we agree with the importance of professional identity and defining one's services appropriately and accurately, we do not advocate for the use of narrowly defined terms that might ultimately inhibit communication and create gaps in services for children and adolescents. Thus, we suggest the following questions for determining whether the counseling services you are considering for a particular student are appropriate for a school setting.

- Do I have the professional competence to provide these services or address the presenting concerns?
- After engaging in a counseling session, is the student likely to be able to return to full participation in the following class period?
- Is the time and effort I put forth with this student similar to the amount of time that I give to other students?
- Are these services consistent with the mission of the school?
- Is the provision of these services consistent with the guidelines of my profession (e.g., American School Counselor Association, National Association of School Psychologists, American Counseling Association, American Psychological Association, or School Social Work Association of America)?
- Would the student's needs be better met within the school setting rather than the community?

If the answer to these questions is yes, it seems appropriate to provide services to the student. A reality of school settings is that they are open to all children, regardless of their ability, history, or diagnosis. That means that

(handwritten margin note:) Is Counseling Appropriate?

many of the students who come through your door may have a clinical disorder or a significant history of abuse. They do not wear signs that allow you to know whether they are going to present you with an issue that is appropriate to address in the schools. For example, an adolescent may present with troubling behavior in the classroom, and through your conversations you find out that she has a history of sexual abuse. Although it would be inappropriate to "treat" the abuse issues in the school, you should not abandon the student after she has shared her most personal secret. Throughout your career, you will need to make these kinds of decisions about whom to serve, how to do so most effectively, and how to help create a school environment that supports the academic, social, and emotional growth of the greatest number of students.

MENTAL HEALTH NEEDS OF STUDENTS

The number of students in the schools who may require additional support services in order to be successful is increasing and represents a growing concern. Many of the students who come to school have very complex needs. According to a report from the National Research Council [NRC] and Institute of Medicine [IOM] (2009), at any given point, between 14 and 20 percent of children and adolescents will experience a mental, emotional, or behavioral disorder (MEB). Of these students, only about one in five (21.3%) will receive services (Substance Abuse and Mental Health Services Administration [SAMHSA], 2007). A recent survey (2005–2006) of students aged 12 to 17 indicated that of the roughly 7 million youth who received services for emotional and behavioral problems, 12 percent received those services in the school, 13.3 percent accessed services through a specialty clinic, and 3 percent received services in a medical setting (SAMHSA, 2008). In real numbers, this means that in a medium-sized high school with approximately 2,000 students, between 280 to 400 students will be experiencing an MEB disorder, and only about 100 of these students will receive services.

These statistics are not meant to indicate that school-based professional helpers must find a way to treat each and every one of these students. Instead, these data highlight a considerable gap in service delivery in our current system. Unfortunately, the level of need does not translate to additional professional helpers assigned to the schools. In fact, in some fields (e.g., school psychology) there is a shortage of practitioners (Curtis, Chesno

Grier, & Hunley, 2004). In school counseling, the student-to-school counselor ratios are often quite high, ranging from 197 to 814, with a U.S. average of 457 (American School Counsel or Association, 2010b). The ratio for school psychologists is much higher, with an estimated 1,621 students per service provider (Charvat, 2005). The ratios for school social workers are more difficult to obtain because only 31 states have a certification process for social workers providing services in the schools (Kelly, 2008). This mismatch between student need and school-based professionals has led to a reconceptualization of our work to align with tiered levels of services. Not all students need the same level of support, and the idea is that if we provide more support through prevention, we may be able to reduce the number of students who require intensive services.

TIERED MODELS OF SERVICES

The growing recognition that we cannot provide effective support services to one child at a time has led to the consideration of alternative methods of service delivery. We must consider ways in which our schools can foster the adaptive functioning and social emotional growth of all children. To do so, we must think about our roles differently and consider how we can create the broadest level of service delivery through our own supports and through our collaboration with others. A growing body of research supports the use of tiered service models such as positive behavioral supports (PBS; Sailor, Dunlap; Sugai, & Horner, 2009) and response to intervention (RTI; Brown-Chidsey & Steege, 2005). These programs emphasize primary prevention, tiered levels of supports or services to address student needs, and school-community linkages.

From this perspective, the greatest amount of effort is directed toward universal treatment with the goal of preventing the need for more targeted and time-intensive intervention strategies. Within these models, guidance lessons and schoolwide programming (e.g., character education, conflict resolution, bullying prevention) would be considered universal or Tier 1 strategies. At the second tier, usually considered to be the level at which students may be considered at risk for a negative outcome, services might include more targeted efforts such as programming delivered to a particular grade level (e.g., transition curriculum for fifth-grade students moving to the sixth grade) or small psychoeducational or counseling group (e.g., divorce group, study skills group). If these approaches are not effective or if a student requires additional support because of an acute crisis, services that are individual and intensive (i.e., Tier 3) can be implemented.

Within a tiered model, it is expected that the percentage of students who require services at this level will approximate 2–5 percent. Furthermore, some of the needs may be so intensive that an individual receives additional supports from a community mental health provider, and the school-based professional helper acts as more of a liaison, consultant, and on-site support as needed for the student. A more in-depth presentation of these tiers is provided in Chapter 15.

WORKING WITH OTHER PROFESSIONALS

Tiered levels of services call for greater levels of collaboration among school personnel. In tandem with the significant transformation of educational practices, the broad fields of counseling, psychology, and social work have also undergone significant change. These changes have created debate in our fields around the types of services that we provide, the nature of our roles, and the degree to which individuals from our fields are relevant to the schools. For example, one of the continuing debates in school counseling is whether the role of the school counselor should be one of providing broad educational support to all students or providing individual student support and crisis intervention (e.g., Paisley & McMahon, 2001; Stone & Dahir, 2011). According to the *Model for Comprehensive and Integrated School Psychological Services* (NASP, 2010b), school psychology is shifting toward more broad, systems level interventions that promote the well-being and academic achievement of students. Although school social workers are also moving toward more prevention and a tiered level of services, a recent survey indicated that respondents spent only 28 percent of their time in Tier 1 activities, while 59 percent of their time was spent at Tiers 2 and 3 (Kelly et al., 2010). As professionals within these three fields continue to define contemporary practice, they face the challenge of establishing their role and professional identity within a shifting framework of services.

Before addressing where the professions are going, it may be valuable to review who we are. One of the most common questions asked by potential program applicants is, "What are the differences between school psychologists, school counselors, and school social workers?" Indeed, there are a number of similarities, but there are also key differences that make our fields unique and important to the well-being of students, families, and other school personnel. Although an entire chapter could be dedicated this topic, we have attempted to highlight with the following table some of the key similarities and differences, as outlined in the *National Model for School Counseling Programs* (ASCA, 1997, 2005), the *Model for Comprehensive and Integrated School Psychological Services* (NASP, 2010b), and the National Association of Social Workers (NASW) *Standards for School Social Work Services* (NASW, 2002). As you can see in Table 1.1, the description and foundation for each of the professions are quite similar. However, differences emerge in the delivery of services and the day-to-day practice of each (presented in Chapter 14).

Table 1.1 Comparison of Role and Function of School Counselors, School Psychologists, and School Social Workers

School Counselor	School Psychologist	School Social Worker
General Description		
School counselors identify and develop a philosophy based on school counseling theory and research/ evidence-based practice to deliver and implement culturally relevant programming in collaboration with others to promote students' academic, career, and personal/social development. • Recommended ratio: 1:250 students	School psychologists provide effective services to help children and youth succeed academically, socially, behaviorally, and emotionally through direct educational and mental health services, as well as work with parents, educational, and other professionals to create a supportive learning environment for all students. • Recommended ratio: 1:500–700 students	School social work is a specialized area within the broad profession of social work. School social workers bring unique knowledge and skills to the school system and the student services team. School social workers support schools in providing a setting for teaching, for learning, and for helping students attain competence and confidence. • Ratios are established by states and districts dependent on the student population served.

(Continued)

Table 1.1 (Continued)

School Counselor	School Psychologist	School Social Worker
Knowledge Foundation		
The foundations of school counseling service delivery are school counseling theory, research/ evidence-based practice, culturally relevant programming, and collaboration.	The foundations of school psychology service delivery are understanding diversity in development and learning, research and program evaluation, and legal, ethical, and professional practice.	Social work practice requires knowledge of human development and behavior, of social, economic, and cultural institutions, and the interactions between these two.
Delivery of Services		
School Guidance Curriculum: structured lessons delivered within the classroom setting designed to enhance student competencies within a systematically designed, developmentally appropriate curriculum. • School counselors may also intervene and advocate at the systems level.	Systems Level Services (schoolwide practices to promote learning): in collaboration with others, school psychologists design, implement, and evaluate effective policies and practices across multiple areas of school functioning (e.g., discipline, school climate) to enhance student learning and well-being. • School psychologists may provide classroom-wide lessons but not typically within a complete, systematic curriculum across all grades.	Work with school, community, and agency personnel to address at-risk student concerns through prevention, intervention, and community/ agency response. • Build student strengths to maximize ability to learn • Help students and families gain access to resources • Collaborate and mobilize resources to support student and family needs

School Counselor	School Psychologist	School Social Worker
Responsive Services: prevention or intervention activities to meet students' needs. • These services may take the form of individual or group counseling, consultation, peer helping, psycho-education, referral to outside agencies, and intervention and advocacy at the systems level. • This area also includes effective crisis preparation, response, and recovery.	Preventive and Responsive Services: school psychologists apply their knowledge of risk and resiliency factors to promote services that enhance learning, mental health, safety, and well-being. • These services are typically provided across the school system (e.g., tiered response systems such as positive behavior supports and response to intervention). • Also includes effective crisis preparation, response, and recovery.	Direct interventions to address the immediate concerns of at-risk students through prevention, intervention, and crisis response. • These services may take the form of case management, individual and group counseling, family counseling, and crisis intervention. • Interventions are to be evidence-based.
School counselors consult with parents, teachers, and other educators and refer to outside agencies as part of their responsive services. They also may have advisory councils that include families, teachers, administrators, and outside personnel who evaluate their school counseling program as	School psychologists consult and collaborate with teachers, administrators, families, and external agencies. These are considered to be practices that permeate all aspects of school psychology service delivery. • Family-School Collaboration	School social workers provide consultation to facilitate understanding among home, school, and community. The following elements represent aspects of their practice: • Home/School/Community Liaison • Community Collaboration • Community Outreach and Mobilization • Interdisciplinary Team Problem Solving

(Continued)

Table 1.1 (Continued)

School Counselor	School Psychologist	School Social Worker
part of the management function of their role.	Services: school psychologists use their knowledge of family systems, culture, and evidence-based practices to develop collaborative partnerships with families in order to support children's learning and mental health.	• Teacher/Administrator Consultation
Individual Student Planning: coordinated activities designed to help students develop personal and educational goals. • General education career planning is unique to school counselors, although school psychologists may assist in transition to postsecondary settings and community agencies for those students who receive special education services.	Student Level Services: school psychologists deliver both instructional support and mental health services to help students develop their academic, social, and life skills. • These services may be direct or indirect and take the form of consultation with teachers, parents, and administrators, individual or group counseling, or use of data to help establish learning and/or behavioral goals.	School social workers build student strengths to maximize opportunities to learn. The following direct services are listed as part of a school social worker's role: • Assessment of student needs to facilitate intervention design • Home/School/Community Liaison • Individual and Small Group Therapy/ Counseling • Conflict Resolution and Mediation • Family Counseling

School Counselor	School Psychologist	School Social Worker
System Support: management of all aspects (e.g., establishing, maintaining, and enhancing) of a school counseling program including professional development, consultation, collaboration, supervision, and operations.	There is no equivalent in school psychology services since school psychologists may function as itinerant staff.	School social workers organize their time, efforts, and priorities to fulfill their responsibilities.
Broad-Based Practice		
Management: school counselors develop and formalize a school counseling program that is reflective of student and school needs. Accountability: school counselors implement data-driven, standards-based, research-supported programs and engage in continuous program evaluation.	Data-based decision making and accountability permeate all aspects of school psychology service. School psychologists are part of a multidisciplinary team that collects and uses student data to identify students' eligibility for special education and other educational services, to assess progress toward academic and behavioral goals, and to evaluate implementation and effectiveness of interventions.	School social workers provide training and educational programs that address the goals of education. They maintain accurate data relevant to planning, management, and services. Additionally, they incorporate assessment into intervention and evaluation plans to enhance student abilities.

Source: Table contents are adapted from the ASCA website (2009) document, "The Role of the Professional School Counselor," the *Model for Comprehensive and Integrated School Psychological Services* (NASP, 2010b), the School Social Work Association of America (SSWAA) website (2009), and the NASW *Standards for School Social Work Services* (2002).

Because there are similarities among the three professions, those who are unaware of the differences might see these roles as interchangeable. They are most definitely not. However, each professional provides distinctive contributions to the school setting that can complement one another perfectly. For example, while the school counselor might focus on delivering specific guidance lessons as part of broader efforts to improve student behavior and reduce bullying, the school psychologist or school social worker could assist in running targeted intervention groups to address students who are at-risk or demonstrating bullying behaviors. Together, all individuals may work to collect data on their efforts to determine whether office referrals for aggressive behaviors have decreased.

When it comes to individual counseling, there are important differences as well. For example, the school counselor may provide short-term supportive services to individuals who have experienced a life stressor that is creating distress and interfering with school functioning. Additionally, school counselors often work with students to help them establish personal goals for their education and future. Conversely, school psychologists tend to work with students who have been identified for additional supports through special education services. School social workers tend to fall somewhere in between with about one-third of their students on individualized education programs (IEPs) and the rest identified as "at-risk" (Kelly et al., 2010). For those students on IEPs, the nature of the counseling services might reflect a longer duration and may include linkages with outside professionals. This brief distinction does not mean to imply that a school counselor should never work with a child who has an IEP or that school psychologists and schools social workers can't meet with students who do not require special education services; instead it is meant as a general guide for understanding the different types of counseling services that are provided by each professional. For all school-based professionals, the focus is on helping the student's performance in learning and social interactions, with an emphasis on the school setting.

ACCOUNTABILITY IN COUNSELING SERVICES

In addition to the growing number of students needing support, all school-based professionals are faced with the challenge of demonstrating the effectiveness of their actions. School-based professionals place great value on demonstrating accountability for their services although the strategies for documenting outcomes have varied. It is not enough to say that the students enjoyed the lesson or that parents seemed satisfied after the meeting. These informal indicators are extremely important, but the real question is whether your services resulted in a positive, measurable outcome. Did students engage in more prosocial behavior after your group? Did Allison begin attending school more regularly after you and she worked individually on goal setting? Have office referrals decreased after you helped implement the schoolwide character education program? Unfortunately, these are complicated questions, and outcomes may be difficult to demonstrate.

School-based professional helpers face many unique challenges to delivering and evaluating the effectiveness of their services. They have a limited amount of time to deliver their services and may be addressing attitudes and behaviors that have been present for a number of years (and therefore, not easily changed or assessed). Some districts place restrictions on the number of times that a school-based helper may deliver services to an individual (e.g., six sessions). This type of mandated limitation creates difficulty in delivering interventions with fidelity if the identified intervention approach calls for a greater number of sessions (e.g., 12–15), as is often the case. Additionally, the implementation of intervention programming may be reliant on a teacher or a team of individuals rather than the school-based professional. The challenge is great, and it is often difficult to justify spending our limited time on data collection rather than direct services. Regardless, there is a greater expectation than ever that school-based professional helpers demonstrate the importance of their services to the overall functioning of school systems.

THE EFFECTIVENESS OF COUNSELING FOR CHILDREN AND ADOLESCENTS

Meta-analyses of research designed to explore outcomes for child and adolescent populations have supported the efficacy of counseling (e.g., Baskin et al., 2010; Kazdin, 2000; Prout & Prout, 1998; Weisz, Weiss, Han, Granger, & Morton, 1995). For example, based on a review of 107 outcome studies of 132 interventions, Baskin et al. (2010) concluded that psychotherapy with children and adolescents in the schools yielded positive effects. Certain variables appeared to increase the effectiveness of counseling including services provided to adolescent populations, single-gender groups, and trained, licensed therapists rather than paraprofessionals or graduate students (Baskin et al., 2010). Further, the modality did not appear to make a difference, as individual, group, and "other" approaches (e.g., classroom) all yielded significant results.

Reese, Prout, Zirkelback, and Anderson (2010) conducted a meta-analysis of 65 school-based psychotherapy and counseling dissertations and found an overall effect size that was very similar to that of Baskin et al. (2010), .44 and .45 respectively. As with previous school-based studies, most of the interventions included those that focused on cognitive-behavioral strategies or skills training and were typically provided in a group format. Of the four published meta-analyses that have focused on school-based mental health services (Baskin et al., 2010; Prout & DeMartino, 1986; Prout & Prout, 1998; Reese et al., 2010), all have reported medium to large effect sizes.

These broad studies can help us to understand which aspects of counseling or psychotherapy have the strongest effects and the areas where we continue to have gaps in our knowledge. For example, we know little about whether the theoretical model of treatment yields different results. Weisz et al. (1995) found that behavioral techniques tended to produce the greatest positive effects in children regardless of age, gender, therapist training, or type of problem. Conversely, Reese et al. (2010) found that skills training had a greater effect size than cognitive behavioral approaches. In the Weisz et al. (1995) study, females tended to have better treatment outcomes than males; however, there were no gender differences found in the Baskin et al. (2010) study. When focusing specifically on 17 school-based studies, Prout and Prout (1998) noted that the positive findings from their meta-analysis reflected group rather than individual counseling outcomes; these findings were not supported by Baskin et al (2010). Finally, Reese et al. (2010) found the largest effect sizes in elementary populations, while Baskin et al. (2010) reported larger effect sizes for adolescents. Prout and Prout (1998) also found the greatest effects at elementary rather than secondary levels. The inconsistent nature of these findings leads us to conclude that ongoing research on school-based interventions is needed to determine which approaches are most effective with whom.

School-based professionals often receive positive feedback from children, teachers, parents, and administrators about the services that they provide. Under these circumstances, it might be easy to conclude that any type of counseling provided in the school will have a positive effect. However, this is not necessarily the case, as demonstrated by Weiss, Catron, Harris, and Phung (1999) who used a randomized clinical trial to determine the effectiveness of child psychotherapy as typically delivered in the schools. Participants included 160 children who had problems related to anxiety, depression, aggression, or attention. They were divided into a treatment or control group that received either "treatment as usual" or academic tutoring for 45 minutes per week. Treatment as usual was provided by mental health professionals (six master's level counselors and one doctoral level clinical psychologist) who reported using cognitive and psychodynamic-humanistic approaches. The treatment extended over two years and did not follow a particular set of guidelines. At the end of the project, the researchers did not find any significant differences between the students in the two groups based on ratings of internalizing or externalizing behaviors, adaptive functioning, or peer relationships across time. Based on these findings, the authors concluded that it will be important to develop and validate effective treatment approaches with children and implement them in school settings.

As school-based professionals, we possess a powerful tool in the form of counseling, but we must use it appropriately by matching strategies that have research support with students' presenting concerns. When this is not possible, we must carefully document the outcomes of our efforts and modify our approaches as needed as described in Chapter 13. Many interventions exist that can promote children's positive development and prevent emotional and behavioral problems (Kellam & Langevin, 2003; Weisz, Sandler, Durlak, & Anton, 2005). The use of these types of programs can help students to develop resilience and cope with the many environmental stressors placed on them (Adelman & Taylor, 2010).

RESILIENCY IN CHILDREN AND ADOLESCENTS

A resiliency framework provides an alternative, more positive way to think about serving youth in the schools. As children develop into young adults, they typically face numerous challenges in the social, academic, and emotional realms. Some of the most significant stressors for children and adolescents reflect "typical" experiences such as advancing to middle school, experiencing puberty, gaining acceptance from peers, and developing a sense of identity. Given a balance of support, adequate problem-solving and coping skills, and a consistent environment, most youth navigate these stressors with little difficulty. On the other hand, children and adolescents who experience too many stressors (either major traumas or daily hassles) often find their coping resources overwhelmed. Of additional concern are the nonnormative stressors experienced by too many of today's children and adolescents such as violence in their schools and communities. When youth are unable to cope with life's difficulties, they become more vulnerable to negative influences, deviant behavior, and suicidal ideation.

Resiliency is an individual's capacity to overcome identifiable risk factors (e.g., poverty, parent depression) and avoid the negative outcomes often associated with these risks such as academic difficulties, delinquency, and mental health problems (Adelman & Taylor, 2010). In other words, resilience can be defined as better than expected outcomes, or competence, in the presence of risk factors (Luthar, Cicchetti, & Becker, 2000). Protective factors in the neighborhood, school, family, and peer network can act as buffers against these risks. Of particular interest to school-based professionals are the school-based protective buffers such as success at school, a supportive school environment, positive relationships with one's teachers and peers, and a strong bond with others (Adelman & Taylor, 2010; Brehm & Doll, 2009).

Many individual factors associated with resilient outcomes including positive self-concept, achievement motivation, social competence, problem solving, autonomy, and sense of purpose are amenable to intervention (Beltman & MacCallum, 2006; Brehm & Doll, 2009). Effective programs exist that help to alter school environments to promote resiliency in students by helping them strengthen interpersonal relationships and promote autonomy and self-regulation (Doll & Cummings, 2008; Doll, Zucker, & Brehm, 2004). By focusing on broad, population-based services, school-based professionals may be able to have the greatest positive impact on students' development.

PROMOTING HEALTHY DEVELOPMENT

Although the field of counseling has historically identified enhanced well-being as the desired outcome of services, this perspective is relatively new to the discipline of psychology. Until recently, mental health was simply considered to be the absence of mental illness. Psychology continues to make great strides in recognizing the positive aspects of human development and optimized life experiences through the study of positive psychology (Seligman & Csikszentmihalyi, 2000). Researchers have directed increasing attention toward identifying the characteristics of healthy individuals, although this line of work is still in its infancy. An outgrowth of this effort is an emphasis on defining the key concepts of mental health promotion and identifying the factors that contribute to healthy development (NRC & IOM, 2009). The term *developmental competencies* is central to health promotion and refers to "young people's ability to accomplish a broad range of social, emotional, cognitive, moral, and behavioral tasks at various developmental stages" (NRC & IOM, 2009, p. 75).

Positive youth development programs have been created to help foster these competencies and have outlined goals such as improving bonding, promoting resilience and competence, and fostering self-determination and self-efficacy (Catalano, Berglund, Ryan, Lonczak, & Hawkins, 2004). As might be expected, the competencies and the factors that promote healthy development differ across the individual's lifespan. Healthy attachment is a critical competency during early childhood, whereas opportunities to belong become much more relevant to adolescents. Smith, Boutte, Zigler, and Finn-Stevenson (2004) identified factors within the school environment that were associated with positive development in middle childhood. These factors included positive teacher expectancies and support, effective classroom management, collaborative school-family relationships, culturally relevant pedagogy, and school policies and practices that reduce bullying. As part of their broad spectrum of services, school-based professionals can implement programming that helps to foster these healthy school environments.

School-based counseling is an important service provided by professional helpers. However, given the imbalance between the number of students and service providers, school-based practitioners will want to adopt a tiered level of services that benefits all students by creating healthy environments, implementing prevention strategies that enhance resiliency, and collaborating with others to support those students with more intensive challenges. It is difficult to know what the future holds, but it is unlikely that we will see a large increase in the number of school-based helpers because too often school leaders tend to marginalize professional helpers and view their work as supplementary rather than integral to the functioning of the school (Adelman & Taylor, 2010). Therefore it is imperative that you find ways to maximize your services and continually reflect on the efficacy of what you do.

Activities

1. Go to the website of your professional organization and review the position statement on scope of practice as related to counseling or mental health services. Consider how the "day in a life" scenarios presented in the Section I introduction compare to these descriptions.

2. Interview a member of the school leadership team. How does the individual view the role of counseling, guidance, or mental health services in the school? Share your findings with other members of your class.

3. Find a current article describing the effectiveness of a specific school-based intervention. What would be some of the benefits and challenges in implementing this type of intervention in your current setting?

Journal Reflections

Reflection #1

What prompted to you to pursue a career as a school-based professional helper? How do you envision your role?

Reflection #2

Sometimes school-based professional helpers might experience "turf battles" over who delivers which types of services and to whom. How will you avoid these types of conflicts and develop supportive collaborative partnerships?

Reflection #3

Consider a continuum of mental health services that begins with universal mental health promotion and continues to intensive, individual intervention. Some people really enjoy the context of the classroom and the system, while others prefer providing individual services to troubled students. Where is your "comfort zone" within this continuum?

Electronic Resources

American Counseling Association: http://www.counseling.org

American Psychological Association: http://www.apa.org

American School Counseling Association: http://www.schoolcounselor.org

Children's Defense Fund: http://www.childrensdefense.org

National Alliance of Pupil Services Organizations: http://www.napso.org

National Association of School Psychologists: http://www.nasponline.org

National Association of Social Workers: http://www.socialworkers.org

School Social Work Association of America: http://www.sswaa.org

Print Resources

Gilman, R., Huebner, E. S., & Furlong, M. J. (2009). *Handbook of positive psychology in the schools.* New York: Routledge.

CHAPTER 2

Working Within School, Family, and Community Systems

Learning Objectives

- Understand the systemic nature of the school setting
- Develop strategies for entering the school system
- Learn how to plan for the school year
- Develop skills in bringing closure to a counseling relationship

---

The moment professional helpers walk into a school building, they have entered a system. Systems are defined as an "orderly combination of parts that interact to produce a desired outcome or product" (Curtis, Castillo, & Cohen, 2008, p. 888). In the instance of a school, the combination of parts includes everything from the building, the teachers, support staff, administration, parents, students, and any other component that contributes to the day-to-day functioning of the school. As the school-based professional, you become a part of this system, and your interactions with others will be a key component to creating the "desired outcome." Of course, one of the desired outcomes within a school context is positive academic, social, and emotional functioning among students.

To complicate matters, schools are part of larger systems (e.g., a school district, community) and also house any number of smaller systems (e.g., classrooms, grade level teams, parent volunteers). As part of your role, you will also regularly interact with systems outside of the school such as families and community agencies (see Chapter 14). Each of the parts of these systems influences other systems, and a change in one part will likely affect the entire system. This interactive effect is known as reciprocal influence. As might be expected, certain changes (e.g., the school principal leaving midyear) will likely have a much greater influence than a single child moving away to a new school. However, from a systems perspective, any change always influences the system to some degree (Curtis et al., 2008).

Knowledge of a system is especially relevant when you are considering any type of change to a system such as implementing a new program or modifying a policy. No matter how minor, change is difficult. Last year, in an effort to reduce student arguments at recess, the P.E. teacher at one of my schools (R. S. H.) investigated the standard rules of four square, typed and laminated them, and distributed the rules to each of the teachers who served as playground monitors. Rather than being met with a big thank-you for his initiative, his efforts were met with disagreement and debate for weeks. When you consider implementing a larger, more meaningful change, you can begin to understand why it is so important to understand the interactive nature of systems.

Systems within and outside of the school have slightly different goals or valued outcomes based on the members' unique perspectives. For example, a group of third-grade teachers may have a desired goal of successfully covering the curriculum and helping their students meet the achievement standards appropriate to their grade level. To accomplish that goal, they recognize that they must present material at a certain pace and that their students must be assessed regularly to ensure that they are making progress. Conversely, the school wellness team may have a goal of ensuring that all students participate in 30 minutes of exercise each day and receive weekly classroom guidance lessons on effective problem solving to enhance physical and social wellness. Both systems share the desired outcome of more adaptive functioning for students, but their strategies for achieving these goals may compete with one another.

FINDING YOUR WAY IN THE SCHOOL SYSTEM

The school setting offers a number of challenges to both new and seasoned professionals. Sometimes the school system can seem like a well-oiled machine that hums along smoothly. At other times it can seem chaotic and ill-defined.

Certain aspects of the school day are structured such as beginning and end times, the daily curriculum, and other scheduling aspects that must be rigidly followed in order to manage hundreds of students moving from one point to another throughout any given day. However, within this structure there are any number of unpredictable elements that new professionals must understand, adapt to, and overcome in order to become an effective part of the system. One of the main tasks for the new school-based professional is to enter the school system. This step, referred to as *entry into the organization* within the consultation literature (Brown, Pryzwansky, & Schulte, 2011), describes both the formal and psychological components in which the actions of the consultant are both sanctioned and accepted (Brown et al., 2011). Although entry issues are more relevant to those who are external to the school setting, in your first year you will navigate some of the challenges associated with system entry.

Entering the School System

For a new school-based professional, the learning curve is steep. One must learn the names of the teachers and what grade or subject they teach, the daily schedule, developmentally appropriate lessons and activities, data management programs, established programs (e.g., character education program, schoolwide discipline programs), and district policies and procedures. This type of information, though massive, is relatively easy to learn as it is written in schedules, handbooks, and policy manuals. Part of your first few days in the school should be spent gaining access to these materials and reviewing them to make sure you are familiar with the information. If you are embarking on your first field experience in a school, it is likely that your site supervisor can provide you with these documents and also facilitate your entry into the school system.

The more challenging task is to learn the unwritten practices and policies and to merge them with best practice as indicated by your professional organization. What are some of the unspoken or informal rules that apply to this school? What is the principal's leadership style, and what expectation does this individual have for your role? Which teachers are most open to integrating your lessons into their schedules? What is the overall philosophy of the school in regard to students, and how does it fit with your own? What are some of the contradictions between practice, tradition, and the stated school philosophy?

It is helpful if your supervisor can introduce you to members of the school but if not, venture out on your own. You want to present as friendly and approachable, yet professional. Schools are small places; do not put your foot in your mouth. As a professional, you never want to make an offhand comment about another faculty member. These kinds of comments can be taken out of context,

Take the time to meet everyone, including the support staff (e.g., custodian, secretary, faculty assistant). These individuals help make the school run effectively and can be lifesavers during an emergency.

are likely to be repeated, and do not reflect well on you. Instead, take the time to observe, talk to people, and figure out the relationships and hierarchies before you ask about implementing a program or changing a policy. It is not expected that you will have the answers figured out during your first week. Through open communication, positive relationships, and collaborative teaming, you are more likely to experience a smooth entry into the school system.

It is important to have an understanding of roles and expectations when you enter a new system. Whether interviewing for a practicum, internship, or job, it is helpful to clarify the expectations of those in leadership roles for your position in the school. If their expectations are much different from your own, it will likely be best to keep searching until you find a closer match. Otherwise, you may find yourself at constant odds with your principal, which can be extremely frustrating for a new school-based professional. Even if you find a school or district that seems "perfect" for you, there will be times when you disagree with a program, a policy, or a procedure for working with a student. Although all parties may want what is best for students, they may see the course of action for achieving this goal quite differently. By establishing open conversations about basic ideas, principles, and goals with your principal and colleagues, you will have a better understanding of your expected role, the areas where you might like to expand your services, and the ways that you can integrate your services into established practices. When inevitable differences arise, you will have laid a solid foundation for working through any disagreements.

Building relationships is critical to success in a school setting. One of the worst things you can do as a new professional is isolate in your office. Although a few staff might seek you out, the majority won't know who you are or what services you provide. Making yourself visible, engaging in helpful acts, and volunteering for committees are all valuable ways to learn about the school and allow others to learn about you. The more school personnel understand who you are and what you can provide, the more quickly you will be able to integrate into the school community. Even if you are not typically an outgoing person, it is important to go out of your way to greet people in the mornings, check in with the office staff if you're going to leave early or be unavailable, ask questions about the school and the staff, and spend time in the teachers' lounge.

We often hear seasoned professionals grumble about avoiding the teachers' lounge at all costs. We disagree with this perspective. Sometimes new professionals are tempted to use lunch time as a time to catch up on paperwork, conduct "lunch bunch" groups, or return e-mails and phone calls. Although this may seem like a good strategy, it can create a perception that you are aloof or unfriendly. Make an effort to eat lunch in the school lounge at least a couple of days per week. It provides a wonderful opportunity to get to know the teachers, it allows you to know what types of global and specific concerns they have, and it helps to establish you as part of the school culture.

Carefully consider how you will spend your days and the strategies you will use to meet the needs of students. In order to maximize the services that you can offer, we encourage you to develop a mental health curriculum that includes a flexible blend of well-planned services in the form of classroom, group, and individual services provided throughout the school year. As you are doing so, it is important to ask, "Who are the students in my school, and what are their needs?"

Planning for the School Year

The effective school-based practitioner carefully makes plans for services throughout the course of the school year. By knowing the school schedule, you can effectively meet the needs of the greatest number of children and reduce the number of unexpected or abrupt endings. A significant proportion of your day will be allocated to guidance lessons if you are a school counselor. According to the *ASCA National Model* (2005) approximately 45 percent of your time if you are at the elementary school level and 25 percent at the high school level should be spent in guidance activities. As a school psychologist, approximately 47 percent of your time is spent in assessment activities (Larson & Choi, 2010). With the remaining time, school-based professional helpers must find time for consultation, crisis management, direct intervention (e.g., groups and individual counseling), team collaboration, and program evaluation.

Creating a yearlong plan can be helpful in allocating your time toward ensuring that you have aligned your practice with the *ASCA National Model* (2005) or with the broad range of activities outlined in the *NASP Comprehensive Model* (2010b). Once you've marked out holidays, teacher work days, meeting times, and classroom guidance or assessment activities, you will have a better idea of the flexible times in your schedule when you could meet with student clients to provide direct services. For secondary school counselors, long-range planning will include career fairs, financial aid workshops, and so forth. School psychologists will want to identify IEP and special education team meeting times. Other potential meetings include standing meetings with the school principal, faculty meetings, book study groups, and participation on any number of school teams (e.g., building leadership team, problem-solving team, health and wellness team, schoolwide positive behavior support team, crisis team). Additionally, you will likely have team meetings at the district level that may be discipline specific or combined with the other school-based professional helpers. As you begin to pencil in your various meetings and obligations, it is amazing how quickly the days fill up.

As you are planning for the school year, consider the ASCA (2005) recommendations around how the proportions of your time are spent. A chart outlining the recommended percentage of time spent in each domain is available in Chapter 13. For school psychologists, the guidelines are less specific, and you are encouraged to spend your time fulfilling a variety of functions consistent with your role. A recent survey of school psychologists suggested that approximately 22 percent of respondents' time was spent in a combination of counseling, intervention, and preventive services. An additional 23 percent was spent in consultation or collaborative meetings (Larson & Choi, 2010). Although school social workers reported spending approximately 60 percent of their time in individual or group counseling, they reported wanting to move toward more prevention activities (Kelly et al., 2010). With these guidelines and estimates in mind, consider how you are building in these blocks of time so that you can deliver a broad range of services. It is important to "block" this time in so that you don't find that you are spending approximately 40 percent of your time on administrative tasks rather than in guidance or direct services.

Another consideration when you are developing your master schedule is the timing of seasonal school breaks. When you are establishing groups, you will want to consider the length of time they might last (e.g., six to eight weeks), and then be sure to begin them an appropriate amount of time prior to winter or spring break so that there is not a disruption in group process. It is best to avoid beginning a counseling relationship with a student toward the end of a school year, right before a school break, or when a student is expected to transfer to a new setting. It doesn't mean that you can't lend support to students in transition, only that you may need to carefully monitor the intensity level of your work with these students (e.g., check-ins versus counseling sessions).

Be sure to build in unscheduled blocks at different times of day. If you are able to set the timing of weekly meetings, try to establish them such that some occur in the afternoons and others in the morning or over the lunch break. In this way, you'll have greater flexibility in offering group or individual counseling or consultative services. Scheduling groups with students who are in different classes or grade levels can be especially difficult as you will have to find times that work for each of the students. A specific time may work well for three of the students but conflicts with the literacy block for another student. Through careful planning, compromise, and patience, you can figure out these service delivery puzzles.

As you are assembling your schedule, you will want to consider the schedules of other school-based helpers. On which days are other professionals (e.g., school psychologists, school social workers, interpreters, home-school liaisons) in the building? There are at least two important reasons for determining this information. One, it allows you to coordinate your services with these individuals. Which services are being offered and on which days? Are there certain activities you might want to provide together? Perhaps you want to offer a problem-solving group to young students who are experiencing behavioral challenges. Needless to say, having a coleader will make this task much easier.

The second practical reason for coordinating with others is to make sure you have a place to provide your services. Because professional helpers might divide their time between two or three schools, they are sometimes housed together in the same office. If you share an office and a computer with another school-based helper, you will want to know each other's schedules to allow for the most effective use of that shared space.

> Good communication is key to successful coordination. Post your schedule, alert your office mate to any changes or needs in advance, and be mindful of the fact that the space is shared. Also, be aware of other rooms in the building that might not be used during certain times of the day so that you have an alternative meeting space if needed.

DAY TO DAY IN THE ACADEMIC YEAR

As noted in the introduction to this section, there is no typical day in the life of a school-based professional helper. Despite all of your best planning and organizing, unexpected events will happen, and it is your job to help address sudden crises, to support a faculty member in calling social services, and to intervene when one of your student clients is having a tough day. Part of the skill in managing these abrupt changes is knowing which aspects of your day are flexible and which ones you need to get someone to cover for you so that you can attend to the planned activity. For example, if you have a monthly meeting around the school's character education program, your committee members will understand your absence if an emergency arises. However, if you have had a long-scheduled meeting with parents who have been difficult to reach, it would be best to meet with them if possible. There are no hard and fast rules, and often these decisions must be made with very little "think" time. Knowing your school, your coworkers, and other resources in the building will assist you in figuring out your priorities, the demands of the situation, and alternatives for when you simply cannot be in two places at once.

A school year tends to have a more predictable flow than a single day. During the start of the year, the weeks are filled with possibilities. Both you and the faculty will be rested after a summer break and full of new ideas about what will be accomplished in the coming year. After the first exciting month or two, it seems the days settle into a bit of a routine until the holidays approach. If you are in an elementary school, you will probably find that Halloween has become one of the major holidays. From the end of October through December, there are a number of events including parent conferences, parties, and assemblies in the build-up to the winter break. After everyone returns in January, a new round of planning often takes place. Depending on the size of your school, you might provide two sequences of guidance lessons. Based on the success of your first set, there may be modifications in scheduling or lesson planning. If you're in a secondary school, students are beginning to think about their college plans and are looking for information, guidance, and support. There is also scheduling as well as supporting those students who had a difficult time over the break.

At some point during the school year, a major event occurs that seems to disrupt every aspect of school functioning. The high-stakes testing window opens. In some states this occurs during the fall, and in others it occurs in early spring. During this time, the halls are empty, younger students are kept as quiet as possible, and the faculty are tense. Often those who are not assigned to classrooms are asked to help proctor or administer exams. There are very few—if any—groups, guidance lessons, or services provided during this two- to three-week window. Once the exams are completed, it almost seems that there is a sigh of relief. Some schools plan a break at the end of this assessment period.

After spring break, there are roughly two more months of school. This period generally becomes quite busy as planning for next year begins. It is also a time when students may begin to act out a bit more and teachers are often worried about certain students because they have not made expected academic gains.

By the last few weeks of the school year, it is clear that faculty are tired and ready for their break, as are the students. Students who are transitioning to another school setting or perhaps graduating are especially difficult to keep on-task. Although there is a great deal of fun and celebration, it is also a time of change and transition. Some teachers may not be renewed, and others may announce plans to move on.

As the end of the year approaches, it is a good time to reflect on your year and the roles, processes, and groups that worked well and those areas where you could make improvements. You will want to engage in this reflective process both individually and with your teams. This is an excellent time to discuss any lingering questions with your supervisor because in the next year, you will be facilitating this process on your own.

Just as a school year has a certain rhythm and pace, there is also a certain life cycle to individual counseling. You must establish rapport with your student clients, develop an understanding of their concerns or issues, and help them develop strategies in accordance with the student's needs and your own theoretical stance (discussed in Chapter 4). Although you will provide supports at many different levels, it is important to understand how individual counseling services fit into your yearly and daily role and function.

THE COUNSELING CYCLE

How do you get started seeing students? Believe it or not, the answer to that question comes very quickly. Teachers, parents, administrators, and even other students will refer students to you. You may also have a list of students who were seen previously, and you will likely follow up with them. No doubt, as you deliver your guidance lessons, observe on the playground, and perform lunch duty, you will see students who appear to be at odds with their world. As a school psychologist or school social worker, there may be some students that have your services written into their individualized education programs (IEPs). Additionally, you may choose to have a locking drop box on your office door where students can request a visit with you.

Because of the number of students who need services in the schools, some school professionals develop rigid policies related to the number of sessions allowed per student. We don't recommend this practice as this type of pressure might interfere with the professional's ability to build a strong therapeutic relationship. It also does not recognize the individual needs of students and the varying rates at which they are able to develop skills and meet their goals. The presenting concern should also help to dictate the number and length of sessions. For example, many students simply need a quick "check-in"; others may be experiencing conflict with another student, and one or two visits is enough for them to discuss their concerns; and still others will have a more troubling pattern of behaviors that warrant ongoing supports through a blend of counseling, group, and check-ins.

When making decisions about which students to serve and what issues to address, we want to emphasize the importance of considering your skills, professional guidelines, and context rather than relying on inflexible role definitions. In addition to time restrictions inherent in a school day, there are also times when you will be unavailable to a student because of a weekend or holiday. If this type of schedule does not seem appropriate to the level of student need, it may be best to refer a student to a community agency that can provide that level of support.

In a typical counseling cycle, early sessions serve to help the counselor develop rapport and begin to understand the student client's concerns. This stage is sometimes called the "exploration stage" (Hill & O'Brien, 2004). The middle phase of counseling is sometimes described as the "insight stage," where student clients engage in a deeper level of exploration and understanding around the presenting concern. We recognize that children may not necessarily achieve "insight" in the traditional sense, and we sometimes consider this component of counseling as a working stage. Finally, there is the "action stage" where the student client develops a plan to address the concern. As the individual gains confidence in his or her ability to handle the particular situation or stressor, you may reduce the frequency and length of your sessions as you move toward termination. The stages of counseling as proposed by Hill and O'Brien (2004) provide a helpful framework as you think about your counseling progress and establish goals for each session. However, it is also important to keep in mind that these stages were developed around adult clients and are generally seen in longer courses of counseling. Counseling with children, especially in a school setting, is likely to follow a more sporadic progression.

TERMINATING THE COUNSELING RELATIONSHIP

In schools, as in community agencies, there comes a time when it is appropriate to discontinue focused work with each student client. This process of bringing closure to the relationship, summarizing a student client's progress, or referring the individual to another therapist is referred to as termination. As easy as it might sound, it is a critical component of the counseling relationship. It represents a healthy model for how to become independent, say goodbye, and end a relationship. Unlike agency settings, termination in schools sometimes occurs abruptly as breaks in the school calendar or school transitions necessitate the end to the therapeutic relationship, regardless of the individual's progress. Further, termination is not as "final" as in an agency setting; for example, school counselors continue to work with previous student clients in other capacities.

Knowing When to Terminate

When working in any setting, it is important to consider whether the time has come to terminate a relationship. This is especially critical in the schools, as there are many students in need of counseling services. School-based mental health professionals cannot afford to see students longer than needed or to see students who do not appear to be benefiting from services. So, how do professional helpers know when termination is appropriate? In a typical situation, the counseling relationship comes to an end when the student client has met his or her goals. In addition to meeting goals, he or she might also show signs of increased openness, healthier problem-solving strategies, increased involvement with peers, and a better relationship with parents (Thompson & Henderson, 2007). Further, teachers and parents might comment on how much better the child is performing in class and in unstructured settings (e.g., on the playground, in the lunchroom). Termination may occur before an issue is fully resolved. However, if students appear to be "on the right track," and believe they can continue the new strategies on their own, termination may be appropriate (Murphy, 2008).

As mentioned earlier, sometimes termination occurs because of external events. Although some children will be ready for termination by the end of your field experience or academic term, others may have just started trusting you and sharing their concerns. This type of premature transition is not only difficult for the child or adolescent but also for the professional (Orton, 1997). This may be one of the first times that you have experienced a warm, trusting relationship from a child (other than your own or a relative's child). In turn, your feelings may translate into a sense of responsibility for helping this child. Unlike the end of other academic learning experiences, you may find it more difficult to see this one come to an end. Additionally, the child may respond to termination with grieving behaviors such as crying, sadness, or acting out (Orton, 1997). As a pre-service professional, you may feel sadness and guilt. You will need to work closely with your supervisor during this time to manage your own feelings and ensure a smooth transition for your student client to a different professional within the school or an appropriate community resource.

When a counseling relationship is abruptly going to end due to an unforeseen change (e.g., family move, child placed in a new foster care setting), it is especially important to bring closure to the relationship and facilitate transition to the new school if possible. A termination session might focus on the student client's progress to date, the types of goals that have and have not yet been reached, and a review of any strategies or skills that the student client has learned that facilitate successful coping with this transition. Depending on the student's age, it is recommended that parents or guardians are involved so that they can support the student in these transitions and help establish services in the new setting.

Sometimes the parents of a student client may decide to discontinue counseling services. In these instances, it is best to speak with the family about the importance of having one or two more sessions in order to bring closure to your work with the student. Orton (1997) noted that the emphasis of these final sessions is on saying goodbye to the child and helping him or her deal with the feelings of sadness, anger, and helplessness. These types of abrupt endings might also be prevented through regular check-ins with parents when working with their child to determine whether there is any growing dissatisfaction or concern with their child's progress. Additionally, school professionals can provide educational materials in the form of brochures or articles in the school newsletter that describe the process of counseling at different stages (e.g., building a relationship, working on school concerns, and termination).

There is one more instance of counseling termination that is unique to school settings. Sometimes students have individualized education programs (IEPs) that include counseling as part of the special education services. In these instances, students receive a certain amount of services directed toward specific goals in accordance with the plan. Services provided under these circumstances tend to be very structured (e.g., minimal number of service minutes per month, directed toward specific objective goals or outcomes), and progress is formally documented on a quarterly basis. If the child has met the goals or if a parent decides that these services are no longer necessary, services may be reduced or discontinued with parental permission. Unlike less formal services, these services are legally mandated by the IEP, and the educational program must be amended to reflect a different level of service.

Because of the lack of predictability in schools, Murphy (2008) recommended treating every counseling session as if it were the last session. To do so, the school-based professional could provide a brief summary of progress, a review of unmet goals, reinforcement of the student client's efforts, and a review of the strategies learned at the end of each session. The professional helper will need to leave a little time at the end of each session for this type of closure. You do not want an abrupt ending and a statement such as, "Oh, we'll get to that next time we meet" to be the last memory that a student takes away from your counseling.

Special Considerations in Terminating With Children

Regardless of the reason for terminating counseling with a child or adolescent, this transition can be difficult. This relationship may reflect the one time in a child's life when he or she receives the focused attention of a caring adult (Thompson & Henderson, 2007). Therefore, certain considerations should be in place prior to termination (when a termination date is known or expected). Children, especially younger ones, should be given ample warning that the relationship is coming to an end. That means a child client should be alerted three to four weeks prior to the end of counseling. In these final sessions, the student client and counselor can discuss plans for the final sessions, reflect on the child's progress, and perhaps even talk about the need for a follow-up session. It is helpful to place an emphasis on the degree to which a child has grown or the amount of progress made rather than focusing on the end of the relationship. You might introduce the topic of termination by stating something like,

> We've been working together for four weeks now. *When* you first started talking with me, you were feeling left out at recess and not sure how to approach other students. *Now* you've learned some great skills for how to talk to other kids, and you're even going to have Katy over to your house this weekend. You've worked so hard, it seems like it may be time for us to wait a bit until we see each other again, maybe two to three weeks?

At the final session, the counselor may choose to give a student a small token reflecting their work together. For example, students in my (R.S.H.) practica have given their child and adolescent clients such items as a stress ball that the client and counselor made together, a special stone that reflected an adolescent's inner strength, or a homemade "book" that reviewed relaxation techniques. These tangible items not only support the work of the student client and professional helper but also serve as a reminder of a special relationship in the child's life. As noted by Thompson and Henderson (2007), these types of informal methods demonstrate that the professional's caring does not end with the formal counseling relationship.

Sometimes children and adolescents wonder about maintaining contact with a school-based helper over the summer break or during school vacations. This question would likely receive a variety of responses. Some would see this as inappropriate because it runs the risk of crossing a professional boundary between professional helper and student client. Others would not see any

Table 2.1 Counseling Termination Ideas for Children and Adolescents

Focus of Counseling	Type of Activity or Transitional Object
Aggression	• Bookmark of calming strategies • Excerpts from *Don't Pop Your Cork on Mondays* (Moser & Pilkey, 1988)
Stress/Worry	• Stress ball (preferably homemade) • Homemade book of relaxation techniques • Worry stone or beads • Affirmation poem
Self-esteem	• My wish for you . . . card with affirmations • Blank journal (either homemade or store bought) • Certificate designed for the child
Transition (e.g., parental divorce, moving)	• Coping strategies (e.g., homemade book, bookmark) • Certificate with symbol of work
Friendship Skills	• Hope, wish, challenge . . . card • Pages of skills bound in a homemade book
Study Skills and Organization	• Cue card for test taking • Sharpened pencil • Organizer
Career Choice Resolution	• Token of career • Goal-setting collage

problem with this as long as the helper had parent approval and did not attempt to befriend the student client or establish dependency. Examples of minimal contact might include a phone call or quick note. It is also important to determine the policy of the school or district in which you work to determine whether this type of contact outside the school year would be acceptable. Additionally, this is an important issue to discuss with a site-based supervisor to ensure that the purpose is consistent with a student client's needs rather than those of the professional helper.

What If a Student Does Not Want to Terminate?

School-based helpers do their best to make sure that students do not become dependent on them. In our work, we attempt to empower students and families by reinforcing their independent efforts to improve and grow, by noting how *their* efforts are making a difference, and by weaning our support once students begin to develop and implement successful strategies on their own. Despite our best efforts, some students may resist ending the counseling relationship even though they have met their goals. This resistance may come from anxious feelings related to fear of failing or disappointing others. It will be important to address these feelings and others related to termination during counseling.

When a student demonstrates this type of resistance, together you may develop a plan for decreasing the frequency of meetings. It may be that the student simply needs a little more time to build confidence in his or her newly acquired skills. Murphy (2008) also suggested letting the student know that you need to provide services to a number of students within the school and asking if the student would be interested in participating as a peer mentor in the future. Through these actions, the school-based helper can reinforce the student's progress, help that individual build empathy for the other students who may need services, and empower the student to help others. You can also reassure the student that you have an "open door" policy should there be a need to check in for support. Again, you'll want to be vigilant that the student does not become dependent on this type of informal drop-in (e.g., coming to your office two to three times per week). Additionally, we encourage school-based professionals to consider other resources available within the school setting (e.g., peer counselors, mentors, afterschool programs) that can serve as either a supplement or a transitional step for students who are terminating from more intensive counseling services. (See Chapter 15 for more information on creating a continuum of care for students.)

As the end of a school year approaches, some student clients transition to a different school. If a student needs to continue working with a supportive professional, a smooth transition can be facilitated by the current helper. Although technically you do not need a release of information to talk with another school-based helper within the same district, it represents best practice. Families should have a say in whether their child receives supportive follow-up in the next school placement. Further, it is important that they know how that follow-up might take place and with whom. You should first obtain a release from the parents of the student client so that you can openly share important information with the other professional helper in the next school setting.

Another strategy for easing transitions is to arrange an opportunity for the student client to visit the new school and the new school-based professional. This process may reduce the student's stress around this transition. Within large schools, there may be three or more counselors who take responsibility for different grade levels. Again, efforts can be directed toward setting up times to allow the student to meet and "get to know" the helper that will be providing support in the coming year.

REFERRING TO COMMUNITY SYSTEMS

As noted, there are times when students' needs for services are greater than what can be provided appropriately in a school setting. Examples of issues not appropriately treated in a school setting might be when a child reports a history of sexual or physical abuse, severe psychopathology (e.g., hearing voices, continual suicidal ideation), or a presenting issue that is beyond the expertise of the school-based helper. Unfortunately, there are no formal criteria for when to refer to an outside agency (Hughes & Theodore, 2009).

You can facilitate this referral process by being familiar with mental health service providers in your community. As a school-based professional, you can create a list of individuals in the community who specialize in working with children and adolescents, who have expertise in specific types of issues, and who accept different types of insurance or payment (e.g., sliding fee scale, Medicaid). Sometimes these types of resource lists are available through community agencies such as United Way or a local family advocacy and resource center. It is best if more than one resource is provided so that it does not appear that you are promoting a particular individual's business. Instead, if you provide families with three to four community resources who provide the type of counseling needed, they can more easily select a therapist who meets their particular needs (e.g., location, cost, scheduling).

Depending on the needs of the family, you might provide further support with this transition by reviewing with the family what to expect at their first meeting (e.g., informed-consent paperwork, intake), helping the family make the phone call for the appointment, or agreeing to meet them at the new location for their appointment. You would reserve this type of support for those families who might have difficulty arranging for this type of transition (e.g., parents who are low functioning, experiencing instability) yet seem invested in pursuing support for their child. Additionally, you would want to obtain the family's permission to contact the new therapist so that you can communicate openly about the student's progress and provide support in the school as appropriate.

In an urban or suburban setting, you will likely have established relationships with outside agencies to which you can refer students with abuse and other significant concerns. You may even be lucky enough to work in a school where individuals from the local mental health center come to the schools to provide therapeutic services to students. In a rural district, this type of referral service becomes much more complicated as you may be the only mental health professional within a 100-mile radius.

WORKING IN THE SCHOOLS: A DELICATE BALANCE

Over the last 15 to 20 years, there has been a growing emphasis on developing students' academic skills rather than their social and emotional skills. Legislative changes such as the No Child Left Behind Act (2002) have implemented greater accountability for academic outcomes. As a result, some educational professionals believe there is no time for support services such as counseling, and they are reluctant to allocate time and resources toward these nonacademic efforts. Additionally, a growing social conservatism has given greater focus to the rights of parents to provide for their children's education and to ensure that children are not exposed to services or curricula that may run counter to their beliefs. Therefore, some school-based professionals have found it increasingly difficult to obtain parent permission to provide small-group counseling. Others have encountered teachers who were reluctant to release students from class and schools that have attempted to omit all curricula that are not specifically focused on an academic area such as reading or math.

Operating in a school means finding compromise and helping others to understand how the social-emotional health of individuals and classrooms enhances the academic learning of students (Adelman & Taylor, 2010; Merrell & Gueldner, 2010). It also means being an active member of a team but also one who maintains certain boundaries and confidentialities. For example, at the end of a tough day, a group of teachers might be blowing off steam about how "wild" the students were or how frustrated they are about a new curriculum that doesn't seem to be working. It might be tempting to join in with some stories from your "tough day"; however, that would be unwise because you could violate confidentiality or invite questions that you could not answer.

School-based helping professionals hold a unique role within a school setting. Because they do not have a dedicated classroom, they are often perceived as available for most any task that needs doing or worse yet, as not doing anything. Therefore, self-advocacy and visibility are necessary to let people know what you do and to see the value of your role. Your perspectives on and methods for helping students achieve academic and social goals are different from others in the school, so you must work consistently as part of a team to interweave your guidance lessons, groups, and individual work into the daily fabric of the school day. As part of a school faculty, you will want to develop close, collegial relationships, but you must also be aware that as the local "mental health professional," some school personnel might seek you out to provide support, advice, or even counseling on personal issues. As a professional, it is critical that you are aware of the boundaries between supportive colleague and becoming someone's personal therapist.

In an agency setting, a practitioner is generally free to work with individuals to help them achieve their goals, with the only constraints being time and perhaps insurance restrictions. Working together, the counselor and the client make decisions about the goals for their work and the type of therapeutic strategies that will be used. They decide when their work is complete. In contrast, school-based professionals make decisions with a team (e.g., When can I provide my guidance lessons? What would be a good time to have this student come to my office and for how long? What types of groups will be provided this year and when?).

Although ultimately you will talk with the family and the student about the goals of counseling, you will often find that you get a lot of "helpful" advice from teachers and administrators about potential therapeutic goals (e.g., "He just needs someone to talk to," "Tell her to stop being so sensitive," "If he could just stay in his seat and focus, there wouldn't be a problem"). Finally, in an agency setting, the client's attendance at counseling sessions and the content of the sessions remains confidential. In contrast, there is always a certain awareness in the school system about who is seeing the counselor. Because you are often removing a student from class, sending a pass down to the office, or simply observed entering your office with a student, at least a few other individuals are aware of who has come to see you. While not necessarily a problem, it may invite queries from teachers, administrators, and sometimes other students (e.g., "I saw Janie going into your office yesterday, what's going on with her?"; "Thanks for seeing BJ today. What did you find out?"). Some of these topics will be visited again in more detail in subsequent chapters, but it is helpful to understand from the beginning that providing counseling services in the schools is vastly different from setting up a private counseling office that just happens to be located in a school.

> ✱ You can minimize the potential "stigma" of students coming to your office if you are involved in a variety of activities that are not related to counseling (e.g., afterschool clubs, advisor to student council).

Once you have built relationships, it will facilitate the collaborative teaming that is an integral part of the school setting. Bryan and Holcomb-McCoy (2010) defined collaboration as a partnership in which the school-based professional and parents, teachers, administrators, and community members "work jointly and mutually to develop and implement school- and community-based prevention and intervention programs and activities to improve children's chances of academic, personal/social, career, and college success" (p. ii). Within schools, much of the decision making occurs through committee and group processes. For example, a school may have an established building leadership team that reviews, recommends, and selects programs that will be established within a particular school. As a professional helper, you will likely be a member of one or more of these collaborative teams.

All too often, school-based programming and services designed to address student needs are fragmented and poorly coordinated (Adelman & Taylor, 2006). In some instances, district leadership might have mandated a specific program that is not well accepted or appropriate for the different needs of students across school settings. Other school-based programming may have been in place for years, and certain staff may have taken great pride and "ownership" of the program. In another scenario, individual school-based professional helpers (i.e., school counselors, school psychologists) may be duplicating services because they do not have clear communication with one another.

Although school personnel direct a great deal of effort toward supporting students and their families, a more systemic, comprehensive process is needed to address barriers and maximize learning. For example, many schools have adopted schoolwide positive behavioral support (SWPBS) programming (Horner, Sugai, Todd, & Lewis-Palmer, 2005). A school-based helper needs to have knowledge of the existing programs, who is served in these programs, the effectiveness of these efforts, and how well the program is perceived in the school (e.g., face validity). Adelman and Taylor (2006) recommended resource mapping as a strategy for organizing this type of information so that you, and your team, can analyze areas of overlap and gaps in these services. By working as an active team member, you can gather this knowledge and make informed decisions about how to proceed when introducing ideas for new programming or services.

This brief overview of the unique aspects of working in the school setting was designed to provide a glimpse into the role of school-based professional helpers. It is a complex and challenging job that can be exciting and frustrating but almost always rewarding. Each day will be different. You will find yourself fulfilling multiple roles as you negotiate the balance between professional helper, staff member, colleague, and child advocate. As you advance in your career, you will be able to play a greater role as a leader and a change agent. For now, we recommend learning everything you can, establishing yourself in your new setting, and pacing yourself as you find balance between your professional and personal roles.

Activities

1. Talk to an established member of your school's building leadership team. Ask about the various student wellness programs, how they were selected, goals of the programs, and how the outcomes are measured. Bring this information to class and compare with your peers. What are the common types of programs?

2. Download the Resource Mapping and Management to Address Barriers to Learning packet available at http://smhp.psych.ucla.edu/pdfdocs/resource-mapping/resourcemappingandmanagement.pdf. Develop a resource map of your school. You may need to work with a supervisor or others who are more familiar with school resources to complete these forms.

3. Develop a potential script of what you might say during the final session with a child or adolescent. Be sure to include your experience of working with the student. Ask the student about what he or she remembers, and discuss plans or skills to use in the future.

Journal Reflections

Reflection #1

Consider your own strengths and areas for growth in relation to entering a new system. Which do you think might serve you well, and which might be disadvantages?

Reflection #2

Describe an ideal day in your work as a school-based professional helper. What would you be doing? How does your day compare to the guidelines put forth by your professional organization?

Reflection #3

Sometimes a professional helper has difficulty terminating when it is appropriate to do so. The individual may really enjoy working with the child and be tempted to prolong a close counseling relationship. How will you monitor your needs versus the child's?

Electronic Resources

Center for Mental Health in the Schools: http://smhp.psych.ucla.edu/

Edutopia: http://www.Edutopia.org

The New School Counselor: http://www.school-counselor.org/topics/new-school-counselor.html

New School Psychologist Support: How to Avoid Crashing and Burning your First Year: http://www.eric.ed.gov/ERICWebPortal/search/detailmini.jsp?_nfpb=true&_&ERICExtSearch_SearchValue_0=ED454483&ERICExtSearch_SearchType_0=no&accno=ED454483

School Psychology Resources: http://www.schoolpsychology.net/

Print Resources

American School Counselor Association. (2004). *ASCA national model workbook: A companion guide for implementing a comprehensive school counseling program.* Alexandria, VA: Author.

CHAPTER 3

Understanding the Developmental Worldview of Children and Adolescents

Learning Objectives

- Understand how child and adolescent development across cognitive, physical, and social/emotional domains potentially affects counseling interactions
- Understand concepts of risk and resilience and the application of this knowledge to school-based support services
- Understand the importance of children's development in the context of home, school, and community

During medieval times, children were considered to be miniature adults who were the same as their larger counterparts in every way except size. Much later, Rousseau (1762/1955), the French philosopher, put forth the romantic notion of the child as a noble savage who was naturally endowed with an innate sense of right and wrong that would be harmed by adult interference. These mixed notions of childhood resulted in a relatively late understanding of the difficulties that children experience and the subsequent application of adult theories and strategies to treat identified issues. As the field of developmental psychology has advanced, we not only have a much better understanding of how the minds, bodies, and emotions of children develop, but we also understand that they view the world differently than adults do. With this knowledge, we can create developmentally appropriate counseling programs and adapt our skills to meet the needs of children and adolescents.

SCHOOL-BASED SUPPORT
FOR CHILDREN AND ADOLESCENTS

Mental health professionals cannot stop children from experiencing stress or negative events in their lives. However, the timely provision of preventive and intervention programs can go a long way toward reducing the incidence of emotional and behavioral difficulties (NRC & IOM, 2009). When parents find that their children are struggling, they often turn to their family physician or to a school-based professional helper. Given the position of schools as one of the lead agencies in delivering mental health support to children and adolescents, it is critical that those in positions to provide these services (e.g., school counselors, school psychologists, school social workers) are well-prepared to engage in prevention, early intervention, and crisis response as needed. The most efficient place to deliver these types of services is in schools where children and adolescents spend their days.

There is a wide range of effective prevention and intervention strategies that may be used by a school-based professional on any given day. Counseling is one of the foundational skills used either in isolation or as a component of one of the other approaches (e.g., consultation, guidance). Within the *ASCA National Model: A Framework for School Counseling Programs* (2005), individual or group counseling is one of the key elements in a responsive delivery system. Recently, the National Association of School Psychologists also adopted a *Model for Comprehensive and Integrated School Psychological Services* (2010b) that promotes the use of "interventions and mental health services to address social and life skill development" as one of the key domains of school psychology practice. Clearly, the provision of counseling services to children, adolescents, and families is an important role for school-based helpers.

To be an effective helper, you must consider both the presenting issue and students' developmental level when selecting and implementing counseling interventions. There can be serious limitations to traditional counseling approaches that rely too heavily on language or oral expression, especially when working with a younger population or students who have disabilities. School-based professionals need to be familiar with and skilled in the use of developmentally appropriate approaches that match the students' cognitive, verbal, and emotional levels.

UNDERSTANDING THE DEVELOPMENT
OF CHILDREN AND ADOLESCENTS

Developmental theories relate to almost every aspect of children's functioning. Although we have presented each of the different developmental domains separately (e.g., physical, cognitive), it is important to understand that these areas are intertwined. Advances in one area are only made possible by growth in another area (e.g., moral development is made possible by advances in cognitive skills). It is also important to keep in mind that not all students develop at the same rate. The suggested age ranges reflect typical development, but by no means do they signify that there is something wrong with students if they are not yet ready to perform age-appropriate developmental tasks. Additionally, there are differences across culture in how development within these domains is experienced. For the purposes of this chapter, we focus on those developmental domains that are most likely to be relevant to a counseling relationship: physical, cognitive, language, moral, and social-emotional.

Physical Development

As children develop, physical changes will be apparent to the casual observer. What is less obvious are the many important physiological and neurological changes occurring that will facilitate the other areas of development. During infancy and early childhood, children develop an incredible number of synapses, or branches that reach between neurons. Shortly after this fantastic cycle of growth, many of these synapses disappear. Those that are used more frequently remain. This process is known as *synaptic pruning*. The process of growth and shedding takes place over the course of several years (McDevitt & Ormrod, 2010; Nelson, Thomas, & de Haan, 2006). It is hypothesized that the overgrowth of synapses prepares young children to adapt to their environments. Once it is determined which synapses are used and which are unnecessary, the excess connections disappear, allowing the brain to work more efficiently (McDevitt & Ormrod, 2010).

A process known as myelination also begins early in a child's development. In this process an insulating layer of fat covers nerve cells. The insulating layer increases the speed at which neurochemical information moves along the axon, facilitating more rapid and efficient information processing (Travis, 1998). At the earliest ages, those nerves that involve sensory development become myelinated, followed by those neurons responsible for motor development. The final area of the brain in which myelination occurs is in the cortex with the neurons associated with complex thinking skills (Nelson et al., 2006). This pattern of brain growth continues through late adolescence.

> When working with adolescents, a common thought experienced by professional helpers is, "What were they thinking?" We must remember that the nerve cells that connect adolescents' frontal lobes with the rest of their brains are still developing. This means that this part of the brain, which manages such complex skills as planning, impulse control, and reasoning, can be accessed but not always quickly.

Attention span has also been linked to myelination. Therefore, children's ability to concentrate and attend to novel stimuli increases with age and brain development. Because of these important development differences, the school-based practitioner needs to be aware that younger children may need shorter sessions and more "think time" to respond than an adolescent.

As noted, children also experience relatively rapid growth in their bodies. By the time a girl reaches 12, she will likely have entered a period of rapid physical development, including the onset of menarche (Schaffer, 1999). Boys lag slightly behind and begin their developmental changes around the age of 13. The timing of puberty can be a great source of stress for young adolescents particularly if it is significantly before or after that of their peers. For example, early maturing girls are more likely to report a variety of internalizing and externalizing symptoms than their same-age, same-gender peers who experienced average pubertal maturation (Ge, Conger, & Elder, 2001). Regardless of the timing of puberty, it can be a difficult time in which young adolescents feel anxious, self-conscious, and awkward (Vernon, 2009).

Cognitive Development

Overall, children's thinking develops in a predictable pattern, but the unique interpretations that children apply to their worlds along this path can be surprising. Indeed, children and adolescents have their own way of structuring information that is sometimes highly distinct from adults. Additionally, the development of cognitive abilities is idiosyncratic and inconsistent; therefore it is impossible to make sweeping generalizations (Schaffer, 1999).

Both Piaget (1970) and Vygotsky (1978) have contributed much to our understanding of how children develop and build on their cognitive skills up to the highest levels of reasoning. McDevitt and Ormrod (2010) asserted that both theories considered together provide a more complete picture of cognitive development than either theory alone. From this perspective, they have organized the theories of Piaget and Vygotsky according to common themes.

One of the first common components for both theorists is the idea that children *construct their own knowledge* rather than absorb it (McDevitt & Ormrod, 2010). While Piaget described distinct stages through which children pass as they organize their thinking, Vygotsky asserted that children had their own unique ways of internalizing information based on their social contexts. For the school-based professional, this may mean that part of your role is helping student clients to develop their understanding of and the ability to internalize concepts that are unfamiliar to them. You may find yourself teaching as well as counseling. At the youngest ages, it is important that we talk to children about their experiences and the meanings that they apply to them. If children don't understand the relationship between two items or events, they are just as likely to make up an explanation without considering whether it is plausible or not (Dehart, Sroufe, & Cooper, 2000).

As students progress through the grades, you can provide different levels of learning supports to assist their understanding. For example, in the early elementary grades you may need to use pictures, games, or puppets to teach new ideas and concepts. In the intermediate grades, you may discuss more abstract ideas (e.g., jealousy, empathy) but will likely need to supplement these concepts with concrete examples. By adolescence, students are generally able to use flexible, abstract thinking but may be inconsistent in their application of logical reasoning. For example, many adolescents are better at applying cause-and-effect reasoning to others' situations than to their own (Vernon & Clemente, 2005). Thus, school-based helpers can help adolescents apply cause-and-effect reasoning to their own lives

Regardless of the student's age, it is important to explore the meaning that he or she assigns to an event or situation. Take time to understand the student's perspective and help correct any misconceptions.

A second common theme in children's cognitive development is that of *readiness* (McDevitt &

Ormrod, 2010). Both Piaget and Vygotsky recognized that there were certain limitations to children's cognitive abilities that did not allow them to engage in more advanced cognitive processes until they had reached a point where they were "ready." In Piaget's description of *accommodation*, children were able to comprehend new concepts by assimilating this information into existing cognitive schema. Vygotsky (1978) saw this process as more flexible and introduced the *zone of proximal development*. From this perspective, children were continually adding new skills and abilities to their repertoires and were able to access more advanced knowledge with adult support and guidance, as long as the new information was within this "zone."

There are many different areas where the professional helper can assist student clients in obtaining higher levels of thinking. For example, young children sometimes have difficulty understanding that a person or event can be viewed in different ways (e.g., as having both positive and negative aspects). By introducing other perspectives, the school-based helper can guide the child toward a better understanding of an abstract issue (e.g., divorce, a tragic event). Students may need visuals or hands-on activities to help them "see" different aspects of a concept. Many times when asked what they're feeling, children will respond with a single word, such as "mad," "sad," or "happy." When attempting to help children understand that they can experience more than one feeling at a time, it may be helpful to provide an outline of a human figure on which they can use colored markers to depict different feelings. These types of visual aids can assist children to grasp complicated concepts (e.g., "When friends do not invite me to play, I feel both angry and sad at the same time").

Another area in which students may need support from an adult helper is in predicting what would happen under hypothetical conditions. In fact, certain theoretical approaches (i.e., solution-focused counseling) require that a student engage in "What if . . ." thinking. Generally, young children are able to engage in this hypothetical reasoning but are better at understanding how to avoid a negative situation rather than to attain a positive outcome (German, 1999). For example, a child may be able to brainstorm other alternatives to fighting with a peer by simply saying, "I wouldn't hit him" or "I'd walk away." In these instances, it is difficult to know if a student client really views this as a possible solution or if he or she is simply repeating a strategy that has been taught.

A professional working with younger children may have to establish with a child that a current situation is not satisfactory before the child is able to engage in hypothetical reasoning about alternative outcomes. As an illustration, consider the case of a young student who routinely engages in fist fights with his peers whenever he perceives that he has been slighted or treated unfairly. It might seem

Ask student clients to think about the positive steps that could be taken to resolve a situation (e.g., "What might be some things you could do in order to get along with Mason?" or "What would it look like if you and Cassidy were friends?"). Use these strategies as a starting point for teaching and practicing new skills.

evident to the helper that if this child is removed from the classroom or receives an in-school suspension (negative consequence), the student's continued use of fighting is not a good solution. However, the student client might not share this perspective and instead view fighting as a way to show his peers that he did not like their actions. It is only through a deeper exploration of other potential negative outcomes (e.g., missing time with favored peers, getting in trouble at home, and recognizing that the problem is not solved) that the student client may be able to acknowledge that his solution (i.e., fighting) is not achieving the desired outcome.

The third common theme shared by Piaget and Vygotsky is that of *challenge* (McDevitt & Ormrod, 2010). When children are challenged to think just beyond their level of understanding, they are able to obtain deeper levels of comprehension (Remmel & Flavell, 2004). Students live in complex worlds where they are regularly expected to learn and adapt to new situations. Counseling dialogue also can serve as a form of stimulation that assists children and adolescents in thinking differently about their current situation, their own behaviors, or their future goals. Both interactions with peers and adults can challenge youth to engage in more complex levels of thinking (McDevitt & Ormrod, 2010). For example, peers can help other students adopt new perspectives on social relationships and other views on the world through peer mentoring programs, while an adult may be best suited to teach students new skills (Gauvin, 2001).

The fourth common theme in the development of children's cognitive development is the *importance of social interaction* (McDevitt & Ormrod, 2010). It is through our daily interactions with others that we come to understand that others think differently about the world than we do. From a very early age (i.e., three–four years old), children begin to make the distinction between thinking and doing as well as their own thoughts versus those of another (Wellman & Lagattuta, 2000). This growing awareness of an internal mental life is referred to as *theory of mind*. It is a relatively new area of research but explains a great deal about how children think about their own and other's thoughts. A child's ability to understand that individuals might engage in behavior according to their own false beliefs increases between the ages of four and six. This knowledge is a good predictor of later social skill development (Jenkins & Astington, 2000). Theory of mind is developed through language, make-believe play, and social interaction (Berk, 2008). This construct is important to the work of a school-based professional because in your various roles as guidance teacher, group facilitator, and individual counselor, you will be assisting students in the process of learning from and working with one another.

One of the key areas where students may need assistance is in changing their maladaptive beliefs. Students are not likely to make these revisions independently, especially if there is any evidence that seems to lend support for their erroneous assumptions. As young people apply their reasoning skills, they can show a bias toward positive rather than negative testing of their beliefs (Remmel & Flavell, 2004). That is, "If this piece of information is true, then my hypothesis is correct" rather than, "If this piece of information is true, my belief is incorrect." Although this trend is also seen in adults, it is especially true for children and adolescents (Remmel & Flavell, 2004). For example, Jaime believes himself to be unpopular and unworthy of friendships. As a result, he tends to see any occurrence of other students failing to greet him or inviting him to join them as "evidence" of his basic unworthiness. A school-based professional can assist Jaime in understanding how "evidence" that seems to support these beliefs may also have alternative explanations. As an alternative hypothesis, a helper might introduce the idea that other students don't ask Jaime to join them because they do not know him very well. The student client can then be challenged to "test out" these alternative explanations through small, supported steps (e.g., introducing himself to a peer whom he views as friendly, offering to share his materials with a student seated next to him).

Although there are a few clear areas where Vygotsky and Piaget differed in their conceptualization of cognitive development, one of the most important was in the area of the role of culture. Whereas Piaget viewed his stages of cognitive development as universal across cultures, Vygotsky (1978) placed great importance on a child's culture and saw it as paramount to the emergence of reasoning skills. Children from different cultures demonstrate differences in the timing of certain abilities, and in some cultures, formal operational reasoning may not appear at all because it has little bearing on everyday functioning (Miller, 1997; Norenzayan, Choi, & Peng, 2007).

Language Development

By the time children reach the age of six, they will have a vocabulary of about 10,000 words (Bloom, 1998). The mechanisms by which young children learn words so quickly and to use them in meaningful sentences is not fully understood (Berk, 2008). Nevertheless, most children will enter kindergarten with the ability to carry on a conversation by taking turns, keeping on topic, and using meaningful sentences—the pragmatics of language. They will have learned most of these skills through their exposure to and involvement in conversations (Berk, 2008).

Younger children assign concrete meanings to words, and it is not until they are in middle school that they will begin to understand the double meanings of words. For this reason, the school-based helper must be careful not to use certain types of humor that may be misunderstood, such as irony or sarcasm. As children develop, they become better able to organize their stories, to provide more detail, and to be expressive in their delivery (Berk, 2008). By adolescence, students are able to use and understand irony and sarcasm in responding to others. All aspects of their language skills continue to develop including vocabulary and grammar. One of the greatest language developments in adolescence is the degree to which students learn to vary their language depending on the situation. An adolescent male may use informal slang with his peers, a slightly more formal tone with his teachers or the principal (e.g., use of titles and last names, appropriate grammar), and a polite, friendly form of communication at his job as a fast-food cashier.

Moral Development

As children's cognitions become more complex and they are able to see the world from another's point of view, their moral reasoning advances. At the earliest stages, Kohlberg (1981) proposed that children are in a *preconventional* stage in which they react to questions of right or wrong based on whether they are rewarded or punished by adults. At the next level, *conventional*, children begin to incorporate a broader, more abstract perspective into their moral reasoning and seek to maintain the social order. At this level, it is important to children to be seen as "good" and to seek favor of those in authority. The final stage described by Kohlberg was the *postconventional* stage in which individuals are able to consider the perspectives of others in their moral decision making. Rather than investing in being "good," individuals make judgments based on broad, moral principles. Historically, it was believed that important gender differences existed with females demonstrating more of a care (i.e., relationship-oriented) focus and males presenting with more of a justice (i.e., fairness and equity) focus (Gilligan & Attanucci, 1988). However, a comprehensive meta-analysis conducted by Jaffee and Hyde (2000) indicated that these gender differences were quite small and that it was more likely that males and females used a blend of both care and justice in moral reasoning.

The stage of moral development must be considered when working with student clients because their level of moral reasoning guides their decision making. That is, a young child may place the greatest importance on whether or not a behavior will result in a negative consequence. Students may be reluctant to tell you about feelings or behaviors because they are afraid that they might be punished. Further, it may be difficult for them to understand the bigger implications of their actions. Your role as the professional helper is to recognize children's developmental level and to encourage them to entertain more advanced levels of moral reasoning. For example, the helper might say, "You're right, if you hit Colton every time he teased you, you would probably get in trouble. So, although that is one idea about how to handle his teasing, I wonder what might be some other things you could try."

Social-Emotional Development

Many different aspects of our personalities, biological makeup, and personal experiences determine how we respond to difficult situations in our lives. For children, temperament is one of the key components that predict their responses. Although we all have traits or characteristics that are considered to be a part of our "personality," children have certain temperaments that, to some degree, determine their reactions to and interactions with others and the environment. There are nine dimensions or categories of temperament: (a) activity level, (b) adaptability (quick vs. gradual), (c) first reaction (bold vs. cautious), (d) predominant mood (pleasant vs. serious), (e) strength of response (mild vs. intense), (f) distractability, (g) persistence, (h) daily biological rhythm (rhythmic/arrhythmic), and (i) sensory threshold (sensitive vs. nonsensitive; Kristal, 2005). Younger children may be more susceptible to responding based on their temperament, and their level of functioning is governed in part by the "goodness of fit" between their temperament and the expectations of their environment (Kristal, 2005). As children develop cognitively, other aspects of functioning moderate these more basic reactions.

Theorists have proposed different methods for organizing a child's social-emotional development including a stage model (Erikson, 1958/1963) and developmental tasks (Havighurst, 1972). Although these stages are helpful in considering broad transitions in a child's social functioning, some of the more recent findings related to social cognition may play a more significant role in guiding one's counseling interactions. Two of the most important aspects of social cognition include self-concept and perspective taking.

Sense of Self. There are a number of ways to describe how individuals think and feel about themselves. Sense of self serves as an umbrella term for these differing constructs (e.g., self-esteem, self-concept; McDevitt & Ormrod, 2010). Self-concept is related to both cognitive and social-emotional development and refers to one's understanding of oneself as an independent person with unique and consistent attributes (Harter, 2006). During the preoperational stage of cognitive development, behaviors and observable attributes define the self ("I can run fast"). As children age, these global, positive descriptions become more differentiated (McDevitt & Ormrod, 2010). Children can talk about themselves as being different across situations and domains ("I am smart in math," "I am good at sports"). A related idea is that of self-worth or self-esteem in which students make a value statement about different aspects of their traits or about themselves as individuals (e.g., "I am embarrassed by the way I look," "I am proud of what a good athlete I am"). As you might expect, those students who see themselves in a favorable light in an area that is important to them tend to report higher self-esteem (McDevitt & Ormrod, 2010). That is, if Chelsea views herself as a good student and achievement is important to her, it is likely that she will feel good about herself. Conversely, if Chelsea believes popularity to be more important than achievement, she may not feel as good about herself if she has only a small circle of friends.

Generally speaking, children and adolescents tend to focus on the things they do well more so than those areas where they are weaker (Harter, 2006). As a result, children tend to feel pretty good about themselves. Further, children and adolescents tend to behave in ways that reflect their perceptions of themselves (Valentine, DuBois, & Cooper, 2004). If a pupil sees himself as a good student, he is likely to attend class, pay attention, put forth effort, and take on challenges in the classroom. Unfortunately, children's competence beliefs tend to decline as they grow older (e.g., Jacobs, Lanza, Osgood, Eccles, & Wigfield, 2002). Another clear pattern is that students tend to engage in behaviors to avoid perceived weaker areas. In some instances, students may actually engage in behaviors that hinder their performance in an effort to protect their sense of self-worth. McDevitt and Ormrod (2010) referred to this behavior as self-handicapping and described it as those behaviors students engage in that provide them with an excuse for failing (e.g., "I'll probably blow this test today because I didn't even read the chapter").

Children tend to base their self-perceptions on their own past performance as well as external evaluations (e.g., adult and peer interactions, group membership; Dweck, 2002; Guay, Marsh, & Boivin, 2003; Harter, 2006). As children get older, they tend to rely more heavily on their peers than their family for their sense of self-worth (Harter, 2006; McDevitt & Ormrod, 2010). Another developmental component of sense of self is that individuals begin to internalize others' criteria for success (Harter, 2006). For example, a young student might want to get an

> Self-handicapping behaviors might include lack of effort, cheating, procrastinating, taking on too much, setting unrealistic goals, and even using drugs and alcohol (McDevitt & Ormrod, 2010).

"A" on a test because it will please her parents. As she reaches adolescence, it becomes more likely that she will want to do well on the test because it is important to her and fits with her self-perception that she is a good student. Despite this trend, some adolescents continue to rely heavily on what others think of them, which can contribute to the "storm and stress" often ascribed to adolescent emotions and behavior (McDevitt & Ormrod, 2010). Adolescents also form subcultures that are defined as small groups of students who have similar interests and shared beliefs. Adolescence is a time of seeking identity. Students at this developmental level try new looks, listen to different music, and generally explore other representations of themselves. For the professional helper, it is important to find a balance in recognizing when students are exploring their identities and when they are involved in a dangerous subculture (e.g., cutting, multiple piercings, sexual experimentation).

The emergence of abstraction allows pre- or early adolescents to integrate differing trait labels into a single abstract concept (e.g., "I'm smart in math and dumb in reading. Overall, I'm about average"). Students may see themselves as a bundle of contradictions ("I am this type of person and a seemingly incompatible type of person at the same time") and may be confused about such contradictions. As youth enter young adulthood, they are able to integrate these different conceptions of themselves into a higher-order abstraction so the self is no longer viewed as contradictory and fragmented (Harter, 2006). For example, the individual views his or her values, behaviors, and attitudes as well as participation in particular religious or social or political activities as reflecting a tendency toward a particular belief system. Overall, these progressive stages involve global attributions that reflect a movement toward a more integrated and fully developed sense of self (Harter, 2006; McDevitt & Ormrod, 2010). For the school-based helper, it can be difficult to keep pace with adolescents who are engaged in this self-exploration as their ideas, values, and goals may seem to change on a daily basis.

Some children view their abilities as traits over which they have little control, whereas others attribute their skills to practice and effort (Dweck, 2002). Children who hold the latter perspective tend to take on more challenges and display more resiliency than children who see ability as innate and fixed. From about middle childhood onward, self-esteem becomes fairly established. As a result, children who have a positive sense of self tend to continue to see themselves in a positive light (Robins & Trzesniewski, 2005). Unfortunately, the opposite is true as well. The professional should remain alert to the development of these negative self-cognitions and help youth differentiate their ideas about themselves, create opportunities for them to challenge negative self-perceptions, and introduce situational factors as alternative explanations for performance.

Just as children attribute certain characteristics to themselves, they also assign attributions to others. Of particular concern are those students who have a hostile attributional bias, meaning that they are more likely to attribute a hostile or aggressive intention to ambiguous behavior (Dodge et al., 2003). For example, if John is walking down the hall during the passing period and is jostled by another student, he is more likely to assume that the student meant to harm him and to react aggressively. A professional working with John should target his attributions and encourage him to explore alternative explanations for the perceived insult. Interventions geared toward reducing aggression and enhancing personal responsibility have been shown to be effective in decreasing aggressive behavior (Hudley, Graham, & Taylor, 2007).

Social Perspective Taking. An important aspect of learning to get along with others is the ability to understand and consider that others may perceive information differently from oneself (Remmel & Flavell, 2004). The foundations for perspective taking begin as early as preschool and continue to develop into childhood and adolescence. One of the first steps in this process is understanding one's own perspective, which occurs by age five. At age six or seven, children come to understand that different people can perceive the exact same thing yet form different interpretations of what they have seen (Selman, 2003).

By middle childhood, children's perspective taking becomes more complex, and they can understand that others not only have distinct views, but those views include an understanding of another child's perspective. That is, not only does Jeannie believe it is unfair that Amanda is the leader of the reading group two weeks in a row, she is able to understand that Amanda believes it to be fair because she missed her week earlier in the year (i.e., perceives the same event differently). Further, Jeannie and Amanda understand that the other has a different point of view (reciprocal understanding). As children enter adolescence and adulthood their ability to understand broader perspectives across multiple levels increases (Selman, 2003). Despite this understanding, aspects of egocentrism continue into adolescence and even adulthood. For example, adolescents often overestimate the amount of attention that other people pay to them, a concept known as "imaginary audience" (Alberts, Elkind, & Ginsberg, 2007). For the professional working with Angelina, a young adolescent with cognitive delays who is struggling to make friends, the focus of the intervention may be on improving perspective-taking ability to facilitate improved interactions with others.

As with other areas of development, culture plays an important role in one's sense of self (Morelli & Rothbaum, 2007). For example, in Western societies, particularly North America, the orientation tends to be more *individualistic*, and children are encouraged to focus on their own goals, motivations, and needs (Markus & Hamedani, 2007). Children are reinforced for being confident and having a strong sense of self-worth based on their own accomplishments (McDevitt & Ormrod, 2010). Other societies place a greater emphasis on families and communities and are considered to be more *collectivist* in orientation (e.g., East Asia). In these societies, an individual's sense of self is considered part of a strong social network that includes their families and communities (Wang & Li, 2003). This distinction may be too simplistic and overlook important differences across culture and domain. Wang and Li (2003) described a more complex structure where a relational orientation remained relatively stable over time, but individualistic goals related to learning and achievement increased as Chinese children progressed in school. It has also been suggested that children who are from collectivist societies may have less need for positive self-regard (Heine, Lehman, Markus, & Kitayama, 1999) in relation to American society and are more able to admit self-limitations (Brophy, 2004).

This brief review of development highlights some of the various ways that children's developmental level can impact their participation in the counseling relationship. In Table 3.1 we have summarized some of the key aspects of development across different domains and provide potential implications for the practice of school-based professional helpers. It is important that we do not talk down to children, but at the same time, we cannot ask them multipart questions, use abstract language, and expect them to respond. We must be careful to break ideas into smaller parts, to use examples and visuals when possible, to pace ourselves, and to be aware of our level of language.

Table 3.1 Developmental Stages and Implications for School-Based Professionals

Child's Developmental Level	Possible Implications for School-Based Professional Helpers
Cognitive	
• Preoperational: Children (ages 3–6*) have difficulty handling more than one concept at a time.	• The professional is careful to introduce only one new idea at a time into a session. • Use concrete examples and manipulatives (e.g., puppets, games) to assist the child's understanding.
• Concrete operational: Children (ages 7–12) are able to apply logic to classify objects (or understand relationships between objects and ideas from more than one dimension).	• Hands-on strategies should be incorporated to help the child understand connections between ideas. • Sand play activities can be incorporated to allow child opportunities to sort, arrange, and group objects (Carmichael, 2006).
• Formal operational: Adolescents (13–adult) begin to use more abstract thinking and are able to formulate and test hypotheses using logical thought and deductive reasoning.	• Children and young adolescents tend to seek information that confirms their beliefs and are less likely to attend to information that would be disconfirming. The professional may need to introduce and reinforce alternative explanations for interpreting events.
Physical	
• As the brain develops, children have an increasing ability to attend, remember, and process new information.	• At younger ages, counseling sessions will likely be shorter (~30 minutes), concepts will need to be repeated, and the helper will need to incorporate "wait time" (that is, give the child time to respond through the use of silence) into the session.
• Timing of puberty	• Helpers will want to be sensitive to students who are significantly different from their peers and provide education and support.
Moral	
• Preconventional stage	• Children may have difficulty judging for themselves the usefulness of their behavior in meeting goals as their judgments will be based on whether the behavior was rewarded or punished.

Child's Developmental Level	Possible Implications for School-Based Professional Helpers
• Conventional stage	• Children may be hesitant to share information with you as an adult and may fear being perceived as "bad." • Professionals must be especially careful not to lead children with questions or suggestions as young children are particularly eager to be seen as "good" (e.g., compliant with adults).
• Postconventional stage	• Adolescents may want to explore aspects of morality from different perspectives and will likely want to know the professional's opinion on controversial topics (e.g., sex before marriage, abortion).
Social/Emotional	
• Temperament	• The professional may consider the "goodness of fit" (Kristal, 2005) for young children who are experiencing behavioral challenges.
• Self-concept	• The professional may need to help children differentiate aspects of themselves versus adopting an "all good" or "all bad" perspective. • Children may seek out reinforcement for negative aspects of themselves, and the professional can help them to identify and change this pattern of behavior.
• Social Perspective Taking	• Young children may not understand that others see situations differently from themselves. • The professional can facilitate reciprocal social perspective-taking when conflict occurs.

*Age ranges presented in this table represent approximations and vary for every child based on his or her own unique pattern of development.

WORKING WITH STUDENTS WITH SPECIAL NEEDS

Students with learning disabilities account for the majority of the school population who receive special education services. *Learning disability* refers to a broad range of difficulties that may affect reading, writing, math, reasoning, and expressive/receptive language. Students who have learning disabilities most often have average levels of cognitive ability but are achieving at a rate much lower than expected. Although the causes of learning disabilities are quite varied and often unknown, they are thought to arise from a cognitive processing problem (Learning Disabilities Association of America, n.d.). As might be expected, learning difficulties affect students across social as well as academic settings. Students with learning disabilities often struggle with poor self-concept and social skills deficits (Raines, 2006).

Counseling programs that address social, personal, and career needs are important to helping students with learning disabilities to achieve their goals (Reis & Colbert, 2004). In their study of elementary-aged children with learning disabilities, Shechtman and Pastor (2005) found that group counseling either on its own or when combined with academic interventions resulted in more positive outcomes for these students than receiving academic intervention only. When counseling students with learning disabilities, it is important to keep in mind that their style and pace of learning may differ from those of their non-disabled peers. As a result, you may need to modify your curriculum, your method of presentation, your pace, and possibly your vocabulary to ensure that your students understand the material. The school-based professional will want to incorporate activities and examples that are meaningful to the student client and ensure that the interactions are both focused and fun.

Children with intellectual disabilities can also benefit from services directed to their specific needs. There are many different levels of ability among children who are intellectually disabled and levels of support needed (intermittent, limited, extensive or pervasive; Wicks-Nelson & Israel, 2003). Students with mild cognitive delays are most likely to be included in the regular classroom milieu and to face social and academic pressures. Some of the most common areas for support include developing adaptive skills, interpersonal relationships, language skills, and coping with emotional concerns (Hardman, Drew, Egan, & Wolf, 1993). Additionally, school-based professionals may want to facilitate specialized skill-building groups such as those that focus on self-advocacy. The school-based professional will want to use clear communication, break instructions down into manageable bits, review information frequently, and be encouraging and respectful of students (Parette & Hourcade, 1995).

At the other end of the ability spectrum are children who are gifted, who also sometimes experience social and emotional difficulties at school. For some gifted students, academic pressures and feeling different from peers contribute to these problems (Peterson, 2003). Many gifted students experience developmental unevenness where specific developmental levels are more advanced or lag behind others (e.g., cognitive versus emotional; Reis & Renzulli, 2004). Several different types of programs may be helpful for students who are gifted as well as those who are twice exceptional (gifted/learning disabled) including individual counseling, strategies for enhancing coping skills, and consultation with teachers regarding the unique needs of specific students (Reis & Colbert, 2004). Further, group counseling with gifted students may help them to realize that there are other students who having experiences similar to their own, and together the group can work toward expressing feelings appropriately, developing coping strategies, and building a supportive network (Reis & Colbert, 2004).

CHILDREN WITHIN AN ECOLOGICAL PERSPECTIVE

Child development occurs within the contexts of their family, school, peer group, and community. Children, especially the youngest, are "extraordinarily dependent on their psychosocial context to achieve adaptive functioning and mental health" (Steiner, 2004, p. 17). They are greatly impacted by their environments, and the contexts of their lives must be considered in developing an understanding of their needs as well as in intervention planning. For example, many changes have occurred in families over the last several decades including high rates of divorce, single parents, same-gendered parents, and children raised by grandparents. It is important to appreciate and respect these new family configurations but also not to be afraid to make suggestions on ways to improve family functioning to help children achieve in school.

An ecological theoretical framework can be useful for understanding these different settings and the relationships between contexts. Bronfenbrenner (1979) examined the social environment in a comprehensive manner and described the multiple spheres of influence that impact children. As shown in Figure 3.1, the influences of family, peers, school, and community are embedded within this ecological model. For example, when we consider risk, it is not just characteristics of the individual that place him or her at risk but the interactions between the individual and the environment (Gordon & Yowell, 1999). A social-ecological model framework such as Bronfenbrenner's (1979) ecological model can also be used to conceptualize service delivery at different levels.

Figure 3.1 Ecological Model

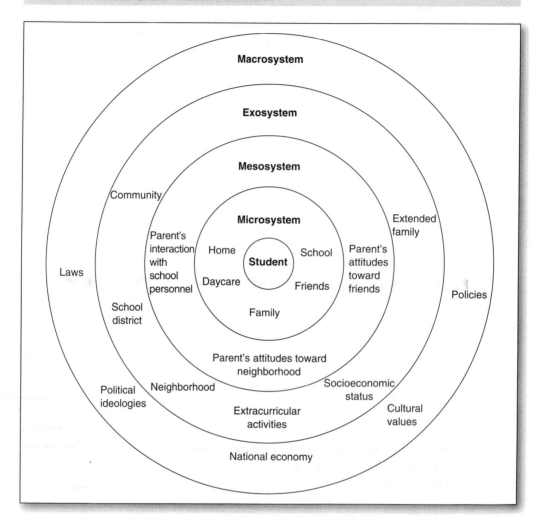

Because of all the complex links between the health of an individual and that of a system, an intervention directed solely at changing the individual is less likely to be successful than one that addresses the needs of the broader system (Weisz et al., 2005).

The ecological model has four contextual environments that impact the individual: the microsystem, mesosystem, exosystem, and macrosystem. The *microsystem* includes environments in which the child interacts on a daily basis, such as the home and classroom milieus. The relationships between contexts (e.g., the parent's *interactions* with the school) are addressed in the *mesosystem.* The *exosystem* might comprise the family's socioeconomic status, the neighborhood, and the larger school system. Finally, the *macrosystem* includes the larger institutions and culture that directly or indirectly impact the individual such as legislation, government programs, and the entire educational system. When considering a child's circumstances, it is important to consider variables at each of these levels and determine the degree of fit between the individual and the environment. As an illustration, consider the case of Ashley, a sixth-grade student in your middle school in a small, rural community.

Ashley is a vibrant, friendly young adolescent who is falling behind her peers academically. A review of her records indicates that she is also starting to miss a great deal of school. Her teachers have not expressed concern, but you have overheard them complaining about the various excuses that her parents have made for her late homework or missed days of school. You decide to meet with Ashley and quickly develop a good rapport. Ashley describes a complicated custody arrangement where she spends a few nights with her father, a few nights with her mother, and weekends with her grandmother. Occasionally, she stays with her aunt because she wants to play with her cousins. Although she does not seem bothered by these arrangements, it becomes clear that she has found ways to take advantage of the situation so that she is able to miss school without her parents' full awareness (e.g., missing one day while staying at her father's house and another while she is with her aunt). Ashley indicates that she has friends, and it is the social aspect of school that she enjoys the most. When you ask her about her interests and her future goals, she does not express any definite career goals and instead seems pretty disengaged from academics and learning. She cannot identify a favorite subject and states that all of her classes are hard.

In your conversation with the principal, you find that she is considering referring the family to the district's truancy officer and that there may be a recommendation for truancy court. The district has a strict policy on attendance, and even though Ashley's missed days of school are excused by a family member, it seems clear that these absences are not necessarily related to illness or appointments.

There are many ways to conceptualize Ashley's situation. She is demonstrating risk of dropping out as she misses many days of school, is academically behind, and does not seem to be engaged in learning. You might envision goals for her that would include improving her attendance, increasing her grades, and possibly developing a greater level of motivation toward school. An ecological perspective provides a framework for organizing all of the important aspects of her context that may play a role in her current situation. For example, at the microsystemic level, you would look at the three contexts of family, school, and friends as these are parts of Ashley's daily life that impact her directly. Ashley has an extended family with whom she is very close. However, because of inconsistent communication patterns between family members, Ashley is sometimes not monitored closely and is able to miss days of school. Additionally, the multiple switches during the week contribute to a lack of organization where a needed book is at her father's house and her backpack is accidentally left in her mother's car. She has good peer relationships and notes that her friendships are an important part of her school attendance.

At the mesosystemic level, you would consider the relationship between the three contexts of family, friends, and school. Little is known about how Ashley's parents feel about her friends, but communication with the school is spotty at best. Therefore, this lack of connection between her family and school may be contributing to some of the problems. As noted, her friends are an important aspect to her school attendance. At a broader level, the exosystem, you consider aspects of her neighborhood, extended activities in the community, and policies and practices in the school district. Ashley does not engage in any afterschool activities, and there are limited opportunities outside of the school setting because of the small size of the community. She does not express any real interests beyond spending time with her family and caring for her younger cousins. As noted, your district has very strict attendance policies, and the principal has been considering referring Ashley's family to truancy court for her poor attendance. Finally, at the broadest level, is a consideration of the laws, policies, and culture that might have an indirect effect on the current situation. Remember, Ashley's family lives in a small, rural community where many individuals do not pursue higher education and instead tend to stay in the community and find work in various service and agricultural positions.

Based on this ecological framework, you decide that rather than just working with Ashley, it might be important to meet with all of the adults in Ashley's life to address some of the attendance and organization issues, as well as to establish better communication. Additionally, although you are concerned with Ashley's lack of investment in school, you wonder about referring her to the child care training program that will be offered as part of your school's 4-H program. It might be a starting point to help establish for Ashley that learning can help her achieve her goals and make her better at something that she likes to do. You also recognize that her friends are a strength and decide to spend some time thinking about ways to build them into a support plan for Ashley.

Although you will certainly talk to Ashley and help her to establish her own goals, you also realize that you now have many more potential interventions.

SPECIAL CONSIDERATIONS IN COUNSELING CHILDREN AND ADOLESCENTS

Children and adolescents present with many distinctive qualities that create both a joy *and* a challenge in counseling relationships. From a practical perspective, it's important to keep in mind that children and even young adolescents do not typically self-refer; they are usually referred by an adult who sees the child as having a particular problem to resolve (Prout, 2007). When this is the case, children may not see that there is a "problem," or the adult's goals for counseling may not match those of the youth. The young person may feel punished by the referral and, as a result, be resistant to working with the professional helper. Additionally, the child may not have a clear view of what is supposed to happen in counseling. If the youth is older, she may have preconceived ideas drawn from media portrayals. In the schools, there may be the stigma of "having to go to the counselor's office." When this is the case, one of the critical aspects of counseling is to build a relationship and come to agreement that some type of change is necessary.

Working With Children

Although we have described several developmental aspects that are key for working with children, it is important to emphasize a young child's limited linguistic development. In many ways, one of the toughest challenges is learning to perform the microskills of counseling while matching the verbal level of a younger child. The degree to which children utilize a concrete interpretation of words can sometimes surprise new helpers. For example, after listening to Shannon relate how she had improved her behavior and academics compared to last year, the helper responded, "You're proud of how much you have grown since last year." The child smiled and responded, "Yes, two whole inches."

It is also important to consider that younger children may lack clarity about time, amount, and frequency. Thus, events that happened some time ago may be presented as recent occurrences, and it may be difficult to draw conclusions around the frequency of behaviors. For a school-based helper, this means that younger students may struggle with the sequence of events or remembering when events happened. They may describe a trip that happened three years ago as having happened the day before. When a child describes going to a place where there were palm trees as having happened over the last weekend, it is often a struggle for the new practitioner to tease out whether the child is remembering a past event, lying, or relating experiences from a weekend trip to the beach.

Finally, the course of counseling may be more unpredictable with children because they are often more reactive to their environments, and their personalities are less established (Prout, 2007). An issue that was of great importance one time may no longer be relevant by the next time you see the child. To accommodate some of these developmental challenges, helpers can use concrete examples, hands-on activities, clear interpretations of rules, and careful explanation of consequences.

When working with children in the schools, you will need to set limits related to noise levels, behaviors, and materials. Although the counseling room should be a place where student clients can be open and explore their feelings, they cannot be allowed to deviate too far from established rules, disturb surrounding classes, or destroy school property. Establishing clear boundaries helps children know the expectations for acceptable behavior, allows them to learn interpersonal responsibility, and keeps them safe (Landreth, 2002; O'Connor, 2000). (See Chapter 9 for an expanded presentation of limit setting.)

Working With Adolescents

Although adolescents are more linguistically similar to adults, aspects of their social, emotional, and cognitive stages present unique challenges to the professional. As with children, there is more unpredictability in the therapeutic relationship with an adolescent, and the professional should be prepared to use a wide range of therapeutic approaches. The professional will want to work quickly to build a strong therapeutic relationship in order to keep the adolescent engaged (Weiner, 1992). One strategy for building rapport includes helping the adolescent feel at ease by explaining what to expect and clarifying any misperceptions. We do not recommend long periods of silence to formulate a response or to allow the adolescent time for reflection during earlier sessions. Be sensitive to nonverbal behaviors that help you identify the underlying

It is important that you do not try to sound "hip" by using terms that are not part of your regular vocabulary, unless you are quoting the client.

affective state (e.g., eye rolling, setting back, crossing arms, tensing body). Some knowledge of current fads, trends, and lingo may also be helpful in the early stages of building a relationship.

We also do not recommend the use of a lot of probing about deep personal feelings or challenging the adolescent to explain misbehavior as this type of interaction may increase a student's resistance. You will want to avoid the use of "why" questions as individuals typically cannot explain their behaviors and this type of question can create defensiveness. Instead, explain your thoughts explicitly, phrase questions concretely, and in general, use a genuine, direct approach. Your therapeutic approach will "look" more spontaneous and conversational. This type of approach also communicates that you like and accept the adolescent (Prout, 2007).

In your work with adolescents, Prout (2007) recommended that you find a balance between dependence and independence. That is, adolescents should not be treated like children, nor should it be communicated that they are free to make all of their own decisions. Also recognize that the adolescent client will likely be curious about you and your attitudes and opinions. Be willing to share, but cautiously (e.g., only if directly asked or using it to explore or open a new area). In this example, the school counselor shares a little bit about her experiences as an adolescent as she believes it will help her student client tell her own story.

Lydia:	I don't like it at this school. All the kids here are mean to me.
School Counselor:	The change to this school has been tough, and the students here don't seem very friendly to you.
Lydia:	They aren't. I try to ignore them, but I feel so left out. I've even started hanging out with the kids who smoke just because they'll talk to me.
SC:	[attentive and nodding]
Lydia:	Yeah, I mean, I know it's stupid. Have you ever smoked?
SC:	Hmm, well, yes, I did try it a couple of times, but I didn't like it. I'm wondering if that is something you have been thinking about so you can fit in with the other kids who smoke.
Lydia:	Actually, I have started smoking, and I know it's dumb.

The school-based professional was brief in her response and immediately returned the focus back to Lydia. In other situations, the professional helper may decide not to disclose information to the student as in the case that follows.

David (a ninth-grade student):	I know why you've called me down here. My grades are in the toilet, and my mom probably called you.
School Psychologist:	It sounds like you have a pretty good idea about why you are here, and you're not too happy about it.
David:	Well, it's so stupid. My mom and dad stopped me when I came home the other night, and they got all mad because they said I smelled like beer. I mean, what's the big deal? Everyone drinks beer. They grounded me for two weeks.
SP:	You're angry with your parents for grounding you and don't believe it is fair because it seems like other kids drink beer as well.
David:	Yeah, I mean, didn't you drink beer when you were my age?
SP:	You're wondering whether that's something I did as well. I'm guessing that if I said I had, you'd feel even more certain that your parents were wrong.
David:	Maybe. I guess I know that they're not wrong, but I just feel like they treat me like such a baby.

Through your interactions, try to determine the motivation behind the question. Sometimes students ask questions because they want to know whether their own experiences are "normal." In other instances, as in the case with David, the student may not really want to know the answer to a question. It is simply a way to deflect attention from a difficult conversation. It is also important to remember that although you are legally obligated to keep information confidential, your student client is not. Do not disclose information that would be harmful to you as a professional if it were to be shared publicly. We provide additional guidelines on using self-disclosure in Tour 3 of the *Practice and Application Guide*.

The dynamic nature of development in children and adolescent populations can create a unique challenge for school-based professionals. With minor modifications, counseling skills can be used effectively with students of all abilities and grade levels. School-based professionals will want to take time to understand the ways in which children interpret their world in order to effectively communicate, build strong relationships, and enlist environmental supports.

Activities

1. Practice introducing the role of the counselor to a 6-year-old, a 10-year-old, and an adolescent. How does your vocabulary change?

   a. How would you define counseling for a very young child?

   b. How might you address an adolescent's challenge that you are someone who will side with the school or with his or her parents?

2. Using information from the vignette, describe the contextual influences affecting the child's current functioning.

   Caleb is an active, sensitive six-year-old who has just moved with his mother to a small apartment near his new school. After years of loud, intense arguing, his mother and father recently divorced, and he is now living with his mother who has taken two jobs to make ends meet. The family had lived in a stable, middle class neighborhood, but Caleb and his mother are now living in an impoverished area of town where he is not allowed to play outside. Caleb also has limited contact with his father who has moved to a new state. Because of his mother's jobs, Caleb spends the majority of his days in the care of others. He attends school during the day and then is at the day care provider into the evening hours as well as all day Saturday. Caleb's behavior at home and school has become progressively more difficult. He is aggressive toward his peers, and when reprimanded, he begins to cry. At home, he is defiant and angry toward his mother. His mother has not been able to attend any meetings with the teacher and has asked the school not to call her at work because she is afraid of losing her job.

3. Role-play strategies for how you might address difficult personal questions. Examples might include the easier ones often asked by children ("Do you have children?" "Are you married?") or the more difficult questions

posed by adolescents ("Have you ever tried _____?" "Did you have sex before you were married?" "Are you gay?").

Journal Reflections

Reflection #1

Think about your own development. What do you remember as the most difficult time and why?

Reflection #2

Students will come to you with many ethical and moral dilemmas such as whether to share something with you that a friend told them in confidence or whether they should talk to their parents about birth control. How do you make your own decisions when faced with morally challenging issues?

Reflection #3

Consider the developmental age of the student clients with whom you will work. What will be some of the specific challenges for you and why?

Electronic Resources

Child Development Institute: http://childdevelopmentinfo.com/index.shtml

A Family Guide to Keeping Youth Mentally Healthy and Drug Free: http://family.samhsa.gov/main/about.aspx

National Institute for Child Health and Human Development: http://www.nichd.nih.gov/

National Institute for Mental Health: http://www.nimh.nih.gov/health/topics/child-and-adolescent-mental-health/index.shtml

Print Resources

Doll, B., & Cummings, J. (2008). *Transforming school mental health services: Population-based approaches to promoting the competency and wellness of children.* Thousand Oaks, CA: Corwin Press in cooperation with the National Association of School Psychologists.
Doll, B., Zucker, S., & Brehm, K. (2004). *Resilient classrooms: Creating health environments for learning.* New York: Guilford Press.

SECTION II

Introduction to Section II

Once you've tentatively decided what counseling is, the next step is to consider how to do it. . . .

Nancy Murdock

Your theory determines what you see.

Albert Einstein

You can see the world through many different lenses, but you shouldn't have to squint.

Harold Mosak

Our students often become proficient with the basic skills learned in their introductory courses and conclude that, indeed, when they "provide a certain type of relationship, the other person will discover within him or herself the capacity to use that relationship for growth and change, and personal development will occur" (Rogers, 1961, p. 33). We recognize and support the idea that a strong rapport or relationship is the foundation for your work with student clients. There are many definitions for the term *therapeutic relationship*. We like the one proposed by Karver and Caporino (2010, p. 223), who described it as "an active and interchanging interpersonal process" between the professional helper and the student client.

School-based helpers facilitate this relationship through specific behaviors such as creating a climate of warmth and empathy, providing a clear expectation of counseling, and encouraging client autonomy (Karver, Handelsman, Fields, & Bickman, 2006). The accompanying *Practice and Application Guide* provides the steps for building this relationship through strategies that are consistent with a client-centered or humanistic approach. However, we also recognize that this relationship may not be sufficient for facilitating change, especially when considering the abbreviated time frames in school-based services.

In this section, we turn to theories that build upon this relationship. We present four theoretical models of counseling that are commonly used in school settings. As you enter your school-based field experience, counseling theories and diverse modalities become increasingly relevant and practical. Your ability to use theory to understand your student clients and to guide your interventions is critical to facilitating the process of change. For many of you, the theory-based chapters in this section will be review. We hope to build on what you learned in your didactic courses and offer a variety of school-based applications.

Throughout the next five chapters, we endeavor to illustrate the application of theories with a variety of examples. We begin this section with an overview of theory integration and case conceptualization. Our goal is to provide you with a framework for defining and applying your theory, regardless of which theory or blend of theories that you use. To create consistency, we introduce two students and then demonstrate the application of the different theories to each of these cases. Additionally, we provide an overview of the therapeutic modalities of play and group, as well as crisis intervention. The first student is Hans, who is in the fourth grade. The second student is Cassie, who is a junior in high school. Let's meet our new students.

HANS

Hans Nelson is a 10-year-old boy who is in the fourth grade. His teacher referred Hans to the problem-solving intervention team in March because he had recently acted out during class. Although Hans typically is an enthusiastic and cooperative student, he has begun to distract other children, and he has initiated several arguments. As the team members discussed plans to help Hans, the school psychologist reflected on her interactions with Hans during classroom activities and recalled antagonistic and sarcastic comments that seemed quite out of character.

The school psychologist observed Hans for 15 minutes during music, during math, and during science. She noted that Hans refrained from singing and appeared to be distracted. Although he did participate in the experimental activities during science class, other students became irritated at him because he hid materials they needed to perform their experiment. He remained attentive as the teacher explained measurements of geometric shapes; however, during the guided practice he drew pictures on his paper and haphazardly attempted to determine dimensions of the various shapes provided.

The school psychologist also investigated his grades. During the first nine weeks of school, Hans had earned As and Bs in all classes. He had received similar grades in third grade as well. Apparently Hans regularly completed and submitted homework. His grades had gradually declined in fourth grade beginning in mid-November. Attendance had not changed; however, two discipline referrals were noted in December, and three had been documented in February.

Given this additional information, the team decided that it would be most appropriate to call Hans' parents before initiating any contact with him. Thus, the school psychologist tried to contact them during the day but was not able to reach anyone. Assuming both parents worked, she tried to call in the evening. Mr. Nelson answered the phone, and the school psychologist asked for an opportunity to visit with him and Mrs. Nelson. Mr. Nelson said he appreciated the call but that he could not visit at that time. He arranged a telephone appointment the following day.

During the visit with Mr. Nelson, the school psychologist learned that Mr. and Mrs. Nelson had encountered marital difficulties during the first semester and that Mrs. Nelson was no longer living with the family; in fact, she had moved to another city in order to obtain employment and make objective decisions about the marriage and family. Mr. Nelson remained in the home with Hans and his brothers and expressed hope that Mrs. Nelson would return to the family once she had some time to herself. Mr. Nelson said that the children were confused, as was he. Although he was doing everything he could to provide stability for the family, he was extremely busy because he was now assuming sole responsibility for the business he owned and had managed with Mrs. Nelson. Mr. Nelson said he would appreciate any assistance the school could provide for Hans and his brothers.

CASSIE

Cassie, a junior in a private high school, lives in a large city. Her mother is an attorney and her father is a dentist. Cassie is an only child who is particularly close with her grandparents, aunts, uncles, and cousins. She enjoys a broad range of friendships with boys and girls and is a star basketball and volleyball player. She is musically talented and has enjoyed participation in school plays. Cassie made an appointment with the school counselor to talk about precollegiate examination results.

The counselor was quickly puzzled. Although Cassie said she wanted to talk about her test scores, she displayed minimal interest in the topic. She missed her first appointment and was late for the second appointment. When the counselor reviewed the profile, Cassie seemed irritated by the results and questioned the value of the test. She expressed uncertainty about college or career plans. She mentioned possibilities of working a year or two because she was burned out. Although she was respectful, Cassie was distant. Before Cassie returned to class, the counselor said, "I have the sense that something other than college is bothering you. I wonder if you'd be willing to meet with me again." Cassie's response was, "Okay. Yeah. Whatever."

In preparation for meeting Cassie again, the school counselor informally observed her when she was not in class and checked school records. During breaks in the school day, the counselor noticed that Cassie was often by herself. When she was with other students, she seemed petulant and impatient. Of course, the counselor had other opportunities to observe Cassie during ballgames. During one basketball game, three fouls were called on Cassie because she was aggressive. When the coach substituted another player, she became angry and sat quietly on the bench during the remainder of the game. Cassie's attendance during the previous three months had been sporadic; in fact, a concern about truancy was noted in her file. Several late slips were documented as well.

The school counselor recognized that a relationship characterized by trust and respect was an essential prerequisite for any assistance he would be able to offer Cassie. Thus, he approached the second session with that in mind. As he waited for Cassie, the counselor glanced at the manipulative puzzles, art supplies, and sand tray miniatures prominently displayed in his office. He was thinking about how Cassie might use them when she knocked on door, which was already ajar.

The counselor reminded Cassie about confidentiality as well as situations that would require him to divulge elements of their conversations. Cassie responded with questions. "What would you tell my mom if she calls? Do kids really trust you with personal things?" She added, "Kids my age get enough criticism, and we have plenty to worry about already. What do you do when you don't approve of something kids tell you?" The counselor respectfully responded to each of Cassie's questions. Ultimately she asked, "So what do we talk about?" The counselor responded with, "I respect high school students a great deal. Usually they know what they need to talk about. My guess is that you have some things you'd like to talk about, and you need to know that you can trust me first."

Cassie seemed pleased with his response. During the next 30 minutes she talked about her concerns about college and making decisions of which her parents would approve. Cassie talked about a variety of career and postsecondary preparation options. She concluded the session by saying, "There's more. But I don't know. I'll think about coming back another time."

The counselor asked Cassie if he could ask her a couple questions, and she agreed. He said that he had a sense that she was depressed some of the time. Cassie didn't know if *depressed* was the appropriate word but did concede that she felt "down in the dumps" pretty often. He posed a scaling question to her: "Let's say that 10 is absolutely, fantastically happy. Everything is going well. Grades are good. Decisions are made. Relationships are all okay. That's a 10. Then let's say that 1 is depressed, so depressed you can't even get out of bed some mornings. You feel hopeless and don't want to be bothered with schoolwork, friendships, family, or anything. You just want to be left alone because you feel sad. You also spend a lot of time crying, and you don't even know why. That's 1. Where would you rate yourself on most days?" After a thoughtful pause, Cassie said she wasn't sure, but she thought she was usually a 6.

Cassie did schedule a third appointment. After exploring frustration with classes, school, and relationships in general she said she wasn't sure about some things. She didn't think she was like other girls. As the counselor reflected her uncertainty and confusion, Cassie began to tell him she wondered if she was a lesbian because she enjoyed "hanging out" with boys, playing ball with them, performing with them, and so forth. However, she felt no romantic attraction to boys. She didn't know how she would recognize romantic attraction to girls. She was confused. She also felt hurt by antigay comments expressed by friends in the school.

At the conclusion of this session, she expressed insecurity. "What do you think? Am I bad? Think you better send me off downtown to one of those shrinks who work with the real losers?" The counselor assured Cassie that he fully respected her and that he admired her courage for talking about a side of her that she feared might be criticized, ridiculed, or attacked. He also asked if Cassie thought there was a relationship between her questions about being a lesbian and her recent difficulties with attendance, grades, irritability, and so forth. Cassie's response was, "Well, yeah!"

For both of these cases, take a moment to consider your initial thoughts, the kinds of additional information you would like to know, how you might obtain that information, and what your next steps would be. We will revisit the cases of Hans and Cassie in the following chapters.

CHAPTER 4

Theory Integration and Case Conceptualization

Learning Objectives

- Recognize the importance of theories
- Understand the process of theory building and integration
- Understand how to choose interventions to match counseling goals
- Develop a process for case conceptualization

Sometimes our preservice professional helpers are confused by the concept, purpose, and application of theories. They may struggle as they begin to identify a theory, or integration of theories, that makes sense to them and that guides their individual or group counseling. They also have difficulty understanding processes such as eclecticism, integration, and case conceptualization. In this chapter, we cover each of these concepts as well as their application to counseling in the schools. Additional information and activities to support you are provided in Tours 4 and 5 of the *Practice and Application Guide*.

Beliefs about the importance of theories, reliance on theories, integration of theories, eclectic practice, and other theory-related notions vary greatly.

Thus, we begin by discussing the role that theories play in your practice. We briefly review literature about theory integration and how it applies to work with children and adolescents in the schools. Finally, we introduce the process of case conceptualization and how it informs your choice of intervention.

PURPOSES, LIMITATIONS, AND EVALUATION OF THEORIES

As mentioned, there is a wide range of beliefs on the usefulness of theories to one's practice. Historically, it was more common for practitioners to rely on one theory to the exclusion of others in order to organize their thinking and guide their work with clients (Mennuti, Christner, & Weinstein, 2009). More recent work describes counseling as a process whereby the professional helper uses a variety of strategies and tools to address the concerns of the client (Cormier & Hackney, 2008). Indeed, it is much more common today for practitioners to use different components of a few theories or to integrate these pieces into their own unique theory (Sharf, 2004).

The ultimate goal is to develop an integrated, personal theory; but this is not an easy task. At this point in your career, you likely have had limited opportunities to apply your theory in practice. Thus, the idea of selecting one or two theories that will guide your work may seem daunting. For this reason, many training programs encourage pre-service professionals to adopt one theoretical model as it is easier than attempting to develop an integrated model of practice without sufficient practical experience. We believe the framework provided by Cheston (2000), which she termed the *ways paradigm*, is helpful in choosing a theory to use in your counseling work with student clients. From her perspective, theory and practice can be organized around three principles: "a way of being, a way of understanding, and a way of intervening" (p. 256).

Consider the first component of this framework. How do you view your role as a counselor? Are you a problem solver, a facilitator, a mirror? As you think about how you want to present yourself in your sessions and the role you want to play in your counseling, you will begin to develop a better idea of the theories that might work best for you. For example, if you see yourself as an active problem solver but really like a humanistic perspective, you may find yourself at odds with your selected theoretical orientation. You'll likely struggle with the underlying belief that clients can solve their own problems if provided with unconditional regard and support. If you do not have a good understanding of the underlying philosophy and beliefs inherent in a specific theoretical model, you risk selecting one that is not consistent with your own values. Further, if applied inappropriately or inconsistently, you risk developing into an ineffective counselor.

It is also likely that certain underlying philosophical systems within these theories make more sense to you than others. For example, if you consider the kinds of explanations you provide when trying to understand an individual's thoughts or behaviors, you may find that you often return to a similar idea. How many times have you heard yourself say, "It's what he's learned" or "She's just trying to establish some kind of control of the world around her" when referring to the behavior of children or adolescents? These kinds of statements reflect the beginnings of a theoretical orientation. In the first instance, a cognitive-behavioral perspective has been adopted and in the second, an Adlerian or choice theory view.

Theoretical approaches differ in the degree of structure, the role of the professional helper, and the explanation that we use to understand the cause of behavior (Betan & Binder, 2010). Theories help us collect and organize information; theories guide the questions we ask as we endeavor to understand the situation. They also help us determine what information is most relevant. That is, should we pay more attention to a student client's behaviors or thoughts? Theories inform questions we ask and information we acquire. Once you have developed and refined your basic skills of counseling, using a theoretical model allows you to apply these skills in an intentional manner (Halbur & Halbur, 2011). Theories guide us in identifying intervention options that will help student clients to address their presenting concerns. That is, if I believed or conceptualized that my student client's depressed and anxious mood was based in negative self-talk and catastrophizing (i.e., based on a cognitive-behavioral perspective), I might decide to ask the client to challenge those automatic thoughts and keep a homework log outlining alternative explanations for these distressing events.

As in the earlier example, theories typically are designed from one viewpoint. Adhering exclusively to a single theory or point of view may result in myopic thinking and professional helpers' failure to recognize rich and dynamic nuances of an individual's personality and situation. In fact, Nelson (2002) concluded that professional helpers have better outcomes when they select interventions that are appropriate for each client's needs and concerns rather than simply relying on their preferred strategy.

Mennuti et al. (2009) presented a useful distinction between being "theoretically eclectic" and "technically eclectic." A theoretically eclectic professional uses several different theories to conceptualize a case (Mennuti et al., 2009). For some practitioners, "eclectic" is not regarded highly as it is viewed as haphazard or "hodgepodge." Others caution that in order to effectively practice in an eclectic manner, one must be highly skilled in the various theoretical models and competent in their application (Norcross, 2005). Those who support technical eclecticism draw their interventions or strategies from a variety of theories to assist clients in overcoming challenges (Prochaska & Norcross, 2007). The decision to supplement with other approaches is based on the specific needs of the client (Mennuti et al., 2009). Therefore, while it may be unlikely that your way of being and your way of understanding will change from client to client, it is quite possible that your way of intervening may vary.

Theories can also be misused. For example, adopting the position that a theory is "truth" may lead to incorrect conclusions and impede your ability to see all relevant data. A variety of viewpoints enriches and diversifies our understanding of each unique individual and broadens our repertoire of possibilities for helping. Theories are resources that must be considered in the context of living human beings' lives, personalities, contexts, and situations. Thus, to be helpful, a theory must be comprehensive yet practical and parsimonious, understandable, and coherent. Credible theories are internally consistent; in other words, there is a clear relationship between problem definition, goals, interventions, and indicators of success. They include a structure for evaluation and research. Finally, a good theory makes sense to the professional helper who uses it. By presenting a few of the more frequently used school-based approaches, we hope to provide you with a good understanding of these different theories as well as the strategies that are consistent with each.

THEORY INTEGRATION

Terminology related to integration is inconsistent and often confusing. *Theoretical integration*, the blending of two or more theories into one conceptualization, is thought to be more systematic and intentional, unlike theoretical eclecticism. In this process of integration, theories are combined to capitalize on strengths each can offer, resulting in an improved approach (Prochaska & Norcross, 2007). Consideration is given to commonalities and unification.

Theoretical integration is our preferred approach because of the intentionality of the process. Certainly no theory is adequate to explain complex, dynamic, and diverse human behavior. Nor is *theory* synonymous with *truth*. Theories are *resources* from which to draw in responding to the unique needs of each student client as well as the unique personality and style of each professional helper. In fact, most psychotherapeutic approaches used today have incorporated aspects of earlier theories or models (Wampold, 2010). Cognitive-behavioral therapy (CBT, see Chapter 5) represents the integration of cognitive and behavioral theories (Mayer & Van Acker, 2009).

WHAT IS THE BEST THEORY?

If there was one theory that was shown to be the most effective across all situations and clients, training programs would likely adopt that model and prepare all new practitioners in its use. Unfortunately, it is not that simple. A prominent contemporary author, Wampold (2001) examined the extensive body of research that had been conducted over the previous 30 years. He reiterated the findings of numerous studies that have shown minimal difference in effectiveness among the various therapeutic approaches. Additionally, he concluded that following specific treatment protocols (i.e., manualized treatment) had not resulted in more effective treatments; in fact, he suggested that adherence to treatment protocols may be counterproductive because professional competence is suppressed.

Clearly, the debate about selecting theories or "best" theories is not settled. A related tension in the field is the emphasis on providing evidence-based interventions (see discussion of evidence-based approaches in Chapter 13). In his updated review of his own and others' meta-analytic studies, Wampold (2010) again concluded that all therapies tend to produce positive outcomes. Other than minor variations, they seem to be equally efficacious across different disorders (e.g., depression, anxiety). In relation to therapeutic approaches with children, he drew a similar conclusion that no one therapy appeared to be superior to another.

Instead, Wampold (2010) suggested that a focus on common factors might provide us with a better understanding of why therapy works. That is, what are the critical elements of counseling that are consistent across theoretical models and might better account for positive outcomes? Although there are many different models for conceptualizing these common factors, generally the focus has been on the alliance between the counselor and the client, characteristics of the counselor, and client factors (Wampold, 2010). There is little doubt that a better working relationship with a professional helper is related to more positive client outcomes, but it has been difficult to show that it is this relationship that *causes* these results. Similarly, despite years of research, we know little about what specific behaviors or characteristics are associated with effective therapists (Beutler et al., 2004). With their recent work, Baldwin, Wampold, and Imel (2007) found that therapists who were able to build stronger alliances with their clients consistently demonstrated better outcomes.

Finally, we turn to client factors. Common sense might tell us that individuals who are most ready for change will make the greatest gains. Truthfully, we know little about how clients make use of therapy. Research with adults has resulted in identification of characteristics such as readiness for change, greater access to psychological resources (e.g., ego strength), and psychological mindedness as associated with better therapy outcomes (Clarkin & Levy, 2004). It is difficult to determine whether these factors would also predict better therapeutic outcomes in child and adolescent populations.

Given all this discussion of theoretical integration, common factors, and equivalent outcomes, where do we go from here? Halbur and Halbur (2011) concluded that it did not matter which theory an individual chooses, as long as one is chosen.

We liked Halbur and Halbur's (2011) analogy of the tool bag. Once you select a theory that fits for you, begin filling your tool bag with the various strategies that are associated with that theoretical approach. In that way, you may begin to implement counseling in an intentional manner. As you gain more experience, you will likely continue to add a variety of tools, some consistent with your theoretical orientation and others that are not. So too, as you gain competency with other theoretical models and techniques, your approach to counseling may change toward a more integrated or eclectic model. At the beginning of your career, we encourage you to adopt a distinction between the theoretical orientation for case conceptualization and theoretical integration in strategy implementation.

CASE CONCEPTUALIZATION

Case conceptualization is a problem-solving process, a comprehensive examination of factors related to the current difficulties and possibilities for their resolution. Another perspective views case conceptualization as a type of working hypothesis about the causes and maintaining circumstances related to an individual's presenting problem (Betan & Binder, 2010). Regardless of your theoretical orientation, you will use a similar process to consider the issues that are relevant to student clients with whom you are working. Berman (2010) recommended starting with a *premise*, as applied to your client, that describes the individual's strengths and weaknesses within the context of the counselor's theoretical model. This first element can be called any number of terms; basically it is your working hypothesis that frames your case conceptualization.

The second major component of case conceptualization includes the *supporting details* (Berman, 2010). When working with children and adolescents, case conceptualization should include a consideration of development (Mennuti et al., 2009). Your case conceptualization should lead into your goals for counseling and your intervention plan. Newer models of case conceptualization also include a step geared toward rethinking one's original ideas based on intervention outcomes.

Case conceptualization includes an examination of the underlying cause of the presenting concern (i.e., the premise). An understanding of the cause likely follows from your own theoretical orientation. That is, if I believe that children's problems are the result of faulty cognitions, I will likely explain or conceptualize a child's presenting difficulty as related to maladaptive thinking. However, I must consider multiple aspects of a student client's situation (i.e., supporting details) before I can come to that conclusion. For example, if I find that a student is being bullied on the playground, I would not want to approach his or her desire to avoid recess as "faulty thinking." When we engage in case conceptualization, it is important that we do not simply plug pieces of information into our theory but instead consider the ways that our theory may or may not apply to a specific student client's situation.

It is also important to keep in mind that conceptualization is not a one-time finite component of counseling (Neufeldt, Iversen, & Juntunen, 1995). Information is combined with theory: the context, student culture and history, and so forth. With that combined information, professional helpers generate hypotheses about how to assist the student. Neufeldt and her colleagues referred to the intervention stage as an "experiment" (p. 14). When the experiment generates anticipated results, the work continues. When the experiment generates unanticipated results ("surprises"), professional helpers modify the theory or modify the hypotheses. This is similar to the solution-focused notion of "if it works, don't fix it. If it doesn't work, do something else."

In Table 4.1, as well as in the *Practice and Application Guide*, we provide an example of a case conceptualization worksheet that can be used to organize multiple aspects of students' lives. We have adapted the cognitive-behavioral model presented by Murphy and Christener (2006) and the model presented by Neufeldt et al. (1995) as well as our own ideas about helpful information that should be integrated to allow for prediction of future behavior. We illustrate an application with Cassie in Table 4.2 to help you understand how to link your

Table 4.1 Case Conceptualization Guide

Student's Name: _____   Date: _____

Student's Age: _____

Significant Adults: _____

Presenting Concerns: _____

_____

_____

_____

_____

_____

Category(ies) of Concerns:

_____ Behavior

_____ Career Decision Making

_____ Postsecondary Planning

_____ Academic

_____ Friendships/Relationship Conflict

_____ _____

_____ _____

(Note: The presenting problem guides direction of conceptualization. For example, career indecision is related to career theory. Relationship problems could indicate the need for interpersonal skill building. Behavior problems may be a sign of limited skills, unmet needs, or distorted perceptions.)

Student's Perception/Explanation of the Concerns:

_____

_____

_____

_____

Teacher's Perception/Explanation of the Concerns:

_____

_____

_____

_____

Significant Adults' Perception/Explanation of the Concerns:

_____

_____

_____

_____

Helper's Perception/Explanation of the Concerns:

_____

_____

_____

_____

Relevant History (Relevant to the Situation and the School):

Grades: _____

Attendance: _____

Behavior Patterns: _____

Other Factors: _____

Potential Factors That Contribute to Maintenance of the Presenting Concern
(e.g., secondary gains):

_____

_____

_____

_____

Hypotheses Regarding Resolution:

_____   Learn New Behavior or Change a Behavior

_____   Change Perceptions or Belief System

_____   Develop Insight and Awareness

_____   Factual Information

_____   Encouragement

_____   _____

_____   _____

(Continued)

Table 4.1 (Continued)

Student's Assets:

_____

_____

_____

_____

Student's Abilities, Talents, and Strengths:

_____

_____

_____

_____

Possible Resources:

_____

_____

_____

_____

Developmental Factors (e.g., cognitive, psychosocial):

_____

_____

_____

_____

Relevant Cultural, Ethnic, Economic, and Contextual Factors:

_____

_____

_____

_____

Relevant Theories and Approaches:

_____

_____

_____

_____

Helping Strategies That Seem Most Plausible to Me:

_____

_____

_____

_____

Helping Strategies That May Be Acceptable to the Student:

_____

_____

_____

_____

Mutually Agreed-Upon Goals and Evaluation Plan:

_____

_____

_____

_____

Initial Plan (Note: Consider who will be involved, level of intervention):

_____

_____

_____

_____

conceptualization to potential intervention and evaluation of outcomes. Consistent with our perspective discussed earlier, we conceptualize Cassie's situation from an Adlerian perspective, but in our intervention strategies, we have used a blend of strategies (i.e., tools) to address her different needs.

Table 4.2 Case Illustration: Comprehensive Conceptualization for Cassie

Student's Name: Cassie   Date: January 18, 2011

Student's Age: 17

Significant Adults: Leonardo and Ezabella (biological parents)

Presenting Concerns: Inconsistent attendance
                        Frequent tardiness
                        Pattern of withdrawing or isolating
                        Irritability with peers
                        Postsecondary questions

Category(ies) of Concerns:

    Yes   Behavior
    Yes   Career Decision Making
    Yes   Postsecondary Planning
    Yes   Academic – grades are slipping
    Yes   Relationship Conflict – irritable with peers, withdrawn
           Possible Identity Questions

Student's Perception/Explanation of the Concerns:
Uncertainty about postsecondary plans
Questioning sexual orientation

Teacher's Perception/Explanation of the Concerns:
None

Significant Adults' Perception/Explanation of the Concerns:
Parents believe Cassie is experiencing normal developmental uncertainty.

Helper's Perception/Explanation of the Concerns:
From a developmental perspective (Erikson): Cassie has encountered an age-
appropriate crisis or combination of crises. It appears that she has not resolved
the developmental crisis of identity versus role confusion. She is endeavoring to
define herself as an autonomous individual. She may be struggling simultaneously
with the tasks in the intimacy versus isolation stage. (For females, particularly,
these two stages may be intertwined.)

From an Adlerian perspective: To some extent, her behavior and possible
depression may be related to tension of age-appropriate separation from parents

and preparing for adulthood. This may be exacerbated by her being an only child who has been particularly close to her family.

Additionally, Cassie may be worried that her relationship with her family would be compromised if she expressed uncertainty about her sexual orientation or about career plans (need for belonging—Adlerian and reality). In other words, would she feel inferior and inadequate in her family context?

We also suspect that Cassie is struggling with acceptance of self, particularly in context of her questions regarding sexual orientation (client-centered). She may not be comfortable with the process of increased self-awareness because she fears the conclusion that she will ultimately draw. In all likelihood, her locus of evaluation and control is shared with parents, teachers, and other significant adults as well as peers. Additionally, her career indecision may be related to questions regarding the meaning and purpose of life, particularly *her* life (existential).

Relevant History (Relevant to the Situation and the School):

Grades:	Grades have historically been strong (A and B range)
	Grades have dropped in last eight weeks (B and C range)
Attendance:	Recent pattern of sporadic attendance (seven absences in past month)
Behavior Patterns:	Some irritability and distancing with peers
	Some irritability during athletic events

Cassie's early childhood may have contributed to her zest for success (Adler). It appears that basic needs were met and that she experienced love, a sense of belonging in her family, and encouragement (Adler).

Potential Factors That Contribute to Maintenance of the Presenting Concern (e.g., secondary gains):
Unsure

Hypotheses Regarding Resolution:

_____ Learn New Behavior or Change a Behavior

_____ Change Perceptions or Belief System

Yes   Develop Insight and Awareness

Yes   Factual Information

Yes   Encouragement

(Continued)

Table 4.2 (Continued)

Student's Assets:

History of good grades

Strong family connection and support

Strong relationships with friends

Student's Abilities, Talents, and Strengths:

Musical

Athletic

Possible Resources:

Family

Coaches

Developmental Factors (e.g., cognitive, psychosocial):

See Helper's Perceptions of Concerns

Psychosocial:	Identity versus role confusion
	Intimacy versus isolation
Career:	Plans not clear
Moral:	Defer
Cognitive:	Abstract

Relevant Cultural, Ethic, Economic, and Contextual Factors:

Cassie's grandparents emigrated from Jamaica.

The family has financial resources for Cassie to attend college of her choice.

The family values professional career activities.

Attending college is an expectation.

Relevant Theories and Approaches:

Individual psychology

Solution-focused brief therapy

Helping Strategies That Seem Most Plausible to Me:

Miracle question

Career exploration activities

Sand tray or art

Helping Strategies That May Be Acceptable to the Student:
She may be skeptical of sand tray.
She seems willing to participate in counseling.
Group counseling may be appropriate later.
Examination of goals of Cassie's behavior

Mutually Agreed-Upon Goals and Evaluation Plans:
Cassie will attend school each day unless she is ill – monitor attendance.
Cassie will complete all assigned work – monitor percentage of completed work turned in.
Cassie will develop postsecondary plans – completion of career inventory.

Initial Plan (Note: Consider who will be involved, level of intervention):
Individual counseling for five weeks – use solution-focused strategies at initial session.

Draw from individual psychology to facilitate development of self-awareness.

Modify lifestyle assessment with focus on purposeful behavior.

Use sand tray or art to examine lifestyle.

Include career inventories (electronic career information and assessment).

Relate career information to results of lifestyle assessment.

Develop an attendance contract.

Based on progress with attendance, focus on grades and task completion.

Conceptualization includes a concise identification of the presenting problem, consideration of the etiology and history of the situation, goals, and procedures for facilitating the attainment of those goals. In this process, attention is given to developmental factors, culture and context, family dynamics, relevant history, and resources. Factors that contribute to or maintain the problem are identified. Hypotheses regarding the resolution of the situation are generated. Professional helpers consider how their chosen theory or theories provide the most useful explanation for the situation as well as a potential sequence of treatment.

Ultimately, an internally consistent, yet flexible, plan for helping student clients resolve challenges is designed. Briefly, this is a process of answering three questions: "How did this person get into this situation?" and "What is his or her ticket out?" An implicit question is "How can I most effectively and efficiently help?"

FROM MAKING MEANING TO ACTION

While case conceptualization will help to organize information about your student clients and guide your understanding of their circumstances, it represents only a first step. Common questions among new professionals are "What do I do now?" and "How does this information guide me toward my next steps?" You must now use this information to decide on and select the most appropriate interventions. Let's consider the following case of a young man who has recently moved to your school (grades 6–12).

> Ben is 15 years old and lives in a small, rural community. He has had some instability in his upbringing with various shifts in his family composition. Most recently he moved away from his mother's home and is now living with an aunt. He described the reason for his move as a result of his "getting into too much trouble." Ben clearly does not fit in at his new school. He dresses like a hippie amongst the other students who mostly wear Wrangler jeans and cowboy boots. Ben is obviously bright and communicative but continues to have academic and behavioral difficulties. He is not completing his schoolwork and says that school is not important. It is also suspected that he is drinking. Last weekend he took his aunt's car without permission. Ben has identified his main goal as "staying out of trouble."

It is fairly easy to see the concerns for Ben—disengaged from school, poor peer relationships, drinking, and defiance. However, he also possesses strengths. He is bright, he can communicate his ideas, and he has a desire to make positive change (i.e., "stay out of trouble"). A professional helper conceptualizing this case from a solution-focused brief therapy perspective would see that goal statement as a starting point by asking him what he will be doing when he is not in trouble. A professional working from a choice theory/reality therapy perspective might ask him the challenging question of how his behaviors are helping him meet his goal. The answers to these questions serve as a launching point for action.

As you engage with student clients and help them identify ways that they may be blocking their own success, you can plan strategies collaboratively to address these incongruities. It is important to keep in mind that as the professional helper, you do not need to do all of the work. In fact, you don't want to. Your efforts should be directed toward engaging individuals in solving their own problems. However, it is helpful to have some ideas about different types of strategies to address different issues.

Case conceptualization can help prioritize areas that the helper may need to address first. For example, Ben is drinking and taking his aunt's car without permission. This behavior is dangerous; thus it rises to the top in terms of priorities. Further, it most aligns (or misaligns) with his stated goal of staying out of trouble. Therefore, one of your first steps is likely to address this issue and create a plan with Ben, and possibly his aunt, around keeping him safe.

From a school perspective, the next most important goals would be to resolve his truancy and lack of work completion, which seem to be signs of disengagement in school. Because these also align with Ben's stated goal (i.e., staying out of trouble), these areas would be a logical place for your next plan of action. There are different ways to approach these issues. One type of intervention is delivered in your counseling by helping him to see how he is sabotaging his own goals. You might also choose to establish environmental supports. Perhaps he would benefit from having an extra study hall during the day because he is not motivated to complete his homework in the evenings. If there is a subject that is especially interesting for Ben (e.g., art), additional opportunities to work with that teacher could be incorporated. You are using a blend of approaches, helping Ben to change his perspective. You are also enhancing the positive qualities of the environment.

There may be other elements in the case that you know are present but decide not to address, at least immediately. For example, Ben does not have friends. You may speculate that because he has good social skills and is a bright, engaging person, as he begins to participate more in school, the friendships will emerge.

Sometimes you may decide not to address certain components of your student client's case because they are not something that is considered appropriate in school-based counseling. For example, Ben appears to have had a lot of

> Just because you know a great strategy for addressing a specific issue (e.g., engaging youth in school) does not mean that it will be a perfect match for your student client. Remain flexible in your use of strategies and make sure it is something that a student client is willing to try.

instability as he has moved back and forth between his parents' houses while he was growing up, and he is now living with his aunt. It is possible that he feels somewhat unloved and finds it difficult to trust adults. Although you may keep that in mind as you are working with him, you do not see it as your role to explore his feelings of loss and abandonment. Instead, you focus on those elements that are most important to address and that are appropriate for a school setting. If it becomes clear that Ben wants to work on these larger family issues, it would be appropriate to refer him to an outside mental health professional.

PROCESS AND OUTCOME
GOALS OF SCHOOL-BASED COUNSELING

In your work with student clients, there are two distinct types of goals. One type is considered a *process goal* and refers to the relationship that is developed with student clients (Cormier & Hackney, 2008). The types of processes that you attend to include the degree of rapport that has been established, the safety of the setting, and the degree to which you have been able to communicate empathy and understanding (Cormier & Hackney, 2008). As we addressed throughout the *Practice and Application Guide*, the success of your counseling depends on your relationship with the student client. This relationship helps to motivate students to attend sessions, to take risks in trying new strategies, and to create the conditions for positive change.

The second type of goal is an *outcome goal* and refers to the actual changes that student clients make based on the counseling process. These goals are typically specific, measurable, and stated in the positive. They are developed collaboratively with student clients (Cormier & Hackney, 2008). As described in the case of Ben, you may have many goals for an individual and need to prioritize. Goals related to safety take priority, typically followed by goals that are relevant to a school-based setting.

There may also be a natural order in which goals need to be addressed. For example, if a student's behavior is so out of control that he is removed from the classroom on a daily basis, we may begin to see a decline in quarterly grades. Although an academic intervention may be appropriate at a later date, your first priority is likely to be directed toward helping the student develop better self-control strategies. You will also want to consider which goals are appropriate to address in your specific setting. If the presenting issue is one that will require long-term treatment, your goal may be helping the student client transition to a community-based agency. We discuss more about goal setting and measurement in Chapter 13.

Both process and outcome goals are important to your work with student clients. As you and student clients set outcome goals, be sure to discuss the kinds of changes that you would expect to see based on your work together. In the case of Ben, the school counselor might work with him initially to set only two goals. The first of these goals would address safety issues with an expected outcome of no more reported incidents of drinking and driving. A second goal would be directed toward increasing school engagement. Together, Ben and the school counselor could set specific expected goals around increasing attendance and work completion.

As noted previously, there are many different ways to meet these goals. As school-based helpers, most of our attention is directed toward outcomes; however, you do not want to overlook your own process goals with each student client. Through personal reflection, journaling, and supervision, you set personal goals around your ability to connect with your student clients, to understand their perspectives, and to create a safe, comfortable environment for counseling.

CONCLUSION

Clearly contemporary counselors and school psychologists have fallen heir to a rich legacy of theories from which we can draw to enhance our understanding of clients and our efforts to facilitate change. Integration of theories and intervention models can expand our therapeutic repertoire, increase our flexibility, and capitalize on strengths of various theories and approaches. However, haphazard eclecticism can result in scattered technicism.

Several years ago Liddle (1982) challenged professional helpers to "periodically engage in . . . an epistemology declaration" to evaluate and articulate "what we know and how we know it, what and how we think, and what and how we make clinical decisions we do" (p. 247). We encourage you to begin that process now and commit to revisiting your epistemology throughout your career.

Activities

1. With the information you have, complete a case conceptualization for Hans (the other student introduced in the Introduction to Section II).

2. What theories and techniques do you believe would be most helpful for Hans and why? How would you evaluate the effectiveness of your work?

3. In a small group, share your current theoretical perspective with others. Describe an instance when it worked well and helped you understand a student better. Share an instance where your theoretical approach did not work as well and you still had questions.

Journal Reflections

Reflection #1

Consider your automatic beliefs about why children act in the ways that they do. Do these vary based on the individual's age, gender, ethnicity, or some other variable?

Reflection #2

At this point in your career, what do you consider to be your theoretical orientation, and why have you selected this one? What makes it a good fit for you? As a follow-up, at the end of your field experience (e.g., practicum or internship), review what you wrote in this reflection. Have your ideas changed? What have you learned in terms of your application of theory to the students with whom you have worked?

Reflection #3

Consider a student client with whom you have struggled to build a relationship and one with whom it was easy to develop a strong rapport. What were some of the student factors that acted as barriers to relationship building, and what factors seemed to facilitate this process?

Electronic Resources

Creating a Personal Counseling Theory: http://pdfcast.org/pdf/creating-a-personal-counseling-theory

Integrative Psychotherapy: http://en.wikipedia.org/wiki/Integrative_psychotherapy

Print Resources

Berman, P. (2010). *Case conceptualization and treatment planning: Integrating theory with clinical practice.* Los Angeles: Sage.

Cormier, S., & Hackney, H. (2008). *Counseling strategies and interventions.* Boston: Allyn & Bacon.

Wampold, B. E. (2010). *The basics of psychotherapy: an introduction to theory and practice.* Washington, DC: American Psychological Association.

CHAPTER 5

Adlerian Approaches to Counseling in Schools

Learning Objectives

- Review essential principles of individual psychology
- Consider applications of individual psychology for work with children and adolescents in schools
- Reflect on individual psychology's relevance to you as a person and as a professional helper

As you probably remember from theories classes, Adler's theory (also known as individual psychology) is rich and comprehensive. Even though the theory was developed early in the twentieth century, Adler's influence continues to be prominent in contemporary approaches and practice (Carlson, Watts, & Maniacci, 2006; Watts & Pietrzak, 2000; Wood, 2003). Adlerian professionals structure the process of counseling, and they often teach or provide psychoeducation. They are directive; however, they collaborate with clients to explore difficulties, motivations, and potential solutions. Thus, many aspects of this theory are particularly useful for school-based professionals (Caterino & Sullivan, 2009; LaFountain & Garner, 1998).

This chapter includes a summary of Adler's premises that hold import for professionals in schools, followed by an overview of the counseling process, assessment strategies, and interventions. We have drawn only a few elements of this comprehensive theory that are particularly relevant to our work in schools; in no way do we wish to imply that other aspects of the theory are unimportant. Additionally, we have examined many elements of the theory in isolation to facilitate understanding; however, Alder's theory is internally consistent. The theoretical underpinnings, assessment procedures, and interventions are complementary.

Adler's own childhood and school experiences in the late 1800s are noteworthy. He seemed to be prone to accidents and illnesses. Because he also had academic challenges, particularly in math, someone recommended that he discontinue formal education to become a cobbler's apprentice. The young Adler could have accepted this point of view and allowed himself to be limited by academic challenges. Rather, Adler became motivated to overcome the challenges. He earned a medical degree by the time he was 25 and sought ways to help others overcome suffering, inadequacies, and disease (Carlson et al., 2006). Additionally, he was an active humanist and advocate for societal reform that addressed needs of people who were poor and disempowered.

ESSENTIAL PRINCIPLES OF ADLER'S THEORY

Alfred Adler (1958) developed individual psychology as a reaction to psychoanalysis and as a reflection of his humanistic beliefs. Even though the theory is called *individual* psychology, Adler's focus was contextual and holistic. He contended that we cannot fully understand people without viewing them in a social context (Carlson et al., 2006; Sweeney, 1989, 1998; Watts, 2000). He also suggested that human beings are primarily social, goal directed, and creative (Dinkmeyer & Sperry, 2000; Kelly & Lee, 2007). Accordingly, personal fulfillment is based on mastery of life tasks related to work, friendship, love, self-acceptance, purpose or meaning, and restorative leisure (Dinkmeyer & Sperry, 2000).

When working from Adler's theory, mental health professionals respond to the unique needs of each student or adult. They ask themselves, "Who or what is best for this particular individual?" (Carlson et al., 2006, p. 10). Thus, this approach is flexible and integrative; at the same time, the "theory is solid" (Manaster & Corsini, 1982, p. 148).

Phenomenology

The concept of phenomenology is central to Adlerian theory. Even in a family, in which the individual members have a shared history, each person has a different perspective and memory of the events in that history. Thus, each human being's experience is unique and must be understood from his or her point of view (Mosak & Maniacci, 1993). Additionally, each child has the task of finding a position of significance in the family context. The same holds true in classroom relationships.

Lifestyle

Lifestyle is "the sum total of all the individual's attitudes and aspirations, a striving which leads him in the direction toward his goal of believing he has significance in the eyes of others" (Grey, 1998, p. 37). Adler suggested that young children draw conclusions from their family experiences about themselves, men, women, and life. Among prominent conclusions are general responses to "I am _____. The world is _____. Therefore _____" (Manaster & Corsini, 1982). Essentially, lifestyle forms the lenses through which individuals view and interpret life experiences. These conclusions, though drawn prematurely during early stages of cognitive development, become blueprints for how children negotiate problems and relationships. They inform responses to frustration, challenges, loneliness, and so forth. Thus, these blueprints contribute to lifelong patterns.

Even though children are highly observant, they miss subtle nuances and often have an incomplete understanding of events and situations. Thus, children and adults may make decisions and base their actions on inaccurate assumptions (Dreikurs, 1964). These faulty or mistaken principles, regardless of their objective accuracy, become guiding principles for values, relationship patterns, worth ethic, and general behavior. For example, a young boy may observe his father caring for a baby sister in gentle ways. He may conclude that the little girl is more loveable or, perhaps, more frail than he. He may also hypothesize that the father loves the daughter more. The boy may grow up believing that his sister is more special to the father. Even though the perception may be entirely inaccurate, the young man could begin acting as if the father loves him less, distance himself, and unwittingly perpetuate a pattern of distance. He may generalize the belief and conclude that he is less loveable than his sister, or even less loveable than women.

Mistaken beliefs become a prominent focus of counseling and consultation when professional helpers draw hypotheses about misbehavior. For example, children may conclude that their significance or importance in a group can only be measured by the amount of attention they receive or the level of power they have. They may believe that their importance will only be recognized when others experience pain or rejection as they have. Discouraged children may determine that they will fail regardless of their efforts and that such efforts are futile.

Overcoming Perceptions of Inferiority and Achieving Significance

Adler suggested that the dependence experienced by infants becomes motivation as they endeavor to compensate for perceived limitations and find significance. Opportunities to experience success help children overcome perceptions of their inadequacy and learn strategies that contribute to their feeling significant. Finding destructive and socially inappropriate ways to overcome or cope with feelings of inferiority can contribute to bullying, manipulation, depression, anxiety, and so forth (Kelly & Lee, 2007).

Within this context, feelings of inferiority are not deemed pathological. Rather, they are a common experience that may be exacerbated for young children as they compare themselves to adults (Mosak & Maniacci, 1993). Strategies for overcoming feelings of inferiority contribute to healthful responses or pathological responses. Of course, children don't consciously say, "I feel inferior. I think I will overcome those feelings of inferiority when I have become an astronaut and I make all of my own decisions about everything I do." At some level, though, children form ideas about what they must do and not do in order to achieve significance.

Courage

Adler, Dreikurs, and others who adhere to this philosophy have emphasized the importance of encouragement and the devastating results of discouragement. Dreikurs (1964) asserted that a "misbehaving child is a discouraged child. Each child needs continuous encouragement just as a plant needs water. He [sic] cannot grow and develop and gain a sense of belonging without encouragement" (p. 36).

Adults inadvertently interfere with the development of courage and independence when they become overly protective or when they do things for children that they are capable of accomplishing independently or collaboratively. Conversely, discouragement becomes prominent when children repeatedly experience failure. Determining when protection and assistance *are* helpful requires adults to be intentional and prudent.

Social Interest

Adler introduced the notion of social interest, which he suggested is a primary measurement of mental health. Social interest is characterized by respect for others, cooperation with others, concern for others, and connection with others. Persons with developed social interest are "responsible, cooperative, and creative members of humankind. Persons high in social interest enjoy and like themselves, others, and life" (Sweeney, 1989, p. 27). Children demonstrate and experience social interest as they develop positive relationships with peers as well as adults. Social interest is also manifest as children encourage others and accept encouragement.

Random Act of Kindness or other kindness initiatives align with Adler's concept of social interest.

Purposeful Behavior

Many Adlerian interventions are based on the assumption that all behavior has purpose. As mentioned earlier, Adler contended that children, like adults, are social beings who are largely motivated by their need to belong and achieve a sense of significance in social contexts. In fact, Dreikurs (1964) suggested that everything a child does "is aimed at finding his [*sic*] place" (p. 14) according to his or her lifestyle (described earlier). Conversely, once behaviors no longer occasion the desired effect, they are abandoned. Thus, well-functioning children and youth are able to develop relationships within groups by becoming cooperative, contributing group members. Children who display inappropriate or less socially acceptable behaviors are endeavoring to achieve a place in groups with mistaken strategies.

Adler suggested that children misbehave to (a) get undue attention, (b) achieve power, (c) express revenge, or (d) display inadequacy. Determining the underlying beliefs and purposes of

Notice the similarity between Adler's suggestions about discouragement and misinformed efforts to achieve goals and the notion of self-handicapping behaviors introduced in Chapter 3.

behavior enables adults to help children effectively and appropriately achieve their goals. Thus, identifying the goal of misbehavior is an important component of assessment.

THE PROCESS OF COUNSELING

Adler recommended four general stages of counseling that include (a) development of the relationship, (b) analysis and assessment, (c) interpretation, and (d) reorientation. Empathy was central to Adler's work with clients; he referred to it as the ability to see with the eyes of clients and hear with the ears of clients (Kelly & Lee, 2007). Empathy and other facilitation skills (as reviewed in the *Practice and Application Guide*) contribute to relationships characterized by cooperation and collaboration. A strong working alliance provides the safety for the other dimensions of this approach. The following sections include basic assessment strategies, examples of interpretation, and techniques for reorientation and effecting change.

Assessment

Formal questionnaires and protocols for Adlerian-based assessment are available; however school-based professionals' assessment procedures are typically less extensive. School counselors and school psychologists consult with adults, talk with children, and observe children in a variety of contexts such as different classes, unstructured time, and group activities. Attention should be given to possible purposes underlying the behaviors and the benefits derived from behaviors. Relationship patterns with peers and adults should also be noted. Indications of social interest, pro-social group behaviors, and cooperation warrant attention as does academic progress.

This perspective is often used when we conduct a functional behavior assessment to gather information and understand the function or purpose of a child's behavior.

Additional insight can be acquired by visiting with children about their view of themselves as well as the goals underlying their behavior. Professional helpers often inquire about perceptions with questions such as, "How do you describe yourself?" and "If I asked you to describe your brother, what words would you use?" Similar questions focus on other family members, friends, and school. Other inquiries relate to fears, pleasurable activities, and dreams.

Responses to these questions may provide adequate background to intervene and assist students. At other times, additional information is acquired through examining the presence or absence of the Crucial Cs (described shortly) or directly exploring goals related to misbehavior.

The Crucial Cs. Bettner and Lew (1996) simplified Adler's identification of children's needs (i.e., to belong, to improve, to find significance, and to be encouraged) with the "Crucial Cs: connection, capability, counting, and courage" listed in the following box. The presence and absence of these attributes can provide guidance in identifying unmet needs, goals of behavior, and areas to intervene (LaFountain & Garner, 1998).

Four Vital Protections: The Crucial Cs

- The need to be connected

  "I believe that I belong."

- The need to develop competence and feel capable

  "I believe that I can do it."

- The essential need for significance; the belief that one counts

  "I believe that I matter and I can make a difference."

- The lifelong need for courage

  "I believe that I can handle what comes."

Source: From Lew & Bettner, 1995, pp. 5–18.

Schools offer extensive opportunities for children to achieve the Crucial Cs. For example, learning to read, perform mathematical operations, and create electronic documents provides concrete evidence of competence. Students have multiple opportunities to acquire friendship skills and achieve a sense of belonging. Opportunities to take appropriate risks in a safe environment can contribute to courage. Contributions to school activities in meaningful ways strengthen students' self-confidence and self-efficacy; they acquire hard data from which they can conclude that they are, indeed, significant members of the school community.

Goals of Misbehavior. Proponents of individual psychology base much of their work on identifying and addressing the purposes of children's behavior that is connected to mistaken beliefs. Asking children why they engaged in a certain behavior is not recommended or helpful. Rather, individual psychologists identify various goals as they inquire about potential purposes. For example, Wickers (1988, p. 72) designed a series of statements for generating hypotheses about the goals of children's behaviors. Conversationally, Wickers (1988) presented the statements (in the following box) to children and asked them to judge the accuracy of each one.

Interviewing Children to Explore Goals of Misbehavior

Recommended by Wickers (1988)

1. I want to be in charge (power).
2. I want people to feel sorry for me (inadequacy).
3. I want people to see what it is like to be hurt (revenge).
4. I want people to stop telling me what to do (power).
5. I think that I have been treated unfairly (revenge).
6. I know I'll mess up so there's no point in trying (inadequacy).
7. I want people to feel sorry for what they have done (revenge).
8. I want people to notice me (attention).
9. I want to be left alone. I can't do things right anyway (inadequacy).
10. I want some attention (attention).
11. I want people to do more for me (attention).
12. I want to get even (revenge).
13. I want people to do what I want to do (power).
14. I want people to stop asking me to do things (inadequacy).
15. I want power (power).
16. I want to be special (attention).

Talking with adults who are concerned about a student's behavior to assist in generating hypotheses about underlying goals is often helpful and more efficient. In this process, professional helpers focus on the feelings experienced by adults. Typical feelings associated with the four goals of attention, power, revenge, and inadequacy are provided in the box that follows. You will find similar tables in a variety of texts and articles. Actually, we are not sure if Adler or Dreikurs originated the strategy of focusing on adults' inclinations for responses to suggest children's goals of behavior. Dreikurs (1957) explained the importance of teachers attending to their own internal reactions to identify possible goals as well as their inclinations for external responses that might "fortify the child's mistaken goal instead of correcting it" (p. 34). For example, a child who is trying to get attention might use the mistaken behavior of acting out during a test. If the teacher strongly reacts with loud verbal retribution, the child succeeds and likely resorts to that strategy again.

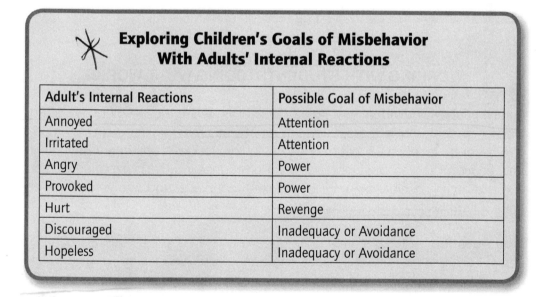

Exploring Children's Goals of Misbehavior With Adults' Internal Reactions

Adult's Internal Reactions	Possible Goal of Misbehavior
Annoyed	Attention
Irritated	Attention
Angry	Power
Provoked	Power
Hurt	Revenge
Discouraged	Inadequacy or Avoidance
Hopeless	Inadequacy or Avoidance

Interpretation and Reorientation

Interpretation and reorientation in school contexts often occur simultaneously. Interpretation is usually directed at increasing insight. Reorientation is the "so what?" component of individual psychology; its purpose is to help clients use the insight to improve their life outside of the counseling sessions. Interpretation and reorientation may occur during individual work with children.

At other times teachers, parents, professional helpers, and other adults collaborate to assist students. For example, interpretation may include questioning to explicate goals of misbehavior. A school psychologist might say, "I have a hunch I want to check out with you. When you argued with your teacher yesterday, I wonder if you were trying to show him that you really wanted to be the boss." He or she might add, "Okay. You would like to feel more powerful in the classroom. I'm wondering how you could do that without doing things that get you in trouble."

> Notice the commonalities between Individual Psychology and cognitive approaches. You may find that cognitive approaches are more efficient when addressing students' faulty beliefs.

If the professional helper believes attention may be the desire that occasions misbehavior, he or she could say, "It sounds like you really like attention. I do too. The problem is that when you try to get attention by interrupting your teacher during a class activity, you typically get in trouble. I wonder how you could get attention by doing things that aren't against the classroom rules."

WORKING WITH STUDENTS: DOING WHAT WORKS

Interventions in individual psychology are not limited to those Adler developed. Rather, professional helpers determine what may be helpful for each individual. We describe techniques that may be useful for work with children and youth in this section. As you develop your style of counseling, gain experience, and explore other possibilities, your counseling technique and intervention repertoire will grow.

The Question. Adlerians often pose questions related to the absence of problems. For example, if a child says she cannot get along with the girls in her classroom, a school-based professional might ask, "What would be different if you were getting along with the other girls?" In response to someone complaining about test anxiety, the counselor could ask, "What would be different if you did not have test anxiety?" Responses to these questions lead to clarification of goals.

The responses may expose other information related to secondary gains of the symptom (Dinkmeyer & Sperry, 2000). Returning to the previous example of test anxiety, a student client may become aware that the anxiety has served as an explanation for low scores. It may be more embarrassing or uncomfortable to say, "I didn't do well because I didn't study" rather than "I didn't do well because I have test anxiety."

Collaborating With the Student. Inviting students to participate in generating solutions to their challenges helps them acquire skills in solving the immediate problem. Additionally, they may increase their sense of competence and courage.

In the following dialogue, notice how the school counselor engages Tariqua with both interpretation and efforts toward reorientation. Tariqua's goal of misbehavior seems to be inadequacy. The school counselor (SC) has other ideas about what may underlie Tariqua's goal.

SC: Tariqua, last week I asked all those questions about wanting people to feel sorry for you or wanting them to leave you alone sometimes. I also visited with a couple of your teachers and talked with your dad. I have a hunch that I want to check out with you. I'm wondering if you leave your work at school sometimes or beg your parents to let you stay home from school because you're tired of trying to do work that just seems to get harder and harder.

Tariqua: What do you mean?

SC: Last week you said you thought it was foolish and really a waste of time for your parents to check your homework every night. I had the sense that you didn't think it would help. It seemed like you wanted your teachers and your parents to leave you alone and let you figure things out for yourself.

Tariqua: Well, yeah. I can't do algebra. I just want to get through the class any way I can. Even if I pass algebra, I won't be able to do geometry, so what's the use?

SC: You're discouraged. Algebra seems so hard, and you're even more afraid of geometry.

Tariqua: It's so easy for everyone else. I just can't do it.

SC: I'm hearing two things. First, you don't think you can do the work in algebra, and you don't want the adults to bother you about it. I doubt that the adults are going to give up because they are worried about you, and they think you *can* pass algebra. So I don't think you are going to be able to change that situation. I wonder if you'd be willing to talk about what happens when you get discouraged with algebra.

Tariqua: Sure. But I don't think it will do much good.

SC: I have the sense that when you start the assignments, you get scared.

Tariqua: Well, yeah. All those numbers and letters are scary.

SC: Okay. And, you've run into things before that were scary.

Tariqua: Like what?

SC: I don't know. You'll have to tell me.

Tariqua: Well, everyone knows that school is scary.

SC: In what way?

Tariqua: That's a no-brainer.

SC: I have to admit—on this one I am brainless.

Tariqua: I can't explain.

SC: I think you can. I wonder if you're afraid of what you'll say and of what I'll think.

Tariqua: Huh!

SC: [waits]

Tariqua: What's the use?

SC: You.

Tariqua: You'll just say I'm dumb.

SC: I can assure you that I won't say you are dumb.

Tariqua: Well, I am.

SC: I have a fair amount of evidence that says you aren't . . .

[Later in the session]

SC: Tariqua, I'm wondering if you would be willing to make a list of things you could do so your teacher and your parents won't worry about your algebra grade. I'd like us to write ideas no matter how silly or useless they seem.

Tariqua: I could steal an answer book.

SC: There's one possibility. What else?

[Later in the session, after at least six alternatives, some of which are plausible, are generated]

SC: I'm wondering which two or three of the ideas you think might work.

Tariqua: I suppose I could work with the teacher like he wants me to do.

SC: Okay, that's one possibility. What else might be?

Tariqua: I could do a couple problems and then ask Mom to see if I'm on the right track.

SC: Okay. That's another. Another?

Tariqua: I could move closer to the front of the room so I can hear better.

SC: Okay. Would you be willing to try any of these during the next week?

Tariqua: I'm not asking Mom.

SC: This is your plan. What would you do?

Tariqua: Okay. I'll talk with the teacher.

SC: That could be scary.

Tariqua: I'm not scared of him.

SC: You've already made a huge step. Congratulations.

Between-Session Interventions. Tariqua's agreement to talk with the teacher is one example of a homework assignment, which is typical for working in this model. Homework can be direct, as illustrated with Tariqua. Assignments can also be subtle behaviors with the goal of simply having students do something different to alter behavior sequences and increase flexibility in both behavior and thinking. For example, "You're having trouble getting to school on time. We've talked about several things that might be helpful. I wonder if you'd be willing to run an experiment and try two things differently this week—like,

You will also see an example of this strategy used in Chapter 6 as part of a cognitive-behavioral approach.

listening to different music on your way to school and coming on a different street than you usually use. I'll be interested in what that's like for you when you come next week."

Acting As If. Adler often asked clients to select a portion of their week to act as if the presenting problem were alleviated (Sweeney, 1989). An example might be, "I'd like to ask you to do something that may seem strange. I'm wondering if you would be willing to pick two days this week when you will act as if you *have* found a way to get along with your social studies teacher *and* that it works well."

WORKING WITH STUDENTS' IMPORTANT ADULTS

Because of the holistic and contextual nature of individual psychology, parents and teachers are often asked to assist in helping children and youth overcome challenges they encounter. Work with significant adults is usually in the form of consultation and psychoeducation (as opposed to counseling). In this section we include contextual interventions related to goals of misbehavior, encouragement, and consequences. More attention will be given to working with parents and adults in Chapter 14.

Encouragement

An integral aspect of Adlerian counseling is the skillful use of encouragement. In fact, Dinkmeyer and Dinkmeyer (1989) suggested that encouragement "is the most important technique for promotion of change" (p. 31). Encouragement reinforces intrinsic motivation when it is communicated with sincerity and congruence (Sweeney, 1989).

Encouraging adults actively attend to children. However, encouragement is more than nonverbally attending or giving random praise. Effective encouragement is focused on behavior as well as effort, progress, or learning. Usually encouragement is given prior to or during an activity. On the other hand, praise is often given after performance of a task and is focused on the product or outcome. Praise may be focused on broad, personal attributes. Notice the difference in the examples provided in Table 5.1.

Table 5.1 Comparison of Encouragement and Praise

Encouragement	Praise
You have spent 35 minutes on that complicated algebra problem, and you have almost got it.	You got that problem right.
You're disappointed that you didn't win; yet I saw how persistent you were during training and how focused you were during the race.	You came in third! Congratulations! I'm so proud of you!
I really appreciate the way you welcomed Sally to the group. When you introduced each member, you mentioned something special about her. The members were pleased, and Sally had many new things to talk about.	You are such a nice girl.
You worked hard to bring your grades up. You stayed after school and worked with the teacher even though you wanted to go home and watch TV.	Congratulations! You got three Bs.
I appreciate your being so conscientious when you organized the books. Placing them in categories was a great idea.	You were such a good child to clean the bookshelf!

Encouragement offers several advantages. Students have clear information about what they have done that was useful or appreciated. Success is framed as a process rather than a single event (Sweeney, 1989). Encouragement also assists in the development of goals, desirable attitudes, and competence (Sweeney, 1989).

Addressing Goals of Misbehavior

As mentioned earlier, inappropriate behavior is recognized as purposeful, though misinformed, efforts to achieve attention, power, revenge, or inadequacy. When it appears that the goal is *attention*, adults can ignore the inappropriate behavior when that is possible and avoid giving attention with punishment, rewards, or coaxing. At times when the child is acting appropriately, it is important for adults to give attention.

When it appears that children are trying to gain *power*, adults can intervene by withdrawing from conflicts and avoiding power struggles. Endeavors to facilitate cooperation and avoid competition may help children achieve power without misbehaving.

Though it is difficult, adults are encouraged to take steps so they *don't* experience being hurt when it appears that *revenge* is the goal of misbehavior. Adults should also avoid punishment and retaliation. Endeavors to develop relationships based on trust and consistently communicating love may alleviate a need or desire for revenge.

To counteract displays of *inadequacy*, it is important to avoid criticism and temptations to become discouraged with the child. Simultaneously, it is important to intentionally encourage efforts as they are displayed. Calling attention to children's strengths is also recommended.

Natural and Logical Consequences

Another individual psychology practice that is particularly relevant in schools is an emphasis on natural and logical consequences. In this regard, proponents suggest that rewards and punishment are ineffective strategies for helping children learn adaptive behavior. Rather, when logical or natural consequences are employed, children experience direct relationships between their behavior and the outcome. Therefore, they also have an opportunity to recognize that they are active decision makers who choose to avoid or experience a consequence.

Natural consequences are "negative outcomes of an ill-advised behavior which follow without the intervention of another person" (Sweeney, 1989, p. 83). Although these consequences are not arranged by adults, adults can interfere with them. For example, if a child leaves his or her bicycle in the yard rather than in the garage where it is secure, the bicycle may be stolen or run over. Adults can interfere with the natural consequences by placing the bicycle in the garage for the child, or replacing a damaged or stolen bicycle, thereby preventing the child's opportunity to learn to be responsible for his or her belongings.

Of course, natural consequences have limitations. The bicycle may not be stolen or hit. Thus, adults design logical consequences to teach children how to be responsible. Effective logical consequences are age appropriate. The relationship between the behavior and the consequence should be clear, and the consequence should be consistently enforced. Logical consequences should be established and communicated prior to the infraction. A logical consequence for leaving a bicycle in the yard would be to have it restricted for a week. A logical consequence for failing to submit an assignment would be loss of free time (during which it *can* be completed).

Consequences can be challenging for teachers, parents, and professional helpers. Adults may be tempted to "rescue" students who are struggling. The temptation may be particularly strong for school counselors and school psychologists who have added insight about children's challenges, limitations, and pain.

ADDITIONAL INDIVIDUAL PSYCHOLOGY CONCEPTS FOR WORK WITH ADOLESCENTS

As mentioned earlier, Adler suggested that each individual has life tasks related to work, friendship, love, self-acceptance, purpose or meaning, and leisure (Dinkmeyer & Sperry, 2000). Mastery of these tasks contributes to psychological well-being (Carlson et al., 2006). Though the foundation for these tasks is laid in early childhood, they become prominent during adolescence.

Professional helpers who work with adolescents may follow structured assessment guides to acquire understanding of progress toward achieving life tasks, as well as goals of behavior. Additional areas of inquiry often address adolescents' view of purpose in their lives and sources of motivation. For example, counselors and school psychologists could use incomplete questions related to happiness, fear, peer groups, career plans, and so forth.

Based on the understanding of adolescents' lifestyle, their beliefs and assumptions about themselves and others, professional helpers can help them deconstruct motives underlying behavior. As assumptions are identified, they can be challenged or examined. Reframing may help adolescents accept more useful perceptions and meanings attributed to experiences. Identification of mistaken approaches to achieve goals and needs may render the actions unacceptable, which Adlerians often call the "spitting-in-the-soup" technique. For example, a counselor might say, "I wonder if you're making that funny noise to get my attention. If you just say, 'Would you talk to me?' I'd give you my full attention, and your throat would be happier." In a group or classroom, a professional helper might explain that people resort to angry temper tantrums when they are caught in a difficult situation and feel powerless. The helper could frame inappropriate displays of anger as "a chicken's way out of a difficult situation" with loss of self-control as an unfortunate price to pay, thereby placing outbursts in a less than desirable context.

BEYOND COUNSELING AND PSYCHOEDUCATION: IMPLICATIONS FOR SCHOOL CLIMATE

In a broader purview, the work of Adler and Dreikurs holds critical implications for school climate (LaFountain & Garner, 1998). We encourage professionals who work in schools to consider the importance of an environment that encourages children and youth and promotes connections, friendships, and positive relationships. Students who experience a sense of belonging are more likely to thrive—regardless of the context.

Additionally, Adler (1964) suggested that schools are a primary place where children develop the capacity for social interest. He directly addressed the interwoven relationship between development of social interest and school experiences by saying,

> Plainly . . . the school is the proper place to increase children's social interest by judicious handling, so that they do not leave as enemies of society. . . . There can be no question that success at school also depends chiefly on the children's social interest; indeed, the social interest they show at school gives us some idea of the form their subsequent life in the community will take. . . . The school has it in its power to awaken and foster the spirit of fellow feeling. If teachers are familiar with our point of view they will also be able, by friendly conversation, to bring to the child's notice his or her want of social feeling; they will show the cause of this deficiency and how it can be removed; in this way they will bring the child into closer contact with society. (p. 48)

Similarly, Adler (1964) contended that "all the problems of human life demand . . . capacity for cooperation and preparation for it—the visible sign of social interest. In this disposition courage and happiness are included, and they are to be found nowhere else" (p. 207). Indeed, schools can become a laboratory for practicing and developing skills

Consider ways you could draw from individual psychology to develop psychoeducational lessons.

for living. We invite you to consider ways you can contribute to an encouraging, inclusive school climate in which children feel psychologically safe as well as physically safe.

EMPIRICAL SUPPORT FOR
APPLICATION OF ADLER'S THEORY

The need for empirical validation for Adlerian interventions is clear (Carlson et al., 2006). The theoretical constructs are supported with research, as are the central assumptions regarding the importance of the therapeutic relationship. For example, empirical evidence supports Adler's notion of social interest and its relationship to appropriate behavior (Watkins & Guarnaccia, 1999). Though less robust, research has also provided support for Adler's beliefs about lifestyle and its assessment.

A sequence of studies designed to assess the efficacy of the Student Success Skills program (Webb, Lemberger, & Brigman, 2008) resulted in significantly improved performance in mathematics and reading across ethnic groups. Additional growth was shown on behavioral rating scale scores. This comprehensive intervention, designed for students in grades four though ten, is grounded in Adlerian constructs as well as research related to skills that equate to academic success and improved social relationships. The sequence of large and small group activities addresses goal setting, progress monitoring, contributing to supportive school communities, strengthening cognitive skills, working under pressure, and developing optimism. Initially the participating school counselors conducted five 45-minute weekly sessions in classrooms. Subsequently they collaborated with classroom teachers to identify students who would benefit from an additional series of eight small-group reinforcement sessions. The smaller groups continued to meet with their counselor on a monthly basis. These authors and their colleagues have provided an admirable intervention that is practical, replicable, and empirically defensible.

Results of research addressing Adlerian-based parenting programs warrant attention as well. For example, Gibson (1999) examined an extensive number of studies addressing Systematic Training for Effective Parenting (STEP) programs and concluded that they are beneficial for parents of children representing a range of diverse groups. Changes noted included attitudes about parenting, empathy, recognition of children's goals of misbehavior and implementation of appropriate consequence, and increased communication skills. In studies focused on children, increased self-concept and decreased behavior problems were shown.

Similar results have been shown for Active Parenting programs. For example, families who participated in the Families in Action program (as opposed to the control group) demonstrated increased family cohesion, decreased discord, stronger connection to school, and enhanced self-esteem one year after the program was conducted (Active Parenting Publishing, 2006). Another study was focused on children whose behavior was observed while their parents participated in an Active Parenting class. Diminished negative behaviors as well as increased positive behaviors, when compared to the control group, were noted.

RESPONDING TO CULTURAL DIFFERENCES

Respect for diverse backgrounds and circumstances is a hallmark of this approach. In fact, Adler was an advocate for marginalized groups and social equity long before professional groups called attention to culture and diversity (Watts, 2003). His theory reflects respect for cultural values and diverse members of society. The work is collaborative, action oriented, and flexible.

Herring and Runion (1994) reviewed individual psychology's relevance for working with students representing diverse ethnic groups, with specific references to Native Americans. The authors suggested that Adlerian concepts were particularly responsive to experiences of marginalization, educational inequities, and inappropriate cognitive assessment. Additionally, Adlerian professional helpers capitalize on cooperation, which is a value of many cultural groups.

As mentioned earlier, school-based professionals who use the theory to its greatest advantage carefully consider what works with each student client under what conditions. Thus, respecting and learning about each person's unique perspectives (i.e. phenomenology) lays a foundation for intervention. Professional helpers consider and attend to social context, which includes culture and ethnicity, and opportunities to promote social interest. Student clients make decisions about changes they make; thus, their values and beliefs guide goals as well as strategies for their achievement.

Cultural differences as well as implications of culture warrant cautious attention during any form assessment, particularly related to Adler's notion of lifestyle. Many elements of Adlerian psychology are based on Western culture. Caution must be employed when drawing hypotheses and conclusions about lifestyle, goals of behavior, and so forth when working with students having non-Western ancestry.

CONCLUSION

Individual psychology is a common-sense approach that provides a rich source of perspectives, guidelines, and resources for school-based professional helpers. Contemporary proponents of individual psychology have championed prevention through psychoeducational programs for students, parents, and teachers. Their books and course materials are easily read, practical, and believable. Encouragement is central—encouragement for children as well as adults.

Adler has become an influential icon; as you study other theories, we encourage you to consider aspects that resemble elements of individual psychology. Because Adler's theory is so extensive, theorists have emphasized components of individual psychology to create new theories and approaches. For example, perspectives and mistaken beliefs were central to Adler's work. Cognitive approaches have focused on those elements without attention to childhood influence, lifestyle, and so forth. You will find many of Adler's interventions in solution-focused brief therapy. Undoubtedly, you will also find elements of individual psychology that seem most relevant and practical for you in your schools. Remember, you are becoming an informed consumer of theories!

Case Illustration of Individual Psychology With Cassie

If we were to work with Cassie from an Adlerian perspective, we would initially gather information that would help us generate hypotheses about her lifestyle. The counselor has talked with Cassie, he has reviewed her school records, and he has conducted informal observations. In order to draw more informed hypotheses about Cassie's lifestyle (especially goals of her behavior), we would acquire more information about her childhood and things that are important to her (e.g., doing well, having lots of friends, making her own decisions). We would probably ask to meet with her parents in order to obtain additional information. Using the information we have, we can generate ideas related to the Crucial Cs.

Cassie seemingly feels connected with her family and her peers. However, she may believe that the connection would be threatened if she were to disclose her questions about sexual orientation. Cassie has a fair amount of evidence to conclude that she is competent. She seems to believe that she counts in her family—that she is significant to her parents, her teachers, and her peers. She has shown courage, although she may be discouraged at this time.

(Continued)

(Continued)

Within this framework, we would share our hypotheses with Cassie and ask for her evaluation of each suggestion. Together we would define a focus of our work and identify a goal. Perhaps Cassie would become attracted to the topic of purpose and meaning. She may want to explore her role and her significance within the family context.

School Counselor (SC): In the short time we've worked together, I have asked you lots of questions. I also visited with your parents and teachers. I'd like to share some of my thoughts, and then I'll want to know your reactions to my thoughts. Okay?

Cassie: Okay.

SC: It's clear to me that you love your parents, and your relationship with them is strong. They are proud of you, and you don't want to do anything that will interfere with their pride. You and they feel good about your many accomplishments. This is the part I wanted to check out with you. It's just a hunch and could be completely off-base. You value your parents' love and pride so much. One of the things that scares you as much as anything else is that you might lose their devotion, particularly if you even mentioned your thoughts about possibly being a lesbian.

> Ultimately, we would help Cassie clarify her concerns by asking, "What would be different if you...?" This would lead to identification of goals, which would be related to school performance and self-understanding.

Cassie: Mmm. Let me think about that a while.

SC: Of course. That's quite a bit for you to think about. We can talk about it next time we meet.

SC: I'd also like to be sure that our work is helpful for you. I've assumed that you want to get back on track with your friendships and your grades. You've also said you'd like to figure things out about yourself and if you are, indeed, different from other girls. I'd like you to think about that and other things that might be bothering you. We can also talk about that next time.

[Following meeting]

Cassie: I thought about your questions, and I want to talk mostly about two problems. I want to talk about my getting mad so much lately, and I want to try to figure out what is going on inside of me.

SC: Let's talk about getting mad first, because I think we will be able to solve that more easily, particularly because you have only felt angry in the last month or two. What would be different, let's say at the game this Friday, if you didn't have a problem with anger at all?

Cassie: I wouldn't get any technical fouls!

SC: So, let's say someone glares at you and maybe even fouls you without getting caught. What will you do to keep from getting a technical?

Cassie: I can just remind myself about how bad I felt when I got benched and keep playing.

SC: Do you think that's all it will take?

Cassie: Yeah. I do.

SC: Are you willing to try it?

Cassie: Well, yeah. It will be easier this week because I'm not so tired, and I'm not as worried about things as I was.

SC: Well, I'll be watching from the teachers' section and cheering for you!

With goals established, we collaboratively devised plans for Cassie to achieve them. Depending on the results of the plan she essentially designed, we might explore connections between her behavior and possible goals (such as power or attention).

Addressing her confusion about sexual orientation would take longer and may not be something that can be addressed in a school setting. Initially, we would engage in activities to increase Cassie's insight. We might offer hypotheses about her lifestyle and beliefs she has adopted. We may talk about her perceptions of risk should she engage in an activity that does not please her parents or her friends. We could explore her fears of what might happen if she did not live up to her parents' expectations.

Insight without change is of questionable value. Thus, we might return to "the question" about what would be different if she achieved clarity and then ask her to select certain periods of time during the next week to act as if the difference had already happened.

Activities

1. Working with a partner, identify and rehearse ways you can verbally and nonverbally express "I appreciate your . . ." "I admire your . . ." or "You are important to me because . . ."

2. Working alone or in groups, list ways you could draw from individual psychology as you begin your career in a school.

Journal Reflections

Reflection #1

For one week intentionally watch for opportunities to encourage others with verbal expressions such as,

- "I really enjoyed being with you today because . . ."
- "I appreciate your help because . . ."
- "Your cookies taste wonderful. Will you teach me to make them?"

Other encouraging activities include the following:

- Sending a birthday card to a friend
- Listening empathically to someone
- Demonstrating patience (adapted from Sweeney, 1989, pp. 140–141)

Keep a journal of your observations and experiences.

Reflection #2

Think about someone in your life who has done something that is frustrating or annoying to you. Use Adler's framework for hypothesizing goals of behavior to explain the other person's behavior and your reactions to it.

Electronic Resources

Active Parenting: http://www.activeparenting.org

Adlerian Psychology Association of British Columbia: http://adlercentre.ca.

North American Society of Adlerian Psychology: http://www.alfredadler.org/Links.htm

Systematic Training for Effective Parenting (STEP): http://www.steppublishers.com/

Print Resources

Bettner, B. L., & Lew, A. (1992). *Raising kids who can: Using family meetings to nurture responsible, cooperative, caring, and happy children.* New York: Harper Perennial.

Herring, R. D., & Runion, K. B. (1994). Counseling ethnic children and youth from an Adlerian perspective. *Journal of Multicultural Counseling and Development, 22,* 215–226.

Lew, A., & Bettner, B. L. (1995). *Responsibility in the classroom: A teacher's guide to understanding and motivating students.* Newton Centre, MA: Connexions.

McKay, G. D., & Maybell, S. (2004). *Calming the family storm: Anger management for moms, dads, and all the kids.* Atascadero, CA: Impact.

McKay, G. D., McKay, J. L., Eckstein, D., & Maybell, S. (2001). *Raising respectful kids in a rude world: Teaching your children the power of mutual respect and consideration.* Roseville, CA: Prima.

Nelson, J. (1987). *Positive discipline.* New York: Ballantine.

CHAPTER 6

Cognitive-Behavioral Approaches to Counseling in Schools

Learning Objectives

- Review essential principles of cognitive-behavioral interventions
- Consider applications of cognitive-behavioral interventions for work with children and adolescents
- Increase knowledge of cognitive-behavioral strategies

With the heightened emphasis on evidence-based practices, cognitive-behavioral therapy (CBT) has become an approach that is frequently used in the schools (Mennuti, Christner, & Freeman, 2006). Many of the common difficulties with which children and adolescents struggle such as anxiety, eating disorders, or anger and aggression are readily addressed through a combination of cognitive and behavioral strategies (Reinecke, Dattilio, & Freeman, 2003). Cognitive-behavioral interventions focus on understanding how individuals interpret their experiences and the effects of these interpretations on their emotional and behavioral functioning (Freidberg & McClure, 2002; Reinecke et al., 2003). The emphasis in this approach is on understanding and changing the cognitions, beliefs, and behaviors that are impacting the student client's current situation.

Philosophers have long held a belief in the importance of cognition to our daily lives. Behavioral approaches appeared much later in our evolution and originally were based on animal models (DiGiuseppe, 2009). Initially, the role of thoughts was not welcomed into behavioral discourse because they could not be observed or measured. But beginning in the early 1970s, cognitive theorists introduced their models of therapy and began integrating behavioral techniques into their approach (DiGiuseppe, 2009). These two models grew in popularity at about the same time and experienced increasing levels of integration as they emerged. Today, cognitive-behavioral interventions represent an integration of behavioral approaches, cognitive therapies, and self-regulation research as well as consideration of environmental and contextual factors (Mayer & Van Acker, 2009). There is no one, agreed-upon approach; instead cognitive-behavioral interventions refer to a number of different strategies that are consistent with this theoretical orientation.

Because the approach is broadly defined, there are multiple strategies that can be used to address students' mental health needs (Christner, Mennuti, & Pearson, 2009; Mayer & Van Acker, 2009; Mennuti et al., 2006). For example, Ariel is a 15-year-old who presents with sad affect. She has difficulty getting along with her peers and is increasingly isolating herself. The emphasis in a cognitive-behavioral approach to counseling would be directed toward her automatic thoughts (e.g., "No one likes me. They all think I'm a loser"), her beliefs (e.g., "If everyone doesn't like and accept me, I'm not worthwhile"), and her behaviors (e.g., avoidance of social situations). From this perspective, behavior is mediated by one's internal thoughts; therefore efforts to facilitate change might include thought logs, role-plays, and other strategies in an effort to introduce alternative thought patterns. Additionally, student clients might be given behavioral homework assignments (e.g., engage in a manageable social activity).

ESSENTIAL PRINCIPLES OF COGNITIVE-BEHAVIORAL APPROACHES

As the name suggests, cognitive-behavioral models focus on both thoughts and behaviors. We first explore the cognitive aspect of this approach. From this framework, our major question is how does the individual perceive and interpret events in his or her world? Cognitions are defined as an "organized set of beliefs, attitudes, memories and expectations, along with a set of strategies for using this body of knowledge in an adaptive manner" (Reinecke et al., 2003, p. 3). These two aspects of cognition are important. That is, the helper does not want to just focus on the "contents" of the individual's thoughts but also on the manner in which information is represented in memory, how thoughts are used to mediate new information, and the degree to which an individual can control his or her thought processes.

Dobson and Dozois (2010, p. 4) outlined the three fundamental propositions of cognitive-behavioral therapy:

1. Cognitive activity affects behavior.

2. Cognitive activity may be monitored and altered.

3. Desired behavior change may be effected through cognitive change.

Different cognitive processes such as problem solving, coping strategies, interpersonal skills, and affect regulation can be viewed as skills that can be taught or acquired similar to other skills. Because of the central nature of cognitions, change in cognition is viewed as a precursor to behavioral change.

From a cognitive-behavioral perspective, our emotional and behavioral responses in everyday life are guided by how we perceive events (Friedberg & McClure, 2002; Reinecke et al., 2003). Additionally, our previous experiences, the attributions we make about events, and the ways that events affect our view of ourselves play a role in how we react. As children develop, they acquire underlying beliefs about themselves and their world based on both experiences and these different cognitive processes (e.g., perceptions, memories). Over time, they develop an overarching belief or schema through which they filter life events and make meaning of these internal and external experiences (Reinecke et al., 2003).

Ariel, described earlier, views herself as a "loser" who is not accepted. She pays heightened attention to evidence that seems to support her beliefs. For example, if someone does not greet her in the hallway, she is likely to interpret this event as confirmation of her basic worthlessness. In turn, she is more likely to behave in ways that actually invite a negative response from her peers. For example, she may walk through the halls with her head down and without making eye contact with others. Her perception of being rejected is reinforced, and she becomes even less likely to reach out to her peers. Thus, she is presented with few opportunities to change her thinking.

Maladaptive Thoughts and Beliefs

These thought patterns or beliefs have different names, depending on the underlying cognitive theory but are viewed as central to the individual's maladaptive responses. For example, Ellis (1994) developed rational-emotive-behavioral therapy (REBT) based on the idea that emotional problems resulted from irrational and illogical thinking patterns. He believed that humans could be taught to control their thoughts, feelings, beliefs, and actions. From this view, if students have a rational belief system, they will likely be well adapted to their environment and able to manage the unpredictable, uncontrollable events that occur. However, if students have an irrational belief system, they may view themselves as inferior and unlovable. Consequently, others will always fall short of their expectations.

Ellis (1979) viewed people as innately irrational and self-defeating. From his perspective, these irrational thinking patterns are reinforced early on through parenting practices, teacher behaviors, and other experiences in the environment. Thus, these irrational beliefs begin to develop early and are present in children. The irrational thoughts are usually identified by the inclusion of the words "must" and "should" (e.g., "Everyone must like me," "I should not make mistakes"). Ellis (2005) described this pattern as demandingness, when individuals come to believe that what they want is the same as what they need. In turn, this expectation can lead to other faulty beliefs such as catastrophizing ("It will be the worst thing ever if I'm not invited to this party"), an inability to tolerate frustration ("I simply cannot stand it anymore"), and global ratings or labels placed on oneself ("I am stupid and incapable").

At about the same time, Beck (1976) also noted negative thought patterns among individuals he was treating for depression. He described these thoughts as "automatic" because they seemed to appear immediately in response to situations. This pattern of erroneous or exaggerated thinking is referred to by the umbrella term *cognitive distortions* (Mennuti et al., 2006). Children and adolescents who have a number of cognitive distortions, or for whom these operate strongly, tend to have more internalizing difficulties (e.g., anxiety, depression).

Although many examples of cognitive distortions exist for adults (e.g., Beck, Rush, Shaw, & Emery, 1979; Burns, 1999), less is known about how these distortions manifest themselves in children and adolescents. Christner and Stewart-Allen (as cited in Mennuti et al., 2006, p. 7) provided a helpful list of common cognitive distortions seen in children that included such patterns as "dichotomous thinking, overgeneralizing, disqualifying the positive, and labeling."

In the previous example, Ariel might engage in "disqualifying the positive" by discounting anyone who said hello to her in the hall and by thinking, "That person must not have any friends, that's why he said hello to me" or, "She just feels sorry for me." In this way, Ariel does not have to challenge her own negative view of herself.

Cognitive Deficiency

Another model of CBT focuses on cognitive deficits. From this perspective, there are some individuals who have not developed the skills needed for adaptive coping. These cognitive deficiencies are believed to contribute to some children's social and emotional challenges because they may have difficulty processing information (Kendall & MacDonald, 1993). For example, they may not use forethought or problem-solving strategies. Instead, children and adolescents with a cognitive deficiency may respond with impulsivity and attention problems. Strategies for addressing deficits in this area include social problem solving (Kendall, 2006) and self-instructional training (Meichenbaum, 1993).

Behavioral Models

From a behavioral perspective, the observable actions of the individual are the most important component of change. Early work in this field focused on the application of operant principles into therapeutic models such as behavior modification and applied behavior analysis (Akin-Little, Little, Bray, & Kehle, 2009). There is little doubt that these behavioral models are effective in changing behaviors, but there are potential drawbacks to these approaches. Professional helpers cannot always be available to reinforce desired behaviors, and unless extensive planning for generalization takes place, it is not likely to occur. As a result, some behaviorists began to teach individuals to reinforce their own behaviors. They also began to incorporate certain cognitive techniques into their practice. Today, many behavioral therapies incorporate some cognitive interventions as well (DiGiuseppe, 2009).

The behavioral component of CBT is incorporated to help teach and reinforce new behaviors. Rehearsal is one of the best ways to incorporate new patterns of behavior into one's repertoire. Because thoughts might be considered a form of behavior, the principles of operant conditioning (e.g., reinforcement, rehearsal) should result in positive changes in these as well (DiGiuseppe, 2009). Behavioral intervention includes the use of positive reinforcement, shaping, and extinction. The effectiveness of these approaches can be enhanced when there is consistency between home and school environments (Crawley, Podell, Beidas, Braswell, & Kendall, 2010).

THE COUNSELING PROCESS

In consideration of these different types of cognitive factors, distortions (or irrational thinking), and deficiencies, a school-based helper who uses a cognitive-behavioral approach helps student clients acquire new skills in both thinking and behaving while also facilitating a change in cognitive processing (Mennuti et al., 2006). Further, professional helpers who use cognitive-behavioral interventions stress the importance of taking responsibility for one's thoughts and behaviors.

School-Based Helper's Role

School-based helpers who adopt a CBT orientation have been described as coaches who act as consultants/collaborators, diagnosticians, and educators (Kendall, 2006). As a "consultant/collaborator," the helper adopts the stance of one who does not have all the answers. Rather, a school-based helper presents ideas about things to try and creates opportunities for the student client to do so. Together, the helper and student client use a problem-solving model to determine the best approach to reaching the student's goals (Kendall, 2006).

Kendall (2006) also described helpers as diagnosticians because they use their knowledge and experience to identify concerns. Sometimes children are referred to school-based helpers with a vague description such as, "This student seems depressed" or "I can't work with the child because his behavior is so out there. I'm sure he has ADHD." Because of your role in the school, you are able to make observations and gather more information from parents and teachers that answer questions such as these: Is this child's behavior appropriate for his age? Does her behavior seem different from other students in her class? What is school like for this student? Through these processes, school helpers engage in a process of "figuring out" whether the presenting concern is accurate and complete.

As an "educator," a helper considers the strategies that will best help a student learn new thoughts and behaviors (Kendall, 2006). That may mean that the helper teaches these new skills, but she will also encourage student clients to think for themselves. The professional helper will consider the best strategies for communicating new information to ensure that the student client understands and is able to apply these concepts. Most importantly, the helper as educator observes the student perform the new behaviors and provides feedback (as a consultant).

Developing a Therapeutic Alliance

Although the focus of cognitive-behavioral approaches is on thoughts and behaviors, this emphasis is not to the exclusion of the therapeutic relationship. In fact, Beck et al. (1979) noted that one of the most common errors in the therapy process was "slighting the therapeutic relationship" (p. 79). The helper works to establish an empathetic and empowering relationship that encourages students to explore their own thoughts and feelings. In fact, Kendall and Southam-Gerow (1996) found that the therapeutic relationship was viewed as one of the most important components to children who had completed CBT. When a trusting, safe relationship exists, youth are more likely to attend sessions, to stay with the counseling until they have met their goals, and to experience better outcomes (Hawley & Weisz, 2005).

Cognitive-behavioral interventions do not take place in a vacuum. School-based professionals must develop therapeutic relationships with their student clients even if they are using a very structured cognitive-behavioral intervention. This relationship was considered unnecessary in early behavioral treatments (e.g., Eysenck, 1960). However, it is now well established that the therapeutic relationship is important to treatment outcomes, especially for young clients who may not have "chosen" counseling (DiGiuseppe, Linscott, & Jilton, 1996). School-based professionals must also consider the role of the social and family context in their delivery of cognitive behavioral interventions.

Attending to the Social Context

Children are more reliant on their environments than adults. They may not have the freedom to make their own choices or the independence to act on decisions. Therefore, school-based professionals working from a CBT model must attend to both the internal and external factors that affect student clients. Because all cognitive development occurs within a social context, proponents of the model place a great deal of emphasis on learning and environmental influences that shape and reinforce certain patterns of thought. At times, these environmental factors may be negative and place individuals at risk for developing behavioral and emotional problems.

Because parents are one of the most significant influences in children's lives, it can be beneficial to include the adults in a student's life in the counseling (Crawley et al., 2010). Parents might act in at least three different roles to support their child's counseling: consultant, coclient, and collaborator (Kendall, 2006). If parents are working with the counselor to determine the nature of the concern, they might be considered "consultants." At times, parents may be unknowingly contributing to the concern. In these instances, they might be considered "coclients." That doesn't necessarily mean that you would see the families for counseling. Rather, through consultation, education, or possibly a referral, you would recognize that the parents may require education or support to help change their interactions with the student client. Finally, at times CBT-oriented helpers enlist the help of families in implementing an intervention with a child, especially younger children. In these instances, parents would be viewed as "collaborators" (Kendall, 2006). With family and student client permission, this approach may be expanded to include the teacher or another important adult at school as a collaborator.

Structure of CBT Sessions

Whether provided in an individual or group format, the structure of CBT sessions tends to follow a similar format. The session begins with a review of the previous week. Based on the issues that arise, the school-based helper and student client engage in goal setting and session planning. Much of the counseling session focuses on a collaborative form of learning. As such, the professional helper focuses on methods for involving children and helping them identify those areas that they would like to change in their lives.

A variety of strategies are used during the session (some of these are described shortly) but might include teaching, problem solving, modeling, and role-play with feedback. With children, you'll want to choose active, fun tasks that are appealing and developmentally appropriate. Treatment components may be introduced using workbooks, stories, puppets, drawings, and other types of hands-on activities (Kingery et al., 2006). At the end of the session, homework is often assigned to help the student apply the new skill or strategy. Increasingly, there are manualized forms of treatment that provide a step-by-step guide for selecting and implementing strategies to address a specific concern (e.g., anxiety, depression). Kendall (2006) cautioned that helpers remain flexible and not overlook the relationship when using a manual-guided intervention. It is also important to keep in mind that just because a therapeutic approach is evidence-based and standardized, does not mean it will necessarily be effective for the specific student with whom you are working. You may find that you need to make slight modifications in the treatment from what is presented in the manual. In fact, flexibility in using manualized treatment is important to helpers (Kendall & Chu, 2000).

There is not a "manual" for all the various issues and concerns that you will encounter in the school. Therefore, you will want to be familiar with the various techniques that are available within a CBT model. Together with your student clients, you will decide on and practice those strategies that you believe will work best to help them reach their specific goals.

STRATEGIES: DOING WHAT WORKS

Cognitive-behavioral therapy is directed toward four systems of response (cognitive, affective, behavioral, and physiological) that are considered within the context of the individual (e.g., family, school, community, and culture). Therefore, the techniques associated with CBT include strategies to address one or more of these four systems. For example, cognitive and affective interventions such as (a) challenging distorted thinking, (b) self-talk, (c) problem solving, and (d) thought stopping might be used when a student struggles with continual negative thoughts or irrational fears (Mennuti et al., 2006). Behavioral principles and interventions such as contingent reinforcement, shaping, role playing, and modeling might be incorporated into sessions to address behavioral excesses, deficits, or physiological responses (e.g., anxiety). A blend of these cognitive and behavioral strategies can be used to teach students new techniques such as social skills, self-evaluation, and self-monitoring, in addition to techniques for managing stress (Thompson & Henderson, 2007).

Cognitive and Affective Strategies

One of the primary strategies in a cognitive-behavioral approach is helping student clients to change negative, automatic thought patterns. Working collaboratively, the school-based helper attempts to understand which maladaptive thought patterns are present and demonstrates the emotional and behavioral impact of these thoughts. After collecting data through journaling or maintaining an "automatic thought log," the helper and student client work to create alternative or replacement thoughts. For Ariel that might be, "Rather than assuming that students are not greeting you in the hall because they do not like you, perhaps they do not know you, and that is why they do not say anything." Beck et al. (1979) described this process as cognitive restructuring to

To adapt this approach for younger children, use visual images (e.g., characters with thought bubbles over their heads) and hands-on materials such as puppets to make concepts more concrete.

help change negative thoughts, impressions, and beliefs. These methods were developed for adults but have been shown to be effective with children and adolescents (Kendall, 2006; Stark et al., 2006).

To help student clients effectively use cognitive strategies, the additional techniques of positive self-talk and thought stopping might be introduced. You may think of the popular *Saturday Night Live* skit that parodied the technique of positive self-talk ("I'm good enough, I'm smart enough, and gosh darn it, people like me"). Although this technique may seem silly, consider approaching your next counseling session with the following thoughts: "I am going to fail, I will not know what to say, and all of my efforts will be ineffective." Now, imagine that you enter your next session with the alternative ideas: "I'm really pretty good at counseling. I'm able to listen to the students and understand what they are trying to say to me. I think I have some good ideas and strategies for helping students to be successful." You can easily see the difference in how you might approach each session based on these different messages. The same holds true for children and adolescents who struggle with negative thought patterns.

Self-talk can also serve as a form of self-instruction. For example, Ariel often walks through the hallway with her head down and avoids making eye contact with other students. She and her school-based helper could develop a homework assignment for her to try walking through the hall looking at other students and smiling at one or two of them. She is to journal about the experience and bring her entry to their next session. The school-based helper models the behavior that she and Ariel practice a few times. As part of her practice, they develop a script she will say to herself (e.g., "I'm going to look up when I walk through the hall. I'll find someone who looks friendly and is looking toward me. I will turn toward that person, smile, and say hi"). Sometimes individuals have ongoing negative thoughts that inhibit their ability to try new behaviors. Through "thought stopping" an individual is taught to become aware of when these thoughts are happening and literally interrupt them, sometimes in an abrupt manner (e.g., shouting "stop" to oneself).

An REBT-oriented school helper would also use an active process to identify, challenge, and replace maladaptive thoughts (DiGiuseppe, 2009). Ellis promoted the idea that individuals come to understand themselves as having strengths and weakness and that these aspects of themselves are unimportant to their overall value as a person (Ellis & Bernard, 2006). This approach supports a blend of accepting oneself unconditionally, challenging negative thoughts, and engaging in behaviors that are contrary to damaging ideas (e.g., acting "as if"). For example, Ariel's homework assignment might be to walk through the hallway "as if" she were one of the most popular girls in the school.

Skill Development

In addition to the cognitive strategies mentioned earlier, school-based professionals might provide specific instruction in any of these four skill-building strategies: problem solving, affective education, relaxation training, and role play/modeling (Crawley et al., 2010). Different skills are typically used together in a variety of combinations depending on the needs of the student client. School-based professionals can assist students to learn these important skills through individual or group counseling as well as classroom guidance lessons (e.g., Mayer & Van Acker, 2009; Weist, 2005).

Problem Solving. The focus of this component is to help student clients work through the process of problem solving. Individuals are first helped to learn how to solve a problem when the "problem" is not serious. For example, what could you do if you forgot your homework at home? By working with students around situations that are not anxiety provoking, they can learn the steps in problem solving. Once they have accomplished this relatively simple task, they will be ready to begin practicing these skills using increasingly more stressful examples (e.g., "What could you do if you were at a party and found out people were using drugs in the bathroom?"). If you were using this approach as part of your individual counseling, you would focus on applying the problem-solving strategies to events or situations in the student client's life.

A related concept is that of social problem solving in which individuals apply a problem-solving model to resolve social conflicts. Originally, these social problem-solving models were used with aggressive youth (e.g., Spivak, Platt, & Shure, 1976). The first step in this model is to identify or define the problem that exists and then to generate alternative strategies for addressing the problem. Once this list is created, the school-based helper and student client explore each alternative and consider the possible consequences of each action. Based on their analysis, a strategy is selected, and plans are made to implement the solution. Social problem solving is effective as an intervention for aggressive students (e.g., Sukhodolsky, Golub, Stone, & Orban, 2005) as well as a prevention program (Daunic, Smith, Brank, & Penfield, 2006).

Affective Education. One of the important roles of cognitive-based interventions is to help student clients to learn how to identify and express emotions appropriately. Younger students often have a very limited emotional vocabulary (e.g., mad and sad), but through explicit instruction, they can learn many important concepts about emotions. For example, school-based helpers might teach about different types of emotions, what they might feel or look like, and how to handle these intense feelings. They can help students understand the connection between their thinking and emotion. Most importantly, students can learn that emotions can be changed (Southam-Gerow & Kendall, 2000).

As with many of the cognitive-behavioral techniques, these skills can be taught in an individual, group, or classroom setting. In fact, many established programs such as I Can Problem Solve (Shure, 2001), Second Step (Committee for Children, 2010), and the Incredible Years (Webster-Stratton & Herman, 2010) are based on cognitive-behavioral principles and were designed to be delivered in the context of a small-group or classroom setting (Mennuti et al., 2006).

Relaxation Training. Another key skill in a cognitive-behavioral model is the use of relaxation training. The goal of relaxation training is to help an individual manage or control the physiological response that might accompany anxiety or high levels of arousal. School-based professionals introduce this strategy as a type of coping skill that can be used when a student is anxious, angry, impulsive, or simply overwhelmed (Crawley et al., 2010). There are many different models available, and a school-based professional may select from scripts for progressive muscle relaxation (Ollendick & Cerny, 1981), guided imagery (Koeppen, 1974), or simply practicing the use of deep breathing exercises.

Role Playing and Modeling. Although the emphasis of a cognitive-behavioral approach is on thoughts, advocates of this approach emphasize the importance of performance-based procedures as the best method for achieving the goal of correcting distorted cognitions or remediating skill deficiencies (Kendall, 2006). Within the counseling session, the helper provides opportunities for role plays and rehearsal and then gives student clients encouragement and feedback to teach and shape skills. This technique is especially useful in social skills training approaches. Depending on the developmental age of the student client, you can use modeling and role play by incorporating puppets, other members of the group, media, or switching the roles of the helper and the student client.

Homework

At the end of a session, students are typically assigned some type of homework to practice their new thinking or behaviors in the broader school environment. School-based helpers may assign homework with the goal of encouraging student clients to make observations about their thoughts and behaviors or apply their learning to "real-life" situations. This homework might take the form of journaling (structured to note situations, thoughts, feelings, and alternative ways of thinking), practicing positive self-statements, or increasing one's exposure to feared situations.

> Homework assignments might be limited to 15 or 30 minutes at first and then increased as the student client becomes more engaged in the change process.

Behavioral Contingencies and Contingency Reinforcement

Behavioral intervention strategies can be incorporated into your counseling approach. For example, behavioral contingencies might be established to increase the likelihood of a student client performing a certain behavior. A contingency refers to any type of an if-then statement that occurs between an environment and behavior (Skinner, Skinner, & Burton, 2009). In other words, if Brandon appropriately asks to take a break when he is starting to feel frustrated, he is allowed to take an additional five minutes to relax and enjoy materials in his "break bucket." As students are learning to use new ways of thinking and behaving, you may need to incorporate additional strategies to help them use these behaviors on a more regular basis and to create a supportive environment. Another strategy, shaping, can also be a helpful behavioral tool when you are attempting to help a student client to learn a complex skill. By breaking a complex skill down into smaller parts and reinforcing the performance of each component, students may be taught to independently engage in multistep behaviors (Alberto & Troutman, 2006). A school-based professional may not choose to use this approach with all student clients, but these strategies can be effective for younger students or students with cognitive delays.

Positive behavioral supports and classroom reinforcements (e.g., coupons) distributed randomly for appropriate behaviors are among the many activities used to influence positive behavior.

COGNITIVE-BEHAVIORAL STRATEGIES APPLIED

In the following exchange, the school psychologist uses a blend of basic skills and cognitive-behavioral strategies to ensure that she understands the student client's presenting concerns. Once the professional helper has a clearer idea, she checks out her ideas for goals and interventions with the student client, Maria, who is 15 years old and in the tenth grade.

School Psychologist (SP): Hi, Maria. What brings you here today?

Maria: Umm, I've missed a lot of days of school, and the attendance monitor said I needed to come talk to you.

SP: So, it's been tough for you to make it here to school every day. What's going on?

Maria: Well, I . . . umm . . . I don't know. I just don't like it here very much (looks down).

SP: This is difficult for you to talk about (pause).

Maria: Yes, I feel kind of dumb telling anyone. I . . . well . . . I just kind of freak out sometimes when I'm at school.

SP: Freak out?

Maria: Yeah, I start shaking, and it's hard to breathe. I don't know what's going on, but when I stay home, it doesn't happen.

Anxiety

SP: That sounds frightening. How often would you say this happens?

Maria: Well, it's not every time when I come to school. Like today, I've done fine. But other days, I'll think everything is okay and BAM! It starts happening. I guess, maybe every couple of weeks.

SP: Have you noticed whether it happens during a particular class or in a certain situation?

Maria: No, not really. I just start looking around and well . . . I get freaked out by all the students around me. It feels like they're looking at me. I mean, I know I'm different from them because my family isn't from here and we don't have very much money.

SP: You're worried that the other students won't accept you, and you feel different from them. So tell me a little bit more about what happens when you start feeling this way.

Maria: Well, the room gets kind of weird, and I feel like I'm outside my head. I start to breathe fast. I get really hot, and my heart beats fast. I just have to get out of there. So far, teachers have been nice and have let me go to the nurse's office or to the bathroom, but I just feel like one day I'm going to lose it in front of everyone. Every time it happens, I stay home a couple of days and I hope that will help.

SP: Sounds like you're scared to come to school because of what might happen, and it just feels better to stay home.

Maria: Yeah, I just don't know what to do. My parents really want me to do well at school, but I just can't come here.

SP: I think I'm getting a pretty clear picture of what is going on. I just have a couple more questions. How long has this been going on?

Maria: Hmm, I guess it started around the first of the year, right after we came back from Christmas break.

SP:	Can you think of anything that would have happened around that time that might be related to what is happening to you now?
Maria:	No, not really. You know, little things happen all the time. Some of the guys tease me, and a lot of the girls just kind of ignore me. I have a cousin in the school and we hang out, but other than that, I just keep to myself.
SP:	Let me see if I understand. When you came back after winter break, you started having these really uncomfortable experiences where you feel kind of "panicky." These events happen about every two weeks or so and only take place when you're at school. There's no exact time when they occur, but it seems to be when you're in the classroom surrounded by other students.
Maria:	Yeah, that's about it. I'm weird, huh?
SP:	It seems like you're going through a tough time right now, and you're reacting to the stress. Sometimes it is easy to figure out what's behind why you're feeling this way, like if something traumatic happened. Other times, we don't really know. People can just start feeling really anxious for what seems like no particular reason.
Maria:	I just want it to stop.
SP:	I can imagine. You feel horrible here at school, but if you stay home, it means the attendance monitor talks to you and your grades drop. That's quite a bind. It seems like if we could figure out a way to stop these "episodes" from happening, you would be able to come to school more regularly.
Maria:	Yeah, it's not my favorite place, but I kind of like some of my classes, and I want to graduate.
SP:	Okay, so, let's start with the goal of figuring out how to reduce or get rid of these episodes all together. Maybe a second goal would be to think about some ways to make school a better place. What do you think would be some things that would help you like school better?

Maria: I don't know, I wish the kids were nicer, and sometimes it feels like I'm wasting my time. I really like to draw, and I know I want to be a graphic artist, but I spend all my time learning history and science and other things that I'm never going to use.

SP: Hmm, so an additional goal might be finding some more friends and, then, looking at your schedule. I can't do anything about having to take history and science, but maybe we can look at getting you involved in more classes and activities that seem more relevant to what you want to do in life.

Maria: That sounds good. I'd like to be able to just come to school and finish it like a normal person.

SP: I have some ideas about how to start working on your first goal of reducing your stress and your "episodes." I'd like to teach you some strategies to use when the room first starts feeling "weird." I'd also want you to begin keeping track of what happens during these episodes. For example, what is happening, what are you feeling, and what are you thinking? That might help us figure out a little bit more about what is going on. Are you ready to start?

Maria: Sure, I guess.

In this brief transcript, we have highlighted some of the components of a cognitive-behavioral approach. The helper is playing a diagnostic role by gathering more specific information about Maria's problem. This effort is not for the purpose of diagnosing Maria but simply to get a better understanding of what she is experiencing and if necessary, preparing to refer her to an outside agency or her family doctor. Additionally, the helper strives to educate her by explaining about stress reactions in the body. Finally, the helper collaborates with Maria through the session by eliciting her goals and checking with her about the strategies that might be used to intervene. In subsequent sessions, the helper would want to find out more about Maria's relationships at school, her family context (e.g., are there new stressors at home?), and to continually evaluate whether the strategies are helping her meet her goals.

EMPIRICAL SUPPORT

The increased emphasis on accountability in our professions has led to a growing movement toward the use of evidence-based interventions. Over the years, CBT has acquired a large body of research that suggests it is an effective approach with children and adolescents (Ishikawa, Okajima, Matsuoka, & Sakano, 2007; Klein, Jacobs, & Reinecke, 2007; Watson & Rees, 2008). It has been demonstrated to be effective in treating adolescent depression (Clarke, Lewinsohn, Rohde, Hops, & Seeley, 1999), children's anxiety (Barrett, Dadds, & Rapee, 1996; Flannery-Schroeder & Kendall, 2000), posttraumatic stress disorder (Wells & Sembi, 2004), substance abuse (Waldron & Kaminer, 2004), and aggression (Daunic et al. 2006; Stark et al., 2006) in child and adolescent populations. Because cognitive behavioral interventions tend to be very structured and each session is goal oriented, the model lends itself to empirical study.

Much of the early research has been conducted in clinical rather than school settings, leading some to question whether the relatively longer courses of treatment, the structured implementation, and skill level required of the helper were realistic for real-world contexts (i.e., schools). However, current research suggests that CBT delivered in a school setting yields similar outcomes to delivery in clinical contexts (e.g., Bernstein, Bernat, Victor, & Layne, 2008; Shirk, Kaplinski, & Gudmundsen, 2009).

RESPONDING TO CULTURAL DIFFERENCES

Regardless of the therapeutic approach used, school-based professionals must demonstrate respect for the students and families with whom they work. Although cognitive-behavioral approaches have some research supporting their effectiveness with diverse populations (e.g., Waldron, Slesnick, Brody, Charles, & Thomas, 2001), the results are sometimes mixed, and study samples have not generally included sufficient numbers to determine whether this model is equally effective across youth groups. Ortiz (2006) suggested that school-based helpers must first develop cultural sensitivity to recognize what cultural factors play a role in treatment planning or intervention. For example, one study found that the development of a therapeutic alliance was especially important to Hispanic populations, indicating that it accounted for 45 percent of the variance in treatment effectiveness (Bernal, Bonilla, Padilla-Cotto, & Pérez-Prado, 1998). By developing knowledge about the differing needs of diverse groups and learning to recognize when cultural factors are impacting treatment, school-based professionals can become more responsive to specific student client needs.

CONCLUSION

Cognitive-behavioral approaches represent a good fit for the schools because they tend to be of a shorter duration and focus on positive change (Mennuti et al., 2006; Reinecke et al., 2003). Additionally, because this framework promotes a "therapist as coach" model where learning is emphasized, it represents an approach that is consistent with the goals of school. The concepts of CBT can be delivered in multiple formats, and all students can benefit from learning problem-solving strategies, coping skills, and the connection between thoughts and feelings. Further, there is substantial empirical evidence that supports the use of CBT for many of the difficulties experienced by child and adolescent populations.

Case Illustration

As we reviewed aspects of Cassie's story, we saw that there were many issues going on for her. We decided to focus on her sadness and anxiety because we believed they were contributing to her erratic behavior. We've described a potential interaction based on a cognitive-behavioral approach. There is a great deal of research that supports the effectiveness of this strategy with depression and anxiety. Additionally, we suspected that Cassie might have "distorted" thinking about what is going on in her life. In this particular vignette, we highlight the use of a thought journal, which is often used in CBT. The purpose of this journal is to help students develop an understanding of how their thoughts affect their feelings. It also serves as a starting point in helping the student client to challenge their nonadaptive thoughts.

Cassie: Hi, Mr. Jackson. Well, I've been thinking about some of the things we've been talking about.

Mr. Jackson: [nods his head]

Cassie: You know, those things about how I automatically think people are going to reject me. You may have a point.

Mr. Jackson: You're finding that some of what we talked about last time might fit for you. Tell me more.

Cassie: Well, I got that thought journal, and I started looking at the kinds of things I tell myself whenever I'm with my friends or on the basketball court. I get really angry, and I think, "If these people really knew me, they wouldn't hang out with me anymore."

Mr. Jackson: You're afraid friends will reject you if they knew that you liked to hang around girls rather than guys. When you think about it, you become angry. We've also talked about some of the ways you have become aggressive and irritable with your friends. I wonder if that's a way for you to reject them first.

Cassie: I guess so, you know, maybe if I push them away, it won't matter if they won't accept me.

Mr. Jackson: It's a way of protecting yourself, but it seems like it also has a negative effect because you're pushing away your main support system. Rather than thinking that your friends will reject you if they knew the "real" you, what are some other ways of thinking about this situation?

Cassie: I don't know, like what?

Mr. Jackson: Well, what if instead of thinking that everyone would reject you, you told yourself, "I may lose some friends, but anyone who is my real friend will accept me the way I am."

Activities

1. Keep a journal of your thoughts over the course of a week. In a small group, discuss your findings. What did you learn about yourself? What was difficult about keeping the journal? How might you adapt it for students of different ages?

2. Reflect on a difficult conversation that you have had or need to have with someone. Working with a small group, practice role-playing elements of this conversation. If you cannot think of a difficult topic, consider practice role plays around the following situations.

   a. Someone seems to be acting more distant from you lately, and you want to find out what is wrong.

   b. You are working with a partner on a project, and you do not believe he or she is putting forth as much effort as you.

   c. Your roommate borrowed money from you a month ago and has not made any effort to pay you back.

3. Throughout this chapter, we provided an example of an adolescent female named Ariel who was struggling with her own sense of worth and her social interactions. Design a counseling plan for her using cognitive-behavioral approaches. Feel free to add other strategies that are not covered in this chapter, but be sure to identify your purpose in using each of the strategies that you have selected.

Journal Reflections

Reflection #1

Mind reading is an example of an automatic thought (e.g., "I know what she's thinking"). Monitor your own tendencies to interpret motivations of people with whom you interact.

Reflection #2

What are some of your own irrational beliefs?

Reflection #3

If you were developing a positive self-talk or self-instruction to assist you with a difficult situation, what would you say?

Electronic Resources

Promising Practices Network on Children, Families and Communities: http://www.promisingpractices.net/default.asp

Print Resources

Friedberg, R. D., McClure, J. M., & Garcia, J. H. (2009). *Cognitive therapy techniques for children and adolescents: Tools for enhancing practice.* New York: Guilford Press.

Kendall, P. C. (2006). *Child and adolescent therapy: Cognitive-behavioral procedures* (3rd ed.). New York: Guilford Press.

Mennuti, R. B., Freeman, A., & Christner, R. W. (Eds.). (2006). *Cognitive-behavioral interventions in educational settings: A handbook for practice.* New York: Routledge.

Vernon, A. (2002). *What works when with children and adolescents: A handbook of individual counseling techniques.* Champaign, IL: Research Press.

Vernon, A. (2009). *More what works when with children and adolescents: A handbook of individual counseling techniques.* Champaign, IL: Research Press.

CHAPTER 7

Solution-Focused Brief Therapy in Schools

Learning Objectives

- Review essential principles of solution-focused brief therapy
- Consider applications of solution-focused approaches for work with children and adolescents in schools
- Reflect on the relevance of solution-focused approaches to you as a person and as a professional school psychologist or school counselor

You have had many opportunities to learn a variety of skills needed to be a professional helper. We invite you to pretend that one night next week, or perhaps the following week, a miracle happens while you are sleeping. Even though you don't know the miracle happened, you immediately become proficient in foundational and advanced counseling skills. Your work is obviously based on a respected theory. Your reflections are crisp and accurate. You ask questions that help students progress toward their goals. Your working alliances are solid.

What will be happening the next day when you begin working with children or youth that will give you some clue that the miracle did, indeed, take place?

What will you see yourself doing during your first individual counseling session? What will you hear yourself saying? How will students with whom you are working respond? What will your colleagues notice?

Of course miracles rarely happen overnight. They usually take more time. We're guessing that your miracle has been occurring for some time already. So, think about progress from where you are now in your maturation of individual counseling skills. What will be the early signs that let you know you have accepted and integrated the next step of your miracle?

This chapter features an overview of solution-focused brief therapy (SFBT) and applications of that approach to school settings. Steve de Shazer, a leader in the family therapy field, is credited as the originator of solution-focused therapy (Presbury, Echterling, & McKee, 2002). He derived his approach from work with Milton Erickson and professionals at the Mental Research Institute (O'Hanlon & Weiner-Davis, 1989). The model was further developed by his wife, Insoo Kim Berg (2005), Bill O'Hanlon and Michele Weiner-Davis (1989), and other colleagues at the Brief Family Therapy Center in Milwaukee.

Solution-focused approaches offer distinct advantages for professional helpers in schools (Berg, 2005; Davis & Osborn, 2000; Legum, 2005; Mostert, Johnson, & Mostert, 1997; Murphy, 2008; Sklare, 2005). Optimism is central. The language empowers and fosters hope. Precise, concrete language contributes to rapid resolution of challenges. Problem resolution is facilitated by changing behavior, changing perceptions, or activating strengths and resources that already exist.

ESSENTIAL PRINCIPLES OF SOLUTION-FOCUSED BRIEF THERAPY

The central philosophy of SFBT can be summarized with three guiding principles (de Shazer, 1987, p. 59):

1. If it works, don't fix it.

2. Once you know what works, do more of it.

3. If it doesn't work, don't do it again. Do something different.

Working from this framework, solution-focused therapists facilitate identification of exceptions to presenting problems; exceptions are "whatever is happening when the complaint is not" (p. 58).

Solution-focused therapy is based on premises that are responsive to schedules and challenges professional helpers in school encounter (Legum, 2005; Sklare, 2005). Legum (2005, pp. 33–34) adapted essential assumptions from clinical-based solution-focused therapy to school-based counseling:

1. School-based professionals should view students as competent and able to implement positive change.

2. There are exceptions to every problem. In other words, there are instances when the problem did not occur. Students should focus on what worked when the problem was absent.

3. Students should construct their future goals and visions. Goals should be stated in the positive, should never contain negative words (like *can't*), and should state what the student is willing to change. These goals are in the student's control, independent of others.

4. Positive change is expected immediately (between sessions one and two).

5. Small change is considered a major success. Eventually, small changes lead to larger changes.

6. There is no need to focus on the past and the causes of the problem.

7. There is no need to understand the "why" of the problem. The focus should be on what works for students and doing more of this.

COUNSELING PROCESS:
THE SESSION AS AN INTERVENTION

Precision in the structure of sessions, the use of language, and targeted interventions contribute to brevity and rapid resolution of problems. Solution-focused therapists use language that is positive. They focus on what is working. Their actions and language communicate their belief that the situation will be resolved, clients have the resources to find workable solutions, and change is inevitable (de Shazer, 1985; O'Hanlon & Weiner-Davis, 1989). Solution-focused therapists create expectations for change by consistently focusing on problem resolution (de Shazer, 1985).

Typical components of SFBT sessions include (a) developing rapport (often called joining), (b) describing the problem, (c) identifying exceptions when the problematic behavior does not occur, (d) articulating and visualizing goals, (e) giving feedback (often called compliments), and (f) assigning tasks. Community mental health professionals who work from an SFBT model may take a break before giving feedback and assigning tasks.

Developing Rapport

As mentioned previously, SFBT features precise and intentional language, structure, and interventions. This level of intentionality, however, will be reduced to gimmickry without a strong working alliance, whether the student is in kindergarten or twelfth grade. In this regard Presbury et al. (2002) spoke of "the centrality of the counseling relationship" and emphasized that there are "no magic tricks" (p. 39). The intentional language, then, is used in addition to, rather than instead of, foundational counseling skills reviewed in the *Practice and Application Guide.*

Skillful SFBT helpers, regardless of their setting, consistently communicate the core conditions of respect, unconditional positive regard, and empathic understanding (Murphy, 2008; Presbury et al., 2002). Because SFBT helpers recognize that empathy does not exist unless students with whom they work *experience* it, introductions of any form of problem solving are predicated upon a solid relationship and ample opportunity for students to express and explain their concerns. They respond to students' subtle messages when they do not feel understood or sufficiently validated. They recognize invitations to proceed, and they introduce transitions with accurate summarizations.

Describing the Problem

Although therapists working from solution-focused models place less emphasis on problems, professional helpers would be remiss to proceed without a thorough understanding of students' concerns, or the concerns of adults in students' lives. A difference may be in the way the initial question about concerns is asked. For example, a solution-focused professional helper may ask, "What were you hoping would happen when you asked to meet with me?" or "What are you hoping to accomplish in our work together?"

In identifying the primary concerns, it is also important to grasp an understanding of how the student client experiences and explains the concerns. A professional in schools might ask, "What concerns you most about this situation?" or "What is the hardest part of this for you?"

Identifying Exceptions

Identification of exceptions is the problem-solving description's close companion. For example, a school counselor might say, "Tell me about a time last week when you *did* feel successful in one of your classes" or "Tell me about a time last week when you *didn't* dread getting up and coming to school or didn't dread coming as much."

By identifying the exceptions, student clients begin to see that the situation is not pervasive, constant, or all-encompassing. As appropriate, solution-focused professional helpers encourage and empower students by asking, "How did you get that to happen?"

Articulating and Visualizing Goals

Rarely do professionals using SFBT ask, "What are your goals for our work together?" Rather, they facilitate the development of clear and specific mental images of resolutions to the previously discussed difficulties with precise language that may border on becoming tedious. They might subtly introduce the notion of a goal with a series of questions such as,

"What will you be doing differently when you enjoy coming to school again?"

"Who will be the first to notice?"

"What will he or she see you doing?"

If the response is stated in a negative form such as, "I won't be frowning and complaining as much," a solution-focused professional helper would inquire,

"When you aren't frowning and complaining, what will you be doing instead?"

Remember, though, that it is important to allow adequate time for responses to which you actively listen and then reflect. For example, you might say,

"Okay. Your friend might see you laughing in the morning when you come to school. What else will she notice?"

The miracle question is a hallmark of solution-focused work. For a student client who is dreading school each day, a solution-focused professional helper might say,

"I'd like you to imagine that one night late next week—maybe Thursday, possibly as early as Wednesday, but maybe as late as next weekend on Sunday—a miracle happens in the night while you are asleep, but you don't *know* that it happens. What will happen the next morning that will give you a clue that the miracle did, indeed, take place?"

A typical response to a miracle question is, "I will *feel* better," to which a solution-focused professional helper responds with video language:

"What will other people see you doing when you feel better?"

"Who will be the first to notice that you feel better?"

"How will he know you are feeling better?"

"If I were watching with a video camera, what would I see you doing so I'd know you feel better?"

"Who will notice when you get to school?"

This line of questioning does at least two things. The student client essentially identifies a goal. Additionally, he or she becomes focused on a positive rather than negative picture of the situation.

Once the success image's clarity is achieved, solution-focused school counselors and school psychologists facilitate development of an action plan by saying,

"Rarely do miracles happen overnight. Usually they take a while. What will be some small first steps that will tell you that the miracle has begun?"

Again, vague responses are clarified with video language and may be followed with,

"What else will you catch yourself doing when the miracle begins to happen?"

The miracle question is not appropriate or effective in every situation. It may be more helpful to be straightforward and ask,

"How will you know when you have overcome this difficulty in the morning?" or

"How will you know when you have solved this problem?"

In a parallel fashion, these responses are followed with video language questions such as,

"What will be some first steps that will let you know you have begun to overcome the difficulty?"

Responses to these questions help student clients recognize and feel encouraged by initial progress. Collaboratively, professional helpers and student clients construct goals that are solvable, observable or measurable, and concrete.

Break

Although it may not be appropriate to step out of a room when working with students, it may be useful to intentionally pause and reflect. Working from this model and incorporating a break, a professional helper might say, "We have talked about many important things this morning. Please give me just a few moments to think about the things you have said and then perhaps offer some ideas that may be helpful." Breaks allow professional helpers to ponder and synthesize aspects of these intense and fast-moving sessions. They also give students an opportunity to reflect.

During breaks, solution-focused professional helpers consider exceptions and strengths that will be useful in overcoming challenges and achieving desired outcomes. They are also able to consider recommendations for homework, which is another feature of solution-focused approaches. Typically breaks are near the end of the session and are followed with crisp comments about strengths, usually called compliments, and an intervention.

Giving Feedback

Compliments focus student clients' attention on the strengths that will contribute to their achieving the desired outcomes. Such compliments might include,

"It is clear to me that you are committed to getting through this rough time because you like school and want to do well. You mentioned many things that you want to accomplish this year. I also want to say that you showed courage in scheduling a time to visit with me about the difficult time you are having now and the things you want to do this year."

Notice the similarities between SFBT and Individual Psychology, particularly the concept of encouragement. You might enjoy reading Watts and Pietrzak's (2000) review of similarities between the two approaches. Consider ways that SFBT and individual psychology could be complementary. For example, individual psychology might guide conceptualization, and SFBT might guide your efforts to facilitate change.

Compliments emphasize resources. Additionally, they encourage student clients and energize them to continue working to overcome current challenges.

Assigning Tasks

Solution-focused professionals typically end sessions by assigning a task. De Shazer's generic first-session intervention was to

"Pay attention to what happens during the week when things are going well. I'd like to hear about those times next week."

Of course, the language of the intervention is consistent with the previously identified goals. The language and the task help student clients focus on what is working and on potential solutions.

A PRIMARY TOOL: PRECISION IN LANGUAGE

Most critical to our work in schools is the powerful use of presuppositional language. Solution-focused professional helpers use presuppositional language to communicate their assumptions that change will happen. Their forgone conclusion is, "The situation will be resolved! You will solve the problem!" The language accentuates that there will be change, and there will be small steps that are indicators of greater change to come. Words such as *when* and *will* instead of *if* or *would* help maintain the positive, solution-focused momentum. Examples of questions and comments designed with presupposition language include the following:

"So, you have not learned to do your homework on your own *yet*."

"*In the past* you haven't used your class time to complete work, and you've had lots of homework."

"Who *will* be the first to notice that you have learned to do your homework on your own?"

"How will you know *when* you have learned to use your study period more effectively?"

"*When* you have figured out how to get along with your music teacher, what *will* you be doing differently?"

"What *will* be some small steps you will see to know you have begun to make progress?"

"Who else *will* see a difference?"

Notice school counselor Phillipe's selection of words in the following interaction with three fourth-grade girls who have been referred because of intermittent yet frequent quarrels:

Girls: Our teacher sent us to talk to you.

Phillipe: What happened before she asked you to come to my office?

Girls: We started arguing this morning before school started, and she wants us to work it out.

Phillipe: Okay. Your teacher is concerned about your friendship, and she knows you haven't figured out ways to solve your problems yet. What do you think about that?

Girl A: Well, we do argue a lot. I'm tired of it.

Phillipe: (to the other girls) How about you?

Girls B and C: Me too.

Phillipe: What is it about the arguments that bothers you the most?

Girls: I can't pay attention, and I worry.

I don't like it when my friends are mad at me.

I really don't like it when the teacher is mad at us.

Phillipe: So, in the past your arguments have kept you from paying attention. You don't like it when your friends and your teacher are angry with you. Okay. I'm wondering how you will know when you have found a way to resolve your disagreements.

Girls: We'll get along and play together again at recess.

We'll pay attention to the teacher.

We'll be nice to each other.

Phillipe: Who will be the first to notice?

Girls: Probably the teacher, but maybe one of us.

Phillipe: What will your teacher see you doing?

Girls: We won't argue in the classroom.

Phillipe: When you aren't arguing, what will your teacher see you doing instead?

Girls: We might help each other with our work. We . . .

Phillipe: I'd like you to pretend something with me. Let's imagine that one night next week—maybe on Thursday, or Wednesday, or even Tuesday—a miracle happens in the nighttime at each one of your homes while all of you are asleep—but no one knows about it—not you, not your parents, not your teacher. Because of the miracle, you wake up, and all of the difficulties and disagreements you have had among yourselves are completely gone. You don't want or need to argue anymore. What will you notice the next day that will let you know that the miracle happened?

Girls: We won't fight?

Phillipe: When you don't fight, what will you do instead?

Girls: We'll get along.

Phillipe: When you have learned to get along, what will your teacher or I see you doing?

Girls: We'll laugh together.

We'll help each other when we have problems.

Phillipe: So, when I am watching you I will see you laughing. I'll see you helping one another. I'll see. . . . I'm a bit worried, though. People don't always agree on everything. What will I see you doing if you don't agree on something? Let's say you don't agree on what you will do during the enrichment time you get each Friday afternoon?

Girls: We'll try to talk about it.

We'll figure out how to do a little bit of what everyone wants.

We'll still try not to fight.

Phillipe: Well, usually miracles don't happen overnight. They take longer than a few hours. What will be some very small steps that you may even notice today or tomorrow morning that will let you know the miracle has begun to take place?

Girls: When we come to school, we'll sit in the gym and laugh together.

Phillipe: What else will happen?

Girls: Well, when we come to school, we'll each say "hi" to everyone, and we won't talk about each other behind our backs.

Phillipe: I don't think you expected to get homework when you came up this morning, and I do have an assignment for you. With your teacher's permission, I'd like you to meet with me Friday morning before school. Between now and then, I'd like you to pay close attention to the times when you are getting along, when you are resolving disagreements without arguments, and when you are having fun together. And, I'd like you to talk about that when we meet on Friday.

Constructing Solutions With Scaling

Solution-focused professional helpers use a variety of techniques to help clients and students adopt more useful behaviors. For example, they use scaling to gauge the severity of a concern and monitor progress. For the student who dreads school (mentioned previously), a counselor might say,

"I'd like you to think about your experiences in the morning on a 10-point scale. Let's say that *1* means you absolutely cannot stand the idea of going to school. Your dread is so severe you decide to stay in bed. Let's say *10* is a great day when you are enthusiastic about getting to school. You can't wait to get ready. Where do you rate yourself now?"

After the student responds, the counselor might add,

"Let's say that we decide to meet again next week at this time, and when you come in you rate your previous two days just one number higher, only one digit higher. What will be happening so you increase your rating by one number?"

The scaling question can be revisited each week to monitor progress and enhance anticipation for change. Scaling can also be used in a solution-focused approach to help students identify the problems that are most concerning to them by asking, "Of the three concerns you mentioned, which would you rank as your first concern?"

Changing the Meaning of a Situation by Reframing

Sometimes solution-focused professionals endeavor to help students and clients change behavior patterns. At other times, they reframe situations to help students and clients explore different meanings attributed to a situation. They often do this by reframing, casting a negatively connoted trait in the frame of a positive attribute. For example, someone who is dominating may be discussed as a leader. Someone who is quiet may be described as a good listener. A difficult situation may be discussed as a challenge or an opportunity to learn or grow.

School-based professionals may also cast doubt on the explanation of a situation. For example,

"How do you know the difference between mornings when you are too tired to bounce out of bed and the mornings when you stay in bed because you dread coming to school?"

A more straightforward reframe is,

"That's one explanation for why you are feeling discouraged. Another explanation might be that your work has been so much harder this year, and you have taken on a leadership role."

Relabeling to Avoid Pathological Terms

The terminology that students, teachers, parents, school psychologists, and school counselors use may imply severity or immutability. For example, a diagnosis of ADHD may result in perceptions that the student cannot overcome his or her challenges. Referring to specific behaviors associated with ADHD may increase awareness of actions within the student's control. Solution-focused professionals might inquire about times when the student is able to attend for several minutes. Similarly, they would refer to transition periods rather than crises. They would discuss a child who is highly dependent as one who is learning to become self-sufficient. The focus is on behaviors and symptoms rather than diagnoses or pessimistic adjectives. Again, language is used to instill hopefulness and interpret problems in ways that lead to solutions.

Normalizing

With normalizing, solution-focused professionals place presenting concerns in a category that is solvable without minimizing students' concerns or experiences. An example might be,

> "I've talked with students before that encountered difficulties similar to the ones you have described. Usually after two or three months, they've been able to overcome the stress of a new school. That being the case, we focused on how to navigate those first two or three months."

Be careful not to minimize a student client's concerns when you are "normalizing."

IDENTIFYING RESOURCES

Solution-focused professionals often expand the construction of resources by considering transferable talents and abilities or previous responses to similar situations. For example,

> "I notice you are struggling with math; however, you like English, and you're doing extremely well in that class. I'm wondering what you are doing in English that might be helpful in math."

The search for resources can extend beyond obvious similar situations. Counselors and school psychologists who work from this model may inquire about hobbies and involvement in sports or draw from insight derived from the initial relationship-building conversations.

Students can also draw on their personal history or call attention to current strengths. Referring to the student who dreads school, a solution-focused helper might say,

> "I'm wondering if you can think about a time when you had a similar experience before. How did you get through that situation?"

He or she might also say,

> "You have had a difficult time for the last two weeks. I'm wondering what you have done to be sure you *did* come to school even though you didn't feel like it."

APPROACHES AFTER THE INITIAL SESSION

Even when solution-focused professional helpers use precise and empowering language, they typically see students more than one time. An initial task of subsequent sessions is to consolidate change. Sklare (2005, p. 85) suggested that solution-focused helpers use the acronym *EARS* to sequence additional sessions. *EARS* stands for

- Elicit what's better,
- Amplify the effects of what's better,
- Reinforce how these changes were brought about, and
- Start over again, discovering additional successes.

Referring to the previously mentioned work with the fourth-grade girls, Phillipe might say,

"Last time when we met, I asked you to pay close attention to the times when you were getting along with one another and enjoying being together. What did you notice?"

As the students talk about the exceptional times, he might say,

"Congratulations! How did you get that to happen?"

Using this language, Phillipe draws attention to behaviors that led to the improvements. He would also ask how the relationship changes impacted other situations. He might say,

"Many times when students make progress in their relationships, they find that other areas of their lives improve too. How has that been for you?"

Of course clear positive results are not always recognized. It is important that student clients have adequate confidence in the relationships with their school counselor or school psychologist to disclose setbacks and discouragement. Abandoning the solution-focused approach is not necessarily indicated; however, it is critical to reflect discouragement or frustration with lack of progress.

Professionals who use the SFBT framework are often quite transparent when progress is not apparent. They might say,

"My suggestion last week wasn't a good one. Would you tell me more about what happened on Wednesday when you dreaded coming to school the most?"

Additional information gained during the interim between sessions can guide directives or the addition of complementary approaches. In this phase it is important to reflect discouragement without becoming discouraged or disappointed. Decisions about concluding scheduled appointments are based on the needs of each student with whom we work and the progress that he or she makes. The term *brief* is somewhat ambiguous. It does not translate to an established time period or number of sessions. Rather, the approach is designed for efficient, expedient use of time, which is a hallmark of school-based professional helpers' work.

EMPIRICAL SUPPORT

Just as SFBT is a relatively new approach, the notion of empirical support for interventions is also in the beginning stages (Kelly, Kim, & Franklin, 2008). Monitoring immediate results and results over time was integral to the work done by de Shazer, Berg, and their colleagues as the approach was developed. Examinations of the efficacy of SFBT have been conducted primarily in clinical settings and often with adults. However, school-based inquiries have offered promising support for SFBT.

Franklin, Kim, and their colleagues have provided leadership in outcome research related to SFBT in schools (as well as in clinical settings). Based on a comprehensive review of experimentally designed studies in schools or with school-aged students, they concluded that "SFBT shows promising findings" (Kim & Franklin, 2009, p. 469). However, they qualified this conclusion with an emphasis that additional research is needed before SFBT will achieve recognition as an evidence-based intervention with students in schools. SFBT interventions seemed most useful for addressing students' negative feelings, behavior problems, and school productivity (e.g., credits earned).

Several investigations that have been conducted in schools invite replication. For example, Littrell, Malia, and Vanderwood (1995) provided compelling evidence of positive responses from high school students who participated in one modified solution-focused session followed by two short (15 minutes or less) follow-up sessions at the second and sixth week. The authors provided support for solution-focused counseling particularly when addressing concerns that were developmental in nature or related to behaviors that contribute to academic achievement (e.g., study skills, goal setting, and time management).

Mostert et al. (1997) worked with counselors to develop a two-stage inquiry. First, they were interested in counselors' response to training in solution-focused approaches. Second, they focused on students' responses to solution-focused intervention. Like counselors who were trained as part of the Littrell et al. (1995) study, the trainees expressed enthusiasm for the model, partly because their sense of efficacy generalized to other areas of their work. Additionally, they reported "visible, viable, and desirable affects" (p. 23) when working with students as well as with their parents.

Newsome (2005) amplified SFBT to an eight-session group format for junior high school students identified to be at risk of school failure. Participants' ratings of social skills increased in addition to ratings of classroom behavior and homework completion. Maintained improvements were documented with data collection six weeks after the group concluded. In addition to reporting findings that appear to be promising, Newsome provided sufficient description for professional helpers to replicate the intervention and the inquiry.

In a similar inquiry, Daki and Savage (2010) examined the efficacy of SFBT individual sessions designed to address academic success, motivation, and socioemotional needs of students enrolled in an afterschool private learning center in which remedial reading instruction and tutoring were provided. The 14 experimental group participants' ages ranged from seven to 14 years. While they participated in a series of five individual counseling sessions based on SFBT with complementary activities, their peers ($N = 15$) in the control group received homework support. SFBT techniques were applied to reading skills and academic goal setting. The authors found tentative support for providing SFBT-type counseling to augment remedial reading programs. Participants' literacy skills, attitude, self-confidence, and program engagement showed marked improvement when compared to students in the control group.

Franklin, Biever, Moore, Clemons, and Scamardo (2001) conducted a study to examine the effectiveness of solution-focused therapy in a school setting using single-case design comparing behavior during the baseline (A) and during treatment implementation (B) (i.e., an AB design). In addition to working with the students ($N = 7$) individually following a replicable protocol, they regularly consulted with classroom teachers. They found that this approach contributed to positive changes on a range of behavioral problems and concluded that SFBT showed promise for helping students with academic difficulties and classroom behaviors.

The consultation model was further developed and investigated with a comprehensive quasi-experimental design (Franklin, Moore, & Hopson, 2008). In addition to providing SFBT individual counseling sessions (five to seven) to fifth- and sixth-grade students with documented behavior problems, four masters-level practitioners facilitated a four-hour training session for teachers. During the investigation, the teachers received consultation and attended collaborative meetings. Teachers' posttest ratings on both internalizing and externalizing behavior were significantly higher for students in the experimental group than their peers in the comparison group. In fact, ratings at the conclusion of the inquiry for students in the experimental group were below levels that would be clinical. These results warrant attention of school-based professional helpers. The results also raise an interesting question: To what extent did the teacher training, collaboration, and consultation influence the impressive outcomes?

RESPONDING TO CULTURE DIFFERENCES

Research of solution-focused approaches applied to clients representing diverse groups is also limited (Seligman, 2006). However, proponents of the approach have emphasized the responsiveness that results from the centrality of respect for and reliance on clients' interpretations of problems and decisions about appropriate solutions (Murphy, 2008; Murphy & Duncan, 2007; Sklare, 2005). Authors have described successful use of the model with clients of African, Mexican, and Asian descent and have reported positive responses as well as results. The focus on solutions and action may circumvent outcomes of shame when problems are emphasized.

At the same time, Seligman (2006) cautioned clinicians to carefully examine broad applications of these approaches to individuals representing diverse cultures. The fact that clients' perspectives are prized does not mean adequate attention is given to diversity and cultural factors.

CONCLUSION

SFBT offers useful tools to school-based helpers. This approach is efficient, respectful, optimistic, and empowering. When appropriate, the model can be used exclusively. At other times, the precise use of language can complement other approaches.

Even though SFBT appears simple, the skills are advanced and can easily be misused in the hands of a novice. Conceptualization is implicit, and pacing is essential. Prudence and judicious caution must be employed when designing homework. Supervision is critically important when mental health professionals begin to work with this model.

Of course, SFBT is not appropriate for every situation. For example, asking a miracle question after a child discloses the loss of a loved one or a pet could be insulting and disrespectful. Talking about exceptions with a student whose parent may be abusive could imply that the student is responsible for actions of the parents. Some students may not be able to understand the questions or anticipate indicators of a miracle. Thus, SFBT is but one tool in our repertoire.

Case Illustration

We initially struggled with how we would use a solution-focused approach with Hans and with Cassie. Our initial thoughts about Hans were, "This is not something Hans can solve. Indeed, he is vulnerable, and the outcomes of his situation in terms of decisions that must be made appropriately rest with adults in his life." We might draw from solution-focused language by saying things like, "In spite of the fact that you are afraid and sad and distracted, you have managed to come to school every day, and you've done amazingly well in your classes. How have you done that?" or "This week I'd like you to pay attention to two things: the times you do get along with your friends, even though things are rough at home, and the times you get all of your homework done. I'd like to talk about those times when we meet next week."

Similar implications hold true for working with Cassie. A variety of plausible explanations for her current distress and academic problems are available. If we focused exclusively on solutions for the identified presenting problem, precollegiate examination scores, we would not have said, "I have the sense that something other than college is bothering you. I wonder if you'd be willing to meet with me again." Cassie's anxiety and questions about sexual orientation are 100 percent legitimate, and she could have left the office with no hope of finding resolution in the counselor's office.

Thus, we would use caution in approaching our work with Cassie solely from a solution-focused approach. She could experience the focus on solutions, normalizing, and reframing as insulting and dismissive. At the same time, Cassie is the person who must make the decisions she faces, and she may be focused on failing and giving up, thereby having no image of resolution.

From a solution-focused posture, we would not be concerned about precipitating factors and historical events. We might introduce our work as illustrated in the following dialogue between Cassie and a solution-focused professional helper (SFPH).

SFPH: I'm glad you stopped by today. What were you hoping we could do together that would be helpful?

Cassie: Hi. I need to see my ACT scores.

SFPH: Okay. Let's look at them together.

[Later in session]

SFPH: What else were you hoping we would do that would be helpful for you?

Cassie: Oh, I don't know. I'm kind of tired of it all.

SFPH: That makes sense to me. You have so much going on, and you have worked hard and steady for so long without a break. You have accomplished so much in the last couple of years. Students usually get exhausted and sometimes even burned out when they maintain the level of intensity as you (normalizing).

Based on Cassie's response, we might introduce the notion of a moratorium and use language such as,

- Let's just say that your *slump* right now is your internal wisdom saying to you, "I need a break. I'm tired. I need a moratorium so I can reflect on where I want to go to college and what I want to do" (reframe). How will you know that the much-needed moratorium *has served its purpose* and you're *back on track?* (presuppositional language)
- When you have had times in the past when you didn't feel like doing your work, what did you do to get yourself back on track? (amplifying personal resources)

Because Cassie has multiple sources of stress that have become overwhelming, we would also help her focus on one or two things at a time. We could ask, "What's bothering you the most?" We might expand that question, as illustrated:

- You mentioned several things that are important. You are exploring lots of options and possibilities for next year. You don't know where to start in deciding what to

(Continued)

(Continued)

do and making plans. You want to please your parents, and yet you know that the ultimate decision—and responsibility—is yours. You've been irritable with friends. And you have had trouble motivating yourself to do your best at school. You also have some very personal questions that are bothering you. Sometimes it works better to pick one thing to work on first. Students usually like to start with the one that they can change the easiest. How does that fit for you? (prioritizing)

Her responses to that question would guide our direction. We might invite her to visualize solutions with comments and questions such as,

- You are asking important questions. Even though people around you may not even know you are wrestling with these important questions, who will be the first to notice that something is different, even though they may not know the difference is because you have resolved your questions? What will your parents see you doing? How will your friends know when the real you has reemerged? (focusing on resolution)

- Let's say that one night next week, well, maybe the following week, maybe on Wednesday night, or on Tuesday night—some night fairly soon—a miracle happens while you are asleep, and you don't even know it happened. However, the next morning you wake up with a strong sense of clarity that you can do the hard work to make plans for next year. Not only that, you have motivation and energy to do the hard work involved in the decision-making and planning processes. What will you catch yourself doing so you will begin to figure out that the miracle did, indeed, happen? (miracle question)

- Okay, you will know because you feel more confident and energetic. What will your mom or dad, or even your teachers or friends, see you doing when your confidence and energy are back? . . . How might I know? . . . What else will I notice? . . . What will be some very small first signs that will be your signal that the miracle has begun to happen? (focus on solution and pro-solution behaviors)

Let's assume she prioritizes academic performance. We would probably use the standard first-session intervention by saying something like, "I'd like to spend some time together again next week. If you are willing to do that, I'd like for you to pay attention to the times this week when you come to school, the times you are on time to classes, and the times you are pleased with the work you submit. We'll start next week by talking about what you notice. Okay?"

The work with Cassie would continue until each situation she raises is resolved. Her questions about her sexual orientation may not have an immediate resolution. Particularly at this phase, we would draw from the solution-focused philosophy, "If it is working, don't fix it. On the other hand, if it is not working, do something different." If the solution-focused approach is effective with Cassie, we might assist with questions such as,

- When you have struggled with questions somewhat like this in the past, to whom have you turned for assistance? . . . How have you regained your clarity? . . . What has helped you?
- You may not have an absolute answer to these questions for some time. Although you are concerned and confused, the clear answer may elude you until you are older. I'd like you to pay close attention to the times this week when you are at least more comfortable (or perhaps less distressed) *without* clear answers.

Activities

1. Practice asking presuppositional questions with a peer. What fits for you?

2. Practice asking the miracle question and teasing out behavioral, visual images of solutions.

Journal Reflections

Reflection #1

Consider how your own philosophy or theory of working with children and youth compares to the premise of the following list. Recall memories from your own K–12 education that are consistent with or contrary to the items in this list.

1. Listen, do not label.

2. Investigate, do not interrogate.

3. Level, do not lecture.

4. Cooperate, do not convince.

5. Clarify, do not confront.

6. Solicit solutions, do not prescribe them.

7. Consult, do not cure.

8. Commend, do not condemn.

9. Explore, do not complain.

10. Be directive, not dictatorial.

(Osborn, 1999, pp. 174–175)

Reflection #2
What do you see as the strengths of this approach? The weaknesses?

Electronic Resources

Northwest Brief Therapy Training Center: http://nwbttc.com

Solution Focused Brief Therapy Organization: http://www.sfbta.org

Solution Focused Therapy Treatment Manual for Working With Individuals: http://www.sfbta.org/researchDownloads.html

Solution Focused Thinking in Schools: http://www.btpress.co.uk/0012 Sample.pdf

Print Resources

Berg, I. K., & Steiner, T. (2003). *Children's solution work*. New York: W. W. Norton.

Melcalf, L. (2008). *Counseling toward solutions: A practical solution-focused program for working with students, teachers, and parents* (2nd ed.). San Francisco: Jossey-Bass.

Murphy, J. J. (2008). *Solution-focused counseling in schools* (2nd ed.) Alexandria, VA: American Counseling Association.

CHAPTER 8

Choice Theory and Reality Therapy Approaches to Counseling in Schools

Learning Objectives

- Review essential principles of choice theory
- Apply reality therapy strategies and procedures to students in schools
- Review William Glasser's recommendations for school and classroom environments

William Glasser and reality therapy have been prominent names in schools since the late 1960s when *Schools without Failure* was published. Much of Glasser's pioneer work was derived from his experiences at Ventura's School for Girls, a residential treatment center. With its prominent psychoeducational component, reality therapy and its related choice theory have relevance to counseling in schools, consulting with parents and teachers, climate in schools, and relationships in classrooms.

Choice theory (which was originally called control theory) provides the theoretical underpinnings of reality therapy (Wubbolding, 2009). The term *reality therapy* refers to the way the theory is delivered. This chapter features a review of choice theory, reality therapy, and Glasser Quality Schools. As in other theory-related chapters, we include considerations for working with students of diverse backgrounds as well as a brief review of empirical support.

ACTIVITY BOX

Step 1

In preparation for this chapter, we invite you to participate in a brief activity that you may want to complete as a journal entry. Divide a blank sheet of paper into four quadrants, with the following labels: (a) Belonging and Love, (b) Power or Inner Control, (c) Freedom, and (d) Fun and Enjoyment.

Step 2

Think about names of people (and pets), activities, or situations you *currently have* in your life that contribute toward fulfillment in each of the four identified quadrants.

- Quadrant A: Ask yourself questions such as, "With whom do I have close, dependable relationships?" and "With whom do I share a loving relationship?" (Write your answers in Quadrant A.)
- Quadrant B: Write responses to, "What am I doing right now to feel competent and personally powerful?"
- Quadrant C: Note areas of your life in which you feel free to make choices and exercise autonomy.
- Quadrant D: List enjoyable activities in which you regularly engage.

Step 3

Allow a few moments of reflection and select a contrasting-colored writing instrument. Pause a moment to consider people (and pets), activities, or situations that you *would like to have* in your life. Write your responses to the following questions in each of the appropriate quadrants.

- Quadrant A: With whom would you like to have a caring, close, intimate relationship—one that would contribute to your sense of belonging and connectedness?

- Quadrant B: What accomplishments will result in your feeling competent and confident?
- Quadrant C: In what areas of your life is it important to feel the freedom to explore options, make your own decisions, and act on those decisions?
- Quadrant D: What comes to your mind in response to the word *fun*? What would be incredibly fun and pleasurable for you? What are some activities in which you would like to engage?

ESSENTIAL PRINCIPLES OF CHOICE THEORY

Central to choice theory is the notion of five basic, universal, and genetically structured needs: (a) survival; (b) love, belonging, friendship, caring, and involvement; (c) power, achievement, recognition, and worth; (d) fun, pleasure, enjoyment, and laughter; and (e) freedom, independence, and autonomy. The need for survival, which is present in all life forms, is an inherent drive to live. Many behaviors that contribute to survival are involuntary; for example, our hearts beat automatically just as trees naturally drop their leaves and grow new ones in the spring. The other four needs are psychological; yet they are, according to this theory, necessary and equally important (Wubbolding, 2000). All behavior is directed toward satisfying these essential needs. Glasser has also asserted that relationships are a central component of mental health (Wubbolding, 2011).

The *needs* are genetically encoded and universal. *Wants* are each person's specific ideas for how those needs should be satisfied. Accordingly, individuals intuitively create mental pictures of how each need is met; therefore our wants or desires become images that are stored in metaphoric "picture albums" (also called the *quality world*). Pain, loneliness, and unhappiness often result from perceived discrepancies between "pictures" and reality. Attempts to resolve pain include depressing, acting with inappropriate behavior, or getting sick. (Glasser uses verbs because he views depression, anger, and other emotions as behaviors.)

The quality world (the picture album) influences behavior even though most people are not aware of its presence. Calling attention to universal needs and individual wants is a key feature of reality therapy. For example, a professional helper might ask, "When I talk about relationships that are meaningful, dependable, and loving, what comes to your mind?" or "What pictures pop into your head?" A similar question might be, "With whom would you like to have a close, loving relationship?" Addressing another need, the helper could ask, "What would you like to do so you would feel proud and competent?" When several individuals, ideas, or "pictures" are identified, professional helpers and students can examine them individually and in combination. How extensive is the discrepancy between existing reality (or perceptions of reality) and the pictures (wants)? Are the pictures (i.e., wants) reasonable and attainable? Are they in agreement? Have some become obsolete? Which are most important? How are the pictures connected to the student's behavior?

As mentioned, actions are endeavors to achieve wants and minimize the discrepancy between pictures and reality. Within the choice theory framework, behavior consists of four components: actions, thoughts, feelings, and physiology. To emphasize the diverse elements, professional helpers use terms such as *total behavior* and verbs such as *anxietying*, *depressing*, and *angering*, thereby consistently implying that even feelings are chosen, at some level, and within our control. Focus is primarily on behavior and secondarily on thoughts, which are more readily changed than feelings.

Glasser has consistently championed personal responsibility and individuals' capability of effecting change. Within this framework, behaviors are chosen; thus they can be abandoned, modified, and replaced. Each person is responsible to choose effective strategies for satisfying his or her needs and wants. Goals of therapy include the adoption of appropriate, responsible, and effective strategies for satisfying basic needs.

The notion of personal responsibility is further defined by a list of 14 habits (see the following table), seven of which are "deadly habits that destroy relationships" (Glasser, 2001, p. 7). The other seven habits are "connecting" in that they *contribute* to strong relationships (Glasser, 2001, p. 49). Rapport (2007) provided definitions and word derivation that may be of particular interest to professional helpers who work with secondary students.

Habits That Destroy Relationships	Habits That Build Relationships
Criticizing	Caring
Blaming	Listening
Complaining	Supporting
Nagging	Contributing
Threatening	Encouraging
Punishing	Trusting
Controlling with rewards	Befriending

THE PROCESS OF REALITY THERAPY

Reality therapy trainees in the 1970s and 1980s often followed a sequence of steps that were particularly attractive to preservice and entry-level professional helpers. The sequence included (a) making friends and asking, "What do you want?" (b) asking, "What are you doing now?" (c) asking, "Is it helping?" or "Is it against the rules?" (d) making a plan; and (e) committing to the plan (Glasser, 1983). Within this framework, reality therapists refrained from accepting excuses, punishing, interfering with consequences, and giving up.

The making-friends phase provided opportunities for assessing the extent to which essential needs are satisfied. Professional helpers inquired about relationships (love and belonging), school or work performance (power and competence), ideas about limitations and opportunities (freedom), and leisure activities (fun). Once a tangible goal was identified (in response to "What do you want?"), helpers explored current efforts and the student client's degree of satisfaction with the results. Their dissatisfaction with the results of their behaviors became the impetus for change.

"Make friends" was the prerequisite to other steps in the earlier training models; its centrality continues. Robert Wubbolding (the current director of the Center for Reality Therapy) has used an inclusive term, *therapeutic environment,* that includes trustworthy relationships between professional helpers and students as well as teachers and students, whether the setting is an entire school, a classroom, group counseling, individual counseling, or consultation. Three critical, consistent factors of the environment are "firmness, fairness, and friendliness" (Wubbolding, 2009, p. 232). High expectations, listening, humor, novelty, consequences, and opportunities for decision making also contribute to the environment. Positive relationships among students and between adults and students are encouraged and supported.

Contemporary reality therapists follow Wubbolding's (2000) "WDEP System." Although the model is presented as a cycle, the various components are not intended to be sequential or mechanical. Skillful reality therapists respond to student clients with flexibility and attention to engagement and pacing. In all settings, they recognize trust and an environment of safety as essential precursors of the therapy. While endeavoring to develop rapport, reality therapists might inquire about hobbies and interests (fun and power), friendships and family relationships (love and belonging), dreams (freedom), and school (belonging and power).

WDEP (Wubbolding's Acronym for Reality Therapy)

Wants: Professionals help student clients identify, with clarity, what they hope to achieve.

What are your dreams?

What do you hope will happen when you talk with your instructor?

Direction and Doing: Professionals help student clients anticipate the results of their behaviors and identify the steps (physiological responses, feelings, thoughts, and actions) they are taking to achieve their wants.

What have you been doing to achieve your goal?

What did you say to yourself about that?

When did your headache begin?

Evaluation: Helpers invite student clients to examine and evaluate the effectiveness of their behaviors in terms of attaining their wants.

How did that work out for you?

What happened when you did that?

Plan: Helpers facilitate the development of simple, attainable, measurable, and immediate plans of action.

What's one thing you could do this afternoon that might move you toward your goal?

What would you be willing to do, even tomorrow morning, that might be more effective?

What could you do when you begin to think, "There's no use in even trying"?

Wants

Within the WDEP System, reality therapists focus on (W) *wants*, needs, and perceptions (the picture album or quality world). They remain attentive to unmet needs and wants while assessing commitment to change. Whether or not they explicitly state the question, professional helpers working within this framework raise questions such as, "What do you want that you are not getting?" and "What are you getting that you do not want?" (Wubbolding, 2011, p. 274).

Notice how the school psychologist endeavors to develop a relationship with Ron, identify his wants, and explore the extent to which his needs are satisfied in the following dialogue. Ron is a 17-year-old high school junior who was referred to the school psychologist (SP) after a disruption in a classroom.

Ron: I hate this school!

SP: You really don't want to be here.

Ron: You've got that right.

SP: You've come to school even though you really hate it.

Ron: I wouldn't be here if I didn't have to.

SP: I know you don't want to be at school, and I'm guessing you aren't happy about being in my office [pause]. Would you be willing to tell me more about how it is that you are forced to be here?

Ron: My parents make me come to school. They say I have to.

SP: If your parents didn't say you had to be here, what would you do instead?

Ron: I'd find a job and make some money so I could buy a car and be on my own.

At this point, the school psychologist is trying to establish a relationship with Ron while attending to opportunities for exploring his perception of needs that are not met. Likely, the school psychologist is thinking about ways to inquire about Ron's sense of personal power and competence, freedom, fun, and belonging. It appears that Ron feels restricted and wants to have the freedom to make his own choices. His idea of having freedom (i.e., his wants) appears to be less than realistic. The school psychologist might be thinking about ways to help Ron exercise age-appropriate freedom *and* remain in school. Another goal will be to ascertain if Ron is just angry right now or if his anger and distaste for school have persisted over time.

The school psychologist would likely monitor the degree to which the relationship is established before moving toward efforts to collaboratively work with Ron to identify a goal (his wants) and strategies to achieve his desired outcome without compromising longer-term goals. The school psychologist might work toward the opportunity to say something like, "I'm wondering if you would be willing to explore ways you could make some money, have some independence, and stay in school."

Doing and Direction

Reality therapists intentionally examine students' current behaviors, what they are *doing*, and how those behaviors interface with their wants and needs or the *direction* of their lives (D). They introduce conversations related to *total behavior* (i.e., physiology, feelings, cognitions, and actions) with primary emphases on cognitions and actions. For example, they might say, "You really want to be on the basketball team. What have you tried?" or "What are you doing to let the coach know you are committed to the team?"

Reality therapists often call attention to negative self-talk and its debilitating effects. They endeavor to teach students strategies for replacing negative, self-deprecating, and counterproductive cognitions such as, "I am stuck in this situation, and there's nothing I can do to get out" with self-mobilizing statements such as, "I have some options here, and I can make some changes." To challenge behaviors and thoughts that repeatedly impede growth and attainment of goals, Wubbolding (2004) might offer an interpretation such as, "It seems like you are saying, 'If I'm frustrating myself by doing something which is ineffective or harmful in order to improve, I will do more of what has not helped me'" (p. 213).

While focusing on current behaviors and directions, reality therapists often ask student clients to predict consequences and potential outcomes. They might use overt questions such as, "Let's say you decide that you will continue to miss practice and argue with the coach. What do you predict will be happening in the next three weeks? . . . How do you think this will work out for you in the next year or so?" Rather than questioning, a reality therapist might offer an observation such as, "I'm not sure your saying 'No one can boss me around' is going to help you in the long run. Rules are a part of our school, and teachers are required to enforce them. I'm afraid you're making yourself miserable, and you're not getting the opportunities you want."

Evaluation

Conversations about current behaviors and direction lead to a pivotal element of reality therapy: the *evaluation* (E). Essentially reality therapists ask, "Is what you are currently doing working?" In schools we may ask, "Is what you are doing acceptable within the school's code of conduct?" When appropriate, the question is posed with reference to the law. With this focus, the student client assumes responsibility for evaluating the effectiveness of his or her behavior.

The evaluation may also focus on contents of the picture album, the feasibility of the images, and appropriate alternatives. Accuracy of perceptions, beliefs, and cognitions may also be addressed. As mentioned before, thoughts are a component of total behavior. They are often addressed in the process of identifying changes to be made.

In the following segment with Ron, the school psychologist (SP) invites him to evaluate the effectiveness of his current strategies for gaining independence. Notice the SP's recognition of the tentative nature of their relationship and Ron's guarded investment.

SP: You would like your parents to give you more opportunities to make your own decisions, and you'd also like to have some of your own money so you can feel more independent. Even though they're related, you're talking about two things. Which is most important to you?

Ron: I want to make some of my own decisions. It wouldn't matter if I had money, Mom and Dad would still tell me how to spend it.

SP: So one thing you want right now is to make some of your own decisions. What are some things you have done to make that happen?

Ron: I complain all the time. I tell my folks to get off my back. I've tried to get the teachers to back off too.

SP: How has that worked for you?

Ron: (glaring at the SP) It hasn't. Now are you going to be on my case too?

SP: That wasn't my plan. I would rather try to help you figure out some ways to get what you want without getting in trouble or messing up possibilities for the rest of the year and next year. Is that something you'd be willing to do?

Ron: I don't know. Maybe.

SP: I'll accept that for now. You want to be sure you can trust me. That makes sense. You want to make decisions and have control over the choices you make; I want to honor that. I'm wondering if you would be willing to think about other things that you might have done so you could make your own decisions.

Ron: I guess I can't think of any.

SP: Nothing comes to your mind [pause]. I'd like to shift gears and go a different direction if it's okay with you. [Ron shrugs his shoulders and nods to indicate some level of agreement.] On most days, how is school going for you?

At this point, we know Ron wants more freedom, which is an age-appropriate desire. Without some sense of the *direction* (D) Ron wants his life to go in both the immediate and longer-term future—a frame of reference for examining current behaviors—the SP might become "stuck" in the current status of the counseling session. Thus, the SP has changed the focus to explore Ron's satisfaction related to other needs.

[A few minutes later]

SP: We've talked about several things. You would like to make your own decisions. School's going okay. Even though you don't enjoy it much, you come every day, and you do your homework. I'm wondering what you would like to happen, even in the next couple hours.

Ron: I want to forget about the whole thing this morning and get back to class.

SP: What do you think you could do to make that happen?

Wubbolding (2004) suggested that "when children are obstinate, uncooperative, and resistant, teachers and parents are astounded to see such behaviors diminish or vanish when they ask, 'What do you want right now?' or 'How hard do you want to work at changing your situation?' Of course, interventions based on this question do not produce a magical, immediate, or total reversal of behavior. Rather, such interventions need to be habitual" (p. 212).

Plan

Finally, reality therapists facilitate the development of effective *plans* (P). Within the reality therapy framework, plans should be "SAMIC" or "Simple, Attainable, Measurable, Immediate, and Controlled by the planner" (Wubbolding, 2004, p. 214). "Getting the teachers off my back" is an unacceptable goal because teachers are not within students' control. Planning to "get motivated" is not measurable. Useful plans focus on clearly defined actions.

When identifying goals and plans, reality therapists also assess commitment. They might do that with a straightforward question such as, "How committed are you to making this happen?" and then explore the potential for increasing commitment. To evaluate commitment, Wubbolding (2000, p. 142) explicated five levels that can be shared with students to provide a framework for their self-evaluation. The levels include the following:

1. I don't want to be here. You can't help me.

2. I want the outcome. But I don't want to exert any effort.

3. I'll try. I might. I could.

4. I'll do my best.

5. I will do whatever it takes.

Once a plan is defined, and commitment is ascertained, reality therapists establish an agreement for activating the plan. As appropriate, they prepare contracts or establish agreement with a handshake. They also schedule accountability, perhaps saying, "Stop in tomorrow and let me know how your plan worked."

Passaro, Moon, Wiest, and Wong (2004) adapted the WDEP process for use with students after classroom disruptions or infractions of school rules. They outlined a "plan for improvement" that includes five questions to which students independently write responses: "What happened in class? How does my behavior affect the class? What is my level of cooperation in class? What am I willing to do? Who can help and support me with this plan?" (p. 507). Subsequently, the school-based professional reviews and discusses the answers. Upon completion of the conversation, students return to class.

GLASSER QUALITY SCHOOLS

As mentioned at the beginning of this chapter, Glasser's contributions have been recognized since *Schools without Failure* was published in 1969. Subsequently he expanded choice theory and reality therapy to educational environments, offered a designation for Glasser Quality Schools (Glasser, 1998a, 2001), and provided guidance for classroom teachers as well as school administrators.

A Quality School environment prioritizes attainment of basic needs of adults and students. Positive relationships between and among adults and students is a central feature of Glasser Quality Schools. In fact, Glasser emphasized that "the success of any endeavor rests on people getting along with each other" (Wubbolding, 2007, p. 254).

An essential element of Glasser Quality Schools is the notion of lead management, which is practiced by administration as well as teachers who "always lead" and "never boss" (Glasser, 1998b, p. 1). They consistently demonstrate commitment, hard work, and caring. Lead management teachers establish relevance of content and express confidence in students' ability to master it. They effectively facilitate cooperative learning and peer instruction. Additionally, they invite students' suggestions for creating classroom environments most conducive to learning. Students assess and document their own learning with practice tests according to an individually established testing schedule. They demonstrate mastery of content before advancing. Subquality work is not acceptable, and the calendar does not dictate the curriculum.

Adults and students in Glasser Quality Schools learn about choice theory and reality therapy. Personal responsibility for attainment of the essential needs is emphasized; individuals are held accountable for satisfying their needs without infringing on others' needs. When students engage in less-than-appropriate behavior, adults often respond with the WDEP framework. They typically ask a series of questions such as, "What are you doing?" "Is that within the school's code of conduct?" "What can you do to get back on track?" "What can you do to prevent this from happening again?" Of course, they allow time after each question for a thoughtful response and validate responses by reflecting content (and affect as appropriate).

Educators in Glasser Quality Schools do not accept excuses. They consistently hold students responsible for their actions and refrain from engaging in arguments. When students are not ready to participate in the problem resolution process, they may be asked to wait in a "time-out room" until they are willing (Glasser, 1998a, p. 148).

> Regardless of your theory, holding class meetings is an effective strategy for students to express their ideas, plan activities, or develop solutions to problems.

Class meetings are another feature of Glasser Quality Schools. Ideally meetings are scheduled regularly and arranged so class members can openly discuss identified topics that are often directed toward satisfaction of needs. Teachers or professional helpers lead the meetings, often employing

Socratic-style questions to engage students in intellectual discussions. Diverse opinions are encouraged and respected. Thus, students are empowered to make contributions from their perspectives. They acquire knowledge and interpersonal skills. They also gain appreciation for different perspectives.

EMPIRICAL SUPPORT FOR
CHOICE THEORY AND REALITY THERAPY

The efficacy of reality therapy has been assessed and supported in a variety of studies conducted in diverse settings including schools in Korea. Inquiries have targeted individual counseling, school counseling, and school climate. Positive results have been shown in self-esteem, perceptions of self-control, self-determination, school behavior, and quality of relationships (Wubbolding, 2009; Wubbolding et al., 2004).

For example, Kim (2006) provided group counseling for 16 Korean students who had experienced adverse effects of bullying. The fifth- and sixth-grade students participated in 10 sessions during which they learned about needs and wants, total behavior, effects of thoughts on feelings, assertiveness, and cooperation skills. Based on measures administered at the beginning and end of the group experience, the author concluded that participation contributed to increased personal responsibility and reduced victimization.

Yarbrough and Thompson (2002) provided a replicable design for assessing the efficacy of counseling interventions. Following single-participant research methods, the authors provided a sequence of individual counseling sessions for an eight-year-old boy and a nine-year-old girl. Teachers' concerns for both students related to daydreaming, inattention, and task incompletion. The children were randomly selected to participate in a sequence of five sessions based on reality therapy or solution-focused brief therapy. Following an AB research design, progress toward goals was routinely monitored with goal attainment scaling. Results included significant improvement for both students. The authors concluded that short-term reality therapy or solution-focused brief therapy can be effective in helping students acquire on-task behaviors that contribute to school success. Even though Yarbrough and Thompson (2002) conducted this inquiry several years ago, their design, intervention models, and findings provide support for using reality therapy to promote academic success as well as a practical resource for progress monitoring.

Wubbolding (2009) cited empirical support for reality therapy in schools, particularly within schools where lead management and Glasser Quality School classroom strategies are used consistently; however, he acknowledged that designs are less rigorous than desirable. Studies have shown that implementation of the Glasser Quality School philosophy contributes to improved grades and diminished problems related to disruptive behavior problems.

RESPONDING TO CULTURAL DIFFERENCES

Contemporary leaders (e.g., Glasser and Wubbolding) have contended that reality therapy lends itself to application for clients and schools representing a variety of groups. Additionally, professional helpers in several countries and settings have been trained in choice theory and reality therapy (Wubbolding et al., 2004). Modifications have been made in translation, and attention has been given to cultural mores. For example, the intensity and directness of questions have been minimized for groups that view such interaction as intrusive or rude.

Wubbolding and his colleagues (2004) have suggested that reality therapists respond to diverse backgrounds because relationships with their clients, characterized by friendliness and warmth, are central to their work. These authors suggested that relationships grow when clients are encouraged to teach their professional helper about their culture and practices within their culture.

Based on experiences in working with professionals and clients around the world, Wubbolding (2000) cautioned helpers against stereotyping and generalizing knowledge about diverse cultures at the expense of recognizing each individual's experiences, culture, and preferences. Responsible reality therapists modify their approach in response to cultural and personal differences.

CONCLUSION

Whether or not you work in a school where administration and teachers ascribe to Glasser Quality School principles, you will likely see evidence of Glasser's influence. For example, teachers often use class meetings for problem solving and planning. Others use refocus forms and similar documents that resemble the plan for improvement recommended by Passaro and his colleagues (2004).

Materials for counseling and psychoeducation based on choice theory are available. For example, associates at the Glasser Institute have provided resources and suggestions for classroom activities, including a series of skits that illustrate the application of choice theory concepts to situations students encounter (see resources section at the end of the chapter). Other materials are available from the American School Counselor Association and various publishing companies.

Case Illustration of Reality Therapy With Hans

Choice theory and reality therapy offer possibilities for working with Hans or Cassie. Focusing on Hans' basic needs, we would question his attainment of love and belonging. We can assume that Hans' family has been his primary source of love, support, and connection. Given the instability and ambiguity of his parents' marriage, he would likely experience insecurity and confusion regarding the future of his family and his place in his parents' lives. Possibilities of his intervening are limited; thus he may feel powerless and stuck. Opportunities for fun may be restricted. Glasser might say that Hans' "angering" is his attempt to reconcile discrepancies between the "pictures in his head" and the reality of his family's situation. Glasser might also hypothesize that Hans' behavior is directed toward satisfying his need for power.

From a choice theory perspective, we would also consider Cassie's basic needs. She may fear that her close family relationships would be jeopardized or compromised if she did not continue to excel academically or if she revealed that she questioned her sexual orientation. Although Cassie has a busy high school schedule, she probably enjoys many of the activities. Career options, though a bit frightening perhaps, are abundant. Her "angering" during athletic events and "depressing" may be misdirected attempts to achieve fulfillment of needs for power even though her competence and achievements are not in question. She may also have conflicting wants. Perhaps she wants freedom to explore careers with less prestige than those of her parents; yet she wants to maintain close relationships and sound approval of her family members.

We have illustrated a beginning portion of a reality therapy–based counseling session with a school psychologist (SP) and Hans. In preparation for the first meeting, the SP asked Mr. Nelson to visit with Hans about the plan so he would not be surprised or frightened when called out of class. The SP also asked Mr. Nelson

(Continued)

(Continued)

to assure Hans that he was not in trouble and that going to the SP's office was not the same as a discipline referral or punishment (which would probably not be an issue if this were a Glasser Quality School).

SP: Hi, Hans. Let's see. I don't think you've been to my office before, right?

Hans: [Shakes his head to indicate no]

SP: Sometimes kids are a bit nervous or uncomfortable when they come to my office the first time. We will take our time so you can be as comfortable as possible. I don't want you to worry about what might happen, so let me tell you what we'll do, okay?

Hans: [Shakes his head to indicate yes]

SP: First, I would like to get to know you, so I will ask some questions. I'd like to hear about things you do for fun, perhaps your friends, your hobbies, and so forth. I'm also interested in knowing how school is going for you. We'll talk about your family and what you'd like to have happen so things will be better for you. Does that work?

Hans: [Nods his head to indicate yes]

SP: I'm guessing you might have some questions too.

Hans: [Nods his head to indicate no]

SP: I'm wondering if you'd be willing to tell me a bit about the things you and Dad talked about when he suggested that you come to my office.

Hans: [somewhat reticently] He thought it would help me stay out of trouble.

SP: What do you think about that?

Hans: I don't know. Do I have to talk about that?

SP: Not until you're ready [pause]. Let's shift gears for a few minutes and pretend that I gave you a ticket that said, "You have earned two hours and ten dollars to do things that would be fun for you. You can take three people with you." What would you do?

Hans: I wouldn't be able to do what I want.

SP: For now, it's okay to pretend. The ticket and money were pretend too, of course.

Hans: I'd go to a Rockies baseball game.

SP: Oh, so you're a Rockies fan.

Hans: Last year me and my dad and mom went to nearly every home game.

SP: You really liked going to games with your mom and dad.

Hans: Our seats were right behind the catcher, and we knew all the players' names.

SP: You know their names? You are a huge fan!

Hans: But I can't do that anymore.

SP: You're sad. You miss the games.

Hans: Not really. I miss my mom.

SP: You love your mom, and it's hard to have her so far away. Your dad told me she has a job in another city and that she lives there.

[later]

SP: [Transition summary] During the time we've been together, we've talked about several things. You love doing things like going to games with your parents. Things are hard for you right now because Mom is not home and Dad is so busy. You're worried about Dad and you're worried about Mom. You really want Mom to come home and are worried that she may not. You don't understand what's going on between her and your dad, and you plainly don't like it. Sometimes you feel mad at both of them, and then you worry that they're mad at you too. Then you come to school and get in trouble, and that makes matters worse. More than anything else, you wish Mom would come home and that she and Dad would get along like they used to. You'd like things to be better at school too—you wish you felt like doing your work and getting along with your teachers and friends.

Hans: That's about it.

SP: I don't know if there's anything you can do to change things—either way—for your mom and dad. They're going to have to work that out. Even though school isn't as important to you as your parents and your family, I'm wondering if you'd be willing to talk about school.

(Continued)

(Continued)

Hans: Okay.

SP: You don't like to get in trouble, and you used to like getting good grades. Which would you like to work on?

Hans: I guess getting in trouble.

SP: Okay. What are some things you've tried to do to stay out of trouble?

Hans: I don't know. Not much really. Sometimes Dad talks to me on the way to school and tells me to keep my mouth shut.

SP: How has that worked?

Hans: Then I got in trouble for not answering my teacher's questions.

SP: Mmm. What else have you tried?

Hans: I guess I really haven't tried.

SP: Oh. Okay. I wonder if you'd be willing to try something different—for maybe two or three days.

Hans: Whatever you say.

SP: Not this time, buddy. It really has to be "whatever *you* say" [goal: bolstering need for power and achievement].

Hans: I suppose I could work on paying attention to the teacher and doing what he tells us to do.

SP: How would you do that?

Hans: I'd try to sit still and not talk to my friends.

SP: How do you think that would work?

Hans: I can do that.

SP: Are you willing to do it?

Hans: I can try.

SP: It doesn't sound like you're sure you can or sure that you want to [assessing commitment].

Hans: I don't know about three days.

SP: Would you commit to three mornings?

Hans: How about today and tomorrow?

SP: You're saying you will pay attention to your teacher and do what he tells you for the rest of today and all of tomorrow?

Hans: Yeah.

SP: Are you ready to shake on that?

Hans: [shakes SP's hand]

SP: Okay. How about checking in with me after school today so you can tell me what strategies you used?

Hans: Okay. Can I go back to class now?

Activities

1. Compare the notions of "quality world," needs, and wants to Adler's constructs related to purposeful behavior and lifestyle.

2. Role-play the WDEP process with a peer. It is easier to maintain this role-play if you use a real-life problem. Select an issue that you will be comfortable to discuss with a peer (e.g., problems with a roommate, stress related to school).

Journal Reflections

Reflection #1

To what extent do you think choice theory and reality therapy will be useful to you as a school-based helper?

Reflection #2

Return to the picture album you illustrated before reading this chapter. To what extent do the pictures represent your quality world? What discrepancies between your current situation and your quality world seem significant to you? What might you do to decrease or remove the discrepancies?

Electronic Resources

The Center for Reality Therapy: http://www.realitytherapywub.com

Skits to Help Students Learn Choice Theory: http://wglasser.org/images/glasser_forms/skit_1.pdf

Print Resources

Banks, S. H. (2009). *Choice theory: Using choice theory and reality therapy to enhance student achievement and responsibility.* Alexandria, VA: American School Counselor Association.

Erwin, J. C. (2004). *The classroom of choice.* Alexandria, VA: Association for Supervision and Curriculum Development.

Glasser, W. (2001). *Unhappy teenagers: A way for parents and teachers to reach them.* New York: HarperCollins.

Glasser, W. (2002). *For parents and teenagers: Dissolving the barriers between you and your teen.* New York: HarperCollins.

Wubbolding, R. E. (2011). *Reality therapy.* Washington, DC: American Psychological Association.

SECTION III

Introduction to Section III

Be a good listener. Your ears will never get you in trouble.

Frank Tyger

We cannot always build the future for our youth, but we can build our youth for the future.

Franklin D. Roosevelt

Example is leadership.

Albert Schweitzer

Peoples' reactions when they learn we are school-based professional help-ers are often intriguing. They envision us sitting in our office, providing individual counseling to one troubled student after another. Consistent with media portrayals, they might believe that we use a blend of probing questions and long thoughtful pauses before rendering our sage advice. In reality, school-based counseling can take many forms. The skills of counseling are tools that can be integrated into different types of interactions, with an indi-vidual, a group, or an entire classroom. They can be adapted for individuals of different developmental levels and for many types of situations.

Many of the preservice professionals with whom we have worked have achieved a fair amount of comfort when counseling with individuals who are will-ing and able to articulate concerns. Yet, they experience self-doubt when they recognize the diverse responsibilities they will encounter. We hear comments such as, "I enjoy working with high school students, but I don't have a clue about working with the little ones!" "What if my student client won't talk?" "How can I see all of these students who need support?" "I can't go into a classroom to teach a lesson on stress management; I don't like to present to large groups."

In Sections I and II, we covered a wide range of topics that are important for preservice and in-service school-based professionals. We have tried to present a realistic overview of challenges you will likely encounter as you enter a complex system called a school. Although we have included a fair amount of theoretical perspectives, we have emphasized the importance of tailoring our language and skills to match the developmental level of the students with whom we work. We have added practical perspectives about effective working relationships with students, their families, and colleagues within the school.

In Section III of *Counseling Children and Adolescents in Schools* we introduce nuances of professionals' work with play- and art-based modalities, group work, and crisis response. The theoretical perspectives presented in Section II, as well as the process of conceptualization, continue to inform professionals' work in these different modalities in response to the needs of students and schools. As we have stressed throughout this textbook, school-based professionals must continually be mindful of children's different ages, modifying counseling strategies accordingly.

By incorporating toys, games, or art, you will be more likely to connect with a younger student or an older student who may be able to relax when play is introduced. The topics of play and art therapy will frequently appear in your research literature and at professional conferences. After reading Chapter 9, we hope you will be able to engage in professional conversations about these approaches and that you will be inspired to learn more.

Groups are quintessential elements of school. In fact, schools *are* groups containing multiple intersecting subgroups. Effective school-based professionals contribute to productivity of groups as participants and as leaders. Strategies for leadership and participation are featured in Chapter 10. We introduce types of groups, leadership skills, and group development theory. We also provide foundational information and basic resources for curriculum development.

Just as groups are central to professional helpers' work in schools, crises demand preparation and attention. Just what is a crisis? Individuals experience events in various ways; thus, you will be called on to recognize and appropriately respond to the intensity of each individual's experience—be the event a national threat, a tornado warning, or the death of someone in the school community. In Chapter 11 we provide a foundation from which you can continue your professional development. Our illustrations with Cassie and Hans will be continued throughout each of these chapters.

CHAPTER 9

Play- and Art-Based Approaches to Counseling in Schools

Learning Objectives

- Understand basic principles of and rationale for using play therapy
- Recognize possibilities of using art therapy with students
- Learn about games as a therapeutic modality
- Respect the importance of training and supervision for using specialized approaches

Children, adolescents, and even adults encounter challenges or limitations when asked to work solely with language and words in their efforts to communicate and gain self-understanding. Toys, art, and play activities provide diverse opportunities for less-verbal students to have the same advantages in counseling as their linguistically talented peers. Drama, dance, music, play, sand tray, and art are just a few examples of modalities that mental health professional helpers use in schools and clinical settings.

We have limited the focus of this chapter to counseling with toys, games, and art. The general review is provided to acquaint you with the broad field of play and art therapies. We briefly review the importance of play in child development, reasons for using play-based activities when working with students, a review of the historical context, examples of theory-based play therapies, toy selection, procedures, and techniques. Our attention then shifts to using structured games in counseling and counseling with visual arts.

We have used the generic terms of *play therapy* and *art therapy* because we have drawn from those literatures; however, professionals working in schools often use terminology such as *counseling with toys* or *working with play media and art*. We also call attention to the difference between using play media in our work with students and claiming or using the title of play therapist or art therapist in a school setting. The approaches presented in this chapter are areas of specialization that should be practiced only with requisite preparation, which includes education and supervised experience. Thus, only professionals who hold appropriate credentials should call themselves play therapists or art therapists. Information about training, supervision, credentialing, and organizations is provided later in this chapter.

As you prepare for and begin your work in schools, you will likely encounter divergent opinions about the appropriateness of using these modalities as school-based professional helpers. As you draw conclusions about the place of play and art in your work, we encourage you to explore literature related to professional helping in schools and counseling with toys (e.g., Perryman & Doran, 2010; Ray, 2010). You may also find it beneficial to consult with professionals in your school districts who use play media, as well as professionals who do not. Whether or not you elect to obtain advanced training and supervision in these areas, you will likely have students in your school who receive services of clinicians who specialize in the various therapies. Thus, it is important to have a basic understanding of these approaches.

WHAT IS PLAY AND WHAT IS PLAY THERAPY?

Please spend a few moments to ponder the meaning these quotes have for you:

- "Children are not simply miniature adults" (Rousseau, eighteenth century).
- "Play is the highest development in childhood, for it alone is the free expression of what is in the child's soul. . . . Children's play is not mere sport. It is full of meaning and import" (Froebel, 1903).

People refer to play in a variety of contexts such as *playing tennis, playing cards, playing with a puzzle to figure it out*, and so forth. Sometimes when adults encounter new challenges, they say something like, "Let me play with this for a while and see what I come up with."

Generally, play is voluntary. Play offers choices in how it is enacted. Play is enjoyable. In a pure form, it does not have an extrinsic goal; its completion does not result in a product (Landreth, 2002). Play has been associated with creativity, stress reduction, and general well-being (Honig, 2007; Schaefer & Drewes, 2010).

Play also contributes to various aspects of children's development (Honig, 2007; Schaefer, 1993; Schaefer & Drewes, 2010). While playing, children learn to solve problems, negotiate social relationships, and develop autonomy. They experiment with various adult roles and career opportunities as they play house or pretend to be firefighters. In this regard, Piaget (1962) asserted that play is an essential component of children's development. Building on Piaget's observations, Bruner (1975) placed play in the category of "serious business, indeed, the principal business of childhood" (p. 83).

The meaning of play becomes specialized for mental health professionals. Play therapy is recognized as "the systematic use of a theoretical model to establish an interpersonal process wherein trained play therapists use the powers of play to help clients prevent or resolve psychosocial difficulties and achieve optimal growth and development" (Association for Play Therapy, n.d.).

How Can Play Be Therapeutic?

Instructional time is limited and valuable. Thus, whenever working with children at school, we must justify the investment of time—to ourselves and potentially to others. When providing a rationale for using play in counseling, we draw from developmental theory as well as research.

One explanation is that play provides a bridge between concrete experiences and abstract thoughts or constructs. For example, adults typically develop relationships with verbal and nonverbal communication. They often resolve challenges as they converse with a mental health professional, or even a caring friend or family member. Adults may repeatedly talk about an event that has troubled them or a loved one who has passed away in an effort to find resolution.

Rarely do young children come to our offices, sit down, and discuss their feelings and concerns. Rather, children naturally express themselves through toys and play. Children often recreate situations with toys in the process of achieving resolution. They also develop relationships through toys and play.

The History of Play Therapy

Attention to the psychological health of children has a relatively short history, which can be traced to the beginning of the twentieth century. Freud, Adler, Jung, and others contributed to that history as they offered comprehensive theories about personality development and interventions for interrupted development when working with adults. Focus extended to children as evidenced by the founding of child guidance clinics. At first mental health professionals endeavored to adapt adult treatments to children. Hermine Hug-Hellmuth, Melanie Klein, Anna Freud, and Margaret Lowenfield were among the pioneers who recognized the need to develop age-appropriate therapeutic interventions for children. Working from their separate activities and viewpoints, these women introduced play and toys as therapeutic modalities (Carmichael, 2006) and laid a foundation for the development of play therapy as a broad field with many approaches.

Hug-Hellmuth, Klein, Freud, and Lowenfield worked primarily from a psychoanalytic perspective; although their assumptions and interventions were quite different. During the 1930s a variety of approaches emerged. Some play therapists directed activities to help children reenact traumatic events or achieve catharsis. Others contended that the therapeutic qualities of the relationship, for which toys and play provided a context, were the essence of the therapy. Play therapy's prominence grew from the work of Virginia Axline, a protégé of Carl Rogers, who wrote two wonderful books, *Play Therapy* (1947) and *Dibs in Search of Self* (1964).

> *Dibs in Search of Self* is a delightful, easily read, inspiring book. We recommend it!

DIVERSITY IN APPROACHES

One hundred years after the notion of incorporating play into therapy with children was introduced, the field has grown to include many modalities that range from highly structured, directive, and didactic to child-centered. Some approaches feature extensive parent involvement; others are primarily focused on working individually with the child. Some approaches are manifestations of primary theories such as client-centered, Adlerian, Jungian, Gestalt, or cognitive behavioral. Others, such as Theraplay and developmental play therapy, are based on attachment theory.

With so many sound and well-defined theories from which to draw, contemporary play therapists have many advantages. We now know that play therapy is a robust and flexible approach. We can draw from several theories; combine play therapy with other modalities such as group counseling, family counseling, or parent education; and confidently use play-based activities in a variety of settings.

An Essential Ingredient: Qualities of the Professional Helper

Regardless of the theoretical orientation, or situation presented by the student client, attributes of school-based counselors endeavoring to provide any form of play therapy are critical. Professional helpers who work successfully with younger clients or students are sensitive to ways children view the world. Their work is guided by theory. Their skills are fine-tuned. Their training is current. They follow ethical guidelines. They also maintain their own psychological health (Landreth, 2002).

Selection of Toys and Preparation of the Environment

The qualities of the professional helper are critical and nonnegotiable. However, we have more latitude in the array of toys and the physical environment. I (S.M.) used to dream about a "Cadillac playroom." It was going to be about 12 by 14 feet. It was going to have a sink with running water, a one-way mirror for observation, and recording equipment for supervision. Most important, it was going to have someone to clean it between sessions! (That dream has not come true, at least yet!)

Most of my work has been in the lower-priced compact models. Because my opportunities to work in a room devoted to play therapy have been limited, I have set aside areas for incorporating play in my traditional offices. That is not unusual, and play therapy's effectiveness is not compromised in less elaborate environments. In fact, portable models can be equally effective. I have a portable fold-up doll house in which I pack an adequate collection of toys to conduct counseling sessions and get from the car to the building in one trip. Collections can also be transported in wheeled suitcases or large bags.

Most recently, I limited my play-based materials to a collection of minia-ture figures, as described in sand tray literature (e.g., Homeyer & Sweeney, 1998). The array included people figures representing a variety of ethnicities and career fields, animals, cultural and religious symbols, buildings, bridges, and transportation modes (as illustrated with Cassie at the end of this chapter).

No matter how lean or elaborate, the room or materials are purposefully designed. Intentional selection of materials is based on guiding theories, purposes, and the student clients. A variety of toys and materials are used to facilitate (a) relationship development; (b) expression of thoughts and feelings; (c) examination of life situations; (d) testing of limits; (e) achievement of mastery, success, and efficacy; and (f) understanding of self and oth-ers (Landreth, 2002). Play materials should be unstructured, durable, and washable.

Lists of materials to include in play media collections are provided in basic play therapy texts. For example, Landreth (2002, p. 143) recommended the following materials for a transportable collection. This array could be adapted for schools, although we would not include the rubber knife or any toy that resembles items that children are not allowed to have at school.

Landreth's Recommendations for Portable Play Materials

Crayons	Popsicle sticks	Newsprint	Pipe cleaners
Blunt scissors	Cotton rope	Nursing bottle	Telephone
Rubber knife	Aggressive hand puppet	Doll	Family figures
Clay or Play-Doh	Dollhouse furniture	Dart guns	Doll house
Handcuffs	Transparent tape	Toy soldiers	Medical kit
Costume jewelry	Play dishes and cups	Spoons	Band-Aids
Small airplane	Small car	Lone Ranger mask	Nerf ball
Bendable Gumby			

Regardless of the size of the room or the collection of materials, it is important to consider privacy and safety. Others should not be able to view or overhear any form of counseling; nor should others be distracted by noise created in a playroom. If there are shelves to display the toys, they should be mounted securely so they cannot fall on a child. Play materials should be sanitized regularly. Disinfecting sprays and wipes are often adequate. At other times it is necessary to wash toys in a bleach-water solution.

THE PROCESS OF COUNSELING WITH TOYS

Theories guide every aspect of play therapy, including the introduction to the playroom or play area. Working from a relationship-based approach (such as child centered or Adlerian), play therapists typically initiate sessions by saying, "This is the room where we'll be together today for 30 minutes. You may do many of the things you would like to do." Some play therapists add, "If there is something you cannot do, I'll let you know."

A play therapist working from a directive approach would likely prepare the room prior to the session and begin by saying something such as, "Today I have three things planned for you. First, we will work with the miniature figures. Next, I will ask you to draw a picture. Before we end, we will create a puppet show."

A school counselor working from a cognitive-behavioral approach to play therapy might develop a scenario to generate options for solving an interpersonal conflict. The counselor could invite the child to rehearse resolution strategies with puppets or family figures. As the story develops, consequences of various options could be explored.

Play therapists often use tracking and reflection (reviewed in the *Practice and Application Guide*). For example, they track activities with comments such as, "You are starting with the house and family today. . . . You have decided to make something out of clay. . . . You are building something tall with those blocks." They also reflect feelings with comments such as, "You like the way you built that! . . . Your voice sounded sad when you said that. . . . You are proud because you built that fort all by yourself."

Limit Setting

Limits are an essential component of play therapy. Consistently enforced limits ground the work in reality and help children acquire skills in responsibility and self-regulation. They are invoked to protect (a) the child, (b) the counselor and other important adults, and (c) the office or playroom. Within a school, limits must also be set to assure compliance with school regulations.

Procedures for therapeutic limit setting often differ from children's experiences outside of a professional helper's office. For example, limits are usually established as they are needed or when the helper anticipates a rule may be broken. Limits are specific, concrete, enforceable, and consistently enforced. They are delivered concisely with a firm yet friendly tone of voice and consistent nonverbal communication.

There are a variety of models for stating and enforcing limits. Landreth's (2002) method, shown in the following table, is used by many play therapists. Because of the acronym, ACT, the model is easily remembered.

Landreth's ACT Approach to Limit Setting

Step	Example
A: Acknowledge the feeling or desire	"Beth, you are angry, and you want to break the airplane."
C: Clearly state the limit	"The airplane is not for breaking."
T: Target an alternative	"You may break the egg carton."

When limits are or might be broken, child-centered play therapists respond with something like, "You are angry and want to pound on that chair with the hammer. The chair is not for pounding. It's okay for you to pound on an egg carton or the pounding block." If the limit is challenged again, the consequence is introduced with an explanation: "You want to show me how angry you are by pounding on the chair with the hammer. The chair is not for pounding. If you choose to hit the chair again, I will put the hammer away for today." Some play therapists end the session after a limit is violated. Others prefer to remove the toy that is involved and then only for that session or a portion of that session.

Working from an Adlerian perspective, Kottman (1995) recommended a four-step limit-setting process as outlined in the following table.

Kottman's Model for Setting Limits

Step	Example
State the limit	"It is against the rules to take the sand out of the sand tray."
Reflect associated feelings or hypothesize about the behavior's purpose	"You are angry" or "You wanted to take the sand out of the tray to show me you are the boss."
Collaborate in generating options that are appropriate	"I wonder what you could do to feel powerful and not break a rule."
If the child continues with the behavior, impose a logical consequence.	"You decided to take the sand out of the tray even though I said it was against the rules. I'm going to put the lid on the sand for 10 minutes. When the timer rings, I'll take the lid off the sand tray."

At times it may be appropriate to combine the third and fourth step. In that case, the third step could be, "I'll bet you can find a way to feel powerful without taking the sand out of the tray. But, if you choose to take sand out again, you choose to play without the sand for the rest of our session today."

These strategies can be used for limit setting even if you are not using a play-based approach.

Sometimes professional helpers invite the child to participate in generating consequences. "You chose to take the sand out of the tray, even though it is against the rules. I wonder what the consequence should be if you decide to take sand out of the tray again."

Deciding When Counseling With Toys Is Appropriate and Selecting the Approach

School-based professionals include toys in their offices or work in playrooms for a variety of reasons. For some, the play and toys are used to develop a relationship. Others use play activities therapeutically. Regardless of their purpose, the presence of toys without the requirement of using them allows children to determine if they wish to use the toys or if they prefer to use conversation. The toys also communicate the message that "this is a child-friendly place."

When determining if play therapy is appropriate for children, it is also important to consider the challenges they are experiencing. In this regard, Fall (2001) provided guidelines for selecting approaches based on presenting problems, as summarized in the following box.

Common Problems in a School

Child-centered play therapy for

—children with diffuse anger; sadness.
—children with a lack of a sense of self.
—children with deep scars or hurts.
—children who appear unsafe and afraid of conversation.

Adlerian play therapy for

—children with social problems.
—children with family issues.
—children who exhibit goals of misbehavior such as power, attention, revenge, or inadequacy.

Cognitive-behavioral play therapy for

—children with attentional issues who need to learn how to focus.
—children needing social skills.
—children who lack study skills.
—children who are depressed.
—children who wish to learn specific behaviors.
—children involved in special education. (p. 325)

Play and Toys With Adolescents

Play-based activities recommended for adolescents include drawing or painting, puppetry, drama, games, and facilitated activities. Materials for adolescents include board games and cards, interactive-process games (e.g., the

Ungame), puppets, dartboards, puzzles, modeling clay, and art supplies (Breen & Daigneault, 1998).

The availability of the materials provides adolescents the option of occupying their hands while talking with professional helpers. They also give professional helpers opportunities to structure activities such as, "I'm wondering if you would be willing to use this ball of clay to make a small sculpture that represents your experience with the football team" or "It seems like you're having trouble finding words to explain what's going on. I wonder if it would be easier to draw a picture." Breen and Daigneault (1998) have provided other examples of using play materials with middle and high school students.

Variations and Adaptations of Play-Related Modalities

The modalities discussed in this chapter have prominence in counseling and psychoeducation school groups. For example, puppets are common in elementary school curriculum activities. Challenge courses are often used in team-building activities. Play therapy and sand tray groups have been used across all grade levels to address a variety of presenting concerns.

A variety of play-based strategies have been incorporated in group counseling (Sweeney & Homeyer, 1999). For example, in an introductory group meeting, members might select toys or figures as representations for their introductions. Group members might draw solutions to challenges they encounter. They can practice prosocial behaviors with play activities and puppets.

Child-Teacher Relationship Training (e.g., Helker & Ray, 2009) is an additional variation that warrants the attention of professional helpers. Essentially, teachers and teacher aides participate in training sessions to learn basic play therapy–based concepts and skills. After the didactic and demonstration components, the teachers and aides hone their skills during supervised sessions with one child. Finally, they use the skills during structured, regularly scheduled group activities. They also schedule 15-minute individual play times with each student each week. Weekly 30-minute sessions are provided for children who pose risks for school failure. Regardless of the number of children with whom trained teachers and aides work individually, the acquired skills generalize to the entire group of students; therefore the intervention can have positive results for many students. Preliminary findings from these interventions suggest positive results for adults and children.

GAMES

Games provide another avenue for children, youth, and adults to learn skills, memorize information, relieve stress, and enhance problem-solving strategies. Undoubtedly you, like us, can remember playing learning games in elementary school. We practiced spelling while playing Scrabble or competing in spelling bees. We practiced mathematical facts with drills, races, and musical games. We developed fine motor agility by playing jacks. We also acquired skills related to cooperation and relationships while playing team sports.

Games can also be used therapeutically (Schaefer, 1993; Schaefer & Reid, 2001). For example, games can be used to establish rapport or provide a venue for communication with children and adolescents who are guarded or reticent. They can also be used diagnostically, as professional helpers observe how children or adolescents approach activities, compete, and negotiate wins or losses. Games can lead to self-awareness and provide opportunities for improving social skills.

Traditional games can be adapted for therapeutic applications. I (S.M.) worked with a fifth-grade boy whose competitive drive interfered with participation in team and individual sports, as well as relationships. We played checkers to see who could lose. We race walked to see who could take the longest time to get from point A to point B. These activities were designed to challenge his beliefs about winning, losing, and having fun without winning.

McDowell (1997) modified traditional pick-up sticks games by pairing colors with emotions (e.g., yellow for happy, blue and black for gradations of sad, red and purple for gradations of angry, green for jealous, brown for bored, and orange for excited). As players remove individual sticks without affecting others in the pile, they disclose a time when they experienced the associated emotion. Pick-up sticks can also serve as a metaphor for taking time to consider one's options before making a decision. Block stacking games such as Jenga work well for this purpose.

Games can also be designed to increase attention and memory skills. For example, a professional helper and student can take turns giving one another a sequence of instructions. The child might be asked to "sit down, stand up, and sit back down." When the student successfully follows three commands, the sequence increases: "Sit down, stand up, turn around, and sit back down." The child practices short-term information retention whether giving or receiving the instructions.

A variety of cooperative group activities can be helpful for children and youth. For example, school counselors (Sabian & Gilligan, 2005) built a program for elementary and middle school students around cooperative games. The students with whom they successfully worked had social and academic challenges such as attention deficit hyperactivity disorder (ADHD), Asperger's syndrome, anxiety disorders, and difficulties with social interaction. Sabian and Gilligan (2005) modified the traditional children's game of tag so that cooperation was an essential element of success. They recommended other problem-solving and challenge-course games to promote social skills and a positive self-image.

Schaefer and Reid (2001, pp. 30–31) offered the following guidelines for determining when a game may be appropriate for working with a child.

1. Consider the age of the child and the developmental preference for certain types of games.

2. Consider a variety of games with different complexities to allow for regression or progression, as the child may need.

3. Identify the purpose for using a game or set of games in relation to the child's presenting problems, the goals of therapy, and the theoretical orientation of the therapist.

4. Identify the potential therapeutic ingredients and methods of change contained in the game.

5. Set the ground rules for game play at the beginning of the therapy.

6. Assess the face value of the game from the child's perspective.

7. Choose games that can be played several times within the therapy hour.

VISUAL ARTS

Artistic activities provide another avenue for communicating painful experiences, thoughts, and feelings (Malchiodi, 2003). Art provides another nonverbal modality that has been used to facilitate resolution of academic challenges, conflicting relationships, and developmental transitions. Interventions in this context can be educational as well as therapeutic (Levitt, 2009). Techniques associated with art therapy can be facilitated with individuals, counseling groups, and classroom lessons (Levitt, 2009). Artistic approaches are particularly advantageous for adolescents (Kahn, 1999).

Gladding (2005) described the effect of self-expression through art by saying,

> Visual arts have been a valuable asset to humankind throughout recorded history and before. People represent their worlds visually, not just in their minds, but in drawings, sculpture, and photographs. When individuals come to face and understand the concreteness of what they have created they are often awakened to a new sense of self and a deeper understanding of their intra- and interpersonal relationships. Thus, the visual arts stir up feelings and open up possibilities. (p. 105)

Although art therapy is a relatively new concept, the connection between mental illness and art has attracted interest for some time (Malchiodi, 2003). Various forms of art, primarily drawing, emerged as psychological assessments during the twentieth century. The term *art therapy* first appeared in professional literature and conversations during the 1940s. Four prominent art therapists—Margaret Naumburg, Edith Kramer, Hanna Kwiatkowska, and Elinor Ulman—wrote extensively and provided training during the next few decades, thereby contributing to the development of the field (Malchiodi, 2003). Contemporary art therapists recognize Naumburg as the founder of art therapy, particularly in America.

Early art therapists were strongly influenced by Freud. Contemporary art therapists practice from a variety of theoretical orientations, including traditional approaches such as client centered, existential, and cognitive behavioral. They also use postmodern approaches such as solution-focused and narrative (e.g., Riley & Malchiodi, 2003).

Selection of Materials and Preparation for Using Art in Counseling

Kahn (1999, p. 293) outlined implementation steps that contribute to more satisfactory outcomes when introducing art interventions in a school:

1. Have permanently set up in the office an art station that is visible and readily available to all who enter.

2. Normalize the use of art in counseling. Describe the process to students, faculty, and parents in your initial meetings with them.

3. Explain to parents and teachers the value of using art with clients of all ages. Emphasize the benefits associated with adolescents' developmental needs.

4. Have teachers experience the process personally. For example, at a team meeting have them create and share their career path to this current job through drawing or pasted magazine images.

5. Consistently remind students that this process is about communicating and expressing through art, not about artistic talent.

6. Issues of confidentiality extend to artwork and need to be clearly stated during initial sessions. Art is not shown to teachers, parents, or specialists without the student's permission.

7. Make a decision about the story of artwork during the counseling process (e.g., will it stay with the counselor or go home with the student?).

Offices, space, and other factors guide decisions about preparing therapeutic art centers. Although permanent centers offer advantages, portable stations can be equally effective and can be transported to classrooms and other areas more easily. Particularly when working outside of an office or dedicated space, safety, comfort, and privacy must be assured (Levitt, 2009).

Rubin (1984) suggested that art centers should include materials for (a) drawing, (b) painting, (c) modeling, and (d) constructing. Typical supplies include clay, drawing and painting paper, colored pencils, crayons, markers, brushes, watercolors, finger paints, and pastels. Pictures, glue, paper, scissors, and other materials are included for preparing collages. Again, a variety of materials and options allows for a range of expression modes and developmental abilities. School-based professionals who use art also keep a supply of cleaning materials and paint shirts.

> Art materials may be incorporated in many different ways. Drawing pictures helps to establish rapport and may assist a less-verbal child in telling his or her story. The use of Play-Doh as a "fidget" can be helpful for student clients who become restless during counseling.

Counseling Process

Kahn (1999) encouraged professional helpers to consider goals for including art activities when helping students, and asserted that "the successful use of art as therapy depends on stage appropriate art directives and counselor processing, which reinforce adolescents' self-expression as they move through the process" (p. 295). Guiding questions to explicate goals include "What art activity will enable the adolescent to move through this stage of the counseling process?" and "What needs to be expressed through art in this stage?" Kahn also offered a general recommendation of using less-defined instructions when beginning to work with a student and increasing the structure during later stages with directives such as, "I'd like you to create a picture that illustrates you when you are with friends and another one that illustrates you as an individual." This stage could be followed by a directive such as, "How would you like to be when you are with your friends?"

As mentioned previously, professional helpers who work from a variety of theories can incorporate art (Kahn, 1999). When working from more directive models, materials and activities are typically preselected by the professional helper. They might ask student clients to illustrate stressors, irrational thoughts, or steps to goal attainment. For less directive approaches, professional helpers typically invite student clients to select from an array of materials and perhaps illustrate their feelings and beliefs about something that is concerning them. Drawing from an existential approach, professional helpers might invite student clients to express aspects of themselves by creating a collage, thereby increasing self-understanding.

Art can be incorporated in a variety of sequences as well. Some students may create something with art only once or twice. Through painting a picture, they may gain insight regarding the challenges they have encountered. Others may benefit from repeatedly using art. For example, children who are recovering from a trauma or loss may benefit from repeated opportunities to express themselves and achieve resolution through art.

EMPIRICAL SUPPORT

The efficacy of play, as a therapeutic modality, has been demonstrated empirically. For example, a recently conducted meta-analysis of 94 studies focused on play therapy resulted in evidence of significant positive treatment outcomes (Bratton, 2010; Bratton, Ray, Rhine, & Jones, 2005). Bratton (2010) focused a similar meta-analysis of 51 outcome research studies for play therapy interventions conducted in schools (defined as "using play as the principal means for facilitating the expression, understanding, and control of experiences, and not simply a way of facilitating communication" p. 26). The author acknowledged limitations and challenges in conducting such a meta-analysis. However, she concluded that

> the body of existing experimental research on school-based play therapy equals or exceeds experimental research on other mental health interventions used in the school setting. Play therapy has been shown to

decrease internalizing and externalizing behavior problems, increase self-concept, improve social skills and social adjustment, increase achievement and skills related to academic performance, and reduce ADHD symptoms, aggression, conduct problems, and disruptive behaviors. (Bratton, 2010, p. 50)

Fall, Balvanz, Johnson, and Nelson (1999) conducted a replicable comparison-group study of particular interest to school personnel. Participating children were referred because of coping mechanisms that interfered with learning (e.g., shyness, frustration, and attention-seeking behaviors). Six 30-minute individual child-centered play therapy sessions were conducted with children ranging in age from five to nine years. Pre- and postmeasures included structured observations, a standardized behavior rating, and a self-efficacy scale. Ratings derived from the behavior rating scale and structured observation were comparable for the experimental and control groups. Results of the self-efficacy scale indicated a significant increase for students receiving play therapy and a slight decrease for students in the control group.

Garza and Bratton (2005) conducted a similar study with Spanish-speaking children who had been referred to school counselors because of problematic externalizing and internalizing behaviors. The children, who ranged in age from five to 11 years, participated in weekly 30-minute child-centered play therapy sessions for 15 weeks. The children who exhibited externalizing behaviors showed the most noteworthy change; a moderate change was documented for internalizing behaviors.

RESPONDING TO CULTURAL DIFFERENCES

Because toys, games, art, sand, and play are universal, these approaches can provide a valuable connection for work with children who are learning to speak the dominant language and adjusting to a new culture (Cochran, 1996). However, it is essential that school personnel become knowledgeable about cultural groups within the school to avoid inadvertent expressions of disrespect or misinterpretation. It is also important to learn about perceptions and patterns of play (Coleman, Parmer, & Barker, 1993) or artistic heritage (Gladding, 2005). With understanding of and respect for culturally influenced practices, school personnel can responsively adjust approaches.

Additionally, office decorations and toy collections must include symbols and representations from a variety of cultures, particularly those represented in a school (Perryman & Doran, 2010). Crayons with a variety of skin colors should be in the art materials. Doll collections should be multiethnic.

ORGANIZATIONS AND CREDENTIALS

The modalities presented in this chapter are areas of specialization. Thus, organizations have been established to provide literature, resources, and guidelines for preparation and practice. We encourage you to visit their websites to learn more about these approaches and opportunities for ongoing professional development.

The Association for Play Therapy (APT) was founded in 1985. This organization has established minimum standards for preparation and a credentialing process (for Registered Play Therapists and Registered Play Therapist Supervisors). The organization publishes a journal (*The International Journal of Play Therapy*) and a newsletter (*Play Therapy*). It has also adopted *Play Therapy Best Practices*, which are available on the website. APT also sponsors an annual conference.

The American Art Therapy Association (AATA) was founded in 1969. The organization is "dedicated to the belief that the creative process involved in art making is healing and life enhancing" (American Art Therapy Association, n.d.). AATA promotes quality delivery of art therapy and provides a variety of continuing education opportunities to members, including a national conference in November. AATA publishes *Art Therapy: Journal of the American Art Therapy Association.* The Art Therapy Credentials Board (ATCB) is an affiliate that monitors two levels of registration: (a) Registered Art Therapist and (b) Board Certified Registered Art Therapist.

SUGGESTIONS AND REMINDERS

Before incorporating play- and art-based counseling interventions in a school, it is important to develop your own language for explaining your rationale and approach. You may be comfortable talking about how you use toys or art when working with children. A common approach is to write an explanation. At the end of this chapter, I (S.M.) have provided one that I use as an example. Whether or not you share the document, we encourage you to prepare one; the process of writing it will help you achieve clarity for yourself and language that you might use when talking about using art or toys. (You may use or adapt the format and language we have provided.)

Depending on the degree of freedom permitted in the session, it is important to prepare student clients for their return to classroom activities. If limits in the counseling room differ from classrooms, those differences should be reviewed. For example, "When you are in the play area it is usually okay to hit the bobo and smash the egg carton. Let's talk about what would happen if you hit something or crushed something in the classroom. . . . What could you do instead when you feel like hitting something?"

Documentation and confidentiality must receive attention when using these approaches. For example, a picture is a student client's communication; thus, the picture is confidential (Hammond & Gantt, 1998). Visual productions should not be posted. Similarly, play and sand tray activities, when used as a counseling modality, are confidential; play areas and sand trays should not be viewed by others until all materials are returned to their places of storage. Permission should be obtained prior to documenting artwork and sand trays with photographs.

Decisions regarding ownership of artwork as well as documentation warrant careful consideration (Hammond & Gantt, 1998). Student clients may ask to keep pictures they paint or designs they construct. Mental health professionals may want to keep artwork for documentation. In the absence of clear guidelines, school-based professionals must consider the needs of the student clients, the school context, and ethical codes governing their profession.

As previously mentioned, it is important to consider your level of training, access to supervision, and needs of students before attempting to work in any of the modalities described in this chapter. To obtain information about training and supervision opportunities, we encourage you to contact professional organizations or consult with your professors.

CONCLUSION

Professional literature is rich with information, guidelines, and resources for diverse modalities related to play and art therapies. In addition to the approaches reviewed in this chapter, we have listed several forms of expressive counseling in the final tour of the *Practice and Application Guide.* We encourage you to peruse the literature and explore those that appeal to you and that seem most consistent with your personality, counseling style, and preferred theories.

Case Illustration With Hans

Play therapy has been helpful for children who are coping with stress and transitions; thus, it could be appropriate for Hans. Goals would include promoting independence and confidence as demonstrated in the following interchange based on child-centered play therapy.

School Counselor (SC):	Hi, Hans. We will have approximately 30 minutes today. You may play with many of the toys in ways you like. You already seem to be looking at several of them.
Hans:	What is this?
SC:	You are curious about that.
Hans:	What can I do with it?
SC:	In this room, you may decide what it is. I wonder what you'll decide.
Hans:	But I want to know what it *really* is.
SC:	You are frustrated with me because you want me to tell you what to do with that.
Hans:	I know. It's some food.
SC:	You've decided it is food.
Hans:	(after pretending to prepare a meal) Dinner is ready.
SC:	(using stage whisper) What do you want me to do?
Hans:	Say "okay."
SC:	(using stage whisper) How shall I act?
Hans:	You're happy because it's your birthday.
SC:	Oh, boy! I am so happy to have this dinner because it's my birthday, and you fixed my very favorite food.

We would also consider a directive approach, drawing from cognitive-behavioral theories, because of his transient challenges with peer relationships, classroom behavior, and homework as well as our assumption that he feels disempowered.

School Psychologist (SP):	Hi, Hans. I have an activity planned for today. First we'll go to your classroom while your classmates are in their separate work areas and take some pictures. When we return we'll use those pictures to create cue cards for you to use.
Hans:	Do I get to take pictures?
SP:	Would you like to?
Hans:	Sure.
SP:	Well, then perhaps I will take some and then you will take some.
Hans:	Okay!
SP:	(in the classroom) Where's your chair [desk]? I'd like you to sit in your chair and pretend your teacher is in the front of the room talking to you and your classmates. How will you be sitting so you can pay the best possible attention? . . . Okay. Let me take a picture.

Now, let's imagine that your teacher is leading a class discussion, and you have something you really want to add. How can you show your teacher that you want to say something? . . . Okay. Let me take a picture.

What are some other reminders you'd like to have?

Hans:	How about turning in my work?
SP:	Great idea! How do you want to picture that?
Hans:	In the morning we put our homework in the basket, so I'll do that.
SP:	Okay. Tell me when you're ready.
	[Hans poses, and the SP takes the picture.]
SP:	I have one more idea for a picture. What could you do when you come to school in the morning to help get the day off to a good start?
Hans:	Usually I just walk to my desk and sit down.
SP:	I wonder if you could do something different for a few days, just as an experiment, to see what might happen.

(Continued)

(Continued)

Hans: Maybe I could go to my teacher's desk and say, "Good morning!"

SP: Do you want to do that?

Hans: Why not?

SP: How do you want to get a picture of that?

Hans: Can we take that later when my teacher is here?

SP: Sure. Now you wanted to take some pictures too. Let's do that before we return to my office.

Upon returning to the office, we would print the pictures and create cue cards or a mini poster titled "Hans' Action Plan" or "Hans' Strategies." Captions for the photographs might include, "Start the day with a smile and high five," "Put my homework in the basket," "Pay attention," and "Raise my hand so I can share my ideas." Progress-monitoring strategies would focus on his success in each area.

Case Illustration With Cassie

In our case conceptualization for Cassie, we considered tasks related to her developmental stage. She is, appropriately, wrestling with issues of identity, values, goals, and relationships. It is typical for students to encounter confusion in a variety of areas as they approach graduation from high school and confront postsecondary planning. We illustrate a play-based intervention drawn from career development literature (Sangganjana-vanich & Magnuson, 2011) for helping Cassie achieve increased clarity and self-awareness. In preparation for the activity, we would place one piece of unlined newsprint or sand-colored construction paper, approximately 11 inches by 17 inches, on the table.

School Counselor (SC): I'm wondering if you would be willing to experiment with something today. You are facing some important decisions about course planning, college, and even participation on the team. I'd like to try something that might help you figure out what you want to do with all of those decisions.

Cassie:	As long as you don't ask me to do something weird!
SC:	It may seem a bit weird. If it's too weird, you can let me know. Let's move over to the table.... I'd like you to look at the figures that are on the shelves [or in the baskets]. I'm going to ask you to select several and then put them on the table for now.
Cassie:	Okay.
SC:	First, I'd like you to pick five or six figures that represent you or that represent something that is important to you. With that in mind, just select the figures that seem to attract you. And then, let me know when you're done. [Counselor actively and intently observes without talking.]
Cassie:	(after selecting a ball, globe, heart, Buddha, basketball player, young-adult figure wearing graduation regalia, four adult figures, and two younger female figures) Okay.
SC:	Now I'd like you to arrange them in a way that fits for you. Arrange them here on the left side of this paper.
Cassie:	(nods after arranging the family figures around the ball, globe, heart, Buddha, basketball player, and young-adult figure wearing graduation regalia)
SC:	Ready? Now I'd like you to imagine that we fast-forward the calendar to four years from now. Let's see. How old will you be then?
Cassie:	I'll be almost 22 (smiles).
SC:	I'd like you to look at the figures again. Select five or six or seven that seem to represent things you hope to have or things you hope to have accomplished by then. If something attracts your attention, even though you aren't sure why, feel free to include it.
Cassie:	(after selecting a car, an additional female wearing graduation regalia, a multiple-story building, five young-adult figures, a rock, and a rainbow) Arrange them?
SC:	Yes. Arrange them here, on the right side of the paper.
Cassie:	(completes the arrangement) Now what?

(Continued)

(Continued)

SC:	Are you game for one more time? (Cassie nods agreement.) This time I'd like you to select figures that represent challenges you will encounter and obstacles you will need to overcome in order to get from here (points to the left-side figures) to here (points to the right-side figures).
Cassie:	Oh! That will be easy! (After pondering the remaining figures, she places a line of fences across the center of the paper, adds a flame, and shrugs her shoulders.) That's it, I guess.
SC:	Would you be comfortable telling me about the figures you selected?
Cassie:	(Cassie interprets the scene, explaining that she values the support she gets from her family.) I really tried to leave the athlete and ball on the shelf, but I just had to include them. I guess I love the team even though I've been struggling with it. I wish I could feel peaceful like the Buddha, and I know my family supports me. (Cassie further explains that she wants to be in college, have a car, enjoy friends, and feel grounded.)
SC:	What about these (pointing to fences and flame)?
Cassie:	When I tried to figure out what the obstacles and challenges would be, nothing fit. So, I just put in the fence and fire. It's like, sure there will be fences, but . . . I don't know. And I have no idea what the flame is about.
SC:	Hmm. You may figure that out. Or not. I'm wondering what thoughts you have right now, as you look at the scene you created.
Cassie:	It's kind of interesting. I don't know. I sure couldn't imagine myself without a basketball. And, I really do want to feel peaceful just like that Buddha looks. Just like that rock, I guess.
SC:	May I touch your scene? (Cassie nods, and the counselor places the Buddha and rock beside the fence and connects them with

	a bridge.) Imagine that the Buddha, rock, and bridge could talk. What do you think they might say? . . .
	[later]
Cassie:	May I move something?
SC:	Sure.
Cassie:	(after moving the athlete and Buddha to the fence) With the help of the athlete, the Buddha can just jump over the fence.
SC:	Try it.
Cassie:	("jumps" Buddha and athlete over the fence and smiles)
SC:	What would it be like for you to lay just one section of the fence over on its side?
Cassie:	That would be fun! (as she smacks the fence over onto its side)
	[pause]
	Would it be okay if I go now? I just want to think about this for a while.
SC:	Of course. Would you like to have a digital picture of it?
Cassie:	Not right now. Would you take it and keep it for me until we talk next time? (counselor nods) But, do I need to put these back before I go?
SC:	No, that's my job. (After Cassie leaves, the counselor takes a digital photograph of the scene and returns the figures to their original positions on the shelves.)

Activities

1. In groups of two or three, discuss your reactions to the modalities presented in this chapter.

2. With a class member or a group of class members, discuss your reactions to the case illustration with Hans. What questions do you have about the illustration?

3. With a class member or a group of class members, discuss your reactions to the case illustration with Cassie. What questions do you have about the illustration?

Journal Reflections

Reflection #1
Revisit your own childhood.
What kinds of play did you enjoy most?
What themes were present in your play?

Reflection #2
As you consider your own childhood activities, what kinds of things did you learn from your play experiences?
How do you see yourself and your adult behaviors in context of your childhood play?

Electronic Resources

American Art Therapy Association: http://www.arttherapy.org

Art Therapy Credentials Board: http://www.atcb.org

The Association for Play Therapy: http://www.a4pt.org

Canadian Art Therapy Association: http://www.catainfo.ca

The Institute for Play: http://www.instituteforplay.com

Play Therapy in the United Kingdom: http://www.playtherapy.org.uk

The Sandtray Network: http://www.sandtray.org

Print Resources

Baggerly, J., & Parker, M. (2005). Child centered group play therapy with African American boys at the elementary school level. *Journal of Counseling and Development, 83,* 387–396.

Drewes, A. A., & Schaefer, C. E. (Eds.). (2010). *School-based play therapy* (2nd ed.). New York: Wiley.

Gladding, S. T. (2005). *Counseling as an art: The creative arts in counseling* (3rd ed.). Alexandria, VA: American Counseling Association.

Helion, J. G., & Fry, F. F. (2003). *Interdisciplinary teaching through games and activities.* Dubuque, IA: Kendall/Hunt.

Jones, K. D., Casado, M., & Robinson, E. H. (2003). Structured play therapy: A model for choosing topics and activities. *International Journal of Play Therapy, 12*(1), 31–47.

Malchiodi, C. A. (Ed.). (2003). *Handbook of art therapy.* New York: Guilford Press.

Ray, D., Muro, J., & Schumann, B. (2004). Implementing play therapy in schools: Lessons learned. *International Journal of Play Therapy, 13*(1), 79–100.

Sabian, B., & Gilligan, S. (2005, November/December). Self-esteem, social skills, and cooperative play. *ASCA School Counselor, 43*(2), 28–35.

Schaefer, C. E., & Reid, S. E. (Eds.). (2001). *Game play: Therapeutic use of childhood games.* New York: Wiley.

Shen, Y., & Armstrong, S. A. (2008). Impact of group sandtray therapy on the self-esteem of young adolescent girls. *Journal for Specialists in Group Work, 33,* 118–137.

You're Taking Kids Out of Class to Play?

An Explanation of Counseling With Toys

When you visit my office, you may be surprised to see a variety of toys. Play and toys are prominent features in the work I do with children; in fact, I don't know how I would provide individual counseling for children without toys. Adults often develop their relationships through communication. They use words and nonverbal cues such as smiles or gestures. Adults also resolve difficult situations and solve problems by talking with a friend, family member, or professional counselor. For example, they may repeatedly talk about an event or situation that troubles them, a decision they must make, or a loved one who has passed away.

Young children don't discuss their feelings and concerns as easily. Rather, they express their thoughts and feelings through toys and play. That's because children's natural language is play, and toys are their words. Children develop relationships through toys and play. They re-create troublesome situations with toys in the process of achieving resolution. They use play to relieve stress and boredom, manage their emotions, develop self-efficacy, and gain confidence. Through play, children learn about themselves, relationships, and their environment. They also learn to accept responsibility for their behaviors and find creative solutions to problems.

Play is also a way that children prepare for their future. For example, they experiment with various adult roles and career opportunities as they play house or pretend to be firefighters, teachers, or pilots. As children play, they engage in a series of "dress rehearsals" for adolescence and adulthood.

Toys and play are developmentally appropriate strategies for assisting children during difficult times. However, it is important to note that the use of toys and play

(Continued)

(Continued)

in counseling is a specialization that requires specific training and supervised experience. Additionally, responsible counselors who use toys when working with children draw from well-established theories, guidelines, and standards.

What Happens When a Child Comes to My Office

When I begin working with a child, I consider his or her needs, age, and concerns as I decide which approaches to use. Sometimes I only use toys when we're getting acquainted, and then I become more directive as we identify ways to solve problems. We may establish behavioral contracts or write letters to parents and teachers. We may tell stories with words or by creating scenes with toys.

Typically when children come to my office for the first time, I say something like, "This is where we'll be for the next 30 minutes. You may play with the toys in many of the ways that you like." I carefully observe and listen to children so they experience my full attention and respect. Through my intentionally composed comments I let children know that I *absolutely* believe they have the resources to resolve whatever challenges they encounter.

As we continue to work, I may ask a student to tell a story or make a scene with the toys. I often say something like, "I'd like you to create two scenes. On this (the left) half, I'd like you to show how you are getting along with your friends now. On this (the right) half, I'd like you to show how you will be with your friends when you've learned ways to get along." After the scene is created, we might talk about strategies for moving from the current scene to the desired scene.

Throughout my work with children, I collaborate with parents, teachers, and other important adults. When possible, I visit with parents before I begin individual counseling with their son or daughter. Sometimes I meet with parents, teachers, and the student. I am also available to attend regularly scheduled parent-teacher conferences.

What did I forget? Please share your questions with me so I can try to answer them. You may also visit http://www.A4PT.org.

CHAPTER 10

Working With Groups in Schools

Learning Objectives

- Learn about different types of groups offered within the school setting
- Review skills in effective group leadership
- Explore strategies for developing and delivering psychoeducational programs
- Consider unique situations for school-based counseling groups

B eginning in early childhood, people around the world grow, learn, gain support, and often become frustrated in groups. Within the context of schools, children as well as adults negotiate the dynamics of evolving and overlapping groups. The type of groups may differ slightly for school counselors and school psychologists, but there is also a great deal of overlap. For example, school counselors are most likely to work with groups of students in classrooms and sponsor student organizations. School psychologists may work with groups of parents and attend meetings with colleagues to develop individual educational programs (IEPs). Professional helpers in both fields are likely to provide counseling to smaller groups of students. They participate in response to intervention (RTI) meetings as well as attend faculty and committee meetings. They develop programs in collaboration with other professional helpers. In all of these roles, they have opportunities to use solid group leadership skills to facilitate the group process, participate as effective group members, reinforce role models, maximize positive peer support, and contribute to positive outcomes.

Skills for working with groups are extensive; indeed, entire texts and courses are devoted to group counseling, and appropriately so. This chapter is not intended to supplant courses or texts. Rather, we have endeavored to apply general group theory and practice to our work in schools.

Another word about words: school psychologists and school counselors use different language to identify different forms of group work. The Association for Specialists in Group Work (ASGW) has provided leadership in establishing standards for training, best practices, and research in group work. We have adopted ASGW language for this text.

The Association for Specialists in Group Work (ASGW, a division of the American Counseling Association) has defined four kinds of group work that include (a) task or work (b), counseling, (c) psychoeducation, and (d) psychotherapy. Task groups include committee meetings, planning meetings, and so forth. These groups are often short term and focused around a goal, purpose, or product (e.g., drafting a statement of philosophy). Counseling groups are led by qualified mental health professionals and are designed to facilitate personal growth or problem resolution. Members may have similar concerns, such as anxiety; on the other hand, members with diverse needs and goals may participate in the same counseling group. Psychoeducational groups are also led by qualified mental health professionals; however, the emphasis is on sharing information and teaching skills. Psychotherapy groups are designed to assist individuals who have serious and persistent psychological disorders. Typically the focus is on remediation, resolution of long-term problems, and personality change.

School-based professional helpers' work is predominantly within the first three areas. For example, they may lead or participate in a school-based mental health team that meets regularly to develop collaborative programs, design activities to assist individual students or groups of students, or assess the efficacy of an intervention (task groups). They might lead counseling groups that focus on relationships, conflict resolution skills, study skills, and so forth. They provide psychoeducation for all students, teaching lessons in classrooms or to larger groups of students. They also share resources with parents and provide parent education in group settings.

Skills that are central to individual counseling are reviewed in the *Practice and Application Guide.* Group leaders use the same skills when facilitating task group meetings, working with six students in a communication skills group, or teaching an entire class about anger management. Consider the following examples:

- Reflection of content during a faculty meeting: "Let me be sure I understand. You would like us to change the schedule because students become lethargic by late morning, and you haven't been able to hold their attention."
- Summary and open-ended question in a classroom: "We have talked about careers and three ways to learn more about a career that appeals to you. What questions do you have before we talk about interests?"
- Immediacy in a counseling group: "I would like to check something out with you. A few minutes ago we were discussing ways to avoid negative peer pressure, and everyone seemed to be involved. I felt a strong connection with each one of you and with the group. And then something seemed to happen that interrupted the work we were doing."
- Reflection of content and affect in a student organization meeting: "You're disappointed because you worked hard to make Day of Silence a success, and several of you needed to break your silence because of the tornado warnings."

Effective group leaders expand and build on basic counseling skills. They structure and organize groups, observe interactions, link members' experiences and contributions, design and process activities, encourage involvement, and prevent domination by one or two members. Group facilitation skills, also referred to as group leadership, are described with examples in Table 10.1.

Table 10.1 Summary of Group Facilitation Skills

Skill	Description	Example
Structuring	Establishing procedures and parameters within which the members experience safety and invitation to participate	"Today we will begin with our traditional check-in time. I have an activity that will help us focus on peer pressure. We'll end with role plays."
Modeling	Consistently demonstrating clear communication, respect, receptivity, and other desirable attributes	Accept feedback. Use I-messages. Engage each member.

(Continued)

Table 10.1 (Continued)

Skill	Description	Example
Facilitating	Providing an environment that is conducive to involvement and clear communication; helping members to maintain focus and interact in a productive manner	"I think we got off track. Let's go back to John's experience as a new student in our school. John, you said that you have felt left out and alone many times during the year. How was it for the rest of you to hear John say that our school seemed unfriendly?"
Encouraging involvement	Inviting each member to actively participate in the group activities and interactions	"Jeremiah, we haven't heard from you today. I wonder what thoughts you have about the program for the *Chi Sigma Iota* initiation."
Observing	Intentionally attending to nonverbal communication and interactions among members	Notice: Who sits with whom? Whose arms and legs are crossed? Who appears to be uncomfortable?
Active listening	Attending and responding to verbal and nonverbal communication	Notice: What gestures are inconsistent with words that are spoken? What emotions are communicated with tones of voice?
Reflecting affect (Reflecting feeling)	Demonstrating desire to fully understand members' contributions; communicating understanding of group members' emotional experiences	"You want to remain in the group. Yet, you are frightened because you are often uncomfortable in group situations. You don't know what to say, and you are afraid someone will make fun of you."
Reflecting content	Conveying understanding of the cognitive aspect of members' contributions	"You have already made up your mind. You are going to U of A so you can get a bachelor's degree in business administration."

Skill	Description	Example
Clarifying	Rephrasing members' contributions to remove ambiguity and capture the essential message; helping confused or conflicted members achieve clarity; accurately naming experiences	"I have a hunch I want to check out with you. When you asked Mary if she had tried to talk with John about her confusion in the relationship, my sense was that you meant, 'I think you need to confront John.'"
Reframing	Positively connoting negative or neutral situations	"No one has responded to my question. My guess is that you are thinking about how it applies to you."
Summarizing	Reviewing essential elements of group interaction, often in preparation for a transition	"This afternoon we talked about peer pressure. You practiced saying no, walking away, changing the subject, making a joke, and returning challenges. At first you didn't think you could learn to use these strategies. As we practiced, you became more confident."
Using solution-focused language	Adopting language of solution-focused brief therapy to promote confidence and hope	"Although this is our first meeting, I'd like you to imagine that we are meeting for the last time—after six meetings. How will you know that your participation in the group was helpful?"
Challenging (confronting)	Explicating discrepancies; calling attention to inconsistencies between verbal and nonverbal communication or behaviors and spoken words	"Maria, each week you have talked about how important the group is for you and how committed you are to your group goals; yet you have arrived at least 10 minutes late for the last three weeks."

(Continued)

Table 10.1 (Continued)

Skill	Description	Example
Limit/ boundary setting	Assuring the established procedures are followed	"Eli, you are really anxious to say something, and not interrupting was one of the things we set as a ground rule. I'm wondering if you would be willing to hold your thought until Ania and Zahi are finished."
Linking	Calling attention to commonalities among and between members' experiences and contributions	"Marcheta, your comment reminded me of something Carolina said earlier. You both feel pretty shy and insecure at your new school. Carolina also said she was afraid that no one would become her friend. Although Carolina is Latina and you are Black, you both go to schools where most of the students are White."
Focusing	Helping members remain focused on one person or one issue until changing direction is indicated	"I want to check with Mika about something. I had the sense that you had more to say about how you handle peer pressure."
Reflecting group process	Commenting about the interaction of group members	"You all became animated when Mary talked about dating violence. It seemed that each of you was deeply affected by what she said and that you trusted one another enough to talk about a topic that can be embarrassing or uncomfortable."
Blocking	Intervening, verbally or nonverbally, to interrupt (a) rambling or (b) communication	"Jose, I'm going to interrupt you because I think you've lost contact with the other group

Skill	Description	Example
	and actions that would be detrimental to individuals or the group	members. Monique, I'm wondering if you would be willing to summarize your understanding of what Jose is trying to say."
Evaluating	Assessing the efficacy of the group and the quality of the leadership; measuring outcomes and members' goal attainment	Throughout the group experience reflect on interactions of the group members and progress toward their goals. Continually collect data in response to these questions: (a) To what extent are the group members' goals being met? (b) To what extent is the leader skillful in facilitating attainment of those goals? and (c) To what extent is the group progressing through the stages of group development?

Irving Yalom has been a major force in group counseling. He is a prolific author who has been featured in group counseling demonstration videos. Many years ago, Lieberman, Yalom, and Miles (1973) conducted research to identify attributes of effective group leaders. Even though the research was conducted over 30 years ago, contemporary authors continue to cite the studies and recognize their contemporary relevance. These researchers concluded that effective group leaders consistently demonstrate their *care* for the group and the group members by maintaining a genuine presence and availability. They are attentive to the members of the group, their needs, and their preferences. Effective leaders structure groups with a clear connection to the meaning, purpose, and worth of activities as well as goals (i.e., *meaning attribution*). Additionally, they recognize and draw from members' emotional connection (i.e., *emotional stimulation*), which may be to one another, the group, topics, or purpose. Finally, effective leaders are skillful in providing structure, assuring that time is used well, maintaining focus, and facilitating progress toward the group's purpose (i.e., *executive function*).

THE GROUP PROCESS

A primary advantage of groups, and sometimes a prominent challenge for leaders, is the notion of *process*, or the dynamic ways in which group members interact with and relate to one another (Gladding, 2008). It is important for leaders to consider the process of the group as it develops as well as maintain a focus on the content, the topic, or the task.

An essential element of group process is the group's stages of development. Regardless of their nature or type, groups typically evolve through somewhat predictable phases. These stages are not discrete, and they may be cyclical, particularly in longer-term groups (Donigian & Malnati, 1997). The distinction of phases is affected by groups' duration and purpose (e.g., a short-term committee assignment or a weekly classroom activity). Additionally, members and leaders may not achieve resolution of each phase simultaneously (Donigian & Malnati, 1997) and topics may become recurrent (Johnson & Johnson, 2009).

Counselors often refer to the *forming, storming, norming, performing,* and *adjourning* stages outlined by Tuckman and Jensen (1977). This model is appealing because it is practical and easy to remember. Corey (2010) provided a similar framework with six stages—formation, orientation, transition, working, consolidation, and evaluation and follow-up. A key advantage of Corey's model is that the language provides guidance regarding leaders' responsibilities as the group develops. These models, as summarized in Table 10.2, provide guidance to entry-level school-based helpers, particularly when working with counseling groups.

Table 10.2 Stages of Group Development

Stages (Corey)	Stages (Tuckman & Jensen)	Group and Member Characteristics	Leader Responsibilities
Formation		Sometimes unaware; often anxious; perhaps hopeful; frequently curious	• Plan and organize • Screen, select, invite, and prepare members • Establish schedule and meeting place • Obtain parental permission when needed

Stages (Corey)	Stages (Tuckman & Jensen)	Group and Member Characteristics	Leader Responsibilities
Orientation	Forming	Anxious; tentative; guarded; dependent; skeptical; cautious; concerned about the group's trustworthiness	• Facilitate accepting environment in which trust can grow • Communicate warmth • Introduce members • Explain procedures • Clarify goals • Address anxiety • Provide guidance for optimizing experience • Articulate expectations (leader and members) • Answer questions • Respond to unique needs of members and the group
Transition	Storming	Ambivalent about commitment; conflicted about willingness to take risks; afraid to disclose with authenticity; defensive; resistant	• Guard against becoming defensive • Maintain respectful demeanor • Respond to members' anxiety • Comment on group process • Disclose with "I" messages
	Norming	Cohesive, energized; confident in trustworthiness of the group and the leader; open to experiences; willing to engage	• Provide structure and stability
Working	Performing	Connected; interactive; committed to group and to individual goals	• Reinforce cohesion, desired behaviors, and productivity • Link to promote sense of universality • Model desired behaviors

(Continued)

Table 10.2 (Continued)

Stages (Corey)	Stages (Tuckman & Jensen)	Group and Member Characteristics	Leader Responsibilities
Consolidation	Adjourning	Ambivalence about ending group; sadness; satisfaction with progress	• Normalize ambivalence • Reinforce changes • Provide strategies for relapse prevention and growth maintenance • Facilitate closure, consolidation, and integration

LEADING COUNSELING GROUPS IN SCHOOLS

Counseling groups in school are designed to address students' challenges that interfere with their learning and school success. Elementary school-based professional helpers' groups often address social skills, friendship issues, anger management, academic success, self-control, and family transitions. Middle and high school professional helpers may offer groups related to topics such as stress management, loss, relational aggression, career development, and study skills. Counselors and school psychologists provide group counseling for students who have encountered challenges with grades, career planning, behavior, or personal circumstances with a focus on both prevention and remediation. They also facilitate group interventions for students who may be at risk of school failure or dropping out of school, or who are identified through RTI procedures.

Children and youth often resolve developmental tasks through interaction with their peers. Thus, it should be no surprise that participation in counseling groups is beneficial for many children. Counseling groups, like psychoeducational groups, are designed for prevention, remediation, and growth (Gladding, 2008). Groups typically include between two and 12 members (depending on the age of the students). Generally, groups meet for a series of regularly scheduled sessions.

> Stages of group development may be less noticeable when you are working with younger children.

Formation

A group's success or failure is often connected to professional helpers' preparation. With careful and thorough planning, helpers can circumvent challenges and provide a solid foundation on which the group can work. Corey (2010) encouraged group leaders to start with a written proposal that includes the following elements:

- The purpose and objectives
- Justification/rationale
- General description of students for whom group is designed

  o Number and ages of members
  o Gender
  o Homogeneous or heterogeneous

- Anticipated number of group members
- Recruitment and announcement procedures
- Screening procedures
- Member selection criteria
- Duration of the group and frequency of meetings
- Structure and format of the group
- Strategies for member preparation
- Evaluation procedures

To Corey's list we would add procedures for notifying parents and obtaining permission when required. Preliminary planning should also include the format and activities for each session. Attention to each of these elements, whether or not a proposal is submitted, allows professional helpers to anticipate and circumvent challenges and achieve clarity for themselves.

A variety of strategies are used to recruit members. Sometimes school-based helpers know about students who have encountered similar difficulties. They may become aware of students who are challenged by similar aspects of personal/social, academic, and vocational development. In these cases, they may select the members and purpose prior to designing the group. They may ask teachers or parents to suggest students who would benefit from a group on an identified topic.

Regardless of the procedures used for recruitment, screening is a critical premember selection activity (Hines & Fields, 2002). With intentional selection and screening procedures, professional helpers meet with prospective members to consider if they are appropriate for the group, if they would benefit from the group, and if they would contribute to the group. Professional helpers can also provide orientation to the group experience, discuss confidentiality and its limits, and introduce discussion of goals. Additionally, prospective members have an opportunity to express interest or disinterest in the group.

Orientation

Members' anxiety and uncertainly is influenced by their familiarity, or unfamiliarity, with the group leader and the members. Nonetheless, it is important to establish a structure for the group during the first meeting. Leaders often begin by explaining the group's purpose and facilitating an activity to help members become acquainted with one another and with the group. They may invite members to generate group rules that will be necessary for them to be comfortable (as illustrated at the end of this chapter with a group in which Cassie is a member). Confidentiality should be discussed in age-appropriate language.

For example, a school psychologist might introduce the first group meeting by saying, "I'm glad you could come today. I have several things planned for you. First we will introduce ourselves and try to learn one another's names. Then we will talk about rules that would help each one of you feel comfortable and safe during our meetings, and even afterward." During the discussion of rules, leaders often invite members to generate ideas and then expand on respecting one another, maintaining confidentiality, and participating voluntarily. In discussing confidentiality, it is often helpful to give examples of breaches and generate ideas for consequences to impose when confidentiality is violated. It is important to reiterate limits of confidentiality and stress that you cannot guarantee confidentiality because the responsibility is shared among all group members.

Transition

Because of the nature of a school context, transition stages may be less overt. However, leaders should be alert to fluctuations in energy or interest in the group's topic, interactions among members, and challenges regarding ground rules or leadership. Leaders' responses to evidence of transition depend on the age and unique needs of the group members. At times, it may be appropriate to simply recognize that such transitions are important aspects of group development. At other times, leaders recognize advantages of discussing the changes or related interactions.

Working

As levels of cohesiveness manifest themselves, leaders become cognizant of opportunities to use the group to promote growth and achievement of goals. Particularly in counseling groups, members assume more responsibility for group interactions. They may challenge and encourage one another toward goal attainment.

Termination/Consolidation

Planning is as important for concluding group experiences as it is for beginning groups. The design of a group conclusion depends on the number of sessions a group meets and the nature of the group. When intense cohesiveness and member interaction is present, leaders should begin preparing members for closing before the last session. For task groups or psychoeducational groups, devoting a portion of the final meeting is sufficient.

Termination, sometimes called consolidation or closing, includes focusing on accomplishments and experiences of group members, as well as implications of those accomplishments for behavior changes in other contexts. Additionally, it is important to facilitate expressions of farewell and opportunities for continued growth.

A variety of strategies are used. For example, a group leader might ask each member to summarize his or her experiences throughout the group. Participants may focus on group interactions or on attainment of goals. Leaders often invite members to give feedback to one another, which is typically focused on encouragement or wishes.

In most community counseling groups, arrangements are needed for follow-up or alternative services. Additionally, group members may not see one another again. School-based professional helpers usually remain in the building with the students, who have continued contact with one another; thus, final group meetings can be quite different and sometimes less intense. Nonetheless, attention to closure and continued support remains important.

PROCESSING INTERVENTIONS AND ACTIVITIES

Regardless of the type of group, processing is a critical element of employing interventions and activities (Jacobs, Masson, & Harvill, 2009; Kees & Jacobs, 1990). Processing is often the "so what?" component of a group meeting

Table 10.3 Illustration of the Processing Model: Activity, Relationships, Self

Activity: The Wright Family Plans Their Vacation (available at several websites e.g.,
http://aa.utpb.edu/media/files/driven.pdf and
http://www.moneycrunch.net/planning/iceBreakers.pdf).
Purpose A: To practice and develop listening skills
Purpose B: To assess, develop, and practice group cooperation skills
Age Group: Adaptable for grades five through 12

	Activity	Relationships	Self
Reflecting	**Reflecting-Activity**	**Reflecting-Relationships**	**Reflecting-Self**
Process points	• What just happened? • What did you do as an individual? • What did you do as a group? • What was hard for you? • What was easy for you?	• What did your group, as a whole, do that worked well? • What things happened in your group that didn't work out so well? • What did you notice about group leadership?	• What was this experience like for you? • What did you have to do in order to be successful individually?
Understanding	**Understanding-Activity**	**Understanding-Relationships**	**Understanding-Self**
Process points	• Why was the activity difficult?	• Let's say that a team was successful, both at passing the pennies and at answering the questions. • What kinds of things would this successful group do? • What behaviors would interfere with successful completion?	• What are your thoughts about your participation in the group activity? • What did you do that helped your group succeed? • What did you do that might have interfered with your group's working together?

232

	Activity	Relationships	Self
		• What did your group do that was helpful? • What could you do, as a group, to be more successful?	
Applying	**Applying-Activity**	**Applying-Relationships**	**Applying-Self**
Process points	• What did you learn from this activity?	• Yesterday you did a group project in literacy class. How did your cooperation yesterday compare to your cooperation with this activity? • If your group were to do a similar activity, perhaps a science experiment this afternoon, what could you do in order to be more successful?	• What's one thing you learned about yourself? • I'd like you to think about ways you work in groups. How did your participation today compare to your style of working in groups? • When do distractions keep you from listening? • What distractions interfere with your following directions? • What is one thing that you can take from this activity that will help you with your friendships? • What is one thing you can take from this activity that will help you during school? • People have different styles for participating in groups. Some quickly take a leadership role and may even become bossy. Some people are more comfortable when they collaborate. And others are reluctant to get involved. What about you? How did your style work today?

Subsequent option: After processing the activity according to the PARS model, it is helpful to repeat the entire procedure emphasizing and building on strategies the students learned. A similar story, by the Line Right Architectural Company, is available at http://www.magnuson-norem.com. Other cooperative games can be explored with an electronic search for *cooperative games for kids.*

Source: Glass & Benshoff, 1999

233

or lesson; through meta-communication about the activity as well as reactions to it, members have opportunities to gain insight about their membership in the group and their relationships outside of the group. Processing activities contributes to personalization, practical application, and change.

Glass and Benshoff (1999) developed the PARS (Processing: Activity, Relationships, Self) model, which was illustrated for an adventure-based counseling group (Glass & Shoffner, 2001). This model is particularly useful for school-based professional helpers. It is summarized and illustrated in Table 10.3.

> Professional helpers consider appropriate counseling theories as well as group process theories when designing group sequences. For example, social skills groups are often based on cognitive-behavioral approaches and choice theory. Career exploration groups are based on appropriate theories of career development. Solution-focused brief therapy approaches sometimes provide a structure for problem-solving task groups.

During the first phase of the PARS approach, leaders invite members to explicate the various aspects of the activity. Essentially, members respond to, "What did we do?" and "What was my experience during the activity?" (p. 17).

Attention is given to the group interactions and self-awareness during the second phase. Members respond to, "How well did we work together" (p. 22) and "To what extent did I contribute?"

The final phase is directed toward application and response to "How was my involvement in this activity similar to my behavior outside of the group?" and "What did I learn about myself?" (p. 23). Members may discuss strategies that were conducive to the desired outcome and behaviors that were detrimental. They may also disclose benefits they derived from the experience.

LEADING PSYCHOEDUCATIONAL GROUPS IN SCHOOLS

Again, we would like you to think about your experiences as a student in elementary school, junior high or middle school, and high school. From which teachers did you learn the most? Who were the teachers who simultaneously challenged and encouraged you? In which classrooms did you feel psychologically as well as physically safe? Which teachers facilitated a classroom environment that was most conducive to all students' academic success? As you think about these teachers, try to identify their behaviors, actions, and strategies that contributed to the kinds of experiences you recall when you think about outstanding teachers.

Typical responses to those questions include the following:

- The teacher was passionate and enthusiastic about the content.
- He was always well prepared.
- She was obviously an expert in the field; she knew what she was talking about.
- Those teachers were good speakers.
- Those teachers captured my attention.
- They motivated me to do well.
- They took the time to get to know me.
- I knew he cared about me.

If we were to ask the opposite question, we would likely get responses like these:

- He was boring.
- He sat behind the desk or on the desk the whole time.
- She was disorganized.
- She didn't know what she was talking about.
- They ran out of time.
- They ran out of things to do and tried to keep us occupied with "fillers."
- The person forgot what grade we were in and treated us like babies.

School-based professional helpers have a variety of opportunities to share information, teach life skills, prepare students for transitions, and equip students with knowledge and skills necessary for successful postsecondary activities. Psychoeducational groups can be remedial or preventative; they can be designed to promote growth (Gladding, 2008). Participants include parents as well as students. For example, a school counselor might invite juniors and their parents to a postsecondary planning workshop.

Psychoeducation, called guidance curriculum, is an essential component of the American School Counselor Association's *National Model: A Framework for School Counseling Programs* (2005). Through direct instruction in classrooms, school counselors promote development in three domains: (a) personal/social, (b) academic, and (c) career. Lessons are based on an established curriculum that is comprehensive, sequential, and developmentally appropriate. Thus, each lesson addresses a standard and student competencies. Objectives are clear. Activities are designed to address the objectives and assist students in attaining specified competencies. Methods of evaluation are included.

Curriculum Design

Planning curriculum for a full year can be a daunting task for any new educator. Many teachers use curriculum maps (Jacobs & Johnson, 2009) as a planning framework. Within the curriculum map framework, professional helpers can track the lessons they provide, sequence and scaffold instructional activities, structure their time, collaborate with one another, and explain their programs to administration and teachers. Curriculum maps also provide sound evidence of the thoughtful planning for curriculum activities that are sequential and developmentally appropriate.

School counselors at University Schools in Greeley (a K–12 school with three counselors) began using curriculum maps after attending an in-service intended for classroom teachers (a planning template is provided as Table 10.4). The counselors initially used the template to document their independent activities for that academic year. The template drafts became their organizational tool for planning coordinated theme-based activities to be implemented the following year. The counselors based the themes on results of a needs

Table 10.4 Counseling Program Curriculum Map

UNIVERSITY SCHOOLS
Curriculum Map Plan for 2009–2010 School Year

Month	Theme	Hall Decoration	Personal Social	Career	Academic
August	Welcome!	"Hello" in diverse languages	Meeting people Making friends		Orientation to school programs Goal setting
September	Be Responsible	Study skills posters			Academic success skills

Month	Theme	Hall Decoration	Personal Social	Career	Academic
October	Keep Safe	Bulletin boards Red ribbons RRW posters	Red Ribbon Week Peer pressure reversal Decision making Upstanding Safe touch Homecoming safety		
November	Appreciation	Interactive hall displays	Relationship skills I-Messages (to communicate appreciation)		
December	Act with Kindness		Making a Difference		
January	Respect Others	International flags World map for paw prints	Celebrating diversity at University Appreciating differences Peace circles		
February	Lead the Way	Upstanding strategies	Leadership Bully prevention and intervention		
March	Celebrate Knowledge	Study skills			Academic success Test-taking skills
April	BARKing up the Career Ladder	Career posters Career ladder		Career development (fairs for 6–12)	
May	Invest in Success	Resources for summer programs			Educational transitions Maintaining momentum in June and July

assessment and the school's positive behavior support program (PBS). (The school's PBS program was designed to complement the bulldog mascot; thus they used the BARK acronym to emphasize Be responsible, Act with kindness, Respect others, and Keep safe.)

After selecting themes, the counselors planned collaborative and complementary activities, hall decorations, parent meetings, and celebrations. They cross-walked the themes with the three ASCA domains. They later connected the activities to standards and competencies. With curriculum mapping, their meetings were focused, and their activities were intentionally designed to align horizontally and vertically. They shared their curriculum maps with parents, classroom teachers, principals, and the school director. They also suggested cross-disciplinary activities for classroom teachers. As the counselors implemented their programs, they documented activities; thus, the maps fluidly guided planning in subsequent years, participation in external activities, and purchase of materials. The curriculum map contributed to a relatively seamless transition when one counselor retired.

A variety of packaged curricula and group activities are available, many of which are empirically supported. When selecting packaged materials, school psychologists and counselors should consider the reading level, the cultural representations, the targeted age group, and the unique needs of students in their schools. Materials that have been used successfully in New York City may not be appropriate for students in rural Wyoming. Additionally, excellent materials may not address goals and objectives established for the school. Having witnessed the purchase of costly materials that remained stored, we strongly encourage you to examine materials carefully prior to listing them on requisition forms.

Lesson Preparation and Delivery

Whether presenting a single lesson or a multisession unit, effective leaders establish a foundation by clarifying goals, purposes, and desired outcomes. They rely on their knowledge of learning theory in selecting as well as sequencing activities. They tailor lessons to meet the needs of the group members. They design and organize interesting materials to support their presentation.

When working with children and youth, leaders do not have the luxury of saying, "Wait a minute. I can't find the handouts. I must have left them in my office. I'll be right back." It is difficult for group leaders, especially those who work with children and youth, to recover from such an introduction.

Instead, effective leaders of psychoeducational groups thoroughly prepare every aspect of a lesson, including materials and supporting technology, before they enter classrooms (Cobia & Henderson, 2007). They are enthusiastic and energetic. They are friendly. They quickly engage the group members and provide appropriate supervision that guides behavior throughout the lesson. They establish relevance by making material meaningful to students and by explicating connections between the lesson and applications in real-life situations. They vary their approaches and facilitate involvement of all class members. They move around the room and maintain physical proximity with students. They endeavor to make a connection with each member of the group. They check for students' understanding of each concept. Finally, they conclude the lesson with a summary or provide additional review, motivate action in response to the lesson, and prepare for the subsequent meeting (if the lesson is part of a unit).

Classroom Management

Maintaining appropriate order in a classroom to assure an environment that is conducive to learning challenges many new educators. School-based professional helpers encounter additional challenges of working in teachers' classrooms; actually, they are guests in the teachers' classrooms. They often need to adapt to previously established rules, procedures, and arrangements. Because of the itinerant nature of their work, they may not know students' names. In these situations, a seating chart provided by the teacher can be helpful.

Challenges can be prevented, or at least minimized, by thorough planning and preparation. Developing relationships with students in and out of classrooms can also mitigate disruptions. Other problem prevention strategies include clear presentation of instructions and checking for understanding prior to distributing materials, carefully sequencing and pacing activities to avoid boredom or monotony, developing activities to maintain interest, and using a variety of delivery modalities.

Teachers, counselors, and school psychologists often rely on rituals or cues to guide behavior. School-based helpers can use the common language and universal tools in schools that have adopted a PBS program. As an example from the previously mentioned school, an elementary teacher easily acquired her students' attention by saying "Bulldogs," which prompted the students' response of "bark." A counselor used large paw prints to reinforce attending behaviors. Other strategies include using a soft voice to say, "If you can hear me, clap." A similar strategy is to say quietly, "Give me a clap. Give me two claps. Give me three claps."

We wish we could promise that our recommendations will guarantee that you will not encounter unacceptable behavior or disruptions to your lessons. Actually, providing opportunities to *learn* appropriate group behavior is an important role of schools. Thus, we encourage you to think about responses to inappropriate behavior as remediation rather than discipline. Additionally, we would like to reframe students' initial acting out as energy or excitement related to a new person or a new activity.

Following the notion of remediation, school-based professional helpers respond to students' inappropriate behavior by doing the following:

- Engaging in self-examination ("Why is this bothering me? Would others agree that this is inappropriate?")
- Protecting students' dignity
- Ignoring behavior when appropriate or possible
- Redirecting
- Considering purposes that may occasion the behavior (Adler's theory, presented in Chapter 5, can be used as a guide.)
- Using logical or natural consequences (e.g., "I see that this is not working as a group activity. Please return to your seats.")
- Avoiding power struggles

Other Administrative Decisions

If you are nervous about classroom management, cofacilitate classroom activities with your supervisor. If this is not possible, consider asking the teacher to be present during the first or second session but then to leave the room for increasing amounts of time as you become more confident.

Many school-based helpers have clear beliefs and preferences regarding teachers' presence or absence during classroom activities. Indeed, each position has advantages. When teachers remain in the room, they learn the strategies that are taught by the professional helper, and they can apply those strategies *in vivo* when appropriate. They can also assist with classroom management. That can be detrimental, particularly if the teacher is more strict and authoritarian than the professional helper. Additionally, students may participate more comfortably in helper-led discussion and activities if the classroom teacher is not present.

LEADING TASK GROUPS IN SCHOOLS

Hulse-Killacky, Killacky, and Donigian (2001, pp. 8, 21–22) identified a series of factors that contribute to effective task groups (e.g., IEP or RTI meetings). These components include the following:

- The purpose is clear to all participants.
- Process and content issues are balanced.
- Systems and individual roles within the group are recognized and acknowledged.
- Time is devoted for culture building and learning about each other.
- An ethic of cooperation, collaboration, and mutual respect is fostered.
- Conflict is addressed.
- Members exchange feedback.
- Here-and-now issues are addressed.
- Members are invited and encouraged to be active resources.
- Members' abilities to be influential are encouraged.
- The leader practices effective leadership and interpersonal skills.
- Group members and leaders reflect on their work and interaction.

The authors recommended that task group leaders design meetings with attention to warm-up, action, and closure. During the warm-up phase, leaders prepare themselves and members for the actions to be taken with introductory comments such as, "Before we continue our work on the crisis response plan, I want to thank each one of you for coming to our design meetings each week. Indeed, you each bring experience that enriches our work together as well as the crisis response plan we are preparing. Although I hope we'll never need to follow our crisis response plan, the children in our school will be safer, and the adults will be more confident because we have it. Our target task today is to complete the internal communication tree." Essentially, members become comfortable with answers to three questions: "Who am I? Who am I with you? Is the purpose clear?" (Hulse-Killacky, Kraus, & Schumacher, 1999, p. 116).

With answers to those questions, members are prepared for the action phase, with new questions such as, "Who are we together? Are all matters related to content represented?" (Hulse-Killacky et al., 1999, p. 116). Leadership is needed to maximize individual and group contributions, efficiency, and productivity. Proficient leaders monitor and facilitate group process as well as content.

The final question, "What outcomes resulted from this group experience?" (Hulse-Killacky et al., 1999, p. 116) should be answered prior to ending a task group meeting. Productive closure is achieved with comments about (a) accomplishments, (b) future directions, (c) advantage of the group in context of the goal, and (d) appreciation. The leader of a Gay-Straight Alliance board meeting might say, "Today we completed plans for Day of Silence. John, you are going to take care of the posters. Ana, you offered to get approval from the dean of students. Brandon, you will prepare a notice for the school announcements. What did I forget? . . . We'll meet next Thursday to plan the kick-off. Before we close, I'd like to talk about the meeting interactions and the work we accomplished today. What was your experience? . . . I appreciate all the ways you are helping prepare for Day of Silence. In our silence, we'll make important statements. We'll be able to practice silence because of all the overt communication we're doing now."

EMPIRICAL SUPPORT FOR GROUP INTERVENTIONS

Many variables compound research related to group counseling in schools. For example, school contexts and environments vary, members' challenges and resources are diverse, effects of group dynamics are unpredictable, leaders' skills and styles differ, and maturation influences growth and change. Thus, it is difficult to generalize findings of even the most exquisitely designed studies. As astute consumers of research, school-based professional helpers must carefully and cautiously interpret findings of any study to be sure the approach can be replicated with fidelity and that the findings are applicable in their schools. This is a compelling argument for conducting our own action research! Will you provide leadership in this area?

Many authors have supported the effectiveness of group counseling (Erford, 2011). Results of a meta-analysis of group treatments for children and adolescents conducted by Hoag and Burlingame (1997) indicated that group treatments produced significantly better results than either wait-list or placebo groups. Groups provide a more authentic setting than individual work because students can learn new skills in a supportive environment and then practice them and receive feedback from their peers. Furthermore, group approaches allow school counselors and school psychologists to deliver services to a greater number of students with positive outcomes.

School-based group counseling interventions for diverse issues have been examined and supported. For example, Brannigan (2007) conducted a psychoeducational group for sixth-grade students referred by teachers and parents because of difficulties with organization, testing, and requesting help. Results at the conclusion of the sixteenth session and at follow-up intervals indicated positive results. A similar study, with standardized test scores as outcome measures, was conducted with fifth- and sixth-grade students (Campbell & Brigman, 2007). Significant improved test scores were shown; additionally, teachers reported positive outcomes related to students' behavior.

Groups have also been provided to address personal issues. Hall (2006) examined the efficacy of a group designed to empower middle school targets of aggression and bullying. Results indicated that participating students acquired assertiveness as well as problem-solving skills. Ziffer, Crawford, and Penney-Wietor (2007) studied the impact of a counseling group for students and parents experiencing separation or divorce. Three years after the conclusion of the study, all participating parents reported positive results—for themselves and for their children. Bostick and Anderson (2009) investigated third-grade students' growth after a sequence of group counseling sessions addressing social skills. Outcome measures demonstrated positive results related to loneliness, social anxiety, and academic success.

Research addressing the impact of counselors' curriculum activities is limited (Erford, 2011). One promising study was conducted to investigate middle school students' responses to a set of classroom activities designed to promote career development and academic success (Jarvis & Keeley, 2003). Although desired outcomes were not shown for all variables, statistical significance was shown for growth related to self-efficacy, school engagement, and prosocial behavior.

RESPONDING TO CULTURAL DIFFERENCES

Groups, by their nature, include a leader and members of diverse experiences and backgrounds. Some groups are designed to address needs of one cultural group. Others are designed to increase mutual understanding among members of diverse groups (e.g., Nikels, Mims, & Mims, 2007). For all groups, attention to diversity is important (Merchant, 2009).

Essential qualities of diversity-competent group leaders include self-awareness, caring, and flexibility (Salazar, 2009). We encourage pre- and in-service school-based professional helpers to learn as much as possible about their own cultural heritage while actively and continually examining their attitudes, beliefs, and biases. As they learn more about themselves, other cultures, and individuals within those cultures, they increase their capacity for cultural empathy. Such insight combined with flexibility enables professional helpers to demonstrate responsiveness to diverse groups and group members. Diversity-competent group leaders remain sensitive to culture at all phases of group counseling.

CONCLUSION

Groups are ubiquitous. As you develop and expand your group skill repertoire, you will lead and contribute to productive committee meetings, conduct profitable lessons in classrooms, and facilitate effective counseling groups. Your knowledge of group dynamics and processes will help you make sense of interactions within various groups in your school community. Thus, skills in group work will serve you well (and your school!) in a variety of situations, whether or not you are formally leading a group.

As discussed in Chapter 2, scheduling poses challenges to school-based professionals. This challenge is compounded when forming groups for students representing different grades and classrooms. Nonetheless, group counseling is efficient and effective. At a pragmatic level, there is simply not enough time for school-based professionals to work with students individually. Of equal importance, group counseling offers interventions and experiences that cannot be replicated when working with individuals. Thus we encourage you to advocate for creating opportunities to work with students in group settings.

Case Illustration of Group Counseling With Cassie

Career development is prominent in high school counselors' work with students and is often a source of stress for juniors and seniors. As was the case with Cassie, students often meet with their counselors to discuss test and inventory results. Astute counselors take advantage of these routine encounters with students, remaining alert to students' other concerns.

High school counselors often provide career education and information in large groups. Students who remain undecided or who express interest in further career exploration appreciate the opportunity to participate in a career counseling group. Notice how the school counselor (SC) leads the first counseling group meeting in which Cassie is a participant.

SC:	Good morning and welcome! I enjoyed visiting with each of you when I planned this sequence of group meetings. For a brief introduction, even though you already know one another, I would like you to share the name you want to use during our time together and then tell three words that come to your mind when you think about your "career." I've had time to think about this, so I'll go first. I'm Sandy. When I think about my career, I also think about colleges, vocational schools, and being scared. Who will be next?
	[after the go-around] We'll be together today and then five additional times. I would like you to think about guidelines or ground rules—I call them agreements—that you would like to have in place so you will feel safe and comfortable enough to participate.
Group Member #1:	I'd like us to be kind of relaxed.
SC:	What does "kind of relaxed" mean to you?
Group Member #1:	I don't know. Maybe it would mean that we don't have to raise our hand and get permission each time we want to talk.
SC:	How does that fit for the rest of you?
	(Group members generally agree, and the counselor writes "Keep a relaxed environment" on the flip chart.)
SC:	I'm okay with that, and it usually works best if only one person talks at a time while other group members listen to one another. How can we be sure that two or more people don't talk at once or that everyone gets an equal chance to participate?
Group Member #2:	I think we can just show respect by listening when someone is talking and then waiting for a chance to talk when we have something to say.
Group Member #6:	And not hogging all the time.
SC:	What do the rest of you think about that?
	(Group members generally agree, and the counselor writes "Listen to one another," "Wait until no one else is talking to say something," and "Share time so everyone can participate; refrain from dominating" on the flip chart.)

(Continued)

(Continued)

SC: What else?

Group Member #3: I don't know what we'll talk about, but it doesn't matter. I don't want others to leave and talk about what I say.

SC: What do the rest of you think about that?

(Group members generally agree.)

SC: What do you think about this language: "What is said in the group stays in the group and is not repeated outside the group."

(Group members generally agree. The counselor writes "What is said in the group stays in the group" and "Do not repeat what is said outside of the group" on the flip chart.)

SC: I'd like to spend some time talking about ways the group members might accidentally or inadvertently violate this agreement. Two of you might be in the cafeteria with another classmate who is not in the group. One of you might say, "It's like you said this morning...." Even though it might seem insignificant or unimportant, the agreement would have been broken. You could also be in a classroom during a discussion of a related topic. It might be tempting to talk about something that was said in the group, and that would be a violation of our agreement. What are your thoughts about that?

Group Member #5: I think we need to all agree that we just won't talk about the group topics or group members unless it's just something we learn about careers that is already general knowledge.

SC: How does that fit for the rest of you?

(Group members indicate agreement.)

SC: I also want to mention a few times that I would break our agreement. If one of you says something that causes me to think that you are in danger of hurting yourself or hurting someone else, I would get help from other appropriate adults to keep you and others safe. If I learned that someone was hurting you or someone else, in or outside of the group, I would do what I need to do so all students are safe. Or, if I learn that the school's code of conduct, to which all students agree, is not being followed, I must report that to our principal. It's a school rule that I must follow. What questions or concerns do you have about those exceptions?

Group Member #7: We already knew that.

SC: Maybe so, but I want to be sure you all agree to those exceptions. (Group members indicate agreement.)

SC: I also want to caution you about the confidentiality agreement that we will make. I can't promise you that the agreement will be honored. If there are things that you absolutely don't want others to know—about yourself or maybe even your friends or your family—then I wouldn't share those things in the group, just to be sure your privacy, or the privacy of others, is protected.... Anytime you would rather not answer a question, you can simply say something like, "I'll pass on that one." What questions do you have about that?...(Counselor writes "It's okay to pass" on the chart.) What other things would you like to add to our agreement list?

Group Member #7: I would feel more comfortable talking if I knew that people wouldn't laugh at what I say, well—unless it's funny. We need to respect one another.

SC: What do the rest of you think about that?

(Group members indicate agreement, and the counselor writes "Demonstrate respect for one another" on the chart.) What else?

Group Member #4: Well, we need to be here. I'd wonder what was going on if someone just stopped coming.

SC: What do the rest of you think about that? (Members indicate agreement.) There may be times when someone has to miss. How do you want to handle that?

Group Member #4: If we have to miss, we can just let you know with a phone call or e-mail, and then you can tell everyone else.

SC: How is that for the rest of you?

(Group members indicate agreement, and the counselor writes "Inform Sandy if you must miss, and give her permission to tell the other group members" on the chart.) What else?

(Group members do not suggest additional agreement items.)

(Continued)

(Continued)

SC: Okay. I'd like each of you to make eye contact with another member of our group and say, "I can sign on to our agreement." Before we leave today I'll ask you to sign your name to the flip chart page. At the beginning of each session, I'll let you know if a member cannot attend, and we'll review the agreement. At the end of each session, we'll review the agreement items to be sure we followed them. Does that work?

(Group members indicate agreement, and the counselor facilitates the first activity.)

Case Illustration of Group Counseling With Hans

Although Hans' situation is somewhat ambiguous, his experience is not uncommon. A changing-families group may provide support for him and comfort in the fact that other students are struggling with similar issues. A variety of resources and age-appropriate books can be helpful when facilitating such a group. However, a clear advantage is the opportunity for students to tell their stories in a safe environment and to hear similar stories from their peers, as shown in the following vignette facilitated by a school psychologist (SP). The following illustration is based on a group facilitated for boys whose families are in transitions. Note how students share their common experiences.

SP: Today I would like you to use the materials on the table to create pictures of your homes. As we've been talking about, you have all experienced important changes in your home, and some of you now have two homes. I want you to create or draw the house or place that feels most like home to you. When you're finished, I'd like you to talk with one another about your home and how it feels to be there. (As students design their homes, the school psychologist observes and responds as appropriate.)

SP: Who would like to tell about his house?

Hans: I'll go. This is my house where I live with my three brothers and my dad. That's my dog in the yard.

SP:	What's different about your house from how it used to be?
Hans:	Well, I used to come home and my mom would be there, but now it's just kind of lonely after school. My older brother is there to watch my little brother, but he just stays in his room and plays videogames.
Michael:	(another group member): I know what you're saying. Since my dad moved out, it just feels different.
Greg:	(another group member): I miss my dad too.
SP:	(Reflecting and linking): Greg, you feel lonely like Michael. Michael and Greg, you miss your dads; Hans, you miss your mom. Losing someone as important as a parent leaves you feeling sad and lonely. What are some things you do when you're feeling that way to make yourself feel better?

Activities

1. Consider a group of which you are currently a member (perhaps a class group). To what extent can you recognize a progression from the forming stage to the storming stage, the norming stage, and the working stage? What evidence can you provide for the group's performing at each stage?

2. Consider Hans and Cassie. To what extent do you believe a counseling group would be beneficial for either one of them? What types of groups do you think would be useful?

Journal Reflections

Reflection #1

Authors have written about and proposed models of counseling groups for counselors. As you consider yourself as a school counselor or school psychologist, what benefits might you derive from participating in a counseling group for professional helpers? What concerns do you have about such participation?

Reflection #2

What are some of your attributes that contribute to a productive group—as a leader and as a member?

Electronic Resources

Curriculum Mapping: http://teachingtoday.glencoe.com/howtoarticles/a-curriculum-mapping-primer

Responsive Services: Small Group Counseling Module: A Professional School Counselor's Guide to Planning, Implementing & Evaluating: http://missouricareereducation.org/CDs/ResponsiveServices/SmallGroupCounseling.pdf

Print Resources

Akos, P., & Martin, M. (2003). Transition groups for preparing students for middle school. *Journal for Specialists in Group Work, 28,* 139–154.

Cummings, A. L., Hoffman, S., & Leschied, A. W. (2004). A psychoeducation group for aggressive adolescent girls. *Journal for Specialists in Group Work, 29,* 285–299.

DeLucia-Waack, J. (2006). *Leading psychoeducational groups for children and adolescents.* Thousand Oaks, CA: Sage.

Hines, P. L., & Fields, T. H. (2002). Pregroup screening issues for school counselors. *Journal for Specialists in Group Work, 27,* 358–376.

Kees, N. L., & Jacobs, E. (1990). Conducting more effective groups: How to select and process group exercises. *Journal for Specialists in Group Work, 15,* 24–29.

Marzano, R. J. (with Marzano, J. S., & Pickering, D. J.). (2003). *Classroom management that works: Research-based strategies for every teacher.* Alexandria, VA: Association for Supervision and Curriculum Development.

Salazar, C. (Ed.). (2009). *Group experts share their favorite multicultural activities: A guide to diversity-competent choosing, planning, conducting, and processing.* Alexandria, VA: Association for Specialists in Group Work.

Veach, L. J., & Gladding, S. T. (2007). Using creative group techniques in high schools. *Journal for Specialists in Group Work, 32,* 71–81.

Villalba, J. A. (2003). A psychoeducational group for limited-English proficient Latino/Latina children. *Journal for Specialists in Group Work, 28,* 261–276.

CHAPTER 11

Crisis Response and Intervention in the Schools

Learning Objectives

- Consider the scope of crises impacting our schools
- Understand the essential components of a crisis response plan
- Develop an appropriate and effective crisis response to various scenarios
- Understand the role of the school-based professional in preparing for and responding to crises in the schools

Today's school-based professionals are charged with responding to and managing crises of all kinds. In this chapter we introduce basic components of effective crisis response planning, the many facets of crisis response and management, and the role of school-based professionals in the response to and management of a crisis. The important information in this chapter should be viewed only as representing a portion of the vast amount of available information. Although this introduction will enable you to respond to a crisis with support of your site supervisor, it is not intended to be a complete guide to crisis intervention. You should enroll in the crisis course(s) offered in your training program. If your program does not include such a course, we encourage you to find one offered elsewhere. We also emphasize that crisis prevention is a vital piece of the educational puzzle. As school-based professionals, we are obligated to address crisis prevention and intervention. Due to space limitations, however, prevention will not be addressed in this chapter.

Research highlights the importance of training school counselors to effectively respond to and manage crises. Allen et al. (2002) found that 35 percent of school counselors reported that they received no training in crisis intervention in their graduate education. Further, 57 percent of school counselors surveyed thought they were "not at all" or "minimally" prepared for crisis intervention (Allen et al., 2002).

In recognition of the growing need for this type of preparation, the 2009 Council for Accreditation of Counseling and Related Educational Programs (CACREP) Standards highlighted new expectations for expanded focus on the issue of crisis. These standards build on the position statement on crisis/critical incident response in the schools developed by the American School Counselor Association (ASCA, 2007). It reads, "The professional school counselor's primary role is to facilitate planning, coordinate response to, and advocate for the emotional needs of all persons affected by the crisis/critical incident by providing direct counseling service during and after the incident" (p. 12).

The National Association of School Psychologists (NASP, 2010b) has also identified the need to increase school psychologists' role in prevention, intervention, and crisis response. NASP subsequently identified the following responsibilities in their 2010 standards: "School psychologists participate in school crisis teams and use data-based decision making methods, problem-solving strategies, consultation, collaboration, and direct services in the context of crisis prevention, preparation, response, and recovery" (p. 6).

WHAT IS CRISIS?

School shootings, while terrifying and extremely traumatic for the impacted school, are considerably less common than other crises experienced in our schools every day. Consider the following crises that could impact a school: the death of a student, teacher, or administrator; accidents; illnesses; sexual assaults; bomb threats; weapons at school; a tornado, hurricane, or other weather disaster; and gang violence. Imagine watching out your window, with your students huddled beside you, as the Twin Towers collapse on the morning of September 11, 2001. This may seem hard to imagine and unlikely.

The two most common crises that school-based professionals encounter, however, are suicide and accidents. According to the Centers for Disease Control and Prevention (CDC; 2009), motor vehicle crashes are the leading cause of death for U.S. teens, accounting for more than one in three deaths in this age group. Suicide is the third-leading cause of death for individuals in the 10- to 19-year-old range. The CDC (2009) monitors youth risk through the Youth Risk Behavior Survey, and the most recent statistics showed that 13.8 percent of students had seriously considered attempting suicide, and 6.3 percent of high school students reported making at least one suicide attempt.

Crisis can be defined in many ways. Heath and Sheen (2005) defined crisis as "an event or circumstance that occurs often without warning and initially poses an overwhelming threat to an individual or group" (p. 2). Subsequently, James (2008) expanded on the definition of crisis as "a perception or experiencing of an event or situation as an intolerable difficulty that exceeds the person's current resources and coping mechanisms" (p. 3). The latter definition encompasses the entire crisis event and response whether we are talking about the shootings at Columbine, the death of a beloved teacher, a suicidal student, or any of the other crises previously listed.

ESSENTIAL PRINCIPLES
OF CRISIS RESPONSE PLANNING

Most of us remember or have heard about the violent and senseless school shootings of West Paducah, Kentucky; Pearl, Mississippi; and Columbine High School in Colorado. These may have impacted us more than other stories of violence because of our previously held belief that schools are safe places for children to grow academically, personally, and socially. One of the necessary and positive shifts in the aftermath of these crises is that schools have moved planning for such events to the forefront. In the post-Columbine era, most districts have plans for initiating lockdown and/or evacuation procedures at each school.

Although this is an effective first step, more needs to be done to ensure that students are appropriately and effectively cared for both during and in the aftermath of any crisis. Some schools and districts have gone one step further and created a team to manage crises. These teams may be called the Trauma

Response Team, Crisis Management Team, Critical Incident Team, or Crisis Response Team (CRT). To avoid confusion, we will use the acronym CRT in this chapter.

School psychologists and school counselors play a key role in advocating for the development and implementation of a comprehensive crisis response plan that focuses on strengthening students' resources and helping individuals develop appropriate skills for coping with an event. An effective plan ensures that those most impacted by the crisis obtain relief (James, 2008) and come through the crisis enriched and stronger (Thompson, 2004).

CONSIDERATIONS OF TIMING WHEN PLANNING A SCHOOL-BASED CRISIS RESPONSE

Issues related to timing primarily drive the response within a school setting. Appropriate timing of a response often makes the difference between an average and a poor response. Poor timing results in lingering and avoidable physical and emotional consequences, while an effectively timed response leads to restoring equilibrium. With the introduction of cell phones, e-mail, and social networking sites such as Facebook and Twitter, this aspect of crisis response and intervention has become one of the most challenging to plan for and manage. School and agency personnel have realized this and commonly add "emergency management" to crisis intervention planning.

In terms of timing, let us first consider crisis response and emergency management in the best of circumstances (i.e., with time to plan). A common example of this is when a student is injured or dies during a weekend. The school and CRT have time to plan an effective and site-specific response. Because crisis does not adhere to any schedule, however, we also discuss issues and strategies surrounding a sudden or unexpected crisis later in the chapter.

It is important for you, as a preservice or new professional, to research and understand the specific protocol for such an event in your school and district.

In the case of the death or injury of a student or staff member over a weekend, a series of standard events will likely fall into place. When tragedies occur, typically police officers are involved at some point and to some degree. Police officers are trained to follow protocol in informing people most closely affected. Thus, officers usually notify a school district official or the building principal of such an event, although this process and timing is specific to the town, city, or county. With this information, building principals usually initiate action by the CRT.

Size of Response

How do we determine the number of CRT members we need for our response? In order to answer this question, a number of things need to be considered.

- Who is the victim (or who are the victims)?
- What are the victim's age, gender, and ethnicity?
- How well known is the victim within the school community?
- What are the details of injury or death (i.e., was it sudden or accidental, expected, suicide, criminal, etc.)?
- What is the final result (death, hospitalization, involvement of others, pending legal charges, etc.)?

Once this information has been determined, we can begin to identify students and adults who have been impacted, which will in turn inform the size of the response. Clearly, the bigger the estimated impact on the school community, the higher the number of responders needed will be. Think about the size of the response involving a car accident in which the quarterback of the high school football team dies versus the response to an elementary school where a fifth-grade teacher has lost her long and well-known battle to cancer. Both events will be difficult and impactful, but the size of the responses will be significantly different.

> Remember, we are discussing only the response for a school. The community may also develop a response, sometimes in conjunction with the school, other times separately.

Let us examine these scenarios further to illustrate the differences in response to each crisis. It is safe to assume that the high school football team's quarterback was known to many in the school community. Football has become a mainstay in most American schools, in part due to the accompanying celebration of homecoming. This level of visibility leads to the possibility that a greater number of students, across all grade levels, will be affected by the student's death. Teams and groups of all kinds are inherently based on high levels of member cohesion. Whether it is a sports team, the marching band, or the chess club, it can be expected that the impact will be greater for members. The number of responders on the CRT would need to reflect the sense of overall connectedness within the school. For example, a school with 2,500 students may need fewer responders and support than a close-knit school with 500 students.

Now, let us compare the quarterback scenario to the situation involving the death of a fifth-grade teacher. Elementary schools are often tightly knit communities; relationships are especially strong among teachers, staff, and parents. It is also fair to say that generally the closest connections among students lie within grade levels because the majority of time outside the self-contained classroom (e.g., lunch, recess, specials) is spent with other students of the same grade. With this in mind, who might be impacted most by the teacher's death? This teacher is known by the entire school. However, in terms of the most consistent interaction and closer connections, the students she taught (current fifth graders and perhaps even those sixth graders she taught the previous year) and her coworkers are likely to be affected the most. The CRT for this scenario may require fewer members than the first scenario. However, it is not just the size of the response that needs to be considered.

Type and Length of Response

As you can imagine, the type and length of a response vary widely. In some cases, a response can simply mean having a CRT "on call." If or when the principal realizes an unforeseen or unmanageable impact, the team can be mobilized. Think about the situation involving the fifth-grade teacher. Because of the close-knit community, school officials may initially prefer to handle the impact "in house" with their own school-based professionals. If they subsequently realize that the impact on students and staff is greater than anticipated, the CRT would be called to assist.

On the other end of the spectrum would be a response requiring a large CRT working with students and staff for up to a week. In the case of the high school quarterback, the response is expected to be more complicated and longer. Let us consider why. The death was sudden and unexpected (unlike the situation involving the teacher). This would lead to a more pronounced initial shock and denial for those most directly affected (Thompson, 2004). This level of reaction would inform the initial interventions the CRT would consider.

Interventions would also be guided by the circumstances of the accident. Did the accident occur because of bad weather? Was he driving under the influence of drugs or alcohol? Was someone else driving who survived the accident? If a death is seen as preventable, people often blame and seek to hold someone at fault (Thompson, 2004). Imagine that another student at the same school is responsible for the accident, and he or she will likely be returning to school. The CRT will need to carefully consider these dynamics as they craft the type and length of their response.

An additional consideration that impacts the length of a response involves the funeral or memorial service for the deceased. Often members of the CRT are requested to be available and visible during this time. This phase of the response can be challenging to schedule and plan. For the fifth-grade teacher, the date and time of any services will likely be announced quickly. The number of students expected to attend can be estimated to guide determination of the appropriate number of CRT members that should be assigned to attend the service or event. In the case of an unexpected death, the plans for services may be slower to unfold, and in some cases the funeral may be as much as a week or more after the death.

> What other factors will impact our planning for this phase of the response?

Composition of the Team

In a perfect world, a school district would have multiple CRTs with members who are trained in crisis response and chosen to reflect the demographic diversity of the district. Teams consist mostly of school-based professionals. In the selection process, attention should be given to gender, ethnicity, level experience (elementary, middle, and high), and bilingualism. Although not always feasible, having more than one team is recommended. Imagine the toll on that one and only team if they were called four to five times during the school year! It is also important to have a choice of teams so that members do not have to respond to crises in their own schools. School-based professionals who have been impacted by their own school's crisis need to have the chance to experience their own reactions without being expected to emotionally care for others.

CRT members should have the personal and professional characteristics that make for the most effective crisis responders. According to James (2008), desirable characteristics include poise, creativity, flexibility, tenacity, courage, life experiences, and resiliency. In addition, Kanel (2007) identified "therapeutic awareness"—being conscious of one's own emotions, values, opinions, and behavior—as enhancing a responder's skill in working with impacted clients

(p. 18). It makes sense that a CRT member who has recently experienced grief or loss should temporarily remove him or herself from the team. Similarly, unresolved grief could lead to countertransference, thereby rendering a responder ineffective (James, 2008; Kanel, 2007; Thompson, 2004).

ROLES AND RESPONSIBILITIES OF RESPONDERS

Let's now look at the various roles and responsibilities of the CRT members. The names and responsibilities of the roles discussed shortly are based on our personal experiences in serving on CRTs. These roles and responsibilities vary from crisis to crisis, district to district, or state to state. However, one role that remains consistent in terms of title and responsibilities across crises is the coordinator. The CRT coordinator is often selected for this position because of strong leadership abilities, good organizational skills, and additional training in trauma response and intervention. The work of the coordinator starts well before the other team members are called to respond.

Once school or district officials have been notified of a crisis and a determination is made that a CRT is needed, the coordinator is contacted. A meeting is arranged between the coordinator and school administrators at the impacted school. Often the on-site school-based professionals are included in this meeting. The purpose of this initial meeting is for the school officials to determine, with the guidance of the coordinator, the psychological needs of the school community. The coordinator is there to help school personnel carefully consider the crisis and the needed response through a nonimpacted lens.

Undoubtedly, school officials, professional helpers, the CRT coordinator, and other team members will view a crisis differently.

At this stage it might be helpful to visualize a rock being dropped into water. It is the responsibility for the coordinator to estimate the size of the rock (is it a pebble or a boulder?), the size of the body of water (is it a lake or a bucket?), and the likely result (are there a few small ripples, or are there whitecapped waves?). To accurately gauge the impact, the coordinator must consider all aspects of the crisis and also any unique or special considerations of the school, the students, or the community. Only then will the coordinator have a clear idea about the number, size, and depth of the ripples the school can expect.

During this initial meeting, after estimating the "ripple effect," the coordinator and the school administrator determine the appropriate composition of the

CRT. Additionally, communications to be delivered to students or parents are developed. Unique or special considerations of the school, the students, the community, or the crisis should be discussed and included in the plan. For example, previous or recent trauma, cultural considerations, scheduled breaks, and upcoming holidays warrant attention.

> Prior knowledge of and appreciation for diverse elements of cultural representation in your school will be an asset during this critical phase of the response.

At the conclusion of the meeting, it is the coordinator's responsibility to contact team members and provide accurate details of the crisis, an initial estimated timeline, and instructions for arriving at the impacted school. It is important for CRT members to have an estimate of the expected length of response so they can notify their own principals of their absence. The likelihood of longer responses and time away from our own responsibilities represents yet another reason school-based professionals should advocate for more than one district CRT!

When the CRT arrives at the school (e.g., in our previous scenario on that Monday morning after the death occurred), the coordinator provides pertinent information about the school community (i.e., specific policies and procedures, personnel, daily schedule, etc.) and new information about the crisis. It is critical that responders have accurate and updated information before working with students, teachers, or parents. This helps decrease the number of distorted facts and rumors being spread that could initiate further trauma or retraumatization for students. The coordinator then assigns roles to CRT members. Common roles and responsibilities include the following:

- *First responders:* provide individual and group crisis counseling for students most impacted. This may be in a predetermined space, such as the counseling office, or may simply happen wherever students congregate.
- *Classroom responders:* provide debriefing of crisis for an entire classroom of students or provide class coverage for an impacted teacher.
- *Parent responders:* provide information, resources, and debriefing to parents as needed.
- *Front-office responders:* help school staff manage and monitor students who leave school with a parent (elementary and middle school) or students who leave school independently (high school), provide support, field phone calls, and so forth.

- *Large-group responders:* secure resources and monitor the common area (usually a library or lunchroom) where students may want to write about or draw their memories of the deceased or injured person.
- *Traveling responders:* visit homes where students gather, work with the football team (or any group to which the deceased or injured student belongs) when they meet, or monitor parking lots and other outside areas where students congregate.

Let's compare responses for the two scenarios again to determine which of the roles and responsibilities might be more prominent for each. The role of the coordinator will be the same in both scenarios. However, the consultation with school officials and the subsequent response plan will be very different.

In the first scenario, the fact that the crisis primarily involves high school students presents challenges for responders. The need for individual and group counseling may be high. Once the announcement is made that grief counselors are available, students should begin to request support. The first responders typically engage in a form of "psychological triage" to identify vulnerable, high-risk individuals or groups (National Institute of Mental Health, 2001). They need to consider which students are physically or emotionally closest to the crisis because these students need immediate services. These services include intensive on-site individual counseling or more intensive interventions such as assessing for suicidal ideation or intent. Once students have been identified, effective first responders offer direct crisis counseling, which will be discussed later in the chapter.

> Twitter and text messaging affect dissemination of information and misinformation and must also be considered in all phases of response.

It is crucial to remember, however, that some of the most affected students may decide to not come to school, or not stay at school, to receive services when they hear about the crisis. These students—typically boyfriends or girlfriends, teammates, best friends, and direct witnesses—usually become the primary focus of the response. It is not unusual for these students to gather off school grounds. Thus, traveling and front-office responders become the most important members of the team. The coordinator, with the help of school officials, can secure names of those students who are emotionally closest to the victim and therefore most impacted. Effective front-office responders use any available means to locate these students, including calling parents, to gather additional information. Traveling responders need to be prepared to provide individual or group counseling in homes, parking lots, neighborhood parks, or even on the sidewalk!

Large-group responders are busy too. Some students are affected by the crisis, but to a lesser degree. These students may not indicate a need for intensive individual or group crisis counseling, but they might benefit from expressing their general thoughts and feelings about this crisis or, possibly, previously resolved trauma. Creating cards, letters, or banners is a frequently used intervention that seems to provide solace. Less intensely affected students typically return to their scheduled school activities within a short period of time. Yet large-group responders remain alert for students having a difficult time managing their emotions and offer additional counseling.

> Parents are well-meaning in wanting to be the sole support for their sons and daughters when a crisis has occurred. Sometimes, however, it is important for CRT members to advocate for additional support, which can be provided by professional helpers on the team or in the community.

In the second scenario involving the death of an elementary school teacher, responders' roles and responsibilities are the same but are utilized to different degrees. As mentioned previously, elementary students, teachers, staff, and parents are quite connected and often have close personal relationships with one another. Thus, a response at this level is often more challenging. It is not unusual for the principal to request minimal or "behind the scenes" presence by the CRT. Principals often know their teachers best and may want to care for and support them without bringing in outsiders (Heath & Sheen, 2005). Likewise, there can be a sense of protectiveness on the part of the teachers. Their preference may be to care for their own students. In these situations, the coordinator may remain in a consultant role, outlining expected responses by teachers and students to the given crisis and providing additional resources.

When planning a response to the death of a teacher, the coordinator may advocate for the CRT to be available at the school. Let's look at how the responders would be utilized. It is not unusual for parents, upon hearing of a crisis at this level, to come to the school to offer help, check on their sons and daughters, and subsequently need support themselves. Based on anticipated need, the coordinator determines the number of parent responders needed. The parent responders should secure a room, gather appropriate resources (including the school library's list of developmentally appropriate books on grief and loss), and notify the front-office responder to direct parents to their location.

Classroom responders typically become more prominent in elementary schools as well. The coordinator assigns this role to CRT members who have experience working with the developmental level of the impacted students. Licensed classroom responders may be asked to substitute while teachers take breaks or receive services. In other instances they may be paired with a teacher to debrief the crisis with an entire classroom of children. This process could lead to students being identified as needing more specific individual counseling by a first responder. For this to be an effective and appropriate process for the remaining students, it becomes imperative that responders are knowledgeable about the developmental differences in reactions to grief and loss. A more in-depth discussion about the developmental reactions to trauma occurs later in this chapter.

First responders and large-group responders may also be utilized in elementary schools. For example, first responders may be assigned as a resource for teachers who are most impacted by the death of their colleague. If a group of teachers is highly impacted, group counseling or debriefing could be beneficial. The strength of the relationship between teachers and the deceased determines the type and amount of crisis counseling or debriefing that is needed.

The principal may also be highly affected by the death. It is the coordinator's responsibility to ensure that he or she receives support, counseling, or debriefing. Sometimes this may simply be encouraging him or her to drink water, eat, or take a walk to be alone. Despite their protests, even principals need to engage in self-care during these emotionally difficult times!

In both response scenarios, the coordinator and CRT members have an additional and important responsibility: record keeping. Each time a responder works with a student, teacher, or parent, a record of that contact should be made. This record should include the name of the responder, the name of the person receiving services, the reason for receiving services (including his or her relationship to the victim or crisis), a description of the services received, the date and times of service, and directions for follow-up if needed. These contact logs are reviewed by the coordinator on a regular basis throughout the day and again at the end of each day to determine the need for further response. An example of a contact log follows.

CRT Contact Log

Responder_____

Date_____

Response Site_____

Name	Relationship to Crisis (Reason for Services)	Services Received	Time	Follow-Up Required? What and When?	Notes

Remember, effective responses are tailored to the unique crisis and the school. The involvement of the CRT may vary from a few hours to weeks. Building administrators and the coordinator determine the appropriate time for the CRT to leave the site. The coordinator communicates with the site's school-based professionals throughout the response to facilitate this transition.

Our discussion thus far has focused on crises that occurred with adequate time to plan the response. Consider the following situations and think about how these crises would be managed by the CRT with no time to plan.

- Three high school students were returning to school after lunch. They were speeding to avoid being late. The driver lost control of the car and hit a telephone pole head-on. The driver and one passenger were killed. The student in the backseat survived and was taken to the hospital where she is placed on life support.
- A middle school student brought a gun to school and threatened students in the lunchroom during seventh-grade lunch. He shot the assistant principal and a student and then killed himself. The administrator and other student survived.
- The tornado siren sounded, and the school followed the proper procedures to prepare. Within minutes the tornado hit, and the farthest outlying portable classroom was heavily damaged. The students and teacher in it were injured.
- An elementary teacher was monitoring morning recess. As the students came back into the building to resume classes, he had a heart attack. The paramedics arrived and worked on him for quite some time. However, he did not survive.
- A bus filled with high school students on their way to school one morning broadsided a car that pulled out of an intersection. The adult driver of the car was killed instantly. The students were transferred to another bus and taken to school.

Let's consider the scenario in which three students returning to school were involved in an accident and answer questions about the response. *Who will be most directly impacted and therefore need the services of the first responders?* The close friends, siblings, and relatives of the victims who attend this school would be at the top of the list. Unless they have a closed-campus policy, high schools often experience a mass exodus of students at lunchtime, which leads to an equally large reentry as the lunch break ends. Therefore, we also need to determine if students witnessed the accident or drove by it on their way back to school so that we can connect them with first responders. If these students remain at school, first responders would be assigned to work with them. However, if these students decide to leave the school, the front-office and traveling responders take on more responsibility.

> Remember, as a district CRT is organizing and assembling, the school-based professionals on site will have this responsibility. In fact, until the CRT arrives the school-based professionals may have to assume all of these roles!

Which of the other responder roles would also be utilized, and how? Beyond the close friends, we also need to consider the impact on the victims' classmates. Victims' seats in every class will be empty. The teachers who had these victims in class, and other staff or personnel who may have had relationships with them, are also affected. Thus, classroom and large-group responders are assigned as needed. Remember, these responders constantly evaluate the needs of the people with whom they are working. When more intensive services are required, the coordinator is informed, and a first responder is assigned.

We now address the same questions for the situation with the elementary teacher having a heart attack. *Who will be most directly impacted and therefore need the services of the first responders?* The students who witnessed the event would be prioritized for immediate services. Other people directly impacted by this event include the first adult staff members on scene to help. When we imagine the person who performed CPR on the teacher until paramedics arrived, it seems clear that he or she could also benefit from receiving crisis counseling. No doubt you will think of other individuals and groups within a school who would be immediately affected and with whom first responders might work.

Which of the other responder roles would also be utilized, and how? Large-group responders may be stationed in the library to be available for staff and students who may have been on the playground but not in close proximity to the event. Classroom responders may be assigned to debrief students who were in class at the time of the crisis but heard and saw the emergency personnel arrive. It would not be unusual for children to want to call their parents to tell them what happened. This will require coordination. Front-office responders, in tandem with the school's office staff, often monitor these calls to prevent unnecessary disruption and confusion. To prevent an increase in the level of trauma experienced by these students, front-office responders often initiate the calls and inform parents of the crisis before giving the phone to students. Parents may decide to pick up their children and can be given information about available services and resources provided by the parent responders.

> Because school-based professionals must assume leadership and provide direct services until the CRT arrives, they must be able to make quick decisions about where their services are most needed. Having other personnel in the building who are trained to manage aspects of the crisis (e.g., fielding phone calls and visits from parents, acting as a substitute in the classrooms of any teachers who are impacted) allows professional helpers to be available to provide their counseling expertise.

CRISIS COUNSELING

As a preservice or new professional, you may not believe you are ready to engage in crisis response work, especially as a first responder. Often we hear, "I'll work for a few years in the field first, and then I'll volunteer to serve on my district's CRT." As we know, crises in schools are common. The need to manage them is inevitable. As we just discussed, when there is no time to prepare a response and the CRT is being mobilized, or when schools or districts do not have organized CRTs, school counselors and psychologists are thrust into the role of first responders, and maybe even coordinator! Our professional codes of ethics require us to be prepared for and engage in direct work with students impacted by crisis. It can be very hard and difficult work. It can also be an incredibly rewarding part of our jobs.

With that in mind, let's get more specific about the actual work of the first responders, crisis counseling. In order to further define their responsibilities, we need to better understand the normal and expected emotional reactions to trauma or loss. As mentioned previously, the reactions to trauma by a child or adolescent are different from the reactions of adults. School-based professionals, whether or not they serve as members of a district CRT, need to be knowledgeable about these developmental differences. We have outlined a few considerations and provided resources at the end of the chapter.

According to the National Organization for Victim Assistance (NOVA, n.d.), children's reactions to trauma can include fearing they may die, reacting with guilt if they think they did something wrong that caused the event, manifesting their feelings physically (e.g., with headaches or nausea), and experiencing highly intense and wide mood swings. Additionally, the safe and predictable view of a child's world is temporarily lost (American Red Cross, 2007), which can cause fear, confusion, and helplessness. When children cannot comprehend the issues, they may distance themselves from any feelings because "it doesn't matter" (NOVA, n.d.).

An adolescent's reaction to the same event would manifest differently. The very nature of adolescent behavior is inconsistent. Therefore their reactions to trauma are also inconsistent. This can be challenging for a responder to track and subsequently manage. Anger can turn to rage, and sorrow may manifest as suicidal ideation (NOVA, n.d.).

A classroom responder also needs to consider these kinds of reactions when working with a group of students. For example, the students of a fifth-grade teacher who dies would manifest these reactions individually and as a group.

Equally concerning is that the immediacy of death is in stark contrast to teenagers' desire to see death as part of a far-distant future as well as their inherent sense of immortality. Sometimes their activities center on proving themselves to be more powerful than death. Involvement in risk-taking activities may be exacerbated by the loss of risk inhibitions due to traumatization (Heath & Sheen, 2005; NOVA, n.d.). Adolescents often create memorials to symbolically represent their loss and to maintain a tangible connection to the person who has died or been injured.

The concept of grief is complex and multidimensional. We define grief as the feelings that arise when one experiences a loss (adapted from Kanel, 2007). It is widely accepted that people of any age progress through several stages of grief as they manage a traumatic event (James, 2008; Kubler-Ross, 1969; Schneider, 1984; Worden, 1991). The remainder of this section is focused on the stages and feelings that first responders and school-based professionals most often need to manage.

The main responsibility of school counselors, school psychologists, and first responders is to help students and teachers navigate these early stages. In the initial stage of grief, feelings of shock, disbelief, confusion, and denial are primary (James, 2008; Kubler-Ross, 1969; Schneider, 1984; Worden, 1991). Usually this is followed by a time when people experience feelings of anger or rage (Kubler-Ross, 1969), guilt, yearning, fear, and sorrow (Schneider, 1984).

> School-based professionals are also often involved in or provide referrals for continued grief management.

Although there is no definitive formula for determining how or when a person enters and transitions through these stages, there are common factors about the survivor and the crisis that influence the process. Kanel (2007) referred to these as determinants of grief, while NASP (2010c) identified them as factors that can impact the degree of psychological distress. Two factors that understandably impact the level of grief experienced include the type and quality of relationship between the survivor and the victim. That is to say, a 16-year-old grieving the death of a new best friend may have more difficulty than managing the death of a family member with whom there has been minimal contact or relationship.

Another factor that affects the grieving process is the circumstances or mode of death (Kanel, 2007). For example, grieving the loss of a person who died from natural causes is less difficult than emotionally processing a death that was unexpected and caused by accident, suicide, or homicide.

Additional factors that impact one's grieving process include prior traumas experienced, mental health status, and the amount and quality of available support (Kanel, 2007).

ESSENTIAL PRINCIPLES AND PROCESS OF CRISIS COUNSELING

Using all of the information we have covered as a framework, we will consider the actual process of crisis counseling, when we sit with a child or adolescent in crisis and engage in meaningful and effective crisis counseling. There are many different approaches that have been developed to engage in the process of crisis intervention. Representative approaches and models include the following:

- The Six Step Model (James, 2008)
- The ABC Model (Kanel, 2007)
- Psychological First Aid (NIMH, 2001)
- PREPaRE curriculum (NASP, 2010d)

NOVA has outlined other protocols that can be accessed on their website at http://www.trynova.org.

A synopsis of common steps employed when counseling individuals in crisis is provided shortly. However, we encourage you to explore resources and obtain additional training so you will be competent and comfortable in this role.

Assuring Safety and Building Rapport

The first step of crisis intervention outlined by most approaches underscores the importance of ensuring the physical safety of the person(s) with whom you are working (James, 2008; NASP, 2010d; NIMH, 2001; NOVA, 2010). Obvious examples of this are the case of the middle school student with a gun in the cafeteria and the case of the tornado touching down on school grounds. Before any counseling takes place, all school personnel must assure that all persons involved are safe from further physical harm.

Once we have ensured the immediate physical safety of the student(s), we begin to develop a relationship by building rapport and utilizing basic counseling skills (James, 2008; Kanel, 2007; NOVA, 2010). These basic skills include attending, reflection of content and feelings, paraphrasing, and summarizing (as reviewed in the *Practice and Application Guide*). Building rapport with basic counseling skills, more often than not with a stranger, during a crisis is challenging. Particularly within a high school setting, where students are mobile and consider themselves independent, we need to be able to do this very quickly.

Consider the example of the car accident occurring during the lunch break. If the first responders fail to make contact and build relationships quickly, students in the school may leave the building when they hear about the accident. Then our opportunity to provide services becomes more difficult, or perhaps disappears altogether.

Specialists working with NOVA (2010) furthered the notion of basic counseling and highlighted the importance of "ventilation" and "validation" in the process of relationship building. By providing a calm and compassionate presence, responders allow students to tell their stories. Some students need to tell their story over and over again, trying to find the right words to accurately express their experiences and reactions. It is the responsibility of the first responder to actively listen and confirm each student's perceptions and responses (NOVA, 2010). This is especially difficult when the story includes graphic details of what they saw or heard.

Assessing Suicide and Threat

Once the rapport is established, first responders begin to identify and define the problem (James, 2008; Kanel, 2007). This phase of intervention includes assessment (NASP, 2010d; NIMH, 2010). Responders must assess the student's level of distress, including his or her level of risk for committing suicide or homicide. They must also assess the level of functioning and appropriate coping skills (Kanel, 2007). Remember our psychological triage? Students who present with suicidal or homicidal ideation become the first priority. Thus, it is crucial that responders are knowledgeable, comfortable, and competent in conducting suicide and threat assessments.

Many scales have been developed to predict the risk of suicide. One approach that is easy to remember and effective for new professional helpers is the use of the acronym *SLAP*.

S = **S**pecificity

L = **L**ethality

A = **A**vailability

P = **P**roximity

How much specificity exists in the student's plan to commit suicide? How detailed is the plan? Has the student made the decision to wait until his family leaves this weekend so he will be alone and the garage will be empty? Has the student stated she may commit suicide if her best friend is taken off life support? The student who knows where and when he will kill himself is considered more at risk than the student who presents with an ambiguous plan.

How lethal is the current plan? The more lethal the method, the higher the risk is for suicide completion. This can be the most difficult aspect of the situation to evaluate. A plan involving the use of a firearm is more lethal than planning to jump off a roof. However, if the student has no idea where to get a gun and the roof is 17 stories up, then the level of lethality changes. A plan involving drugs or alcohol is also challenging in this aspect of the assessment. For example, a student who tells you she is planning on "taking pills" could mean taking a handful of aspirin, driving to the store to purchase several bottles of extra-strength pills, or stealing her dad's prescription pain medication.

The next step of the assessment provides additional clarification. The more available the means, the higher the risk. Does the student have available means to carry out the plan? Does the student have access to a gun and ammunition? Can the student access lethal amounts of drugs or alcohol? Can the student drive, and does he have access to a car? Having a driver's license is a major factor to consider when assessing the risk of suicide in adolescents because it means many methods become more accessible—not to mention the lethality of using the car as the means to kill themselves!

> Children are more likely than adolescents to identify family members as part of a support system. Developmentally, adolescents are quick to identify friends as the biggest source of support. While acknowledging the importance of peer support, it is also imperative for school-based professionals to help adolescents identify adults who can fill this role.

The final step of SLAP involves determining the student's proximity to others. Who is in the student's support system? Is the student isolated from adults who are in a position to provide support? Students with minimal or inconsistent support systems are considered to be at higher risk for attempting suicide.

There are a few other things, which do not fall under the SLAP acronym, that should also be considered when assessing for the risk of suicide. A student's level of risk is higher if there is a history of attempted or completed suicides within the family or close friends. The level of risk also increases with certain mental health diagnoses (i.e., depression and substance abuse).

Further, it is helpful to determine stressors in a student's life. Have there been recent losses or significant changes (e.g., death of a loved one, loss of family income, change of schools, deployment of family member, etc.)? The more stressors a student is managing, the higher his or her risk is for attempting suicide.

Assessments of the SLAP nature are not effective in isolation, without some level of existing relationship and without a certain level of comfort on the part of the responder. Assessing the level of risk for suicide can be extremely challenging for beginning professional helpers. It is not only vital to ask the right questions but to do so in a nonjudgmental, empathic, and congruent manner. It is your ethical responsibility to ensure that you can engage effectively in this aspect of work with children and adolescents in schools.

Upon completion of a suicide risk assessment, school-based professionals determine if the student exhibits a low, moderate, or high level of risk for committing suicide. The responder then informs the coordinator, provides documentation of the assessment, and recommends the most appropriate course of action. At the high school level, possible courses of action range from calling parents or the police to recommending further evaluation for possible hospitalization (high risk) to continuing to provide individual or group support (no or low risk). Regardless of the level of risk, parents and guardians of elementary and middle school students should be informed.

Consultation with supervisors and colleagues is recommended whenever risk is suspected. The *Ethical Standards for School Counselors* (ASCA, 2010a, A.7) provide guidance that is relevant to all school-based professional helpers:

Professional school counselors

(a) inform parents/guardians and/or appropriate authorities when a student poses a danger to self or others. This is to be done after careful deliberation and consultation with other counseling professionals.

(b) report risk assessments to parents when they underscore the need to act on behalf of a child at risk; never negate a risk of harm as students sometimes deceive in order to avoid further scrutiny and/or parental notification.

(c) understand the legal and ethical liability for releasing a student who is in danger to self or others without proper and necessary support for that student.

In this regard, the authors of the revised code recognized the complexity in making decisions about potential danger to self or others. In Section A.2, addressing confidentiality, they wrote the following:

[Professional school counselors] recognize the complicated nature of confidentiality in schools and consider each case in context. . . . Serious and foreseeable harm is different for each minor in schools and is defined by students' developmental and chronological age, the setting, parental rights, and the nature of the harm. School counselors consult with appropriate professionals when in doubt as to the validity of an exception.

Prediction and Preparation

The next phase of intervention involves what NOVA (n.d.) refers to as "prediction and preparation." First responders help students answer questions such as, "What happens now?" and "How will I cope with this?" James (2008) identified the tasks of this stage as making plans and obtaining commitment. Responders provide students with information about the grieving process and also normalize the emotional reactions that might occur.

During this phase, responders review the students' coping skills. They not only provide strategies to strengthen existing skills but also introduce new and additional coping skills for students to try. Responders ask students about their plans for the next few hours, days, and weeks. They offer guidance as appropriate. It is also important to help students and adults incorporate as much routine as possible (Heath & Sheen, 2005). Finally, students are provided with appropriate resources for any additional services they may need. These resources include any that exist within the school, as well as any within the community that can address their needs.

> First responders may also be asked to complete a homicide or threat assessment. Imagine you are working with a distraught student whose best friend was just killed in a car accident. He tells you that he is angry and is going to kill the driver of the car that caused the accident. You must determine the level of risk this student has for carrying out his plan to kill the driver. The principle of SLAP would also apply to a threat assessment.

CONCLUSION

Timely and effective crisis intervention minimizes the negative impacts of grief and helps mitigate the development of posttraumatic stress disorder (American Red Cross, 2007; NOVA, 2010). This makes our jobs as crisis responders even more critical. School-based professionals are not immune from responding to crises within the schools. In fact, they are very likely to be asked to advocate, plan, and provide training for crisis intervention within the schools.

Case Illustration of Crisis Counseling With Cassie and Hans

To make this final section as applicable as possible, we have used actual crises encountered by the authors. Of course we have changed identifying information to protect the students' anonymity. Hans and Cassie are the students who have been impacted by our crises.

In the first case, we present the school-based professional's interaction with Cassie. A CRT is mobilized to a high school in response to a student death the previous evening. Linda is assigned the role of first responder and monitors the hallway near the deceased student's locker.

Linda: Hi. I noticed you're upset, and I am wondering if you would like someone to talk to.

Cassie: Who are you?

Linda: I'm Linda, and I'm one of the counselors brought to your school today to talk with anyone who may need some support after hearing about the death of the student.

Cassie: I'm not talking to any stranger.

Linda: I know it can be hard talking to someone who doesn't even know you [pause]. Did you know the student who died?

Cassie: Uh, yeah! So?

Linda: [pause] How did you know Dennis?

Cassie: [looks down but says nothing]

Linda: I am here to listen. Take your time [pause]. Whenever you're ready.

Cassie: He and I were the leads in the school play. Why do you care?

Linda: Well, I know lead actors usually spend lots of time working together and that sometimes they even become good friends.

(Continued)

(Continued)

Cassie: [pauses and then begins to cry]

Linda: [uses minimal encouragers, open body language]

Cassie: I can't believe he's dead! I just talked to him last night. He seemed fine. I had no idea. He told me everything was cool. I can't believe he lied to me!

Linda: Friends aren't supposed to lie, and he told you he was okay.

Cassie: What am I gonna do? [pause] I hate him!

Linda: It sounds like you're not sure what to think or feel.

Cassie: I can't believe he'd kill himself over a girl! He said he was okay with it, that he was over it—you know, ready to move on....

Linda: Going through a breakup can be really hard.

Cassie: Oh my god! [pause] His parents, or his little brother [pause]. Did they find him? Did he leave a note—you know, a suicide note?

Linda: I have not been told if he left a note or not. It sounds like you have lots of questions and not many answers. That can make it really hard to make any sense of anything right now.

Cassie: I wonder what it said—what he said—you know, about why. I wonder if he talked about Marcela breaking up with him. If he left a note, I hope he blamed Marcela. I wish he would have killed that [expletive] instead of himself. Why didn't he just hang on and call me or come over or text me or something? We always said we were there for each other. He is so full of [expletive]! He should have called!

Linda: You two agreed to always be there for each other, and you can't believe he didn't share something this big with you.

Cassie: He didn't even say goodbye [pause]. Why did he do this to me?

Linda: You may never know exactly what he was thinking and feeling when he decided to kill himself, and the worst part is you didn't even get a chance to say goodbye [pause]. Sometimes people commit suicide because they cannot see any other way out.

Cassie: That's crazy. We talked about it sometimes, you know, but we both said it was stupid.

Linda: You said you and Dennis "talked about it." Do you mean you talked about suicide?

Cassie: [looks away]

Linda: I am here to listen and to make sure that you are safe. I am wondering, Cassie, if you have ever talked with your school counselor or any other counselor before.

Cassie: No, why? I am a good student.

Linda: Counselors talk to lots of students about lots of things, and the one thing we need to make sure students know is that what we talk about is confidential. I want to let you know that I am a counselor, and what we talk about is confidential. That means I will not share what we talk about with anyone else. Remember also when I told you I am here to make sure you are safe? The only reason I would tell someone else about our conversation is if I think there is any serious and foreseeable harm. That's kind of a weird way of saying if I think you are in danger of hurting yourself or someone else I need to let someone know so we can keep everyone safe. Does that make sense?

Cassie: Yeah, but just because we talked about it doesn't mean we're gonna do it!

Linda: Right, I know that. Tell me about your conversations with Dennis about suicide.

Cassie: I don't know, we just talked in general about it . . . lots of kids do . . . it's just talk.

Linda: You say you talked about it in general. Cassie, have you ever thought about killing yourself?

Cassie: No! Are you kidding me? I would never do that. I think it is stupid.

Linda: I don't ever want someone to get to the point that it seems like Dennis did. I want to help people see there are other ways to manage what's going on in their lives. It seems like you see that there are lots of other ways to deal with problems.

Cassie: Yeah, suicide's messed up. What a waste, man.

(Continued)

(Continued)

Linda: How *do* you cope with tough things, Cassie?

Cassie: What do you mean?

Linda: I mean you've just found out that your friend Dennis is dead, and I think the next few hours and days and weeks are going to be pretty difficult. How will you cope with all of this?

Cassie: I don't know [pause].

Linda: Anyone who is going through what you are—grieving a loss like this—will experience lots of emotions. You may feel like you are on an emotional roller coaster. Tell me about your support system, Cassie.

Cassie: You mean like my family?

Linda: Your family and anyone else you might turn to for support with this.

Cassie: The whole drama department for sure. We are all real tight, and we're getting together after school to decide when and where we're going to have the candlelight vigil. I called my mom, and she said she would help us buy the candles and paper cups. Do you think we should do it here or at his house?

Linda: That's a good question. Would it be okay if I came to the meeting after school and helped you guys figure it out?

When assessing for the risk of suicide, it is important to ask directly and use clear language. Often preservice and entering professional helpers express discomfort at asking the question so overtly (i.e., killing vs. hurting or harming, or the notion of "planting the seed"). It can be difficult and awkward to ask the questions "Have you thought about killing yourself?" or "Are you thinking about killing yourself?" If a student is experiencing suicidal ideation and intent, imagine his or her reaction if the professional helper asks, "Surely you're not thinking about harming yourself, are you?" Likely the student's response would reflect the helper's need to hear a reply of "No."

In our second example, we introduce crisis counseling with Hans. On Friday afternoon, students in Hans' school attended a celebration of Valentine's Day. Many of the students gave a valentine to Franco, a fourth-grade boy who had been diagnosed with cancer a few months previously and whose illness was progressing rapidly. Franco's parents had decided to homeschool him, beginning after the Valentine's

Day parties. However, Franco died on Sunday morning. A CRT was mobilized before students returned to school on Monday morning. Rob, a classroom responder, was assigned to the classroom of Franco and Hans. The teacher explained that Franco's body was unable to fight the cancer and that he died over the weekend. Hans immediately stood, threw his pencil at the wall, and left. Rob informed the teacher that he would follow Hans and send another responder to the classroom. Rob found Hans sitting in the hallway.

Rob: I'm lonely. Can I please sit here with you?

Hans: I don't care [pause]. What's your name?

Rob: My name is Rob. What's yours?

Hans: Hans.

Rob: Nice to meet you. Thanks for letting me sit with you.

Hans: You're welcome. You aren't a teacher here.

Rob: Wow, you are very observant, Hans. I am a visitor [points to his badge], and I checked in with the front office when I got here this morning. You are in Ms. Ross' fourth-grade class, right?

Hans: Yeah, how did you know that?

Rob: Well, I came into your room this morning to be with you all while Ms. Ross talked to you about Franco. You seemed mad when you left the room just now.

Hans: Am I going to get in trouble again?

Rob: Right now I just want to sit with you and talk some more. Is Franco your friend?

Hans: Uh-huh. He has cancer.

Rob: Yes, I know. Cancer is a very scary disease.

Hans: I'm not afraid. I gave him a Valentine's Day heart with SpongeBob on it, and he put it on his wheelchair.

Rob: That's very thoughtful of you, Hans. I'll bet he liked it [pause]. It seems like you didn't want to hear what Ms. Ross was saying this morning.

Hans: I don't like hearing tough news all the time.

Rob: Tough news?

(Continued)

(Continued)

Hans: Yeah, my dad calls it tough news. It means hearing something hard—like stuff you don't wanna hear, but you have to hear it anyway.

Rob: Oh, that makes sense. Thank you for explaining that. You just told me you hear tough news all the time. It sounds like that would be hard.

Hans: I guess.

Rob: Sometimes it helps to share the tough news with someone else. I am a counselor, Hans, and I talk to lots of kids about their tough news. Sometimes they feel better after we talk.

Hans: You're like Mr. Swan, our school counselor?

Rob: Yes, Mr. Swan and I are both counselors.

Hans: Mr. Swan is cool.

Rob: That's what I think too. I wonder if you would like to share your tough news with me or maybe with Mr. Swan some time.

Hans: My tough news isn't about Franco [pause]. It's about my mom [pause]. Dad says she might not come home.

Rob: [pause] That *is* tough news, Hans.

Hans: She said she was going to come home this weekend, but then I guess she changed her mind. We waited all weekend and everything. I told Dad I was going to make her a SpongeBob Valentine's Day card, and he said we wouldn't even have to mail it because I could give it to her when she comes home. I miss Mom. Dad says we need to be brave and that me and my brothers just have to be strong [starts to cry].

Rob: I'll bet you do miss your mom, Hans. You made a really nice card and thought you would be able to give it right to her yourself this weekend. It ended up that you couldn't do that because she didn't come. You're sad and disappointed.

Activities

1. Do research to compile a list of possible referral sources in your community for adolescents and children experiencing trauma or grief. Bring your lists to class, and discuss the resource lists with your peers.

2. Find out what the crisis plan for your school site currently is. Analyze its strengths and weaknesses and be prepared to discuss it in class.

3. The response by children and adolescents to traumatic events differs from that of adults. Think about the differences in discussing the teacher's death with a first-grade classroom compared to a sixth-grade classroom. Think about the words you would use when talking to six-year-olds versus 12-year-olds about the teacher's death.

Journal Reflections

Reflection #1
What resonates the most with you about managing a crisis in schools?

Reflection #2
To which kinds of crises will you be most comfortable responding? Least comfortable?

Reflection #3
Consider your own personal and professional characteristics in comparison with recommendations provided by James and Kanel.

Reflection #4
How will you prepare yourself so you are ready, willing, and able to effectively assess for the risk of suicide?

Electronic Resources

After a Suicide: A Toolkit for Schools: http://www.sprc.org/AfteraSuicideforSchools.asp

American Red Cross: http://www.redcross.org

American School Counselor Association: http://www.schoolcounselor.org

http://asca2.timberlakepublishing.com//files/PS_Crisis_Critical.pdf

Lessons Learned from the Shootings at Columbine High School: http://www.schoolcounselor.org/files/columbine.pdf

National Association of School Psychologists: http://www.nasponline.org/standards/2010standards/1_Graduate_Preparation.pdf

http://www.nasponline.org/resources/crisis_safety/terror_general.aspx

http://www.nasponline.org/prepare/curriculum.aspx

National Child Traumatic Stress Network National Center for PTSD: http://www.ptsd.va.gov/professional/manuals/manual-pdf/pfa/PFA_2ndEdition withappendices.pdf

National Organization for Victim Assistance: http://www.trynova.org/victim info/readings

National School Safety and Security Services: http://www.schoolsecurity.org/resources/scott_poland.html

Threat Assessment in Schools: http://www.secretservice.gov/ntac/ssi_guide .pdf

Print Resources

Heath, M., & Sheen, D. (2005). *School-based crisis intervention: Preparing all personnel to assist.* Practical Intervention in the Schools Series. New York: Guilford Press.

Lieberman, R., Poland, S., & Cassel, R. (2008). Suicide intervention in the schools. In A. Thomas & J. Grimes (Eds.), *Best practices in school psychology V* (pp. 1457–1473). Washington, DC: National Association of School Psychologists.

Lieberman, R., Poland, S., & Cowan, K. (2006, Oct.). Suicide prevention in the schools. *National Association of Secondary Principals Leadership, 7*(20), 11–15.

SECTION IV

Introduction to Section IV

> All change is a miracle to contemplate; but it is a miracle which is taking place every instant.
>
> Henry David Thoreau

In the final section of this book, we focus on the broad context of the school and how to maximize your efforts within this setting. Up to this point, we have emphasized the context of schools as well as the theories and techniques that you will use in your individual and small-group work with children and adolescents. However, these approaches reflect only one small component of your work within the schools. In order to affect the greatest number of students, you will want to consider other important aspects of your services. In this section, we address the broad issues of legal and ethical practice and issues of accountability. Specifically, we describe ways to incorporate evaluation practices into the services you provide. Throughout this text, we have attempted to refer to the ways that you will work with other adults in the students' lives. To this end, we strongly promote the development of collaborative relationships to maximize your influence in the school. Finally, we propose a new model of service delivery that promotes system-wide prevention and intervention at increasing levels of intensity and focus.

To highlight the need to develop collaborative relationships to serve higher-risk students, we provide you with a fictional school that represents a conglomeration of many of the current problems experienced in some school districts. That is, this is a school in which a number of students who attend experience high levels of risk. Rather than working together, the school staff feels overtaxed and unappreciated. They are unable to support one another. Further, the services that are available are fragmented, and the service providers compete for the limited resources and recognition that are available.

CASE ILLUSTRATION

From the outside, Marley Elementary School appears to be like any other elementary school. It has the same blocklike construction representative of elementary schools built in the 1960s. There is a playground with the requisite swings, tetherball poles, and jungle gym equipment. However, one glance around the surrounding neighborhood tells the casual observer that the school is not well situated. The houses in the surrounding neighborhood appear to be in need of repair. Some have cars on blocks in the front yards, and many have bars on their windows. During the day, there are always a number of men lounging in front yards as there is a high unemployment rate in this area.

Each day, the neighborhood children are escorted to school by their parents or older siblings. On any given day at Marley Elementary, 20 percent of children will be absent or tardy. Over the last three years, the students at this school have performed in the "not proficient" range on their statewide achievement tests. As a result, the state board of education is threatening to take over the school. The school leadership has attempted to bring positive change to the school, but these efforts are not supported because of the frequent turnover of staff.

Not only does the principal struggle with the poor academic achievement of students but also the chronic behavioral problems. Students routinely fight on the playground and in the halls. They do not seem to know how to behave at school, and it is a constant struggle to keep students on-task in the classroom. Many teachers are frustrated and have come to believe that the children in this school do not want to learn. Other teachers simply do not seem to care anymore, and students are not challenged on either academic tasks or regarding their misbehavior.

The school leadership team consists of the principal, vice principal, the school counselor, the part-time school social worker and school psychologist, three teachers who have been at the school for a long time, and one or two parents. Their most pressing issue is to raise student achievement. However, there is no consensus on the best strategy to pursue this goal. In meetings, deep divisions are apparent. The teachers do not feel supported and regularly voice their frustration with the community and the building leadership. The school professional helpers (i.e., school counselor, school psychologist, and school social worker) express their inability to help because of the time and effort they are each extending toward addressing crisis situations. The parents are angry that the school is not providing a better education to their children.

From this brief description, it is clear that this is a school in trouble. We have no easy answers for the school professional helpers who serve schools similar to Marley Elementary. However, we do believe that effective services, strategies that address the needs of youth at risk, a high degree of collaboration, and a systemic perspective represent the types of approaches that are needed to effectively serve those schools in which students experience a number of challenges.

CHAPTER 12

Legal and Ethical Issues in School Settings

Learning Objectives

- Understand the limits of confidentiality and how to handle situations within the school setting
- Learn strategies for documenting your work with student clients
- Apply a decision-making model to ethical dilemmas
- Participate in a supervision relationship and attain needed support and feedback

---

Within school settings, issues related to informed consent, confidentiality, privileged information, and parental rights complicate service delivery but also provide us with important guidelines that protect children and families. As a professional within the schools, you will need to know school policies plus the federal and state laws related to working with minors and families in school settings. Additionally, school-based professionals (e.g., school counselors, school psychologists) have ethical codes that guide their work with children, adolescents, families, and other personnel within the school (e.g., American

Counseling Association, 2010a; American Psychological Association, 2010; American School Counselor Association, 2010a; National Association of School Psychologists, 2010a). This review of ethical issues is not meant to be definitive or exhaustive. Rather, we highlight some of the most important aspects that relate to counseling work in the schools and how these might differ based on your particular discipline. (The full text of these ethical guidelines can be found at the websites listed at the end of this chapter.)

INFORMED CONSENT

One of the most important aspects of your work in schools is an understanding of who you can counsel and whether you need permission to do so. This broad area is referred to as *informed consent* and "means that a person giving consent has the legal authority to make a consent decision, a clear understanding of what it is he or she is consenting to, and that his or her consent is freely given and may be withdrawn without prejudice" (Dekraai, Sales, & Hall, 1998, p. 541). In this area, the ethical guidelines of school psychologists and school counselors differ, and so each professional will be identified as such to ensure clarity.

NASP Principles for Professional Ethics (2010a) state clearly that informed consent must be obtained from an individual who has the authority. Because children do not have legal authority prior to age 18, school psychologists must obtain informed consent and parental permission prior to working with a student in the school. As part of this consent, parents (or adult caregivers) are informed of the limits of confidentiality, other individuals within the school who will be provided with information (usually in relation to assessments), and the possible consequences of your work with the student client. Having provided all of this information, you obtain documentation of this consent. In order to provide informed consent, parents and students must be able to understand the information within the consent form and be able to make a rational decision related to this information (Salo, 2006).

In emergency situations or when a student self-refers, the school psychologist may assist a student client prior to obtaining informed consent from parents or caregivers. The school psychologist may see the student client "one or several" times to explore the situation and determine the nature of the student's concerns. If a student client is "a danger to others, at risk for self-harm, or there is a danger of injury, exploitation, or maltreatment," the individual may be seen by the school psychologist prior to receiving parental consent (NASP, 2010a, p. 4). You have the ability to explore the student client's concerns and rule out any of these conditions. After these preliminary meetings, you should obtain parental consent.

If a student client has been referred for your services by another individual (e.g., parent or teacher), it is important to obtain student assent. In those instances where the services are legally required or the services are considered to be a benefit to students, you do not necessarily need to obtain assent. If you do not obtain assent, students should at least be informed about the services that will be provided. When possible, students should be given a choice about whether they want to receive these services (NASP, 2010a). Further, if you are going to share information about a student client with a parent or outside agency, you should obtain the student's consent.

One of the gray areas in the practice of school psychology relates to the different circumstances when parent permission is not necessary. For example, if you observe in a classroom or consult with a teacher about a specific child, do you need to have parent permission to do so? In the most recent update of the ethical standards, NASP (2010a) clearly stated that permission is not required for these kinds of activities. However, they do recommend that districts include this information in their handbooks (e.g., teachers may consult with school psychologists for support around classroom management) so parents are not surprised if they learn that a teacher has been talking with a school psychologist about their child.

Within the *ASCA Ethical Standards* (2010a), school counselors are to make every effort to obtain informed consent from their student clients, but when it is not possible they can make those decisions on their behalf. The standards state that the "primary obligation of confidentiality is to the student." Consent from the student includes an agreement on the purposes and goals of counseling and well as the techniques and procedures. There does not appear to be a definite answer to the question of whether a school counselor is required to get permission from a student's parents or caregivers to engage in a counseling relationship. The ASCA standards (2010a) have described this obligation of confidentiality as being balanced with parent rights. The answer seems to vary depending on the age of the student, the type of counseling service provided, professional ethics of the specific profession, state law, and district policy (Davis, 2005).

Because the roles and functions of school counselors and school psychologists are so different, each profession has its own guidelines for compliance with informed consent. For example, school counselors may not need to meet the conditions of informed consent because their work is considered to be part of the scope and sequence of a school's curriculum (Remley & Herlihy, 2005). Glosoff and Pate (2002) noted that informed consent is best viewed as a process where initial information is provided globally through brochures, communications, and workshops directed toward parents, teachers, administrators, and students. Additionally, before talking to a student, a brief comment such as this is recommended: "What you say here will be kept between you and me, unless I learn that someone is hurting you or something unsafe is going on. Then I'll need to tell someone else." Glosoff and Pate described this issue as a "complex balancing act" involving the rights of the parents, an individual's expectation of confidentiality, and the legal responsibility of school systems.

As noted earlier, minors cannot legally give consent to receive counseling services (Welfel, 2006). However, school counselors must ensure that student clients are willing participants and involved in all aspects of decision making in the counseling relationship. Because school counselors also seek to involve parents as partners in their work to support the learning of children, some assert that it is best practice to obtain informed consent from parents (Davis, 2005). Also, as noted earlier, some schools have established policies regarding the provision of parental consent for individual or group counseling to students.

Muro and Kottman (1995) have suggested the use of a brochure or consent letter that outlines and explains confidentiality and its limits, as related to danger to self or others and reporting child abuse, in a manner that is easily understandable. A separate form may be developed for children or adolescents to help them understand their rights within the counseling setting. Other types of information included in this brochure or form would include the professional helper's education, training, degrees, and expected therapeutic method. It is also important to include information related to contacting the service provider and types of services (e.g., individual counseling, group counseling, or classroom activities) provided (Thompson & Henderson, 2007).

Once the parents have acknowledged that they have heard and understand their rights and those of their child within this counseling relationship, this creates a sort of contract that permits treatment. When formal informed consent is sought, parents are asked to sign documentation indicating that they have received this information. In all of your interactions with parents and students, the spirit of the law and ethical code is to ensure that they understand their rights and parameters within your work. We promote this mentality rather than a minimalist approach in which one simply attempts to meet the most basic requirements.

When students refer themselves for counseling without the knowledge or consent of their parents this can create a potential difficulty. If your district requires parental consent, they often have established policies so a professional helper may see a child one or two times to ensure that the child is not in danger of suicide. After that, if district policy or professional ethics requires it, formal parental consent must be obtained in order to maintain the counseling relationship.

STANDARD OF CARE AND DUTY TO WARN

When professional helpers enter into a counseling relationship, there are certain responsibilities or "duties" that they are expected to follow in a skillful and responsible manner, consistent with the standard of care maintained by others in their field. This somewhat ambiguous language basically means that when you present yourself as a professional helper (e.g., school counselor or school psychologist), you are expected to behave in a competent manner that is consistent with the standards of your profession. Furthermore, you accept that there are certain duties that you are legally and professionally required to perform such as protecting the welfare of a student client who is a danger to him or herself, informing others if a client is a danger to others, and reporting suspected child abuse.

When a student threatens him or herself, threatens others, or reports being abused, the plan of action is clear. The professional helper must complete an assessment of the situation and inform the appropriate parties. In Chapter 11, we provided an outline of the process for assessing a student's suicidal ideation. Many schools have established threat assessment guidelines that allow you to determine the degree of threat (e.g., specificity of the plan). Based on the level of threat, there are certain actions that should be taken. For example, if a younger person has made an explicit threat toward another named individual, the professional must warn that individual and his or her parents if the child is a minor. Additionally, the student who made the threat may be placed on a safety plan (e.g., backpack check in the morning, escorted to the restroom). The Secret Service and the Department of Education worked together to create an informative document, *Threat Assessment in the Schools* (Fein et al., 2002), that outlines an excellent process for identifying, assessing, and managing students who may pose a threat to others within the school environment.

In instances of child maltreatment, the appropriate authorities must be notified (e.g., Child Protective Services). If a professional helper has any reasonable suspicion that a minor has been physically, sexually, or emotionally abused or neglected, that individual has a legal duty to report this suspicion to the appropriate authority. Although the details and paperwork required vary by state and school district, there is a duty to inform.

When the presence of or potential for danger is vague, as when an adolescent reports considering a sexual relationship with her boyfriend or is experimenting with alcohol, the professional helper will want to consult with a supervisor or use an established ethical decision-making process to guide his or her actions. The laws related to these issues vary from state to state, and districts may place additional restrictions on the scope of information provided in these areas. Therefore, it is always important to have a thorough knowledge of state law and district policy beforehand so you will know how to respond to these unexpected disclosures.

ISSUES OF CONFIDENTIALITY IN THE SCHOOL

Maintaining the confidentiality of the student clients with whom you work is one of the most difficult aspects of work in the school. Professionals have the responsibility to protect the information that is gathered in the context of the therapeutic relationship but also the identity of those who seek counseling. How do students really retain their confidentiality when other students may see them entering your office? Other examples of limited confidentiality may occur when an office helper, who is frequently a student, sees that you're requesting to see a particular student, or teachers see you and a student walking together and talking. By virtue of your role in the school, in each of these cases, the assumption may be made that you have an established therapeutic relationship with that student.

For elementary-aged students, a trip to the school-based professional helper's office is generally not a problem. However, as students approach adolescence, there is often a great desire not to be seen as "different" from their peers, and a visit to the mental health office may be stigmatizing. For this reason, it is critical that professionals address this issue early on. For example, when introducing themselves to classrooms, professional helpers might note that they provide a variety of different services in addition to counseling (e.g., information regarding community resources, college scholarships, assistance with scheduling). Further, you may schedule appointments with students rather than sending a pass to their teachers. It is important to talk openly with students about the possibility that other students may question or tease them about coming to "see" the counselor. It might also be helpful to clarify how the student client would like to handle seeing one another in the halls. At the same time, the professional wants to work with students, teachers, and administrators to create an open atmosphere where seeking mental health support is not stigmatizing and school personnel are made aware of issues related to confidentiality.

The conversations that occur among students, families, and school-based professionals must be closely guarded within the school building. As one of the mental health professionals in the building, you will have access to a great deal of personal information about families and students. In your conversations with others, you must be especially aware of what information you have that is confidential, which information can be shared to benefit the student client, and how to politely but firmly refuse to provide information to those who are simply curious about what is going on with a particular student. Sometimes a teacher refers a particular student to you and then wants to follow up by asking about the presenting issues. Generally, this inappropriate probing is not malicious, but simply out of concern for the student, so it is important to try to understand the teacher's intentions. In the following excerpt, the school psychologist (SP) uses reinforcement and questioning to better understand a teacher's request for information, which allows her to decide the best way to respond.

Mrs. Smith, seventh-grade teacher:	I sent Braden down to you today because he just seemed "off." I wonder if something is going on with his family. He's been so quiet and moody. Did you learn anything?
SP:	Thank you for sending him down. That's great how you are so attentive to the needs of your students. It really shows that you care.
Mrs. Smith:	Well, I know when something's wrong. His family has really gone through a lot in the last year, but I thought everything had gotten stabilized. Did you talk to his mom?
SP:	Hmm, why do you ask?
Mrs. Smith:	Well, last year I had his older sister in my class, and their mom would come in and talk about some of the things that were going on at home. I really worry about that family.
SP:	I can see that. Well, again, thank you for letting me know about this situation. I'll follow up and see how the school can help. Let me know if you see any other changes in Braden's behavior, either for the better or the worse.

In this interchange, the school psychologist is respectful and reinforcing, yet does not relate any confidential information despite the teacher's questions. Of course, this type of conversation would occur in private. If the same type of interaction was initiated in a more public setting, the professional would need to redirect the conversation by asking to get together during the teacher's planning period. School-based professionals are not only required to protect the information shared with them but also can serve as role models for others on how to treat important confidential information. By doing so, professional helpers establish themselves as individuals who can be trusted with sensitive information. This may help in the future as teachers seek you out for support in working with challenging students or parents. They will know that you are someone who does not share or gossip with others.

One of the trickiest aspects of working with children and adolescents is establishing guidelines around confidentiality between parents and children. On one hand, you want an open working relationship with families, but on the other hand, you also recognize that sometimes students will not be as open around what is troubling them if they fear that their parents will find out (even if it is a seemingly benign issue). You'll be working with minors who can't typically own their own confidentiality; it is their parents. Under Family Educational Rights and Privacy Act (FERPA), also known as the Buckley Amendment, parents have the right to review educational records, expect confidentiality related to those records, and request amendments to educational records. It also means that if parents want see your notes from a session, they have a right to review these materials as they constitute educational records. Additionally, some parents want to know the contents of a counseling session, and they have a legal right to this information.

In my initial meetings with families, I (R.S.H.) explain the counseling relationship and that it works best when information is kept between the student client and the professional. I also reassure parents that if anything comes up that I believe is important for them to know, the student and I will together find a way to tell them. By discussing this openly with all members present, I establish that the student has some "right" to privacy but that the parents' needs for information will be respected. Additionally, providing ongoing general updates about the child's progress typically satisfies the parents' desire for information.

There are times when a student shares information that is so concerning that you will need to breach that student's confidentiality. When this occurs, it is usually best for the school-based professional to talk with the student about the need to do so and to seek input from the student client when deciding how best to proceed. The following vignette with Jessica and a school counselor (SC) provides an example of how this can be done while maintaining the therapeutic relationship with a student.

Jessica: I didn't want to come here today, but my friend, Sara, made me.

SC: Something very important is going on in your life right now, and your friend is concerned about you.

Jessica: She said if I didn't come to you, she'd come tell you herself (pause). I . . . I've been . . . I've been feeling really down lately, and well, I told her I wished I'd never been born (pause). It's been so difficult lately (softly crying).

SC: I'm glad you decided to come see me today, Jessica. There is so much going on in your life right now that you're really overwhelmed. You mentioned that you'd been feeling like it would be better if you hadn't been born. Sometimes kids who are struggling like this think about suicide. Jessica, are you thinking about killing yourself?

Jessica: Sort of, not very seriously though. But sometimes I think, well, what if I just walked out in front of this car or jumped off the roof of my apartment building. You know, just thinking about it as a possibility.

SC: That does seem like you've given it some thought. Have you ever attempted suicide before?

Jessica: No, I stood on the roof once before, but I couldn't do it. I just kept thinking that it might hurt (pause). I don't really want to die; I just want things to get better.

SC: Things are so bad right now, dying seems better than having them go on the same (pause). I'm concerned about the things we've talked about today and need to let you know that I'll have to tell your parents about our conversation. It's my responsibility to keep you safe. If you, your parents, and I sit down together, we can figure out how to help make things better and keep you safe until you're feeling better.

Jessica: My mom is going to freak out. She's known I've been down, and well, she used to be depressed. She's going to think it's all her fault.

SC: It is a difficult thing to talk about with your mom, especially when you think she might blame herself. You care about your mother and don't want to hurt her. Let's think about the best way to talk to her.

This abbreviated vignette illustrates how you can let students know that you will inform their parents or others about something they have shared in the counseling session. Ideally, you'll have met with a student beforehand to let him or her know the limits of confidentiality, either through specific informed consent or through the classroom presentations and brochures mentioned earlier. This brief example also highlights one of the most important responsibilities of counselors; namely, ensuring the safety of minors by reporting suicidal ideation or intention to a parent or guardian. In this case, the school counselor has the difficult task of building rapport very quickly with the student, assessing the degree of lethality in the student's suicidal ideation, and formulating the best plan that will keep the student safe, ensure that appropriate notification occurs, and maintain a therapeutic relationship.

The issue of "cutting" or self-harm by students is common and can be complex for school-based professionals to manage, especially in terms of confidentiality. Cutting falls into a gray area and is sometimes difficult to fit into the category of "clear and imminent danger" or "serious and forseeable harm." I (L.B.) consider the comments of our school district attorney when deciding whether to break confidentiality because of an incident of self-harm. The lawyer said, "It's sort of like calling a districtwide snow day. There are definite guidelines to consider, but five inches of snow is not always five inches of snow. Five inches with icy and windy conditions is different from five inches overnight with a forecast of warming temperatures by the time buses are rolling." In other words, there are other variables to consider. A student who has scraped her wrist with a paperclip is different from the student who used a razor blade to carve her boyfriend's initials into her arm.

DOCUMENTATION

The issue of what and when to document is also related to confidentiality. As with many aspects of the practice, there are varying opinions as to the degree of detail to record in your session notes. Some believe that a detailed account that notes the presenting issue, goals, and progress toward goals should be maintained. Others have noted that these records could be viewed by parents (according to FERPA) or subpoenaed and recommend brief notes related to student progress (Davis, 2005). We believe the student records you maintain should be useful to you and help you monitor student progress (e.g., subtle differences in appearance or affect), allow you to continue from the point where you left off in the previous meeting, and provide some degree of accountability related to your work.

As part of your own self-reflection, you might review your notes every few weeks to ensure that you're making progress with student clients, using counseling techniques that are appropriate and effective for a particular student, and being thoughtful from week to week in your services. It is easy to feel rushed in a school environment and to take shortcuts in the form of unplanned sessions, sketchy notes, and shortened meetings. A review of your notes allows you to recognize if this type of pattern is developing and to make appropriate changes.

Pre-service professionals often wonder what type of information should be documented from a session. Sometimes youth in conflict present with long, convoluted stories about their families, friends, or their own lives. Does everything need to be documented? What is the most important information to record? A couple of useful and commonly used techniques for recording sessions use the acronyms *SOAP* and *DAP*. *SOAP* stands for subjective (S), objective (O), assessment (A), plan (P) (Cameron & turtle-song, 2002). *DAP* notes represent a variation of SOAP, with the *D* representing data and reflecting a blend of subjective and objective information from the session.

One of the benefits of using this type of structured approach is that it provides a problem-solving format and helps to organize the professional's thinking about the student client's presenting concern (Cameron & turtle-song, 2002). If written with sufficient detail, the reason for selecting specific strategies will be clear from the subjective and objective components of the notes. The following example illustrates a session note featuring these elements.

Date   Progress Notes

1/8/10 **S.** Met with student for 30 minutes. Student indicated that he is feeling a lot of pressure around schoolwork (e.g., not sleeping at night, unable to relax, wanting to give up). He also noted worries about which colleges to attend and how to afford his education. Student would like to bring his grades up and begin to feel more at ease. Right now he describes his situation as "impossible."

O. Student appeared quite anxious and perhaps depressed. He rubbed his hands on the tops of his legs throughout our conversation. He also did not make eye contact

(Continued)

(Continued)

and did not appear to be as well groomed as usual (e.g., shirt untucked, hair not combed). At the end of the session, he appeared a bit more relaxed.

A. Student appears to be experiencing a great deal of stress related to schoolwork and future educational plans. This anxiety may be interfering with his sleep and result in his feeling tired and down. As an initial baseline, I asked the student to rate the level of anxiety he is experiencing (1 = relaxed, 10 = overwhelmed). He provided a rating of "7."

P. Next week, I plan to explore current stressors with the student. He also expressed interest in learning relaxation exercises that he can practice at home and in class. During the week, he will note those times when he feels most and least stressed.

In the subjective component of your notes, reflect information that the student client has told you. In your narrative, record the student's reported feelings, thoughts, plans, and goals, and the perceived intensity of the problem (Cameron & turtle-song, 2002). It is not necessary to record tangential details about the family or friends unless directly relevant to why the student is seeking counseling. It is also helpful to provide examples of the student's behaviors and define ambiguous terms. Although some have suggested leaving out names of specific individuals in one's case notes, I (R.S.H.) like to add the names of important friends, pets, or siblings so that I can incorporate these names into my sessions. Further, although you should include all pertinent information, your notes should be as brief and concise as possible (Cameron & turtle-song, 2002). You do not want the time spent maintaining session notes to cut into your direct service to students.

In the objective section, note your observations made of the student client during your session. How did she look? What was his affect like? Did her behavior stand out in any way? Did you observe any strengths? This section can also be a place to record the student's responses to the counseling process. In support of your observations, provide examples. For example, what did the student do to give you the idea that he or she was anxious, frustrated, or depressed? You should avoid language that sounds judgmental (e.g., *spoiled*, *needy*), or seems opinionated, or that reflects a label (e.g., *attachment disorder*, *antisocial*) (Cameron & turtle-song, 2002).

The assessment section is the place for you to record your thoughts about the student client's presenting issue or concern. In a clinical setting, you would be expected to provide a diagnosis; however, that is not appropriate in the schools. Instead, you should answer the question, "What do I think is going on with this student based on the information that he provided and what I observed during the session?" This section can also be a place to present your tentative hypothesis, but it should be noted as such. For example, in the sample case note presented earlier, if the counselor was worried about suicidal ideation because of the current situation, she might note, "Although no indication of suicidal ideation presently, given the student's level of distress and hopelessness, it will be important to watch for any signs." There is some debate as to whether these types of impressions should be included in progress notes or kept separate because they are only your personal thoughts or ideas. Cameron and turtle-song (2002) strongly recommended, as do we, keeping one set of notes in which you record both your assessment and your tentative impressions.

The last component of your notes, the plan section, should include your ideas about what interventions you want to use and toward which goals. In developing your plan, it is important that you work with student clients to ensure that these plans reflect their wishes as well. Consider using language that reflects this collaboration. If you assign "homework" during the week, this is also an important place to include that information so that you remember to check with the student about the "assignment." As your work with a student client continues, you should record his or her progress toward stated goals.

Your written notes serve as documentation of your professional work with a student client. It is best to write your notes right after a session in order to assure the most accuracy possible. You should also record attempts to see a student, contact with a parent, and if appropriate, contacts with outside agencies in regard to a particular student. All of this information should be kept in a locked file cabinet. As an alternative, many school-based professionals keep their records in electronic format. In this case, you should make sure that you do not leave notes on your computer screen when you are not in your office. Be sure to close the file and log out of your computer. Your computer should be password protected so that others in the school cannot access your files.

Even though the likelihood is that you will be the only person to see your notes, you should use appropriate grammar and spelling. If by some chance your notes are subpoenaed, they should reflect your professionalism. If you make an error while writing your notes, use a single line to cross out the error, initial, and write in the corrected information. This practice indicates that you are not trying to "cover up" any information, only to ensure accuracy and clarity. Your notes should be typed or written in ink so that they are legible. Finally, sign your notes with your full name. If you are being supervised, you will also want your supervisor to review and sign your notes.

DUAL RELATIONSHIPS

Because of the unique role of school-based professionals, it is important that these individuals maintain clear boundaries between their professional role and other roles in their lives (Davis, 2005). This type of separation is much easier said than done. School-based professionals sometimes serve as advisors of student groups or coaches within their schools. These activities increase the chances that you may end up working with a student who you have seen or will see. When a school-based helper works and lives in the same town, the chances for bumping into students and their parents in the community is quite high. If you live in a rural community, it will be virtually impossible to maintain a strict boundary between professional and personal roles.

In all instances, a reasonable policy is to maintain the clearest boundary possible and to communicate clearly with all parties involved as to your role in certain settings. As long as you are open and honest with students and families regarding the potential issues, you have taken steps to reduce the potential for harm. If for whatever reason, the school-based professional cannot maintain objectivity (e.g., student is the child of a close friend or relative, student assaulted your child who attends the same school), it is critical that the student be referred to another mental health professional (e.g., school psychologist, school counselor) in the school or district or to an outside agency.

ETHICAL DECISION-MAKING MODELS

When faced with an ethical dilemma, it is not always easy to determine the best course of action. There are many factors to consider, and no one answer may seem like the best course of action. In these instances, it is important that mental health professionals have a clear understanding of law related to the issue, their professional ethics, and the school or district policy. When the law is clear on an issue, that tells us how we must act (e.g., reporting child abuse). Generally, the same is true for district policy, unless it clearly violates legal or ethical guidelines.

However, sometimes we need to make decisions based purely on our ethical guidelines, which often have vague or ambiguous language. According to the ASCA's *Ethical Standards for School Counselors* (2010a), a school counselor might follow a decision-making format such as the Solutions to Ethical Problems in Schools (STEPS; Stone, 2001, as cited in ASCA 2010a) protocol described here.

Solutions to Ethical Problems in Schools (STEPS)

1. Define the problem emotionally and intellectually
2. Apply the ASCA *Ethical Standards* and the law
3. Consider the students' chronological and developmental levels
4. Consider the setting, parental rights, and minors' rights
5. Apply the moral principles
6. Determine your potential courses of action and their consequences
7. Evaluate the selected action
8. Consult
9. Implement the course of action

Other models of ethical decision making exist, but most recommend similar components. Sileo and Kopala (1993) provided an easy to remember framework for ethical decision making with their A-B-C-D-E strategy.

A: Assessment—the professional helper considers all aspects of the situation, including those of the client as well as him or herself.
B: Benefit—the professional helper evaluates which course of action is likely to be the most beneficial to the client and others who might be involved (e.g., family members).
C: Consequences and Consultation—the professional helper considers all of the possible consequences associated with different courses of action. Additionally, he or she consults with a supervisor or more experienced professional to discuss these components.
D: Duty—the professional helper must consider to whom he or she is professionally responsible. In most instances this will be the student client, but in some instances

(Continued)

(Continued)

this may lie with another individual as in a situation of needing to warn another individual of pending harm.

E: Education—the professional helper considers his or her education related to the particular issue and refers to texts, notes, and professional ethics to assist in decision making.

At first you will likely need to work through these steps frequently. However, with experience and consistent supervision from a knowledgeable supervisor or mentor, these types of decisions will become more automatic.

COMPETENCY AND SUPERVISION

Competency

As is clear from the previous discussion, a school-based professional can never know the best course of action in all situations. Recognizing this reality leads us to our next two sections that address competency and the need for ongoing supervision. Generally speaking, a competent school-based helper has a solid understanding of child development and family systems, and is skilled in the use of a variety of intervention strategies consistent with his or her theory (Neill, Holloway, & Kaak, 2006). Once you graduate and obtain the appropriate certification or licensure, you are considered to be qualified for your position in the schools but not necessarily competent to address every situation that arises. The ethical guidelines of all school-based professionals stress the importance of possessing and maintaining competency. You may be well-prepared, having received high grades in all of your courses and the highest rating on your internship evaluation, yet you will encounter children, adolescents, and families that present unique issues for which you feel unprepared. Students with any number of issues (e.g., substance abuse, pregnancy, acculturation struggles, questions about sexual orientation) may approach you as the professional within the school who can provide support.

Obviously in your first few years of practice, you cannot expect to be an expert in every one of these areas. On the other hand, you cannot refer every student who presents with a concern that you have not specifically addressed before. There are no clear markers that define competence. A general guideline for identifying yourself as having competency in a specific area is that you have had training or supervision on that issue. Without this type of training, you should consult with or be supervised by someone who has had the appropriate training or supervised experience. You should definitely refer a student who presents with an issue that is beyond the scope of your training, requires ongoing clinical intervention, or has a serious issue that cannot be adequately addressed in the schools (e.g., long history of sexual abuse, severe mental illness) (ASCA, 2010a).

Throughout your career, it is important that you monitor yourself, consult with peers, gather additional information through reliable resources, and obtain ongoing supervision as appropriate. Beyond that, if you are performing a specialized skill or therapeutic intervention (e.g., play therapy, eye movement desensitization and reprocessing [EMDR], dialectical behavior therapy [DBT]), it would be expected that you have completed the additional training requirements and obtained additional certification or licensure as appropriate. As a professional, competency is also defined as keeping up with current research and continuing to grow in your level of knowledge and expertise. We hope you will always be engaged in learning new skills. Additionally, competency means monitoring your emotional and physical health and maintaining wellness (ASCA, 2010a) in order to maximize your effectiveness with student clients. As a part of your ongoing growth, it is likely that you will seek supervision on and off throughout your career.

Supervision

You may have encountered your first clinical supervisor during a counseling skills class or counseling practicum. You will probably have, or did have, a site clinical supervisor as well as a university-based supervisor during your internship. Requirements for postdegree supervision of school-based professionals are regulated by state departments of education and vary from state to state. Regardless of the requirements in your state, we strongly recommend that you become intentional in finding supervisors who will support you during your initial years and challenge your continued growth. We encourage professionals in all sectors to become lifelong learners and to avail themselves of supervision across their professional lifespan.

For university-based practica, one person is usually responsible for administrative and clinical aspects of supervision. The administrative component is focused on agency requirements and procedures, attendance, punctuality, and so forth. Clinical supervision is focused on basic skills, advanced skills, enacting counseling, promoting change, and so forth. In a school setting, principals usually assume responsibility for the administrative supervision. Unfortunately, clinical supervision is often neglected in schools.

Our focus is on clinical supervision. And what is that? Supervision specialists Bernard and Goodyear (2004) captured the essence of clinical supervision by referring to it as

> an intervention provided by a more senior member of a profession to a more junior member or members of that same profession. This relationship (a) is evaluative; (b) extends over time; and (c) has the simultaneous purposes of enhancing the professional functioning of the more junior person(s), monitoring the quality of professional services offered to the clients that she, he, or they may see, and serving as a gatekeeper for those who are to enter the particular profession. (p. 8)

These authors have endorsed the importance of supervision by suggesting that it is "a means of transmitting the skills, knowledge, and attitudes of a particular profession to the next generation in that profession" (2004, p. 2). Other authors have contended that "supervisors are potentially the most critical element of optimal internship experiences that become the apex of a trainee's course of study" (Magnuson, Black, & Norem, 2001, p. 5).

Excellent supervision does not occur accidentally (Magnuson, Wilcoxon, & Norem, 2000). Supervisors ground their work in their own training, supervision of supervision, and continuing education. Like counseling, there is an art and science of supervision; these two factors complement as well as inform one another. Thus, supervisors draw from theories of supervision as they work with supervisees. They also adhere to codes of ethics specific to supervision. They demonstrate excellence as counselors and supervisors and inspire supervisees. They facilitate development of a relationship that is conducive to the growth for supervisees.

Supervisors engage in three primary roles: teacher, consultant, and counselor (Bernard & Goodyear, 2004). As teachers, supervisors provide information and instruction. As consultants, supervisors provide guidance related to clients and supervisees' work with them. As counselors, they invite supervisees to focus on their own experiences as they work with clients. Of course counseling in this sense is qualitatively and significantly different from counselors' work with clients; a therapeutic relationship between a supervisor and supervisee is always unethical.

Evaluation may be subtle and informal, for example, when feedback is given upon review of case notes. It may be formal and structured, such as when final written evaluation is given at the end of the semester or prior to endorsement for a credential. However it is framed, evaluation is a constant component of supervision.

Responsibilities associated with supervision are multiple and daunting. Supervisors' first and foremost responsibility is to protect clients or students and society at large. Additionally, they are accountable to supervisees. They are accountable to supervisees' present and future clients. They are accountable to agencies, schools, or universities within which they work.

Although supervisors have primary responsibilities for structuring and enacting supervision, supervisory relationships are characterized by reciprocity and mutuality. Supervisees *may* have more influence regarding the experience and outcomes than supervisors. Supervisees can empower themselves by becoming informed consumers of supervision (see suggested articles provided in the resource section of this chapter). They can also participate in ways that have been shown to contribute to successful outcomes and avoid actions that have been shown to be detrimental.

Research addressing supervisees' contributions to the success of supervision is limited. Authors of one article, based on data collected during interviews with 12 seasoned supervisors, concluded that supervisees who were considered outstanding reflected a constellation of attributes (Norem, Magnuson, Wilcoxon, & Arbel, 2006). Stellar supervision outcomes and optimal counselor development corresponded with mature, autonomous supervisees who were self-aware, open to experience, motivated, and perspicacious. Rather than manifesting as separate personality components, the attributes became interdependent and synergistic. The authors concluded that

> being open to experience (other points of view and feedback) may be
> an important characteristic that allows supervisees to benefit from
> experience by gaining increased knowledge of other perspectives and
> by reinforcing an acceptance of other points of view. The confidence
> and independence gained from experience may contribute to comfort
> with taking risks and receiving feedback from supervisors. Similarly,
> qualities associated with wisdom (e.g., empathy, acute perception, dis-
> cernment, sound judgment, deep understanding, intuition, and insight)

may contribute to learning from life experiences, as well as being enhanced by life experiences. (p. 46)

These authors also examined supervisees' contributions to unsatisfactory supervision outcomes (Wilcoxon, Norem, & Magnuson, 2005). Again, supervisees' contributions were not described as one characteristic or attribute. Rather, *combinations* of behaviors, attitudes, perspective, and knowledge seemed to result in difficult supervisory relationships and unsatisfactory outcomes. The authors concluded that impeding factors related to limitations in four interactional categories: (a) interpersonal development (e.g., unresolved personal issues or fearful of change), (b) intrapersonal development (e.g., lack of sensitivity, unable to grasp client's perspective, unwilling to accept feedback), (c) cognitive development (e.g., lack of cognitive complexity, unable to conceptualize, rigid), and (d) counselor development (e.g., limited motivation for learning, limited skills and knowledge base, unwilling to grow and change).

As you continue through your professional career, we encourage you to be informed and active consumers of supervision. When supervision does not seem beneficial, we also encourage you to visit with your supervisor and let him or her know what you believe would help you grow professionally.

Activities

1. Compare the ethical codes of your profession to those of another profession.

2. Create a brochure describing the legal and ethical guidelines of your specific discipline (e.g., confidentiality, informed consent) and your services in parent-friendly language.

3. Use either the STEPS or A-B-C-D-E decision-making model to work through the following vignette.

The principal has asked you to see Ceri, a 14-year-old student, who has been falling asleep in class, is not turning in her schoolwork, and doesn't appear to have any friends. Her attendance is generally good, except she has a lot of early morning tardies. She comes to your office with her face heavily made up, a short skirt, and numerous bracelets on her wrists. Rapport is not easy to establish with Ceri as she is very guarded. When you ask her about falling asleep in class, she will only say that she can't sleep at night. Over the half hour, she does warm up a bit and begins to tell you a little bit about her life. She lives alone with her father and was removed from her mother's home when she was quite young because her mom "was a drunk." When you suggest that you'd like to continue counseling with Ceri, she begrudgingly agrees. When you mention that you will need to get her father's permission to continue seeing her, she seems frightened and asks you not to tell him that she talked to you. Instead, she asks that you keep seeing her and promises not to tell her father. District policy requires you to obtain parental permission. You're worried about Ceri and want to continue counseling with her because you are concerned that she may be having serious problems at home.

Journal Reflections

Reflection #1
  What ethical or legal situations concern you the most?

Reflection #2
  As a novice practitioner, consider some of the events that you have experienced over the last few weeks. Which aspects were made more difficult simply because of your inexperience?

Electronic Resources

ACA Code of Ethics: http://www.counseling.org/Resources/CodeOfEthics/TP/Home/CT2.aspx

APA Ethical Principles of Psychologists and Code of Conduct: http://www.apa.org/ethics/code/index.aspx

ASCA Ethical Standards for School Counselors: http://www.schoolcounselor.org/files/EthicalStandards2010.pdf

NASP Principles for Professional Ethics: http://nasponline.org/standards/2010standards/1_%20Ethical%20Principles.pdf

Threat Assessment in Schools: A Guide to Managing Threatening Situations and Creating Safe School Climates: http://www.secretservice.gov/ntac/ssi_guide.pdf

Print Resources

Gibbon, M. M., & Spurgeon, S. L. Applying the American School Counseling Association Ethical Standards. In J. R. Studer & J. F. Diambra, *A guide to practicum and internship for school counselors-in-training* (pp. 147–157). New York: Routledge.

Magnuson, S., Norem, K., & Wilcoxon, A. (2002). Clinical supervision for licensure: A consumer's guide. *Journal of Humanistic Counseling, Education, and Development, 41,* 52–60.

Skovholt, T. M., & Trotter-Mathison, M. (2011). *The resilient practitioner: Burnout prevention and self-care strategies for counselors, therapists, teachers, and health professionals* (2nd ed.). New York: Routledge.

Smith Harvey, V., & Struzziero, J. (2008). *Professional development and supervision of school psychologists: From intern to expert.* Thousand Oaks, CA: Corwin.

CHAPTER 13

Accountability in School-Based Services

Learning Objectives

- Understand the different levels of accountability: child and program
- Design simple evaluation forms to track effectiveness of an intervention
- Learn strategies for program evaluation

Anyone who has watched the news, stepped inside a schoolhouse, or taken a class in his or her respective field has heard the word *accountability*. It is a word that is tossed around repeatedly but one that holds many different meanings. Some believe accountability lies in how a child performs on a single test, whereas others view accountability as upholding one's responsibility through a broad range of actions. We advocate for the latter interpretation and provide a number of ways that school mental health professionals can demonstrate accountability to students, teachers, families, administrators, and their professions.

There are many reasons for the current push toward accountability. As the cost of education has risen, the American public has expected to see a rise in student achievement. Unfortunately, this has not been the case. Comparisons between the academic scores of American youth and those of students in other countries have suggested that the United States is losing ground. Additionally, highly publicized cases in which high school graduates proclaim their inability to read or to have mastered other basic skills have focused the public's attention on the quality of education provided in public schools.

This emphasis on accountability has not been isolated to the educational system; it has spread to other fields as well. The professional organizations for school counseling and school psychology have intensified their focus on implementing evidence-based practices and demonstrating the effectiveness of their programs and their work with students (ASCA, 2005). ASCA has summarized this endeavor into one essential question: "How are students different as a result of the school counseling program?" (ASCA, 2005, p. 59). To best answer this question, school-based professionals must provide reports of immediate program results as well as longer-term outcomes. Further, all helpers must carefully audit their programs to ensure that all standards are met.

There are also pragmatic reasons for demonstrating the effectiveness of one's work. With fewer resources available to meet the needs of more people, we need to know that the ways that we spend our time and energy are resulting in positive outcomes. Further, we need to demonstrate this effectiveness to others in specific and measurable ways.

WHAT DOES IT MEAN TO BE ACCOUNTABLE?

In the broadest sense, accountability refers to being responsible for one's actions and the ability to explain those actions or decisions. In the field of education, this responsibility has been translated into the practice of holding teachers and administrators liable for student learning by linking school ratings and subsequent funding to students' demonstrated progress. Although the main responsibility in education has been placed on teachers, those who work within the schools and provide services are also expected to demonstrate accountability.

We also demonstrate accountability by responding to phone messages in a timely manner, following through on all commitments, assisting colleagues when opportunities arise, and so forth. Seemingly "small things" make large impressions.

Not only are there different levels of accountability (child level and program level), there are also different methods for demonstrating a desired outcome. For example, there is the formal accountability in which professional helpers gather data to demonstrate positive change as a result of an intervention. On the other hand, there are less-formal methods of determining the effectiveness of one's work. This type of informal data collection might include talking with school staff, classroom observations, or "check-ins" with the students and their families. It can be difficult and time consuming to document every change that occurs as a result of your efforts; for that reason it is best to pick out a few key areas where you spend the majority of your time. In collecting data, you'll want to focus on both formal and informal measures.

FORMAL MEASURES OF EFFECTIVENESS

When documenting the effects of an intervention, you are basically trying to show how the student's behavior differs as a result of your services. There are two key components in this statement. Has the student's behavior changed? If so, is the change related to your intervention?

The first question is much easier to answer than the second. For example, a student may demonstrate a positive change in behavior, but was it because she matured? In a given period of time, a child might begin seeing you individually, join the afterschool karate club, and start spending more time with his parents. Which one of these actions resulted in the positive outcome? Practically speaking, we might think, "Who cares?" After all, the student is performing better. On one hand, it may not matter because, after all, the goal is for children to demonstrate improved adaptation to their environments. On the other hand, if we can never really demonstrate that *our* efforts make a difference, it is too easy for others to dismiss the importance of those efforts when critical funding, staffing, and resource decisions are made.

Pre- and Postmeasures

As noted previously, changes in student behavior can be measured either formally or informally. Your outcome measure should be aligned with the goals that you established with the student in your group or individual counseling relationship. For example, if a student expressed the goal of bringing his grades up and "not getting in so much trouble," you could measure the student's GPA from one semester to the next and compare the number of office referrals during that same time frame. Sometimes counseling goals are more difficult to measure. In another example, you may be working with a very shy student who would like to "have more friends." In that instance, how would you know if another student had become a friend? How do you define a "friend"? In this example, you might want to observe the student and note the number of times she approaches other students and initiates conversations or observe the number of playground interactions to determine whether they increase during the time that you are counseling the student.

The two techniques just described entail a simple pre- and postmeasure to determine the frequency that a student performed certain behaviors prior to counseling and the degree to which she is performing them at the end of counseling (or at various points during the counseling relationship). There are a couple of disadvantages to this relatively simple method of evaluation. The professional is not able to fully determine why the change happened, only that it did happen. Additionally, because this type of strategy is often used with individual and small-group counseling, the professional helper is unable to determine the statistical significance of the change. That is, the change may not be "real."

Sometimes we may see an increase or decrease in our targeted behavior. Before we either celebrate or start looking for a new program, we need to decide whether the change is large enough to indicate that real change has occurred. Alternatively, is it a minor fluctuation? While we are not necessarily encouraging you to engage in sophisticated statistical tests to determine the significance levels of each of your interventions, we introduce a few easy models that can be implemented to help you determine whether your outcomes have "clinical significance." That is, have these interventions resulted in real, meaningful change?

Single-Case Designs

Single-subject or small-N designs have long been recognized as an empirical method for evaluating change in individuals (McDougall & Smith, 2006). In fact, The Council for Exceptional Children has promoted the idea that single-case research design is an appropriate model to use in school settings to evaluate the effectiveness of interventions (Odom et al., 2005). As you are developing your evaluation model, keep in mind that the degree of structure and control present in your evaluation design helps you decide on the amount of confidence that you place in your findings. There are a variety of strategies for carrying out single-case studies that help you focus on the outcomes of your intervention and minimize interference from other sources. Unfortunately, in a school setting, strict adherence to experimental design can be difficult if not impossible.

Three commonly used strategies in single-case design include the case study (AB), a reversal design (ABAB), and multiple-baseline designs (Brown-Chidsey & Steege, 2005). It might be easiest to understand these different models within the context of a case vignette. Let's apply each one to our intervention with Gina, a sixth-grade student who is struggling in math. During class, she does not perform well on assignments or tests. She reports feeling very anxious during tests and is unable to remember what she has studied. Additionally, on a daily basis, her behavior is frequently off-task, and she tends to make loud comments, tell jokes, and generally disrupt the classroom. Together, you set three goals related to this problem area: (a) improve her grade in math, (b) feel less anxious during math tests, and (c) improve her behavior in math class.

The most straightforward of the three is the simple case study in which *A* refers to a student's performance prior to intervention and *B* to the student's behavior after the intervention (e.g., counseling) has been implemented for a period of time. In an AB design, the student's performance is measured prior to the intervention. This period of data collection is referred to as the baseline condition. Please note that in some of the graphs provided, we have provided a single point as the baseline in order to simplify the presentation of our data. After the intervention has been implemented, the targeted behavior is measured frequently to determine whether the resulting behavior approaches the desired outcomes. Kazdin (1998) has argued that a case could be made that outcomes are linked to the intervention if the following conditions were met: (a) accurate measures were used, (b) consistent conditions for sampling behavior were used, (c) the intervention was implemented as proposed, (d) and the behavior changed immediately (or nearly so) after implementing the intervention.

> Set SMART goals. That is, goals should be specific, measurable, achievable, realistic, and timed.

We might use this model to determine whether our intervention helps Gina increase her math completion during class. The teacher records the number of math assignments that are given each week and the percentage of these that are completed by Gina. For now, we are not going to look at accuracy; we will simply track assignment completion, which is defined as a paper that is turned in on time with the majority of questions attempted. The vertical line on our chart defines the point at which our intervention was started.

Figure 13.1 Simple graph showing Gina's math completion prior to intervention (Week 1) and after intervention (Weeks 2–7)

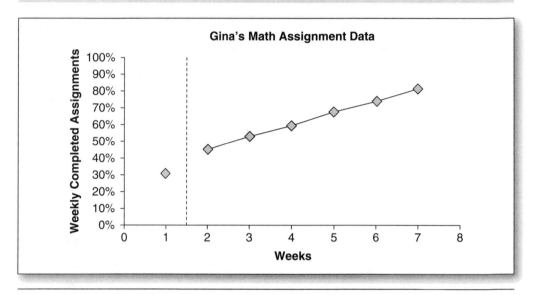

Goal Statement: Gina will increase her weekly math assignment completion to at least 80% each week.

A weakness of a simple case study is that we can never be sure whether the change occurred as a result of our intervention. The second model is the reversal design (ABAB) wherein a student's behavior is measured prior to intervention and then again after intervention has been implemented for a period of time. In the ABAB design, the second *A* indicates that you remove the intervention to determine whether the behavior returns to previous levels. If the student's behavior drops to the previous baseline or near baseline levels, the intervention is implemented again. If the behavior goes up and down in accordance with the intervention (e.g., more behavioral problems when there is no intervention and fewer problems when the intervention is in place), the professional helper can say with confidence that the intervention is contributing positively to the student's behavioral change.

Although a within-series replication (ABAB designs) with high experimental control yields results in which you could place a great deal of confidence, many school-based professionals tend to be satisfied with the simpler design. If an intervention has been working well, very few school-based professionals want to relinquish success for scientific rigor!

In our previous example, we implemented a strategy with Gina to assist her with assignment completion. Perhaps we have also created an intervention plan to help her improve her on-task behavior. Because you believe that many of her outbursts are related to anxiety and task avoidance, you and Gina work on relaxation techniques and positive self-talk during your counseling sessions. You blend these techniques with a behavioral intervention where Gina can "earn" a free pass from one of her math assignments that is worth 20 points or less. She must increase her weekly on-task behavior to 75 percent or higher in order to earn a free pass. The following figure shows hypothetical data regarding Gina's response to this intervention. The intervention (i.e., the free pass) is removed and then implemented again. There are some interventions that you cannot undo, such as relaxation training. However, it is clear from this graph that relaxation training without reinforcement is not sufficient at this point to help her achieve her goal.

As noted, this approach may not be popular in the schools. Further, withholding counseling to determine whether it is having a positive effect would not be appropriate. However, if you wanted to determine whether a certain intervention or technique that is implemented outside the counseling relationship was effective, this might be a strategy to use.

A variation on this type of design is to introduce one intervention and then add a second one and see whether it makes a difference. For example,

Figure 13.2 Graph showing ABAB design for Gina's on-task behavior

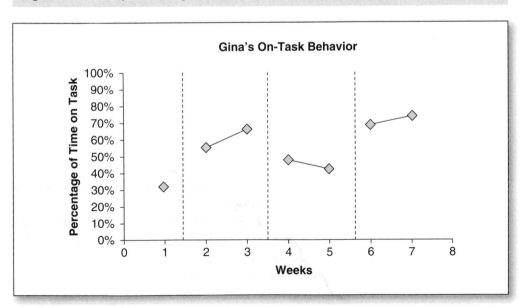

Goal Statement: Gina will increase her on-task behavior during math class to 75% of the time during weekly 20-minute observations.

perhaps Gina has shared that her anxiety during testing is one of her biggest concerns. She does not feel well when she has an upcoming test, she worries that she will do something embarrassing (e.g., throw up), and she forgets everything that she has studied. Although it is possible that with the relaxation strategies she has learned, she may be able to manage her stress in this situation, you also introduce self-talk techniques that are specific to math. Together, you and Gina decide that you want to evaluate whether these self-talk strategies are necessary in addition to the relaxation techniques.

First, you gather baseline data on her reported level of anxiety during the weekly quizzes that her teacher gives during math. Gina routinely rates her anxiety at a 9 or 10 during the first three weeks. During your initial meetings with her, you help her to learn relaxation strategies, and she begins to report a slight decrease in her anxiety, perhaps around a 7 or 8. Next, you help her to write and rehearse positive self-talk related to math tests. Gina again records her level of anxiety using both strategies (i.e., relaxation and positive self-talk). If her ratings of anxiety decrease even further, you might conclude that using both strategies together works best for her. However, by returning to the first condition (relaxation only) and gathering additional data, you can be more confident in your findings. If her anxiety returns to previous levels (in the first condition B), then it is likely that the self-talk is helping. If her anxiety levels remain low, it may be that she is better at implementing her relaxation strategies and does not need to engage in the self-talk. Of course, one of the potential drawbacks of this approach is that you may not be able to fully "remove" the positive self-talk strategy. Although Gina may not report actively using positive self-talk, it is possible that she is more aware of the messages she gives herself prior to tests and does not engage in negative self-talk. In this example, you may not have a definitive answer to which strategy worked best for her, but you have effectively helped Gina to reduce her anxiety. Additionally, you have evidence to suggest that it is your intervention that is creating the change rather than another variable in the environment.

Another model for measuring the effectiveness of an intervention within single-case design is through the use of multiple baselines. This strategy is especially useful because it does not require the withdrawal of an intervention that appears to be working. In this model, the connection between the intervention and the positive outcome is replicated by implementing the intervention across several responses, people, or settings. It is most commonly used across different students.

For example, perhaps you are working with a group of kindergarten-age students, teaching them problem-solving skills using the Social Skills Intervention System (Elliot & Gresham, 2008). In group, the students appear to be making gains, but the classroom teacher is still concerned at the level of aggression shown by these students. You decide to work with the teacher to add a behavior warning system (e.g., green, yellow, red cards) to help them understand when their behaviors are on track and when they are violating the established classroom rules. You implement it with each student at different start times (e.g., one–two-week intervals) in order to evaluate whether the students' behaviors change when this additional component is added to the intervention. The resulting graph shows that each student in the group made gains after the additional behavioral program was implemented. While three of the students demonstrated reduced levels of aggression in response to the new program, one student (Student #2) demonstrated initial gains but then began showing higher rates of aggression.

Determining Clinical Significance

When we conduct one of these single-case studies, how do we know if the result is meaningful? A student's behavior might have changed a little, but was it enough? Scruggs (1992) described the relatively simple technique called percentage of nonoverlapping data (PND) to determine the effectiveness of an intervention in a single-case design. To carry out this technique, the school-based helper collects data during the baseline condition before any intervention has been implemented. In Gina's case, let's simplify this example by just selecting one goal—to improve her behavior in class. During the course of the week, we would observe (or have the teacher note) the number of times that Gina blurts out jokes or wisecracks (targeted behavior) in a given class period.

As noted previously, a baseline should contain at least three data points. Once we have our baseline, we choose the highest or lowest point (in the expected direction of the intervention effect). Using the information in Figure 13.2, only one data point is used to depict her average level of on-task behavior. For this example, Gina was on-task 32 percent of the time on Monday, 28 percent of the time on Wednesday, and 26 percent on Friday. During her highest level of performance, she was on-task for 32 percent of the time in her math class, and this percentage constitutes our starting point. The goal of our intervention is to increase the percentage of time that she is observed to be on-task during her math class. Once we have this data, in a table, we draw a line parallel to the abscissa that extends into the intervention phase.

Figure 13.3 Graph showing multiple baseline data

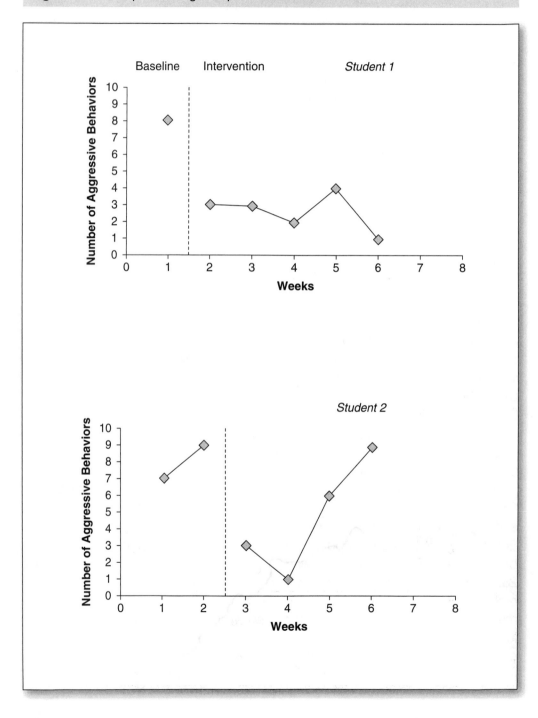

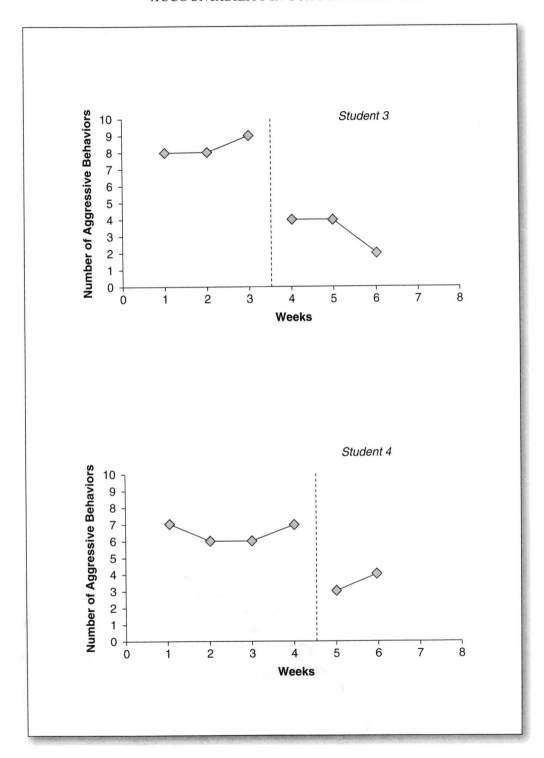

Figure 13.4 Graph showing percentage of nonoverlapping data (PND) for Gina's on-task behavior

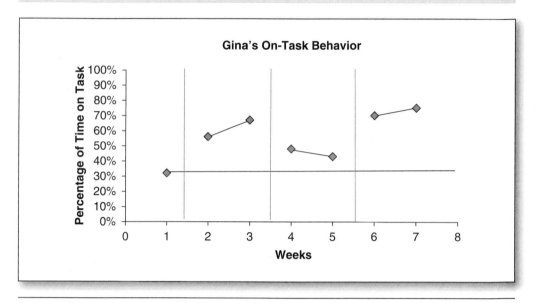

Goal Statement: Gina will increase her on-task behavior during math class to 75% of the time during weekly 20-minute observations.

Observation: Gina's on-task behavior was above her baseline 100% of the time during the 20-minute weekly observations suggesting both the relaxation training and "free pass" intervention were somewhat effective. As noted, the condition with the relaxation training only (Weeks 4–5) resulted in slightly better performance than her baseline. The relaxation training combined with a "free pass" (Weeks 6–7) appeared to help Gina reach her goal.

Regardless of our design (e.g., AB, ABAB, or multiple baseline), we will continue to collect data on Gina's on-task behavior during her math class. In our example, we specified observation data, but there are a variety of ways to measure a student's behavior: self-report, teacher report, or intermittent observation by yourself or a teacher's aide. Using the percentage of time that she is on-task during a weekly observation, we plot her data on a graph. By examining where the data points fall (above or below) in relation to the target line, it helps us to know if our intervention is working. To determine the effectiveness of the intervention, simply count the number of data points that are above 32 percent (Gina's best performance during baseline).

In our example, Gina had 6 data points above the line. This number is divided by the total number of intervention points (all data points), which in this example was also 6, for a score of 1. This number is multiplied by 100.

This statistic provides the percentage of intervention points that do not overlap with baseline points (Bonner & Barnett, 2004), or the percentage of time that Gina was performing at a level better than her baseline performance. Scores above 85 percent suggest a highly effective intervention, and scores between 65 percent and 85 percent suggest a moderately effective intervention. Scores between 50 percent and 65 percent would have questionable effectiveness (Bonner & Barnett, 2004; Scruggs & Mastropieri, 1998).

Goal Attainment Scaling

Some behaviors are more difficult to monitor than others. If you want to monitor multiple goals, the processes described earlier can become quite complex. Kiresuk, Smith, and Cardillo (1994) developed a method for evaluating counseling outcomes called goal attainment scaling (GAS). Using this technique, the professional helper and the student establish one to five goals collaboratively. Next, they decide which goals are most important to the student and weigh the goals accordingly. For example, of the three goals Gina has established, her most important goal is to reduce the anxious way she feels when she is taking a math quiz or test because she believes that is why she is getting a poor grade. Her next most important goal is improving her grade and finally, improving her behavior. The relative weights assigned to each goal should add up to 100. In this example, Gina provides a weight of 60 to anxious feelings, 30 to improved grade, and 10 to improved behavior.

An additional step includes creating five levels of attainment for each goal. These levels of attainment are assigned a value from –2 to +2 based on the student's expectations of worst possible outcome to best possible outcome. A *0* is assigned to the student's expected level of success. See Table 13.1 for an example of Gina's goals and levels of attainment. It is important to note that these levels of attainment can be made more challenging once a student client has started to experience success.

After this chart has been constructed, the school-based professional and the student decide the current level of performance. For example, Gina is currently getting a D in math, is unable to concentrate during math quizzes and tests, and is only on-task about 30 percent of the time during her math class. On your chart, you would note current levels of performance with asterisks in the appropriate cell. A rating for current performance can be calculated by adding up the ratings. In this example, Gina has a –4 on her current goals.

Table 13.1 Gina's Goal Attainment Scale for Math Class

Scale Attainment Level	Scale 1: Grade W = 30	Scale 2: Anxious Feeling W = 50	Scale 3: Behavior W = 20
Most unfavorable outcome expected (−2)	Fail the class, receive a grade of F	Feels so anxious needs to leave the room during quizzes/tests	On-task only 30% of the time or less ***
Less-than-expected success (−1)	Receive a grade of D ***	Feels anxious and is distracted, unable to focus on the test ***	On-task 31–45% of the time
Expected level of success (0)	Receive a grade of C	Feels anxious but is able to focus for the most part	On-task 46–60% of the time
More-than-expected success (+1)	Receive a grade of B	Only feels a little anxious at first, but this feeling goes away	On-task 61–75% of the time
Most favorable outcome expected (+2)	Receive a grade of A	Does not feel anxious and is able to focus the entire time on test	On-task 76% of the time or more during math class

Note: *** = current level of performance

Depending on the degree of specificity you want to have in your ratings, you can weight the scores based on your priorities and derive a T-score that demonstrates the individual's overall progress toward these goals (Kiresuk & Sherman, 1968; Kiresuk et al., 1994). Originally, GAS was designed as an outcome measure to be evaluated by an external rater (Kiresuk & Sherman, 1968). However, the psychometric properties of GAS have been questioned (Donnelly & Carswell, 2002), and creating a well-designed scaling model is more difficult than it may seem. Some of the common problems include multidimensionality on the levels (e.g., measuring more than one behavior), gaps or overlap between the levels of attainment, and not enough detail to facilitate accurate ratings (Kiresuk et al., 1994). Alternatively, Coffee and

Ray-Subramanian (2009) suggested using GAS as a progress-monitoring tool. They have also recommended, if using GAS in this format, expanding the possible ratings from five to seven (–3 to +3).

> When graphing your GAS data, you may want to put your positive rating at the top of your axis and the worse-than-expected rating at the bottom so that it is easier for others to interpret your data.

Using a simple table for each goal, you can develop a grid that has the levels of attainment on the left side and the weeks of intervention across the bottom (adapted from Coffee & Ray-Subramanian, 2009). For each of the goals, you would want to create a separate chart and attach Gina's goal attainment scale so that you can easily refer back to it as you are monitoring her weekly performance on each of the goals (see Table 13.1). To monitor Gina's progress, you might use her weekly grade from the teacher's grade book. During your weekly sessions with her, you might use her self-report to monitor her anxiety during tests and quizzes. Finally, observations (completed by you, the teacher's aide, or another individual in the school) will help you to establish her weekly behavioral performance. Each week, enter data for each of your intervention goals. Place an *X* in the grid that corresponds to the student's behavior according to the student's goal attainment scale.

In our example, Gina's self-rating prior to beginning counseling was a –4. After engaging in counseling for a period of time, Gina and her counselor want to determine where she is on her goals. The first three weeks of the data reflect baseline data and a period of building rapport and goal setting. After about two weeks, the interventions were introduced, and by the fourth week, Gina was beginning to show change. Let's say after six weeks of practicing her new strategies, she rated herself as +1 in her grade (i.e., receiving a B), +1 in her anxiety (i.e., a little anxious, but feeling goes away), and +1 in her behavior (i.e., on-task 61–75 percent of the time during math class). She now has a goal attainment score of +3 compared to her precounseling score of –4. Even without obtaining a T-score, you can determine that she has made growth toward each of her goals. By monitoring her progress along the way, you were in a position to change the intervention as needed if it did not appear to be having the desired effect.

The procedures just described are fairly straightforward, but it might take some time to set up your spreadsheets and graphs so that you can use them as a template for the various student clients with whom you will work. As an alternative, there are commercially available products that incorporate GAS. Two examples of these include the *Academic Competence Evaluation Scales*

Figure 13.5 Gina's weekly progress monitoring data across her three goals

Gina will obtain a grade of C+ or better in her math class.

+2								
+1								X
0					X	X	X	
−1	X	X	X	X				
−2								
Week	1	2	3	4	5	6	7	8

Gina will report an increased ability to manage anxious feelings during math quizzes and tests.

+2								
+1								X
0				X	X	X	X	
−1	X	X	X					
−2								
Week	1	2	3	4	5	6	7	8

Gina will be on task in her math class at least 75% of the time.

+2								
+1								
0						X		X
−1		X		X	X		X	
−2	X		X					
Week	1	2	3	4	5	6	7	8

(ACES; DiPerna & Elliott, 2000) and the *Outcomes PME: Planning, Monitoring, and Evaluation* (Stoiber & Kratochwill, 2001). Additionally, there are new progress-monitoring tools such as the *Behavior Intervention Monitoring Assessment System* (BIMAS; McDougall, Bardos, & Meier, 2010), *AIMSweb* for Behavior (Pearson, 2010), and the *Social Skills Improvement Scale* (SSIS, Elliott & Gresham, 2008) that can make tracking the outcomes of your interventions a bit easier. We do not recommend using standardized behavioral measures (e.g., *Behavior Assessment System for Children*, 2nd edition; Reynolds & Kamphaus, 2004) because they were not designed for this purpose and are not likely to be sensitive to small changes in student behavior.

Using Existing Data

No matter which strategy you use to measure the effect of selected interventions, you will want to make as much use of existing data as possible. Data collection and program evaluation can be time consuming, and for some, these activities are also given lower priority than other tasks. Therefore, you want to ensure that you set up the easiest design possible and that you streamline your data collection. Schools maintain an incredible amount of data on their students. More importantly, as schools have started keeping their data in one location through information management systems such as Infinite Campus, it is easier than ever to access student data. Some of the existing data that you could access to demonstrate the effectiveness of your efforts includes attendance records (including both absences and tardies), behavioral referrals, suspensions, grades, and test results.

INFORMAL MEASURES OF EFFECTIVENESS

Although the procedures described in the previous section have benefits in terms of allowing us to provide a numerical summary of the effectiveness of our efforts, they also have drawbacks. Most of these techniques require a clear behavioral indicator of change. Sometimes that is not possible when working with a child who is experiencing internal struggles. Additionally, these methods do not account for trends in a student's performance and instead measure indicators of rapid change. Data collection can be difficult because of the busy, unpredictable nature of schools.

For these reasons, and others, it is important to supplement your more formal methods with informal techniques of gathering information. These types of strategies would include your general observations of the student in the school setting. Students' self-ratings and self-monitoring can provide you with important information. As we demonstrated with our GAS for Gina, one of her goals was monitored through her self-report. You may also want to talk with the student's teachers and parents. Do they see a difference in the child's behavior or attitude? It is possible that the student client is improving in one area but still struggling in others? Although an indirect indicator, it is also helpful to scan existing data related to a particular student. Does it appear that the student's grades, attendance, and behavioral referrals are improving? Although you might not be working toward these specific goals, these data can serve as general indicators of how a student is functioning overall. Improvements in attendance, for example, may suggest that the student is engaging in school to a greater degree.

PROGRAM-LEVEL ACCOUNTABILITY

The techniques described earlier address child-level accountability. That is, how well did your interventions work for one child or a small group of students? There is another level of accountability that concerns your overall program of service. At the broadest level, this type of accountability asks, "Do students in your school benefit as a result of your services?" Additional questions could be considered replacing the word *students* with *teachers, families,* and *administrators.* Further, do all students benefit or just some? These are important questions to ask. Although your services may be excellent, and all students with whom you work demonstrate tremendous gains, if you only serve 10 students in a semester, you are missing the opportunity to meet the needs of many more students.

There are various ways to establish program-level accountability, and no one way will suffice. Instead, consider program-level accountability as a number of different efforts that you take to ensure that you are spending your time in a manner that is most beneficial to your school and the students within it. Some of these different types of accountability might be demonstrated through the selecting evidence-based interventions, linking interventions to educational outcomes, spending your time efficiently in professional activities, evaluating the effectiveness of your work, and ensuring that the services you provide address the needs of your specific school or district. We will examine each of these in more detail.

Selecting Evidence-Based Interventions

When a school-based professional meets with a student client and learns of his or her concerns, the helper is faced with the decision of what to do. There are a number of intervention strategies from which to choose. Typically, the school-based helper considers his or her theory, the available resources, and the intervention that is likely to be most effective. There is an increasing trend toward using selected approaches for specific problems based on empirically supported treatments (Deegear & Lawson, 2003). With the growing body of research literature that documents the effectiveness of certain interventions for specific problems or issues, it has become much easier to decide which approach to use. The practice just described is sometimes referred to as evidence-based practice. (Additional coverage of evidence-based interventions is provided in Chapter 15.)

Evidence-based practice as applied to the schools refers to the process of selecting and implementing intervention programming based on the best available scientific evidence (Kratochwill, Albers, & Shernoff, 2004). From this perspective, an intervention is evidence-based if there is a body of evidence derived from tightly controlled empirical studies (e.g., randomized controls; standardized, large sample sizes; replicated) to support its use. It is more difficult to implement this type of evidence-based practice in the schools as some of these interventions are better suited to clinical settings. Further, the effectiveness of these interventions has not been measured when applied in a school setting. Most importantly, there is no guarantee that an evidence-based intervention (EBI) exists for the specific issue that a student might present. For this reason, we recommend a blend of both approaches—using the best evidence available to select your interventions. When possible, incorporate those specific EBIs into your work.

The task of selecting an empirically supported group or classroom intervention has become less difficult. There are now helpful documents and websites that make the task of selecting an evidence-based intervention somewhat easier (see Electronic Resources at the end of this chapter). With the greater emphasis on accountability, many of the prepared program curricula are much more likely to research and publicize the effectiveness of their respective programs. Additionally, the school-based professional will want to consider the needs of the school, the demographics of the school population, and the cost (both time and monetary) for the program.

Linking Interventions to Educational Outcomes

By linking educational outcomes with interventions, school-based professional helpers can demonstrate that they are full educational team members who share the goal of student success. The work of Adelman and Taylor (2003) is helpful in conceptualizing and communicating the ways that interventions can reduce barriers to learning. They have organized their framework into six categories:

1. increasing the teacher's ability to handle problems and nurture development;

2. supporting the school's ability to manage transition;

3. preventing crisis situations and addressing them when they happen;

4. increasing participation of family members;

5. integrating the community; and

6. offering special assistance.

When considered from this framework, school-based professionals can clearly delineate how their services (e.g., consultation, classroom lessons, parent training, community outreach) help to increase student learning (or reduce barriers).

Spending Time Efficiently

In our school buildings, we need to consider the manner in which we spend our time. One of our goals should be to provide our services to the greatest number of individuals possible in accordance with the expectations of our profession and our position. As noted in Chapter 1, there may be only one school-based professional for 400 to 700 students, depending on the specific profession. The exact nature of your role (e.g., how you spend your time, activities in which you are expected to participate) varies depending on the district in which you work. Although you want to be flexible and meet the needs of your school, you also want to be sure that the ways you spend your time are consistent with the expectations of your profession.

The *ASCA National Model* (2005) includes general percentage guidelines for how school counselors' time should be allocated. As you will see in Table 13.2, the guidelines are flexible and responsive to students' dynamic developmental needs. For example, more time is devoted to individual student planning as students progress through each level. Less time is devoted to curriculum for middle school students and again for high school students. Ideally, counselors limit system support (indirect activities) to 15 percent of their time, reserving 85 percent of their time for curriculum, individual student planning, and responsive services (direct activities).

Other school professionals do not have these specific types of guidelines. The NASP *Model for Comprehensive and Integrated School Psychological Services* (2010b) indicates that there are 10 domains of service provided by school psychologists and that these services are delivered in a planned manner that meets the needs of students and families in the community. A recent

Table 13.2 *ASCA National Model* (2005) School Counselor Suggested Time Use by Grade Level

Component	Grade Level	Percentage of Time
Curriculum	Elementary	35%—45%
	Middle	25%—35%
	High	15%—25%
Individual Student Planning	Elementary	15%—25%
	Middle	15%—25%
	High	25%—35%
Responsive Services	Elementary	30%—40%
	Middle	30%—40%
	High	25%—35%
System Support	Elementary	10%—15%
	Middle	10%—15%
	High	15%—20%

survey of schools psychologists suggested that they spend the majority of their time in assessment activities, followed by consultation and direct services (e.g., counseling, groups) (Larson & Choi, 2010).

Evaluating the Effectiveness of Your Work

School-based professionals must continually evaluate the effectiveness of their work. There are a number of elements to consider when you are developing a model to evaluate your program. Which components of the program will you evaluate? What outcomes will you measure? How will you organize and maintain your data so that they are easy to aggregate? What is the best format to present this information?

There are a few key concepts to remember in developing your program evaluation plan. First, you will want to develop your evaluation plan from the very beginning of your year. As you consider what types of services you will provide, you will also think about how you can evaluate the outcomes of that work. If you wait until you have already delivered your services, it is too late. You are not likely to be able to demonstrate change. Further, the data that you have access to may not be directly related to the types of outcomes that you wanted to evaluate. This second point addresses another key concept. You want to be able to demonstrate a logical link between the outcomes that you are measuring and the services you provide.

For example, let's say you designed and delivered an intervention to decrease angry outbursts in a small group of third-grade boys. One of the common strategies that I (R.S.H.) have seen school-based professionals use to evaluate their work is a group satisfaction questionnaire. In this case, there is no assurance that a high degree of group satisfaction is linked to a decrease in angry outbursts. It is fine to use group satisfaction as one of your data points, but you also want to know whether your intervention resulted in the desired outcome.

Communicating results of a program evaluation can be viewed as an indirect strategy for professional advocacy. As we inform constituents about the value of our work, we advance our professional fields in addition to helping students learn and grow.

Finally, one of the most important aspects of collecting, aggregating, and analyzing your outcome data is the ability to report it in a clear and meaningful way to others. A full discussion of program evaluation is beyond the scope of this text. However, there are several good articles and texts out there (e.g., Stone & Dahir, 2011) that can help guide you as you develop your service delivery model.

Stone and Dahir (2011) have outlined a comprehensive assessment model that helps school-based professionals demonstrate the effectiveness of their work. The model aligns with the *ASCA National Model* (2005) and is referred to by the acronym *MEASURE* (p. 29):

- Mission
- Elements
- Analyze
- Stakeholders-Unite
- Results
- Educate

Use of this type of comprehensive evaluation model allows school-based professionals to organize their efforts, demonstrate their effectiveness, and participate in meaningful systemic change (Stone & Dahir, 2011).

Meeting the Needs of Your System

Another component of accountability is to ensure that the services you provide meet the needs of your system. There are many different strategies for accomplishing this goal. School-based professionals, working with the building leadership team, might conduct an assessment to determine the greatest needs in a building. This assessment might include a survey of teachers, children, families, and administrators or might focus on one particular group. (See Chapter 15 for additional strategies on conducting a needs assessment.)

Another way to collect information related to the needs of a building is through the analysis of existing data. School-based professionals may examine such indicators as the number of students who are not proficient on achievement tests, the number of office referrals at each grade, the overall attendance rate for the student body, or the school's dropout rate. By comparing this information to district and national data, a decision-making team (of which the school-based professional is a member) can determine the areas of greatest need within their specific school.

Providing Services to All Children

Finally, and most importantly, you want to ensure that you are accountable to the children and families in your school. As noted, this accountability can be demonstrated through your services and the programs that you implement and by ensuring that you are meeting the needs of students in your building. However, there are a number of children in your school who will present with many unique needs and issues.

Have you created a program that truly addresses the needs of all children? We want to remind you that we are not asking, "Are *you* meeting the needs of all children?" Sometimes new professionals attempt to display superhuman powers by individually trying to provide services to every student. Instead, we advocate for an approach in which school-based professionals are mindful of the specific needs that students bring to the school setting and ensuring that there are program resources available that can address these needs.

CONCLUSION

An essential component of any sustained effort at systemic reform must be accompanied by a thorough evaluation that is carefully integrated into all aspects of the model. We must be accountable for our efforts and ensure that they are effective in supporting student achievement. Results evaluation is a primary and emphasized component of the *American School Counselor Association National Model* (2005) and represents one of the domains of competency as outlined in the NASP *Model for Comprehensive and Integrated School Psychological Services, 2010b).* Further, because our time to provide services is limited, we must maximize our efforts to increase the likelihood of positive student outcomes.

Activities

1. Practice creating a goal attainment scale for a student client within your school.

2. If you are able, set up a simple AB design for a student client with whom you are working. Gather baseline data prior to beginning your work or implementing a specific intervention. If possible, monitor the targeted behavior for the next few days and bring the information to class. Discuss with a small group the benefits and challenges to monitoring a behavior. If you do not have access to a student, monitor a behavior in yourself.

3. Keep track of your hours over the coming week and the types of activities that you engage in. How well do your activities match the *ASCA National Model* (2005) or the *Model for Comprehensive and Integrated School Psychological Services* (2010b)?

Journal Reflections

Reflection #1

When you think about expectations regarding evaluation and accountability, what reactions do you have?

Reflection #2

Consider different situations that you have experienced in your school where you have intervened but where it has been difficult to demonstrate the efficacy of the outcome. Think about alternative ways that you might measure whether these interventions were effective.

Electronic Resources

Society for Prevention Research: http://www.preventionresearch.org

Print Resources

Kiresuk, T., Smith, A., & Cardillo, J. (1994). *Goal attainment scaling: Applications, theory, and measurement.* Hillsdale, NJ: Erlbaum.

Parsons, R. D. (2007). *Counseling strategies that work!: Evidence-based interventions for school counselors.* Boston: Allyn & Bacon.

Sink, C. (Ed.). (2006). Special Issue: Research methods in school counseling. *Professional School Counseling, 9.*

Stone, C. B., & Dahir, C. A. (2011). *School counselor accountability: A MEASURE of student success.* Boston: Pearson.

CHAPTER 14

Building Alliances Through Consultation and Collaboration

Learning Objectives

- Understand the difference between consultation and collaboration
- Learn models for enacting consultation
- Learn principles of effective collaboration

School-based professional helpers often assist students indirectly by consulting with their parents or guardians, teachers, and other adults. By working with significant adults, we amplify services. Before exploring consultation and collaboration, it may be helpful to clarify the roles of some of the other professionals within the school setting.

Throughout this text, we have noted that school counselors and school psychologists are trained to deliver counseling services and other affective educational programs to children. In Chapter 1, we described the ways that these two professional roles differ. However, we have not explored how these professional helpers can work together to maximize the available resources within a school or district.

For some school-based professional helpers, it is easy to slip into a mindset in which they assume they are the only ones responsible for solving the problems of the students in their school (Epstein & Van Voorhis, 2010). Collaborative partnerships can reduce this load, but building these relationships can also create additional challenges. Subtle political processes, conflictual *and* collaborative relationships, strengths, and challenges operate within every school system. When we discuss our pre-service professional helpers' roles in their buildings, it is not the specific requirements of their positions that provide the greatest challenge. Rather, it is the degree to which they must maneuver through the complex social and political dynamics. Unfortunately, one of these struggles has included unnecessary turf battles.

Regrettably, the separate disciplines are sometimes viewed as competitive or, worse, interchangeable, especially when education funds become limited. We suggest that systematically configured school-based mental health teams augment the complementary nature of school psychologists and school counselors and, therefore, constitute a wise investment of educational resources. For this reason, and because of our strong belief in the importance of collaboration, we contend that it is important to understand the unique strengths, capacities, and limitations of the roles of the different school-based professional helpers. We have already provided a comparison of the role and function of school psychologists, school counselors, and school social workers in Chapter 1. Therefore, we will briefly recap that information here. Additionally, we focus on the role of the school social worker who also has the responsibility of providing social-emotional supports for students and families in school settings. We begin with a simple definition of the role of each, their education and preparation, and the way each might spend a day in the school.

ROLE DEFINITIONS

School Counseling Services

Professional school counselors are certified or licensed through state departments of education. They are responsible for providing comprehensive programming to meet the needs of all students through a school counseling program. They use a developmental approach to facilitate student growth and address the needs, tasks, and interests related to those stages. The four primary interventions provided by counselors include counseling (individual and group), large-group guidance, consultation, and coordination. Their emphasis is on developing programs that promote and enhance student learning. The majority of their skills, time, and efforts are focused on direct services to students, teachers, and families.

School Psychology Services

School psychologists are also licensed or certified professionals who may work within the school setting. Their practice blends the science and practice of psychology with the educational process to benefit children, youth, families, and learners of all ages. School psychologists provide a range of direct services including psychological and behavioral assessments, intervention, prevention, crisis response, and individual and group counseling. Their indirect services include teacher and parent consultation, program development, and evaluation of services. They emphasize understanding the functioning of children within the contexts of schools, families, and communities. Additionally, school psychologists promote healthy environments through research-based effective programs that enhance the social and academic skills of students (NASP, 2010b).

School Social Work Services

School social workers are also licensed/credentialed individuals who focus their efforts on reducing the contextual barriers (e.g., social, cultural, economic) that may place children at risk for school failure. They promote student achievement, safety, attendance, social-behavioral competency, and family and community involvement. School social workers provide a wide range of services to students, including assessment and screening of social and emotional concerns, individual and group counseling, crisis intervention, family support, advocacy, and classroom instruction. School social workers collaborate with community-based organizations to help students and families have access to needed services. School social workers also provide consultation to families, teachers, and administrators. They assist in the development and implementation of new programs, resources, and policies directed toward maximizing students' success in school (National Association of Pupil Service Organizations, n.d.).

WHAT MEMBERS OF EACH PROFESSION DO

School Counselors

Contemporary school counselors base their programs on the ASCA's *National Model* (2005), which provides a framework for developing and implementing school counseling programs. The model is presented in four distinct but inter-connecting components: the foundation, the management system, the delivery system, and the accountability system.

The foundation includes the philosophy and overall mission of the program, the content standards outlined in the *National Model*, and an articulated focus on three domains: vocational, academic, and personal/social. The management system comprises agreements and action plans for cooperatively designing and implementing the program, an advisory council, and time management.

System support responsibilities contribute to a sound infrastructure for the program. Designing a program requires extensive time. Counselors are also members of the overall school team, which means they make contributions, attend meetings, and serve on committees. Accountable, professional counselors also prioritize their own professional development by attending conferences or receiving supervision.

The delivery system is the most visible component. This is the portion of the *National Model* that provides general guidelines for distribution of counselors' time among (a) guidance curriculum, (b) individual student planning, (c) responsive services, and (d) system support. (In the previous chapter, Table 13.2 outlined the percentage of time spent in each of these areas at the different grade levels.)

School counselors' curriculum design reflects the same level of scope and sequence planning as teachers follow when they teach math, English, or science. The curriculum is intentionally crafted to be developmentally appropriate, sequential, and comprehensive with a focus on prevention. Competencies are identified for students in elementary, middle, and high schools. Indicators are also provided to ensure that students master the competencies. As mentioned earlier, the curriculum domains are academic, vocational, and personal/social.

Typically counselors assist students in attaining the various curriculum objectives through classroom presentations. For example, an elementary counselor may conduct a unit on goal setting as applied to academic performance. The same model for setting goals can be used later in a peer pressure reversal unit. The goal-setting model can also be applied to career planning.

Curriculum activities are also delivered through team teaching activities, small-group activities based on students' needs, and workshops or classes for parents. Many of the competencies parallel or correspond with objectives addressed in other disciplines, thereby inviting collaboration. Some children require additional support to demonstrate mastery of competencies with teachers.

Individual student planning activities include assisting students in transitioning from one level of education to another, assisting students and their parents in postsecondary planning, and completing applications for institutions, financial assistance, and jobs. These activities may occur in classrooms, with individuals in counseling offices, in small groups, or with parents. Time allocated to individual student planning increases as students enter middle school and again in high school.

Responsive services are counselors' responses to the immediate needs of students. Counselors may provide individual or group counseling and consultation to parents or assistance to others who are negotiating a crisis. They may respond to a student who knocks on the office door and says, "I need to talk." The focus of responsive services often includes groups for children whose parents are divorcing, groups of students who are having interpersonal challenges, or individuals who are depressed. Historically, responsive services may have related predominantly to personal and social challenges as school counselors provided more mental health counseling. Contemporary school counselors balance personal/social interventions with academic support and vocational development.

School counselors and their activities are regulated at various levels. Licensure is granted and monitored at departments of education within each state. Requirements vary; however, a master's degree in school counseling is recognized as minimum preparation. Some states require previous teaching experiences, although many do not. Professional school counselors belong to the American School Counselors Association (ASCA) and the branch within their state. Many school counselors also belong to the American Counseling Association (ACA) and to various organizations representing teachers.

School Psychologists

In the newly released *Model for Comprehensive and Integrated School Psychological Services,* NASP (2010b) has outlined the official policy regarding the delivery of school psychology services in the schools. This model is based on 10 domains of practice that are divided into smaller units. For example, there are two domains, data-based decision making and consultation/collaboration, that are considered to be "practices that permeate all aspects of service delivery." Under the broad umbrella of direct and indirect services, school psychologists are to deliver interventions for academic support and mental health services to develop social and life skills. These two domains are considered to be student-level services. The other types of services that fall under this umbrella are systems-level services, which include schoolwide practices to promote learning, preventive and responsive services, and family-school collaboration. The underlying foundation to the entire model includes diversity in development and learning, research and program evaluation, and legal, ethical, and professional practice.

The role and function of school psychologists vary a great deal by the state and district in which they are employed. In more rural areas, school psychologists tend to operate in an itinerant model where they might serve many different small schools in a typical week. In urban and suburban areas, some districts have moved toward a school-based model with a school psychologist serving only one school as a member of the school faculty. The general trend in the field is to move away from the previous diagnostician and gatekeeper role to special education. Instead, practitioners are encouraged to provide a broader range of services with an emphasis on consultation and systems intervention activities. With the publication of the *NASP Comprehensive Model* (NASP, 2010b), the recommended ratio is one school psychologist for every 500–700 students.

School psychologists are prepared at the masters (60+ credit hours), specialist, and doctoral level. They are typically members of either (or both) the National Association of School Psychologists or Division 16: School Psychology of the American Psychological Association, as well as their state organization.

School Social Workers

The role of school social workers is to act as a link among the school, home, and community. School social workers provide services to all students through direct services such as individual and group work, classroom presentations, and crisis intervention. They also provide indirect services through consultation and referrals to community services. School social workers are frequently a part of the special education process as they may help gather information on a student's family and complete some of the instruments to measure social-emotional functioning. The recommended ratio for school social workers to students is 1:400.

Most school social workers hold a master's in social work (MSW). They are regulated through state educational agencies, although only 31 states have a certification process in place for licensing school social workers (Altshuler, 2006). Each state develops its own certification requirements, and some states allow entry into the field with a bachelor's degree (Altshuler, 2006).

Given this brief description of the specific service areas, it is easy to understand why parents and the lay public are sometimes confused about the distinctions among these three professions. Although some of the specific tasks are the same (e.g., counseling, consultation), parents might hold stereotypes for one group over another. For example, parents might refuse to allow their child to talk to a school psychologist because of the idea that he or she is a "shrink" and wants to medicate their child, while welcoming the services of the school counselor or social worker.

Although there is overlap in some of the services provided by these individuals, the perspectives of each group differ and the amount of time spent in providing different types of services varies greatly. For example, school psychologists tend to spend the majority of their time providing assessment and consultation and, to a lesser degree, individual or group counseling. Conversely, elementary school counselors devote the majority of their time to classroom-based guidance lessons, and individual or group counseling, and a smaller percentage to consultation or interpreting educational assessments. Finally, each profession grew out of a different tradition and therefore holds a unique perspective on needs and strategies for addressing student learning. School social workers view their services systemically and tend to focus their efforts broadly on the contexts of students' lives. School counselors' professional roots include education, vocational development, and psychology. The field of school psychology developed at the same time as a clinical model and historically has aligned with a medical-model perspective. That is, the efforts of school psychologists have tended to focus on identifying illness in the individual rather than promoting health in the system, although as noted, there are continued efforts to change this emphasis. At least in some schools, representatives of the three professions have traditionally tended to work alongside one another but separately. The analogy of silos has been used in community settings to describe professionals focused on the same general issues, yet working in isolation. This type of approach does not fit well in school settings. Unfortunately, individuals from all three professions may only be in a school on specific days. This staffing pattern makes it necessary for these individuals to work together to communicate about developing concerns, follow through on parent contacts or arranging meetings, and delegate components of a larger task. Factors such as the professional's expertise, history with a child or family, or availability should help in determining which tasks might be carried out by each team member.

We encourage all professional helpers to refrain from making statements such as, "The school psychologist shouldn't be conducting groups. She only knows about testing." We want professional helpers to rely on their own knowledge, training, and competency in making decisions about the roles they should perform. Further, it is important that they do not assume that other professionals do not share some of that expertise. Our professional identities stem from our overall philosophies, training, and expertise, not from specific roles that we perform.

When professionals from different disciplines work together, they are able to plan for and deliver integrated models of service. Contemporary professionals and administrators recognize the value of these models (e.g., Adelman & Taylor, 2010). Critical aspects of integrated models include consultation and collaboration.

CONSULTATION AND COLLABORATION

The terms *consultation* and *collaboration* appear in a variety of contexts and have become somewhat generic terms. They are generally valued and frequently included in a variety of initiatives. Diverse interpretations of these terms can be found throughout the professional literature. For example, some authors conceptualize models of consultation (e.g., school based, mental health, behavioral, educational, and organizational). Others use consultation and collaboration interchangeably or describe consultation as a collaborative endeavor. Although consultation and collaboration have points of intersection, distinctions assist professional helpers in determining which role is appropriate in various situations (Brown et al., 2011). Despite the frequency with which these practices are promoted, effective consultation rarely happens spontaneously. True collaboration is difficult to practice.

CONSULTATION DEFINED

Simply stated, "Consultation is a voluntary problem-solving process" (Brown et al., 2011, p. 1). Of course, this brief definition does not capture the full purpose of a consultative relationship. Regardless of the model of consultation that is adopted, the goal of consultation is to "assist consultees to develop attitudes and skills that will enable them to function more effectively with a client, which can be an individual, group, or organization" (Brown et al., 2011, p. 1). Because of the broad and diverse contexts of consultation, examples and descriptions of the process may be easier to formulate than succinct definitions.

School-based professional helpers provide consultation in a variety of forms. For example,

- A teacher asks a professional helper for assistance because he is having difficulty with classroom management.
- A principal asks a school psychologist to conduct an in-service on class-room interventions for students who have challenges with attending.
- A counselor may ask a social worker for assistance in identifying community resources for a group of students who have limited access to all forms of health care.
- A mother and father ask a school counselor to assist them in developing strategies for helping their daughter adjust to an impending divorce.
- The school district wants to implement a new program and works with a small group of school-based professionals from various schools within the district to develop an implementation plan.

These situations, though diverse, have three common elements: (a) the consultant who may be a school counselor, school psychologist, or school social worker; (b) the consultee who is the direct recipient of the consultation, such as a parent, a teacher, a school-based professional, an administrator, or the entire system (i.e., school district); and (c) the focus of the consultation, for example, a child, a group of teachers, or a family (Dougherty, 2009). Typically, the consultant's role is indirect, and the consultee holds primary responsibility for following the recommendations or intervention plans.

A twofold purpose of consultation is to empower adults, and even children, to (a) solve immediate problems and (b) acquire knowledge and skills to address similar problems in the future. Thus, the process can be efficient, and the results can be empowering and long lasting. For example, when a classroom teacher acquires skills to more effectively address the needs of one child, all children in the classroom—both present and future—are beneficiaries. Providing an educational program to a small group of parents has an impact on many children, possibly over generations (Dinkmeyer & Carlson, 2006).

Similar to other consultation experts, Brown et al. (2011) described the following processes that are inherent in consultation (p. 2):

1. It may be initiated by either the consultee or consultant.

2. The relationship is characterized by authentic communication.

3. Consultees may be professionals or nonprofessionals.

4. It provides direct services to consultees, assisting them to develop knowledge and skills that ultimately make them more effective with clients (broadly conceived).

5. It is triadic in that it provides indirect services to clients.

6. Consultation is goal oriented, often pursuing two goals simultaneously (consultee's and client's).

7. Types of problems considered during consultation are work related when the concept of work is broadly conceived.

8. The consultant's role varies with consultee's needs.

9. The locus of the consultant may be internal or external.

10. All communication between the consultant and consultee is confidential.

A Not-So-Subtle Reminder About Basic Skills

Although consulting and collaborating are distinctly different from counseling, the basic helping skills presented in the *Practice and Application Guide* are transferable and directly applicable to consulting and collaborative relationships. Indeed, when school-based professionals are not able to fully understand the request and situation of someone requesting consultation, or fully appreciate the perception of a collaborating colleague, the value of the relationship is compromised. In our example below, Enrique, a novice school-based helper, responds to Cassie's English teacher. Consider the potential effect of Enrique's words.

High school English teacher: I don't know what to do with Cassie. She isn't doing her work, and I'm afraid she is going to fail.

Enrique: How old is Cassie?

Teacher: She is 17, a junior.

Enrique: Let's see. Do I know her? What color is her hair?

Teacher: She has long dark hair.

Enrique: Is she the girl who tried out for cheerleading last year?

Teacher: I don't know.

Enrique: Isn't her mom a lawyer?

Teacher: I think that's right.

Enrique: What class are you talking about?

Teacher: Juniors' Advanced English.

Enrique: What is Cassie doing?

Teacher: Well, I'm more concerned about what she is *not* doing. She isn't turning in her homework, as I mentioned. She usually comes to class—sometimes late, but she doesn't participate. In fact, she just sits without really participating.

Enrique: Do you think she has a problem?

Teacher: Well, I really don't know.

Enrique: Have you talked to her about it?

Teacher: No.

Enrique: Do you think that would be a good idea?

Teacher: Well, I'm not sure. I don't want to embarrass her or pry.

Enrique: Why not?

Teacher: Well, I don't know really.

Enrique: Well, what is it you are hoping I can do?

Obviously, Enrique is not providing a good example of using his basic skills to help his consultee express his concerns. In the dialogue that follows, Sebastian, another school-based helper, uses reflection skills and still acquires information. He is careful to balance reflection responses with questions and ensures that his questions are relevant.

Teacher: I don't know what to do with Cassie. She isn't doing her work, and I'm afraid she is going to compromise her scholarship opportunities.

Sebastian: You're obviously concerned about her.

Teacher: I really am. She was a strong student last semester and was always involved. Now she doesn't participate in class discussions, and she's missed several assignments.

Sebastian: I'm wondering if you have any ideas about what might be going on.

Teacher: I don't. I haven't directly talked with her because I wanted to consult with you first. She hasn't mentioned any problems at home, and when I see her during breaks, she is usually involved with her friends.

Sebastian: It sounds like you're stumped at this point and just don't know what Cassie needs from you in order to get back on track.

Teacher: Bingo. I was hoping you might have some ideas.

Sebastian: Perhaps if we talk about it together, we can generate some ideas to try. It would be helpful for me to know a bit more about Cassie. How old is she?

Teacher: She's 17.

Sebastian: That's right. You said she was a junior in Advanced English.

Teacher: Yes.

Sebastian: It sounds like she has been a fairly strong student prior to now. When did you begin to notice changes?

Teacher: She did really well last semester. She was involved in class discussions and always turned in her work. It was usually well done. In fact, I'm sure she got As the first two quarters. I'm trying to think . . . I guess her grades started dropping shortly after we returned from winter break. It wasn't until last week that I realized she had not been turning in her assignments, and that's when I became more aware of her reticence during class discussions.

Sebastian: So, as you see it, her performance has gradually declined since the beginning of this quarter.

Teacher: Yes. That's right. I didn't think much about it until last week when I realized she hadn't turned in several assignments. And then I began thinking about her grades and class participation.

Sebastian: What other thoughts do you have?

Teacher: I am really puzzled. I can't imagine what may be distracting her. Because she's been such a good student, though, I am sure something has happened.

Sebastian: You are just perplexed by all of this. From the information you have now, nothing makes sense.

Teacher: That's right. And I haven't felt comfortable talking with her. I don't want to interfere or get in over my head.

Sebastian: How would you like us to work together to help Cassie?

MODELS AND STRATEGIES FOR CONSULTING WITH TEACHERS AND PARENTS

In schools, consultation is often focused on assisting other professionals as they endeavor to promote development of students or provide a school environment that is more conducive to students' personal and academic growth. More specifically, consultation is often enacted to effect change of students' behavior or academic performance. School-based consultants also assist with an examination of schools' systemic nature and offer suggestions for school improvement.

As mentioned previously, mental health professionals, because they are human beings, have insidious and untested beliefs (or theories) about children, appropriate behavior, and human nature. Thus, it is important that their work be grounded in established theory to prevent the inadvertent imposition of their personal theories, life experiences, and so forth. Just as there are theories to guide one's counseling, there are numerous theories of consultation. Some of the most commonly used forms of consultation include (a) mental health and consultee-centered (Caplan, 1970; Knotek & Sandoval, 2003), (b) behavioral and conjoint behavioral (Bergan, 1977; Sheridan, 1997); (c) Adlerian (Dinkmeyer & Carlson, 2006); (d) solution-focused (Kahn, 2000); and (e) systems (Beer & Spector, 1980) to name a few. It is beyond the scope of this text to provide a detailed description of each of these approaches; additional resources are provided at the end of the chapter.

Models provide a structure and organization to assist the consultant in gathering information and designing interventions. Theories inform the content and direction of consultation. Although interventions should be theory based (e.g., Adlerian or behavioral), they also need to be designed to meet the unique needs of each child, teacher, or family. Successful consultants translate theory to practical intervention strategies (Dinkmeyer & Carlson, 2006).

Because consultation is viewed as a problem-solving process, the steps that reflect that process can be applied to consultation, regardless of one's model (Brown et al., 2011). Dougherty (2009) captured the essence of the consultation process with his generic four-stage model that includes (a) entry, (b) diagnosis, (c) implementation, and (d) disengagement. Dougherty's model implicitly underscores the temporary, short-term nature of consultation. Brown et al. (2011) described a similar process by outlining eight stages: (a) entry into the organization, (b) initiation of a consulting relationship, (c) assessment, (d) problem definition and goal setting, (e) strategy selection, (f) strategy implementation, (g) evaluation, and (h) termination.

Eight Stages of Consultation

We have adapted consultation stages proposed by Brown et al. (2011) and suggested language for verifying that tasks within each step have been accomplished, transitioning between steps, providing information or amplification, and initiating action. In Table 14.1, we provide an outline of the eight stages in the consultation process and some of the possible phrases a professional helper might use in consulting with a teacher.

Table 14.1 Stages of Consultation and Possible Language

Stage and Accompanying Goals		Possible Language
Stage 1	**Entry Into the Organization**	
	Exploration and information exchange	• Tell me about your goals for our work. • Let me tell you a little bit about how I would see our work together.
	Clarifying confidentiality	• Our discussions about Student X will generally be confidential. However, there are times when I would need to share information with others.
	Arrange for a convenient meeting time	• I'm glad we're going to work on this together. I would like to get a more complete picture of what is going on. When will be a good time for us to meet?

(Continued)

Table 14.1 (Continued)

Stage and Accompanying Goals		Possible Language
Stage 2	**Initiation of a Consulting Relationship**	
	Establish rapport and treat consultee as an equal	• We will each bring our own ideas and expertise to this situation, and together, I'm sure we can come up with a good plan.
	Structure the roles	• We will work together over the next four–five weeks to figure out a solution to X. My role won't be to tell you what to do. Instead, we'll work together to figure out a plan. Depending on what we come up with, I may help with parts of the plan. If it is successful, we can start meeting less often. How does that work for you?
	Use your basic counseling skills	• You've described a lot of different issues that are concerning about Student X. It seems like his defiance is the issue that is hardest for you. You worry that he is undermining your entire class structure.
Stage 3	**Assessment**	
	Examination of the factors that are relevant to the problem (varies depending on consultation model)	• What is usually going on in the classroom when Student X makes a defiant comment toward you? (behavioral) • What will it look like when Student X is acting in a respectful manner toward you? (solution-focused) • It seems like Student X is really able to push your buttons. You generally aren't bothered by this kind of behavior, is there something different about Student X? (consultee-centered)
	Consider cultural variables	• Student X's family is Muslim. What role, if any, do you think that might play in this situation?

Stage and Accompanying Goals		Possible Language
	Help the consultee view the problem in a more complex manner	• I know it may be easy to assume that Student X is defiant toward you because you are a woman, but let's keep trying to think about other factors that might be impacting his behavior.
	Summarize the information	• To summarize . . .
Stage 4	**Problem Definition and Goal Setting**	
	Clarify the problem	• Tell me specifically what it looks like when Student X is defiant toward you. • Is this a recent problem, or has this been going on all year? • Have there been any other changes in Student X's life that you know about?
	State what the problem is	• Let me see if I have this right. When you make an instructional demand, usually during reading, Student X blurts out a defiant comment such as "No" or "Why would I do that?" When he engages in this behavior, his peers laugh, and he is asked to leave the room.
	Agree to desired outcomes or goals	• What we would like to see happen is that when you give a direction to the class, Student X will comply without a comment. • Right now, he is making comments six–eight times per day. It is not realistic to expect him to stop right away. What might be a goal that is somewhere between where he is currently and where we'd like him to be?
Stage 5	**Strategy Selection**	
	Consider different strategies that will help consultee achieve goals	• There are a few different ways to address this issue. What are some of the things you've either tried or considered?

(Continued)

Table 14.1 (Continued)

Stage and Accompanying Goals		Possible Language
	Encourage the selection of a strategy that is empirically supported	• We've considered a few different options. Behavioral contracts and increasing reinforcement for positive behavior have shown good results in research and in the schools. Let's take a closer look at these.
	Explore issues related to strategy implementation	• Both of these approaches will require some extra work on your part. Which one might work best for you? What barriers might you see to implementing this strategy?
	Explore issues related to strategy acceptability	• What are your thoughts about this approach? Does it seem like something that you could try?
Stage 6	**Strategy Implementation**	
	Plan for implementation and follow-up	• You mentioned you'd like to start with our plan on Monday. That's great. I'll check in with you on Wednesday to see how it's going. Often we think we've covered all of the bases, but we find that there is some detail or part of the plan that needs to be adjusted to work well.
	Check for regular implementation	• How has the plan been going? I noticed on Student X's data card that there wasn't any information for Thursday or Friday.
	Problem-solve and adjust plan as necessary	• Sounds like the end of the day isn't a good time for you to give him his reinforcements. When might be another time in the day that would work?
	Encourage fidelity to the plan	• I know it is a really busy time of the year, and I've noticed that Student X hasn't always been getting his reinforcers at the end of the day. It is important to stick with the plan consistently while we're trying to help him learn a new behavior. Is there another time of day that might work better for giving him his reinforcers?

Stage and Accompanying Goals		Possible Language
Stage 7	**Evaluation**	
	Develop a strategy to evaluate the effectiveness of the plan	• We identified that we would see an increase in Student X's compliant behavior and a decrease in his comments. How do we want to measure that? If Student X is more compliant, then we would expect more of his in-class work to be completed. In class, there should be fewer comments, and as a result, his referrals to the office should decrease.
	Establish responsibilities	• Let's see, after you've implemented the plan for a couple of weeks, I'll come in during reading time and gather some information on both his comments and the amount of time it takes him to get started on his work in reading.
	Generate evaluation criteria and methods	• We agreed that there would be fewer than six–eight comments, and you said four would be a good initial goal. In terms of complying with requests, you mentioned that it generally takes him five minutes to get started. We decided if he started in two–three minutes, we would consider that to be compliance with teacher request, right?
Stage 8	**Termination**	
	Conduct a review session at a specified time	• From your perspective, things are going much better. That's great. Let's set up a time to look at the data and see if it is time to set a new goal.
	Review data and analyze the results	• Student X has really been doing a great job. He is averaging less than one defiant comment per day, and he is complying with teacher requests fairly quickly (30 seconds to one minute). Even though

(Continued)

Table 14.1 (Continued)

Stage and Accompanying Goals		Possible Language
		we mostly focused on the reading block, it seems like his behavior has improved throughout the day.
	Move toward termination	• You've really helped turn Student X's behavior around. Maybe we're ready to change our meetings from every week to my checking in after three weeks? How does that sound?

Solution-Focused Group Consultation

The value of consultation is often strengthened when students, their parents, and perhaps a teacher participate as a group. Many of the models described earlier tend to focus on work with the individual. We present an alternative model that incorporates a small group of individuals (e.g., parents, student, three teachers who work with the student) and follows a solution-focused approach. Expertise and authoritative leadership are critical to assure that a meeting of diverse individuals is beneficial. Indeed, this can be a daunting responsibility. For a group consultation, the structure of solution-focused sessions as explained in Chapter 7 may be helpful. The framework is quite similar to individual or group counseling.

1. Join with every person present and establish structure.
   • Emphasize the importance of each group member's contributions.
   • Capitalize on positive effects of parent and school collaboration.
   • Summarize purpose and provide overview of meeting.
2. Establish a brief description of the concern on which members agree.
3. Inquire about exceptions.
4. Inquire about previous attempts to address the situation and the results.
   • Invite members to generate ideas for new strategies.
5. Establish goals with presuppositional language.
   • How will you know when Joe has learned to manage his anger?
   • What will be the first small steps that will let you know he has begun managing his anger?

6. Consider taking a break.

7. Identify ways each member has contributed or will contribute to solution.

8. Suggest a task.

   - As a consultant, you may determine that interventions based on behavioral, Adlerian, or other approaches would be beneficial.
   - You may also recognize the need for additional information.

9. Determine schedule for an additional meeting or follow-up.

In organizing a group consultation, professional helpers must consider who should be present in the context of their schools and the overall mission of the school. They should refrain from involvement in relationships and personal difficulties of students' parents; the focus should remain on students and their academic success. For this illustration, we will assume that Mrs. Nelson cannot attend because of her current living situation. School-based professional helpers, however, should not dismiss her important role in Hans' life.

Consultant (Joining and structuring):	Thank you for coming today. Mr. Nelson, I appreciate your rearranging your schedule so you could attend. Mr. Teacher, I also appreciate your arranging your class responsibilities so you could be with us. And, Hans, I'm always glad to see you. Sometimes it's kind of scary for kids to be in a room of adults, especially when they know that the conversation may be about them. How are you doing?
Hans:	Okay.

Consultant: I wanted to be sure you all knew that I had contacted Mrs. Nelson, and she was not able to come today. However, Hans, she wanted me to start by saying that she loves you very much, and she wants to do whatever she can do to help you during a time that's usually pretty tough for kids.

> Notice how the consultant has engaged Hans in order to support him, help him feel comfortable, and actively involve him in the consultation process. Including students during structuring establishes their role as participatory rather than observatory.

Hans: Okay.

Consultant: After we visit today, Hans, your dad and I will call your mom on the speakerphone, and we'll tell her about our meeting. Is that okay with you?

Hans: Sure.

Consultant: I am not big on surprises; so let me talk a bit about what we'll do today. I'll probably ask a lot of questions, and I hope each of you will have ideas about answers to those questions. First of all, we'll talk about how Hans is doing in school and some of the things that are going on for him. Then we'll talk about what needs to happen so that Hans will feel supported and encouraged to get back on track. At that point I'll probably take a short break so I can think about recommendations that may be helpful. When I return, I'll share those with you, and we'll decide together what our next steps will be. What questions do you have before we start?

> Notice that permission is asked. If Hans had not granted permission for the consultant to start with him, it would have been important to honor his response with something like, "Okay. Let's put Dad on the spot first."

[With this introduction, the consultant has established a structure for the session and has implicitly stated that each person will be involved.]

Consultant: Hans, may I start with you?

Hans: Okay.

Consultant: Thanks, Hans. What's your understanding of why we are meeting?

[This question is asked of each member present and followed by a paraphrase. A summary is provided once each person has responded.]

Consultant: As I understand it, then, each of you has noticed that Hans has not seemed to be happy in school lately. He hasn't sung as much as he usually does. He hasn't laughed as much as he usually does. He has had some difficulties with his friends, and his grades have dropped. Dad, you believe that Hans' difficulties right now are related to the problems between you and his mom. Hans, what do you think about that?

[Later]

Consultant: I'd like to ask a different question now. What were each of you hoping would happen as a result of our meeting together today?

[Later]

Consultant: Even though things have been difficult for Hans, I'm guessing there have been times, even during the last week, when Hans did his homework, when Hans got along with his friends, or when he participated in a class activity. Mr. Teacher, when have you noticed that? . . . Dad, when have you noticed the *real* Hans? . . .

[Again, the consultant reflects and paraphrases: "So even though Hans felt sad that morning, he got his books together and had everything ready for school. Hans, how did you get that to happen?"]

Consultant: I don't want to minimize the difficulty of this time for Hans. He loves his mom. He loves his dad. He doesn't know how things are going to be for his family. Of course he's worried. Of course he's confused. When kids, and adults, are confused, it can be hard to concentrate. It can be hard to go on as if nothing is wrong—when so much is going on. Hans, I'm going to ask you a question that may be hard. I'd like you to think about things your teachers can do, things your dad can do, things your mom can do, and things I can do to help you stay on track even though things are tough for you right now.

Hans: I don't know. Maybe my teacher could help me be sure I have everything I need when I go home at night.

Consultant (to the teacher): Is that something you are willing to do?

Teacher: Sure. Could I suggest something else?

Consultant: Let's ask Hans.

Hans: Sure.

Teacher: Sometimes I think it would be helpful for you to have a break. If you

> The miracle question may not always be appropriate and was not used in this consultation. Hans cannot control his parents, and he has little influence on their decision. Thus, the consultation is focused on assisting him during a time when he is extremely vulnerable.

could give me some clue, I would understand that you're going to the reading center just to have a few minutes by yourself.

Consultant: Hans, what do you think?

[This process continues with several ideas being generated.]

Consultant: Okay. We've talked about several possibilities. The teacher could help with organizing homework each evening. Hans could let the teacher know when he thinks a few minutes by himself would be helpful. Dad and Hans could spend 40 minutes each evening doing homework without the television. Dad and Hans can play chess each evening for 10 or 15 minutes. We can ask Mom to visit with Hans each evening on the telephone. What else? . . . We have several ideas. Which do you think will be most helpful?

> Even in consultation, a break is appropriate to consider the session as a whole, each person's contributions, and the plausibility of the plan. The consultant also thinks about feedback that will encourage each participant.

[In this stage, the group evaluates the ideas and determines the best strategies to follow.]

Consultant: Once again, we have talked about many things during our time together. Would it be okay if I step out for a few minutes to reflect? There may be something I have forgotten.

Consultant: Thanks. In the short time I was gone, I thought of many things that you are already doing to support Hans. Hans, first of all, let me say that you were brave to participate in our meeting today. I appreciated your thoughtful responses to questions that I asked. You care about your mom, your dad, and your friends. You seem to want to keep things on track even though you are having a tough time right now.

Dad, your concern and love for Hans are beyond question. Even though you are also having a difficult time, your commitment to assist with homework and devote time to Hans each evening is clear. And, Mr. Teacher, you too have made yourself available to give Hans a bit of space to help himself when he feels irritable or stressed, to help him get materials together each evening, and so forth. My sense is that he isn't going to need that extra support long, but he will appreciate it for the short time it will take for him to manage uncertainties and confusion with his family [pause]. What do you think about meeting again?

SOME FINAL THOUGHTS ON CONSULTATION

Just as you develop and practice your theoretical application to your counseling skills with student clients, you will want to develop your expertise in delivering a theoretically consistent model of consultation. We also caution new school-based professional helpers to clearly distinguish counseling from consultation. There are definitely some similarities. You will be discussing a problem or a concern with an individual and will likely be using some of the same skills (e.g., reflection, summarization) and the same theoretical approaches. Nevertheless, you do not want to confuse the two services. With counseling, you develop a therapeutic relationship for the purpose of empowering an individual to accomplish his or her goals. In consultation, you may also be working with individuals to help them accomplish their goals. However, your work is on behalf of another. For example, your ultimate goal is directed toward helping a teacher to work more effectively with a student, educating parents on how to establish more effective structures for their adolescent, or facilitating systems change to benefit all students.

COLLABORATION DEFINED

School-based professional helpers also work collaboratively. Conversely, in the process of collaboration, they may provide components of consultation. However, there are essential differences between consultation and collaboration. In consultation relationships, professional helpers have primary responsibility for the structure and many phases of the process. The recipient of the direct consultation—the consultee—holds final responsibility for the outcome. In collaboration, the responsibility for the process, decisions, execution of plans, and outcomes is shared. Brown et al. (2011, p. 3) articulated the difference by stating that "collaboration involves pooling the expertise of the collaborators and using the information as the basis of problem solving." Thus, collaboration involves a shared responsibility for the outcome of the problem-solving process. Collaboration can occur among different groups of individuals, both professional and nonprofessional. To be effective, Homan (2004) suggested that those who collaborate must have clear communication, trust, established and clear roles, a process for monitoring outcomes, and recognition of one another.

An appropriate response to such a definition is, "Well, isn't that the way we are with people all the time? We collaborate when we prepare dinner." Although people may think collaboration is simple, they often experience challenges and distress in their efforts to work collaboratively. In this regard, Stone and Dahir (2006, p. 184) asserted that

> collaboration is not for the faint of heart. It involves risk, relationship build-
> ing, personal interaction skills that are above the norm, a spirit of coop-
> eration, leadership ability, mediation skills, a thorough understanding of
> the nature and function of schools, likeableness, the ability to think on your
> feet, flexibility, a willingness to compromise, confidence, and an attitude
> and sincere belief that you can and will make a difference regardless of
> the attestations of the naysayers.

"Collaboration is harder than working alone" is an obvious conclusion that can be drawn from such a description. At the same time, experts have sug-gested that collaboration may be "more suitable as a systemic change strategy than consultation" (Brown et al., 2011, p. 4). Because of the shared responsibil-ity for designing and enacting interventions, collaboration offers distinct advan-tages in schools (Brown et al., 2011). Indeed, if school-based professionals want to be successful in the large-scale system change suggested in Chapter 15, the ability to develop collaborative relationships is a must.

MODELS AND STRATEGIES FOR SCHOOL-BASED COLLABORATION

Effective leaders in collaborative relationships draw from recommended models and strategies. Many of the models described for consultation can work equally well for collaborative partnerships (Brown et al., 2011). Other hallmarks of collaboration include voluntary engagement, equality of partici-pants, mutual goals, shared responsibility, shared resources, and shared decision making.

Consistent with the perspective of collaboration as problem solving, Rubin (2002) developed a 12-stage model that can be used to guide the efforts of collaborative groups. The first three steps in this model address the issues of identifying, assessing, and recruiting potential collaborators. For example, if you were looking at increasing the safety in and around your school, you might decide that you want to hold a "town meeting" and invite parents, police, local businesses, and school officials to come together to address this issue. From this meeting, you might determine which attendees were most invested, offered a unique perspective, and would be able to dedicate the time to this issue.

The next five stages of Rubin's (2002) model address the work of the collaborative group. These steps include identifying the different roles for the collaborators and then establishing connections among these individuals. Once these steps are in place, the group works to develop an action plan with short-term objectives. At this point, this group also reaches out to the community and other potential stakeholders in order to assist with the implementation of the plan. The final four stages occur after the plan has been in place and the group is starting to see positive outcomes. These steps include celebrating the success of the plan, gathering additional information, reporting the findings, and working with the collaborative group to determine next steps (Rubin, 2002).

Despite attention to each step of the model, outcomes may be compromised because of a variety of interpersonal interactions and reactions. To mitigate negativity, Homan (2004) suggested the following "tactics and tips" (p. 420):

- Communication at every level and stage (Homan suggested that consistent communication and participation are easiest when groups are small.)
- Clear agreements and mutual understanding of expectations (preferably documented)
- Leadership (Even in collaboration, leadership is a prerequisite of productivity; however, the style of leadership is collaborative.)
- Agreed-upon decision-making parameters and styles (Consensus is preferred.)
- Communication of recognition and appreciation (public and private)
- Trust (which is based on each member's trustworthy actions)

With attention to those factors, professional helpers can provide collaborative leadership that increases productivity. We agree with Stone and Dahir (2006) who asserted that collaboration is critical, but collegiality is collaboration at a different, deeper, and more professionally satisfying level. Collegiality results in a school that taps the collective talents, experience, and energy of its professional staff. . . . The achievement of strong collegial relations is a remarkable accomplishment; it is not the rule, but the rare, often fragile exception (p. 196).

School-based professional helpers have the knowledge and skills to influence the culture of a school to move toward more collaborative practices, or to assure that a collaborative culture is sustained. The benefits of collegiality among significant adults in a school are unquestioned and immeasurable. Thus, we encourage you to consider ways that you will contribute to a collegial, collaborative school environment.

COLLABORATION WITH PARENTS

Supporting parents' and significant adults' efforts to prepare their children for success in school and for entry into adulthood has become central to the work of school-based professional helpers (Bryan & Holcomb-McCoy, 2010). Historically, this work might have included brief individual meetings with families related to their children's needs or possibly providing parent training. Current perspectives on family collaboration and participation have expanded this view. Because parental involvement is an important component of student success, school-based professionals are now encouraged to enhance their efforts to promote family input, collaboration, and decision making at all levels (Patrikakou, Weissberg, Redding, & Walberg, 2005).

It is important to consider the difference between collaborating and supporting families and providing family therapy. When you are working with families, keep in mind that your focus is on the student client. Your role is to act as an advocate and support for the student.

Therapy with families is a specialization for which many school psychologists and school counselors are not trained, although they often consult with parents. It is important for all professional helpers

If you find yourself discussing a parent's personal concern, you can usually get the conversation back on track by asking a question such as, "What kind of effect do you think this might have on Jason's (student client) current behavior?" This kind of a question helps both parties remember that the student is the focus.

to work within the parameters of their training and supervised experience and to recognize times when referrals to credentialed family therapists are needed.

Family Systems Theories

Amplification of theories and approaches used in family counseling is beyond the intent or possibilities of this text. However, we include a few systemic concepts that warrant the attention of school-based professional helpers as they prepare to work with families, whether in consultation activities designed for work with individual families or for parent education programs. A basic understanding of family systems principles and approaches is advantageous for school-based helpers as they consult with parents, coordinate referrals, and collaborate with community service providers. Partnerships with parents and families can be strengthened by attention to basic tenets of family systems theories and the diverse ways families function effectively.

Systemic therapies are drawn from general theories about systems. In this regard, principles of biological, mechanical, and social systems extend to families. This way, any set of components or parts that are interrelated in mutually contributory ways constitutes a system—a circulatory system, an automotive system, or a family system. As we discussed in Chapter 2, a change in one part of the system influences the entire system and its components. Additionally, each individual part's value is considered in context rather than in isolation. For example, a carburetor is of little value unless it is connected with the other components of an engine. A heart is interdependent with other parts of the human body.

Systems are thought to be redundant and predictable; thus, they engage in fairly consistent sequences of behaviors, which often become the focus of systemic therapy. Systemic therapists explicate patterns rather than blaming any one entity such as parents, teachers, or students. For example, a systemic perspective of two friends in a counterproductive pattern would be, "John wants to spend time with Jill, and Jill is busy with homework and play rehearsals. John calls Jill and leaves notes for her. Jill doesn't have time to deal with John and ignores the calls and text messages. John sends more text messages and calls more often. Jill doesn't know how to respond without devoting time she does not have; thus she ignores John's overtures. John escalates his attempts to connect with Jill." Interventions would be designed to interrupt the pattern.

Just as individuals encounter challenges as they negotiate developmental stages, families must also respond to changes that parallel individual members' development. For example, families change dramatically when the first child goes to school and when the last child begins school. They must respond to changing needs of children as they reach adolescence and prepare for emancipation.

Family systems theories and approaches are diverse, just as are the models used in individual and group counseling. Some theorists emphasized intergenerational legacies and patterns. Others focused on communication patterns and reciprocal interactions. Minuchin (1974), who originated structural family therapy, examined the nuclear family, its subsystems and hierarchies, the external and internal boundaries, the family's rules (explicit and implicit), and the communication styles. Structural family therapists view problems in context of the structure and address them with changes in the structure. For example, structural family therapists empower parents to assume their responsibilities as leaders in the home.

Many concepts from the structural approach are applicable to our work in schools. Children function best when they have clear guidelines regarding behavior that are consistently followed. They also benefit from nurturing relationships with adults characterized by clear respect for boundaries. Sexual abuse is an extreme and highly destructive example of boundary violation. However, conversations with children that should be limited to adults are another example of a boundary violation.

It is important to remember that families must negotiate the interface of several systems—their family, the school, the community, the classroom, and so forth. In all likelihood, functioning in the various systems requires students to learn which rules (spoken and unspoken) are in place in each context. Additionally, they encounter diverse values that contribute to expectations. Sensitivity to these challenges assists professional helpers as they respond to needs of students and families in their schools.

Family Involvement Theories

Epstein (2001) developed a helpful theory that outlines the important ways that families and schools can merge their efforts in order to promote student success. This theory is referred to as *overlapping spheres of influence* and posits that "students learn more when parents, educators, and others in the community recognize their shared goals and responsibilities for student learning and work together rather than alone" (Epstein & Van Voorhis, 2010, p. 1). The overlapping contexts in this model refer to home, school, and community. This model helps to guide the school-based professional in ways of enhancing family-school partnerships by creating organizational structures, policies, and processes that engage families (Epstein & Van Voorhis, 2010).

One of the most helpful features of this model is the expanded definition of family involvement. In the past, parental involvement tended to be defined in fairly narrow ways (e.g., attendance at parent-teacher conferences, participation in the Parent-Teacher Organization). Epstein (1995) articulated six types of involvement that include parenting, communicating, volunteering, learning at home, decision making, and collaborating with the community. These categories represent distinct, valuable areas for parental involvement and partnership.

School-based professionals can use this framework to think in systemic ways (Epstein & Van Voorhis, 2010). For example, consider the different avenues for parent involvement in your own setting. How many of the six types of involvement are covered? What additional actions might you take to increase involvement of other types? Many schools have established clear communication strategies through e-mails, newsletters, and homework hotlines. Schools also typically have a parent volunteer program. However, the area of decision making is sometimes not reflected in parent-school partnerships. School-based professionals might work with their building leadership team to include parent members on important committees to facilitate this type of involvement.

One of the frequent complaints among those who seek to increase parent involvement is that they often see the same small group of parents. Sometimes it can seem that your efforts are only reaching a handful of parents. A challenge for school-based professionals is to reach out to those parents whose voices have not been heard. School-based professionals can work to create a welcoming school environment that encourages parent involvement and attendance at school events (Epstein & Van Voorhis, 2010). In all of your efforts, you will want to measure your results. Are more families attending your "back-to-school night"? Have you increased participation in parent-teacher conferences? Do you have parent representation on important school committees?

CONCLUSION

Through collaboration and consultation, school-based professionals can maximize their services and help the greatest number of families, teachers, and students. These efforts do not happen overnight. As a new school-based professional, you may spend your first few years enhancing your consultation skills and becoming comfortable in this role. However, we also encourage continued efforts toward enhancing your collaboration efforts. Working with your school-based team, we encourage you to create realistic yearly goals toward increasing school-family-community partnerships.

Activities

1. In groups, consider how you, as a consultant, would respond to one of the following vignettes. As you compose your responses, attend to relevant legal and ethical issues.

2. What ethical and legal considerations will be relevant to you in this capacity?

3. How would you respond (draw from one of the models presented in class)?

Vignette 1: Your high school principal meets with you. The principal has been the main administrator in the school for several years. The school has experienced an influx of new students, which has required the addition of portable classrooms. The principal moved three veteran and two new faculty members to these portable buildings. The principal has noticed a distinct change in faculty unity. There is more gossip, more sarcasm, and more verbal altercations among the faculty. The principal has recently had a conference with each of the new faculty members. One cried and expressed a feeling of isolation at being "out there in the boondocks." The other expressed a sense of abandonment in being assigned to the portable classroom. The three veteran faculty members have been more distant and noticeably cooler to the principal. The principal is unsure how to bring harmony and unity back to the faculty. The principal asks you for assistance.

Vignette 2: A few days later, you are contacted by Mr. and Mrs. Martinez. They are concerned about their child's misbehavior at home and at school. They report that the child frequently interrupts family members at home and classmates at school. The parents are puzzled at the behavior, which is quite inconsistent with the child's previous relationship patterns.

Vignette 3: And, that same week, Mr. Washington, a teacher, requests consultation. He tells you, "I am not very organized in the classroom. I am so disorganized that I cannot find my car in the garage. My disorganization is interfering with my otherwise pretty-doggone-good teaching."

Journal Reflections

Reflection #1

As you visit schools, attend to your initial reaction. How do you feel as you enter the building? Why?

Reflection #2

How do you recognize a collaborative culture? What do you notice about interaction among colleagues?

Reflection #3

What will you do to assure that guests are welcome in your schools and that their initial reactions are positive?

Reflection #4

What values related to your concepts of "good family" and "good teaching" will you need to monitor as a consultant?

Electronic Resources

National Alliance of Pupil Service Organizations: http://www.napso.org/

http://www.partnershipschools.org

School Social Worker Association of America: http://www.sswaa.org/

Print Resources

Bradley, C., Johnson, P., Rowles, G., & Dodson-Sims, A. (2005). School counselors collaborating with African-American parents. *Professional School Counseling, 8,* 424–427.

Bryan, J., & Holcomb-McCoy, C. (Eds.). (2010). Special Issue: Collaboration and partnerships with families and communities: The school counselor's role. *Professional School Counseling, 14.*

Davis, T. E., & Osborn, C. J. (1999, January). The solution-focused school: An exceptional model. *NASSP Bulletin, 83,* 40–46.

Dinkmeyer, D., & Carlson, J. (2006). *Consultation: Creating school-based interventions* (3rd ed.). New York: Routledge.

Epstein, J. L. (2001). *School, family, and community partnerships: Preparing educators and improving schools.* Boulder, CO: Westview Press.

Friend, M., & Cook, L. (2007). *Interactions: Collaboration for school professionals* (5th ed.). Boston: Allyn and Bacon.

Mullins, F., & Edwards, D. (2001). Consulting with parents: Applying family systems concepts and techniques. *Professional School Counseling, 6,* 116–123.

CHAPTER 15

Creating a Continuum of Care

Learning Objectives

- Understand the different levels for providing services (universal, selected, targeted)
- Learn strategies for maximizing the services you deliver in the schools
- Develop a needs assessment for your school
- Understand how to create seamless services through linkages between comprehensive school-based services and community resources

It seems we are not able to open a newspaper or turn on a news program today without hearing about the shortcomings of our students and our schools as related to academic achievement. Yet many of our approaches to increasing academic achievement have overlooked one of the basic prerequisites— attending to the social and emotional needs of children. In fact, at times, counselors and teachers have found themselves at odds over such issues as children missing instructional time and allocation of funds for "extra" services versus academics. Despite these perceived differences, research supports that the two goals, academic achievement and social-emotional health, are inextricably intertwined (Adelman & Taylor, 2010; Merrell & Gueldner, 2010).

The challenge to education is to find a model of service that incorporates strategies for supporting healthy social-emotional development for all children, providing targeted, evidence-based services for children who need higher levels of support, and incorporating and aligning these services to be congruent with the context of schools and the goal of increased academic achievement.

A broad continuum of mental health care is a critical component of today's educational environments. Every day, children come to school unable to focus on their academics due to family and peer conflict, environmental stressors, and increasing rates of mental health problems (Christner, Mennuti, & Whitaker, 2009). Unfortunately, the resources available to meet these growing needs are limited, partially due to the lack of school-based professional helpers within the school (ASCA, 2010b; Curtis et al., 2004). Given the daunting statistics related to student needs (cited in Chapter 1), we simply have to recognize that school-based professionals do not have the "person power" to counsel each student individually.

Approaching student well-being from a systems perspective holds promise. How can we create programs that promote students' strengths and resiliency? What sorts of programs are needed to reduce or prevent negative outcomes (e.g., bullying, truancy, school dropout)? How can you help your school leadership team decide which programs will be best for your school? Clearly, we can't answer all of these questions in a single chapter. Our goal is to provide a framework that encourages you to think about providing your services across varying levels of intensity, with a focus on prevention.

LEVELS OF PREVENTION

Over the last 20 years, the fields of education, counseling, and psychology have grown increasingly more interested in the area of prevention science. Quite simply, prevention works. Research tells us that there are many programs available that can promote children's positive development and prevent emotional and behavioral problems (Kellam & Langevin, 2003; Weisz et al., 2005). Furthermore, the positive outcomes associated with these programs appear to last for many years after the programming has ended (Weisz et al., 2005). One of the most widely accepted models of prevention outlines three levels: universal, selected, and indicated (Barrett & Turner, 2004). To better understand these different levels of intervention, we review and provide examples of each.

Universal Prevention

At a primary prevention level, no students are identified as having special needs or problems; instead a positive foundation is created that supports the greatest number of children. The goal of primary or universal prevention is to enhance the environment so that it promotes the learning and well-being of all students. As noted by Rutter and Maughan (2002, p. 470), "[p]upil achievement and behavior can be influenced (for better or worse) by the overall characteristics of the school environment."

One of the most common school-based programs is that of schoolwide positive behavioral supports (SWPBS; Sailor et al., 2009). Sugai and Horner (2008) estimated that when a school has a supportive, safe environment in which social and behavioral expectations are clearly communicated and consistently followed, 80 percent of students respond favorably and need no additional supports. When schools engage in the development and implementation of SWPBS, they are able to reduce behavioral referrals, increase academic achievement, and increase the degree to which school personnel work together (Bradshaw, Koth, Bevans, Ialongo, & Leaf, 2008; Horner et al., 2005; Lassen, Steele, & Sailor, 2006).

This method requires a collaborative team approach in which a group of individuals (e.g., parents, teachers, administrators) come together to (a) review the data; (b) analyze, describe, and prioritize the problems; and (c) create specific measurable desired outcomes for the schools. Then, the team selects various evidence-based approaches to meet these goals. These approaches will be preventive, will address the needs of the broadest range of children, and will be considered evidence-based. The school-based professional helper is an ideal individual to act as a "coach" for these efforts by coordinating the team, acting as a consultant, supporting accurate and sustained adoption and practice, as well as assisting with the monitoring of the implementation and outcomes.

Selected Prevention

Despite our best efforts at creating environments that support the needs of all students, some children will require greater levels of support due to both internal and external factors that place them at higher risk. For example, there may be some students in your school who are engaging in bullying and other aggressive behavior. Perhaps there is another group of students who is struggling to cope with the aftermath of a friend's suicide. When this is the case, we adopt a secondary level of prevention in which a problem is identified and additional supports are provided. These services might include individual and group counseling for those students who are at risk for increased difficulties.

Secondary prevention actions are sometimes referred to as selected interventions. These types of intervention are not delivered to the entire school but are provided to a student or group of students based on exposure to risk factors. Sometimes, students may be showing early signs of a problem (e.g., aggressive behavior). Selected interventions can be provided through individual or group approaches.

Sometimes the students who are selected to receive secondary prevention programming are identified through screening measures. Efforts to identify groups that might be "at risk" can be quite minimal. Teacher referral is one of the most common ways that school-based professionals become aware of a student who is struggling. Unfortunately, this strategy tends to overidentify those students who are acting out. We also want to have methods in place to identify those students who are experiencing less visible emotional challenges. Sudden changes in attendance, grade point average, and health office visits are important screening tools that can help you know when a student is experiencing a difficult time.

Several effective targeted prevention programs have been identified for use in school and community settings. One of the most common types of programs at this level is skill-building groups. These types of programs usually consist of a series of structured lessons that incorporate role plays, adult and peer modeling, and applied practice in real-life contexts (e.g., Greenberg & Kusché, 2006; Shure, 2001). Another common program, a part of SWPBS, is Check In-Check Out (CICO; Todd, Campbell, Meyer, & Horner, 2008).

This targeted intervention includes a daily report card established around the school's PBS program and the student's own goals. Each morning the student checks in and sets a daily goal. At the end of each day, the student checks out with a mentor to discuss how the student performed on his or her goals and the number of points earned. Results suggest that it is effective at reducing problem behavior (Todd et al., 2008).

Indicated Prevention

Further along the continuum of care, focus is directed toward those individuals who are demonstrating early signs of challenging behaviors, having difficulty managing their emotions, and isolating from others. These behaviors may be seen as early indicators of more serious problems. Therefore, programs designed for the indicated level of prevention tend to be more comprehensive and to target many different aspects of the individual's environment. In some instances, intensive, focused services through school/ community networks are necessary for the small percentage of children and their families who are experiencing significant mental health and/or behavioral challenges (Horner et al., 2005).

Students at this level of intervention have not responded to previous prevention programming and have greater severity in their behavioral or emotional symptoms. Therefore, a great level of time, effort, and resources is required. Although some elements of the programming may be delivered in a small group, there is typically an individual component as well. Despite this cost in terms of time, energy, and programming, these types of programs are considered to be cost effective in the long term (NRC & IOM, 2009).

Aggression, in particular, appears to be a long-standing problem and if not addressed by Grade 3 is likely to persist into adulthood and result in negative outcomes (Crick et al., 2006). In fact, Petras et al. (2008) concluded that if you want to reduce adolescent risk behaviors, the single best generic risk factor to target in elementary school is aggression. Thus, if we intervene earlier, we reduce the likelihood that patterns of aggression, substance abuse, and social isolation will become a chronic challenge for this relatively small number of students who do not respond to universal prevention programming.

Prevention for those behaviors that pose significant risk to individuals can be implemented at any age. However, the majority of evidence-based programs focus on preschool and elementary age populations (e.g., Fast Track, Conduct Problems Prevention Research Group, 1999; Incredible Years, Webster-Stratton & Herman, 2010). The Olweus Bullying Prevention Program (n.d.) is also evidence-based and is highly recommended.

Indicated programming is not only for aggression and externalizing behavior. There is a growing body of research that supports intensive programming to reduce internalizing behaviors as well (e.g., Cuijpers, van Straten, Smit, Mihalopoulos, & Beekman, 2008; Horowitz & Garber, 2006). In fact, intensive programming may be more effective for internalizing behavior than universal interventions. Horowitz and Garber (2006) found that prevention efforts directed toward reducing depressive symptoms did result in positive outcomes (i.e., lower levels of depressive symptoms). However, in this meta-analytic study, selected and indicated programs were found to be more effective than universal in decreasing these symptoms. More recently, Cuijpers et al. (2008) found that preventive interventions for adolescents reduced the incidence of depressive disorders by 23 percent. These two studies included a variety of approaches that were mostly based on cognitive-behavioral interventions.

At the greatest level of need, some students and their families may require expanded services through community agencies. Two promising models are a *system of care* philosophy (Stroul & Friedman, 1996) and, as a part of this model, the development of a wraparound team process (Eber, Sugai, Smith, & Scott, 2002). A system-of-care model emphasizes the development of a range of services to comprehensively address the needs of a student client and his or her family. To accomplish this goal, partnerships with parents and a variety of community service agencies (e.g., social services, community mental health, juvenile justice) must be established. Through this model, children and families receive individualized, comprehensive, and culturally competent care that is designed at the local level using the best available research evidence (Stroul & Friedman, 1996). A wraparound team assists families in building natural community supports to meet their needs. Both a system of care and wraparound model allow for more effective communication between all stakeholders around the needs of the child and family and ensure that duplication of services is avoided and gaps are addressed. School-based professional helpers can be active participants in the wraparound team and system of care.

ELEMENTS OF A SCHOOL-BASED CONTINUUM OF CARE

In addition to the depth provided through tiered levels of services, school-based professional helpers want to create a model that reflects best practices and meets the needs of the broadest range of children. From this perspective, this type of model would (a) help school personnel build positive, schoolwide behavioral supports that provide a sound foundation of high expectations, positive peer relationships, and a reinforcing school climate; (b) provide an increased number of evidence-based services to children through individual and group counseling, consultation, and other modalities; (c) build capacity through collaboration and interdisciplinary professional development opportunities; and (d) strengthen relationships with families and community agencies to address the needs of children, including those with the most severe mental health needs.

Positive Schoolwide Social, Emotional, and Behavioral Programs

One avenue that holds promise for meeting this difficult goal incorporates a systemic, preventive approach while providing resources to address a broad range of mental health needs. Nastasi (2004) has advocated for a public health model to provide school mental health services to children and adolescents.

The public health model endorses a continuum of services available to meet the broadest needs, with an emphasis on prevention. Doll and Cummings (2008) promoted a similar model that focuses on school environments and broad population-based services rather than on individuals. These ideals are consistent with the *ASCA National Model* (2005) and the *NASP Model for Comprehensive Services* (2010b) in that the majority of your services are directed toward the greatest number of students through guidance and systems interventions.

In our conceptualization of a continuum of care, one end of the continuum would feature schoolwide prevention programs that create a positive educational climate focused on learning. As Greenberg et al. (2003) noted, "well-designed, well-implemented school-based prevention programs can have a positive influence on a diverse array of social, health and academic outcomes" (p. 472). We conceptualize this seamless set of services that is able to promote student wellness and address student needs as a "continuum of care." Ideally, this continuum is woven into the fabric of the school to promote positive school environments, expand partnerships, implement prevention programs, and improve school-based mental health care for all children. Systemic approaches to change are effective but represent a long-term approach that is sometimes difficult to carry out in a school.

As we discussed in the previous section, many school districts have already incorporated prevention programming through the implementation of schoolwide positive behavioral supports (SWPBS; Sailor et al., 2009) and response to intervention (RTI; Brown-Chidsey & Steege, 2005). These approaches provide frameworks that emphasize prevention and universal programming to address the needs of the greatest number of students. These models are also considered to be tiered because they provide for a greater intensity of services based on student needs. We encourage new school-based professionals to plan their services to emphasize prevention programs delivered at the universal level to meet the greatest number of student needs.

Increased Access to Evidence-Based Services

School-based professional helpers must not only provide services to the greatest number of students, we must also ensure that those services are likely to have the desired outcome. All aspects of our services should reflect processes (e.g., consultation, intervention) that are supported by research. The term *evidence-based practice* refers to programs or interventions that are based on sound scientific knowledge and that have been demonstrated to be effective through rigorous research (Hoagwood, Burns, & Weisz, 2002). By indicating that an approach is an evidence-based practice, we are saying that it has robust, empirical evidence to support its use with a particular issue or population. Unfortunately, there are many gaps in our knowledge about what works with which population and in what setting.

Because of the clinical nature of research, it is often difficult to adapt some of these approaches to "real world" settings. Further, the dynamic nature of schools and the limited availability of resources (e.g., time, expertise) make precise delivery of these interventions challenging. School personnel do not tend to select programs that have been appropriately evaluated or that have been shown to produce the desired outcomes (Ennett et al., 2003). The end result has been that it is difficult to integrate evidence-based practices (EBPs) into schools (Hoagwood & Johnson, 2003). In fact, Zins, Weissberg, Wang, and Walberg (2004) reported that although a typical school-based professional will deliver an average of 14 separate programs that address social-emotional issues, most will not be evidence-based.

As training programs, professional organizations, and professional literature continue to focus on evidence-based practices, it is likely that we will continue to see a shift toward more of this type of programming integrated into educational settings. No doubt your generation of school counselors and school psychologists will become leaders in the integration of evidence-based prevention and intervention programming in school settings.

BUILDING CAPACITY THROUGH COLLABORATION

Capacity building refers to efforts that are "designed to enhance and coordinate human, technical, financial, and other organizational resources directed toward quality implementation of evidence-based, competence-building interventions" (Spoth, Greenberg, Bierman, & Redmond, 2004, p. 32). Long-term prevention and intervention programs rely on systems that are able to support and sustain these efforts. The basic elements of capacity building include collaborating in ways that educate and empower others. In order to meet the second part of this goal (i.e., educating and empowering others), ongoing professional development is an important element to enhancing the skill and knowledge of your team members, including families. Many of these components of capacity building are already part of your role as a school-based professional helper.

Collaborative Teaming for Education and Empowerment

One of the first steps in creating a systemic approach is to join or help build a team with a group of individuals at your school and in the community who are interested in working toward the same goal. As discussed in the previous chapter, working with others helps to increase the level of services that you can provide. Students' needs may be most expediently addressed when school-based professional helpers and representatives of other mental health professions (e.g., school social workers, community mental health practitioners) collaborate to meet the social, emotional, behavioral, and academic needs of all students (Adelman & Taylor, 2006).

School-based professional helpers have effective communication skills that allow them to work with individuals from a variety of backgrounds. Consultation and counseling skills can be put to good use when facilitating working groups in which individuals with differing perspectives must come together to develop a plan. By implementing the steps of a problem-solving process, professional helpers can identify needs, help establish goals, and decide on a potential plan to meet these goals. We recommend a collaborative teaming model that includes teachers, administrators, families, and other school-based professional helpers.

Ongoing, Interdisciplinary Professional Development

To facilitate systemic change, training of caregivers, service providers, and those individuals who can make a difference is a necessary component. Parents, classroom teachers, and community members (e.g., religious leaders, afterschool program leaders, athletic coaches) represent significant influences in a child's life, and mental health professionals can share their expertise with these individuals to help them more effectively communicate with children, create healthy environments, and identify children who are in need of additional mental health services.

Your professional development activities may be designed to match the levels of prevention activities (e.g., primary, secondary, tertiary). That is, consider what preparation all stakeholders need in order to create an appropriate context for the implementation of a program. If you are working to implement whole school reform, what information or skills are needed in order to increase the chances that your efforts will be successful? For example, if your school team has decided that a SWPBS approach would decrease the levels of aggression among students, there are certain steps that your group might take in order to prepare the school and community members for implementation of such a program.

The initial goal for your professional development will be to help make others aware of the issue and the importance of taking action. Next, you will want to help all school staff and families understand the program and the types of changes that are required. Once the program is officially implemented in the school, the trainings may become more focused. For example, you might collaborate with teachers at different grade levels to adapt aspects of the programming to meet the developmental needs of students. Another aspect of your work might be training other school staff (e.g., bus driver, custodian, office administration, lunch room staff) to help them understand how to implement aspects of the program within their own contexts. At the narrowest level, you may "troubleshoot" to address the needs of individuals who are reluctant or struggling to implement the program or doing so in a manner that is contrary to your efforts.

At the secondary level of prevention, it is important for school staff to learn more about how to meet the needs of students who are struggling. As a part of the professional development in this area, the school-based helper could provide information on identifying children who are at risk or who are experiencing mental health problems. Another potential training would be directed toward developing positive behavioral support plans for individual children who need additional supports in order to function in the school environment.

At the tertiary prevention level, professional development opportunities should extend to community mental health providers to help establish interagency teams and extend our collaborative relationships with community resources. Through these partnerships, you can help teachers and administrators develop a greater level of awareness of resources for families.

Strengthen Relationships With Families and Community Agencies

Communities play an important role in the development of youth. They can be vital, supportive environments or unsafe targets for violence and aggression. It is important for school-based professionals to help build safe and healthy school environments and develop close, collaborative relationships with resources in the community in order to best meet the needs of students and their families. (See Chapter 14 for more information on school-community collaboration.)

We can no longer afford to have separate programs within schools and communities that are structurally and philosophically independent. Instead, we should direct our efforts toward developing seamless supports that identify and support the academic, social, and emotional needs of children.

Professionals and representatives from community agencies can work together to achieve the goals of the project and to develop a better understanding of how to align their efforts.

CONDUCTING A NEEDS ASSESSMENT

The tasks described in this chapter may seem daunting. One of the most common concerns is, "Where do I begin?" If you are in a school that has a number of concerns such as low academic achievement, poor attendance rates, identified behavioral challenges, and low teacher morale, it may be difficult to identify any one area to target. Everything may seem equally important to address. In other schools, there may be one clear area of concern (e.g., bullying), but you need more information to understand why it is occurring and what types of strategies might be most effective in addressing the identified concern.

A useful framework to guide your efforts to identify the needs of your school is one that focuses on existing risks and protective factors. What risk and protective factors are associated with this specific area of concern? Which ones can be modified? As you identify a specific area of focus (e.g., school dropout), you will also be able to determine those factors that might be contributing to this issue (e.g., low school engagement, below-average academic performance). Further, consider the factors that help make students resilient to negative outcomes. In the case of school dropout, having peers who are engaged in school and a close relationship with a teacher or other adult in the school helps students to stay academically engaged.

Your interventions are designed to target the related risk and protective factors. That is, your program would be designed to strengthen the protective factors and reduce the risks. Issues such as bullying and victimization, academic underachievement and failure, poor peer relationships, violence, and substance use are all risk factors that are associated with disorganized and unsafe neighborhoods and schools (NRC & IOM, 2009). If you are working in a school or community where these problems are prevalent, there is much that you can do in your school setting, working together with community supports, to ameliorate the occurrence and the negative effects of these risk factors.

In addition to the formal measures mentioned shortly, self-created questionnaires can also be helpful for gathering important information regarding your school's specific needs.

Fortunately, many organizations have already carried out the work of identifying risk and protective factors associated with some of the most common negative outcomes in youth (e.g., school dropout, teen pregnancy, violence). For example, the Substance Abuse and Mental Health Services Administration (SAMHSA) has developed a survey, a prevention manual, and a community leaders' guide that can help communities identify a broad range of risk and protective factors in their youth and implement effective programs to address concerns. The *Communities that Care Youth Survey* can be administered in 50 minutes to sixth- through twelfth-grade students and used to help identify youth who might benefit from more targeted interventions. Additionally, there is an accompanying prevention guidebook that provides information on over 50 programs that have evidence to support their use with students from different developmental levels, to address specific risk and protective factors, in different domains (e.g., individual, family, school, community) and at different levels (e.g., universal, selective, indicated). All resources associated with the *Communities that Care* program (e.g., survey, prevention guide, leader's manual) are available for free at the website provided in Table 15.1.

An alternative, offered through the Centers for Disease Control, is the *School Health Index: A Self-Assessment and Planning Guide*. This simple self-assessment tool consists of eight modules that cover topics such as nutrition, school safety, physical activity, health services, health promotion, counseling, psychological and social services, and family involvement. The self-assessment is completed by a group of school stakeholders such as the principal, nurse, school counselor and/or school psychologists, as well as parents and community representatives (e.g., health department, community mental health, American Cancer Society representative). After responding to the series of discussion questions for each module, the group completes an overall scorecard for the school, chooses their top five priorities for action, and then uses the materials provided on the website or from other sources to begin addressing their goal areas.

The Collaborative for Academic, Social, and Emotional Learning (CASEL) also lists a number of needs and outcome assessments. These instruments vary in the range of behaviors that they assess. Most are focused on a broad range of health behaviors (e.g., *California Healthy Kids Survey*, Youth Risk Behavior Surveillance System [YRBSS]). However, if your team was interested in measuring a very specific type of outcome, the Child Trends Youth Development Outcomes website is an excellent source for these focused measures. On this site, a list of possible outcomes that you might be interested in measuring (e.g., parent-child relationship, mental health, school engagement) are provided. By familiarizing yourself with these websites, you can quickly access existing assessments that can help you and your team gather important information about potential problem areas as well as the types of risk and protective factors that are unique to your setting and your student population.

School-based professionals may be able to access important information about the youth in their community through the county health department. The Centers for Disease Control (CDC) has developed a youth risk survey (YRBSS) that is used to monitor the degree to which youth are engaging in specific behaviors that are associated with health risks. Questions regarding seat belt and helmet use; exercise; use of sun protection; tobacco, alcohol, and illicit substance use; engaging in sex; and perceived safety and aggression (e.g., fighting, carrying a weapon) are all part of this survey. The information is used for a variety of purposes, but the current focus for the CDC is to monitor the degree to which the United States is meeting its goals for the *Healthy People 2010* initiative. Individual states and counties have used the data for such

Table 15.1 Websites of Needs Assessment Instruments

Program	Resources and URL
Communities That Care	Survey, Prevention Guide, Leader's Manual http://ncadi.samhsa.gov/features/ctc/resources.aspx
Centers for Disease Control *School Health Index: A Self-Assessment and Planning Guide*	Self-assessment, Modules covering many health behaviors, Meeting agendas, Ideas for team members https://apps.nccd.cdc.gov/SHI/Default.aspx
Collaborative for Academic, Social, and Emotional Learning (CASEL)	Broad-Based Needs and Outcomes Assessments http://www.casel.org/
Child Trends Youth Development Outcomes	Focused Needs and Outcomes Assessments http://www.childtrends.org/what_works/clarkwww/compendium_intro.asp
Centers for Disease Control, Youth Risk Behavior Surveillance System	Surveys, Fact Sheets, Data http://www.cdc.gov/HealthyYouth/yrbs/index.htm

purposes as developing a health curriculum and programming within educational settings or using the information to support community-based programs to increase physical activity (Centers for Disease Control and Prevention, 2010). If your state or county uses these types of surveys, it may be relatively simple to access the data for your community in order to develop a better understanding of the kinds of risk and protective factors that are present among youth in your community.

APPLYING A CONTINUUM OF CARE

We return to Marley Elementary School introduced earlier (Section IV Introduction) to provide an example of what happens when we address the needs of the system. We realize we have skipped over a number of steps and details in this case. A full step-by-step description is beyond the scope of this text. However, we hope that this illustration demonstrates the importance of continually expanding your efforts by working with others to create positive systemic change.

Case Illustration

Marley Elementary School is located in a neighborhood with high unemployment and unsafe conditions. The school has been identified as not meeting academic goals, and as a result, there is low morale among the staff. The students as well seem to have given up on themselves and were disengaged in the classroom. As a member of the school leadership team, you have decided to approach this situation from a systemic perspective.

The one overarching goal for the school leadership team is to improve student achievement outcomes. There are several ways to support improved academic outcomes including the use of evidence-based programming and communication of high expectations. However, academic interventions may not address all of the concerns. Clearly, a number of students are engaging in challenging behaviors that are interfering with their own and others' learning. Therefore, your team also has to consider a broad behavioral intervention that will help students demonstrate more appropriate learning and social behaviors. Your team recognizes that you cannot accomplish these goals on your own and decides to invite parents, local business owners, and other community leaders to a planning meeting.

(Continued)

(Continued)

You develop a working team that selects the goals of improved student behavior and increased academic achievement. As a school-based professional, you decide to work with the team that will focus on improved student behavior because you believe your expertise is best suited to this group. In your role as a group member, you help research potential programs, assist in developing a needs assessment around student behavior and safety, and help facilitate the meetings.

After reviewing various programs and discussing the advantages and disadvantages of each, your team decides to implement a schoolwide behavior support program. Because you have invited diverse members to your team, you are able to obtain broad support for your efforts. The parents on the team help you to design communication that will inform other parents. Community business members agree to help provide incentives to reinforce positive student performance. You know it is going to be a lot of work, but for the first time in a long time, you sense a renewed, positive energy in the halls of Marley Elementary.

CONCLUSION

School-based prevention programs that are directly linked to the central mission of the school and are aligned with goals to which school personnel are accountable are more likely to be successful (Greenberg et al., 2003). Creating sustainable, systemic change is not an easy task and requires a great deal of time and training. When stakeholders share a common vision, feel empowered, and have support, systemic change will occur.

It is not expected that you will accomplish this type of change in your first year, nor that you will do it alone. Instead, we encourage you to use your current skills to build the foundational structures. As you begin your journey, we encourage you to see yourself as a part of this continuum of care. In your efforts, we challenge you to become a leader and a change agent. Through systemic interventions, collaborative approaches, and the use of evidence-based practices, we can have the most positive impact on the greatest number of students.

Activities

1. Working in a group, create a list of local service providers and/or other services in your community that specialize in services to children and adolescents. Costs? Pro bono? Specializations? Languages? What gaps do you see?

2. With a small group, develop a needs assessment for an elementary, mid-dle, or high school (select one). Use some of the needs assessments presented in this chapter as a model.

Journal Reflections

Reflection #1
As a new school-based professional, what might be some initial steps you could take to become involved in systems change?

Reflection #2
Consider the idea of a "continuum of care." At which points are you most comfortable working?

Electronic Resources

Child Trends Youth Development Outcomes: http://www.childtrends.org/what_works/clarkwww/compendium_intro.asp

Collaborative for Academic, Social, and Emotional Learning (CASEL): http://www.casel.org

Communities that Care Program: http://ncadi.samhsa.gov/features/ctc/resources.aspx

School Health Index: A Self-Assessment and Planning Guide: https://apps.nccd.cdc.gov/SHI/Default.aspx

Youth Risk Behavior Surveillance System: http://www.cdc.gov/HealthyYouth/yrbs/index.htm

Print Resources

Algozzine, B., Daunic, A. P., & Smith, S. W. (2010). *Preventing problem behaviors: Schoolwide programs and classroom practices* (2nd ed.). Thousand Oaks, CA: Sage.

Lane, K. L., Kalberg, J. R., & Menzies, H. M. (2009). Developing schoolwide programs to prevent and manage problem behaviors: A step-by-step approach. New York: Guilford Press.

Parsons, R. D. (2007). Counseling strategies that work!: Evidence-based interventions for school counselors. Boston: Allyn & Bacon.

References

Active Parenting Publishing. (2006). *Over twenty years of evidence: Active Parenting works!* Retrieved November 1, 2010, from http://www.activeparenting.com/Research_summary

Adelman, H. S., & Taylor, L. (2003). On sustainability of project innovations as systemic change. *Journal of Educational and Psychological Consultation, 14,* 1–26.

Adelman, H. S., & Taylor, L. (2006). Mapping a school's resources to improve their use in preventing and ameliorating problems. In C. Franklin, M. B. Harris, & P. Allen-Meares (Eds.), *School services sourcebook: A guide for social workers, counselors, and mental health professionals* (pp. 977–990). New York: Oxford University Press.

Adelman, H. S., & Taylor, L. (2010). *Mental health in schools: Engaging learners, preventing problems, and improving schools.* Thousand Oaks, CA: Corwin.

Adler, A. (1958). *The practice and theory of individual psychology.* Patterson, NJ: Littlefield, Adams.

Adler, A. (1964). *Social interest: Adler's key to the meaning of life.* Boston: Oxford.

Akin-Little, A., Little, S. G., Bray, M. A., & Kehle, T. J. (2009). Introduction. In A. Akin-Little, S. G. Little, M. A. Bray, & T. J. Kehle (Eds.), *Behavior interventions in schools: Evidence-based positive strategies* (pp. 3–10). Washington, DC: American Psychological Association.

Alberto, P. A., & Troutman, A. C. (2006). *Applied behavior analysis for teachers* (7th ed.). Upper Saddle River, NJ: Prentice Hall.

Alberts, A., Elkind, D., & Ginsberg, S. (2007). The personal fable and risk-taking in early adolescence. *Journal of Youth and Adolescence, 36,* 71–76.

Allen, M., Burt, K., Bryan, E., Carter, D., Orsi, R., & Durkan, L. (2002). School counselors' preparation for and participation in crisis intervention. *Professional School Counseling, 6,* 96–102.

Altshuler, S. (2006). Professional requirements for school social work and other school mental health professions. In C. Franklin, M. Harris, & P. Allen-Meares (Eds.), *School services sourcebook: A guide for social workers, counselors, and mental health professionals* (pp. 1129–1146). New York: Oxford University Press.

American Art Therapy Association. (n.d.). *About the American Art Therapy Association.* Retrieved June 22, 2006, from http://www.arttherapy.org/index.html.

American Counseling Association [ACA]. (2010a). *ACA code of ethics.* Retrieved December 13, 2010, from http://www.counseling.org/Resources/CodeOfEthics/TP/Home/CT2.aspx.

American Counseling Association [ACA]. (2010b). *Definition of counseling.* Retrieved November 20, 2010, from http://www.counseling.org/Resources/.

American Psychological Association [APA]. (2010). *Ethical principles of psychologists and code of conduct.* Retrieved December 13, 2010, from http://www.apa.org/ethics/code/index .aspx.

American Red Cross. (2007). *In the aftermath.* Retrieved December 10, 2010, from http://www .redcross.org/preparedness/educatorsmodule/EDU_In_the_Aftermath/Aftermath%20Back ground.pdf.

American School Counselor Association [ASCA]. (1997). *The national standards for school counseling programs.* Alexandria, VA: Author.

American School Counselor Association [ASCA]. (2005). *The ASCA national model: A framework for school counseling programs* (2nd ed.). Alexandria, VA: Author.

American School Counselor Association [ASCA]. (2007). *The professional school counselor and crisis/critical incident response in the schools.* Retrieved December 8, 2010, from http:// asca2.timberlakepublishing.com//files/PS_Crisis_Critical.pdf.

American School Counselor Association [ASCA]. (2009). *The role of the professional school counselor.* Retrieved July 14, 2011, from http://www.schoolcounselor.org/content.asp?pl=325& sl=133&contentid=240.

American School Counselor Association [ASCA]. (2010a). *Ethical standards for school counselors.* Retrieved December 13, 2010, from http://www.schoolcounselor.org/files/Ethical-Standards2010.pdf.

American School Counselor Association [ASCA]. (2010b). *Student/school counselor ratio by state, 2008–2009.* Retrieved December 6, 2010, from http://www.schoolcounselor.org/files/ Ratios%202008–09.pdf.

Association for Play Therapy. (n.d.). *About play therapy.* Retrieved October 27, 2010, from http://www.a4pt.org/ps.playtherapy.cfm.

Axline, V. M. (1947). *Play therapy.* New York: Ballantine.

Axline, V. M. (1964). *Dibs in search of self.* New York: Ballantine.

Baldwin, S. A., Wampold, B. E., & Imel, Z. E. (2007). Untangling the alliance-outcome correlation: Exploring the relative importance of therapist and patient variability in the alliance. *Journal of Consulting and Clinical Psychology, 75,* 842–852.

Barrett, P. M., Dadds, M. R., Rapee, R. M. (1996). Family treatment of childhood anxiety: A controlled trial. *Journal of Consulting and Clinical Psychology, 64,* 333–342.

Barrett, P. M., & Turner, C. M. (2004). Prevention of childhood anxiety and depression. In P. M. Barrett & T. H. Ollendick (Eds.), *Handbook of interventions that work with children and adolescents: Prevention and treatment* (pp. 429–474). West Sussex, England: John Wiley & Sons.

Baskin, T. W., Slaten, C. D., Crosby, N. R., Pufahl, T., Schneller, C. L., & Ladell, M. (2010). Efficacy of counseling and psychotherapy in the schools: A meta-analytic review of treatment outcome studies. *The Counseling Psychologist, 38,* 878–903.

Beck, A. T. (1976). *Cognitive therapy and the emotional disorders.* New York: International Universities Press.

Beck, A. T., Rush, A. J., Shaw, B. F., & Emery, G. (1979). *Cognitive therapy for depression.* New York: Guilford Press.

Beer, M., & Spector, H. (1980). *Organizational change and development: A systems view.* Santa Monica, CA: Goodyear.

Beltman, S., & MacCallum, J. (2006). Mentoring and the development of resilience: An Australian perspective. *International Journal of Mental Health Promotion, 8,* 17–28.

Berg, I. K. (2005 July/August). Keeping the solutions inside the classroom. *ASCA School Counselor, 42*(6), 30–35.

Bergan, J. R. (1977). *Behavioral consultation.* Columbus, OH: Merrill.

Berk, L. E. (2008). *Infants, children, and adolescents* (6th ed.). Boston: Pearson.

Berman, P. S. (2010). *Case conceptualization and treatment planning: Integrating theory with clinical practice.* Los Angeles: Sage.

Bernal, G., Bonilla, J., Padilla-Cotto, L., & Pérez-Prado, E. (1998). Factors associated to outcome in psychotherapy: An effectiveness study in Puerto Rico. *Journal of Clinical Psychology, 54,* 329–342.

Bernard, J. M., & Goodyear, R. K. (2004). *Fundamentals of clinical supervision* (3rd ed.). Needham Heights, MA: Allyn & Bacon.

Bernstein, G. A., Bernat, D. H., Victor, A. M., & Layne, A. E. (2008). School-based interventions for anxious children: 3-, 6-, and 12-month follow-ups. *Journal of the American Academy of Child and Adolescent Psychiatry, 47,* 1039–1047.

Betan, E., & Binder, J. L. (2010). Clinical expertise in psychotherapy: How expert therapists use theory in generating case conceptualizations and interventions. *Journal of Contemporary Psychotherapy, 40,* 141–152.

Bettner, B. L., & Lew, A. (1996). *Raising kids who can.* Newton Center, MA: Connexions.

Beutler, L. E., Malik, M., Alimohamed, S., Harwood, T. M., Talebi, H., Noble, S., et al. (2004). Therapist variables. In M. J. Lambert (Ed.), *Bergin and Garfield's handbook of psychotherapy and behavior change* (5th ed., pp. 227–306). New York: Wiley.

Bloom, L. (1998). Language acquisition in its developmental context. In D. Kuhn & R. S. Siegler (Eds.), *Handbook of child psychology: Vol. 2: Cognition, perception, and language* (5th ed., pp. 309–370). New York: Wiley.

Bonner, M., & Barnett, D. W. (2004). Intervention-based school psychology services: Training for child-level accountability; preparing for program-level accountability. *Journal of School Psychology, 42,* 23–43.

Bostick, D., & Anderson, R. (2009). Evaluating a small-group counseling program—A model for program planning and improvement in the elementary setting. *Professional School Counseling, 12,* 428–433.

Bradshaw, C. P., Koth, K., Bevans, K. B., Ialongo, N., & Leaf, P. J. (2008). The impact of school-wide positive behavioral interventions and supports on the organizational health of elementary schools. *School Psychology Quarterly, 23,* 462–473.

Brannigan, M. (2007). A psychoeducational group model to build academic competence in new middle school students. *Journal for Specialists in Group Work, 32,* 61–70.

Bratton, S. (2010). Meeting the early mental health needs of children through school-based play therapy: A review of outcome research. In A. A. Drewes & C. E. Schaefer (Eds.), *School-based play therapy* (2nd ed., pp. 17–60). Hoboken, NJ: Wiley.

Bratton, S. C., Ray, D., Rhine, T., & Jones, L. (2005). The efficacy of play therapy with children: A meta-analytic review of treatment outcomes. *Professional Psychology: Research and Practice, 36,* 376–390.

Breen, D. T., & Daigneault, S. K. (1998). The use of play therapy with adolescents in high school. *International Journal of Play Therapy, 7*(1), 25–47.

Brehm, K., & Doll, B. (2009). Building resilience in schools: A focus on population-based prevention. In R. W. Christner & R. B. Menutti (Eds.), *School-based mental health: A practitioner's guide to comparative practices* (pp. 55–85). New York: Routledge.

Bronfenbrenner, U. (1979). *The ecology of human development: Experiments by nature and design.* Cambridge, MA: Harvard University Press.

Brophy, J. E. (2004). *Motivating students to learn* (2nd ed.). Mahwah, NJ: Erlbaum.

Brown, D., Pryzwansky, W. B., & Schulte, A. (2011). *Psychological consultation and collaboration: Introduction to theory and practice* (7th ed.). Boston: Pearson.

Brown-Chidsey, R. & Steege, M., (2005). *Response to intervention: Principles and strategies for effective practice.* New York: Guilford Press.

Bruner, J. (1975). Child development: Play is serious business. *Psychology Today, 8*(8), 81–83.

Bryan, J. A., & Holcomb-McCoy, C. (2010). Editorial introduction: Collaboration and partnership with families and communities. *Professional School Counseling, 14,* ii-v.

Burns, D. D. (1999). *Feeling good: The new mood therapy* (Rev. ed.). New York: Avon.

Cameron, S., & turtle-song, i. (2002). Learning to write case notes using the SOAP format. *Journal of Counseling and Development, 80,* 286–292.

Campbell, C. A., & Brigman, G. (2007). Closing the achievement gap: A structured approach to group counseling. *Journal for Specialists in Group Work, 32,* 67–82.

Caplan, G. (1970). *The theory and practice of mental health consultation.* New York: Basic Books.

Carlson, J., Watts, R. E., & Maniacci, M. (2006). *Adlerian therapy: Theory and practice.* Washington, DC: American Psychological Association.

Carmichael, K. D. (2006). *Play therapy: An introduction.* Upper Saddle River, NJ: Prentice-Hall.

Catalano, R. F., Berglund, M. L., Ryan, J. A. M., Lonczak, H. S., & Hawkins, J. D. (2004). Positive youth development in the United States: Research findings on evaluations of positive youth development programs. *Annals of the American Academy of Political and Social Science, 591,* 98–124.

Caterino, L. C., & Sullivan, A. L. (2009). Applying Adlerian therapy in schools. In R. W. Christner & R. B. Mennuti (Eds.), *School-based mental health: A practitioner's guide to comparative practices* (pp. 273–298). New York: Routledge.

Centers for Disease Control and Prevention. (2009). *Trends in the prevalence of suicide-related behaviors*. Retrieved May 10, 2011, from http://www.cdc.gov/healthyyouth/yrbs/pdf/us_suicide_trend_yrbs.pdf.

Centers for Disease Control and Prevention. (2010). Youth risk behavior surveillance—United States, 2009. *Morbidity and Mortality Weekly Report, 59* (SS-5). Retrieved May 12, 2011, from http://www.cdc.gov/mmwr/pdf/ss/ss5905.pdf.

Charvat, J. L. (2005). NASP study: How many school psychologists are there? *Communiqué Online, 33*(6). Retrieved April 9, 2011, from http://www.nasponline.org/publications/cq/cq336numsp.aspx.

Cheston, S. (2000). A new paradigm for teaching counseling theory and practice. *Counselor Education and Supervision, 39,* 254–269.

Christner, R. W., Mennuti, R. B., & Pearson, L. M. (2009). Cognitive-behavioral approaches in a school setting. In R. W. Christner & R. B. Mennuti (Eds.), *School-based mental health: A practitioner's guide to comparative practices* (pp. 181–200). New York: Routledge.

Christner, R. W., Mennuti, R. B., & Whitaker, J. S. (2009). An overview of school-based mental health practice: From systems service to crisis intervention. In R. W. Christner & R. B. Mennuti (Eds.), *School-based mental health: A practitioner's guide to comparative practices* (pp. 3–22). New York: Routledge.

Clarke, G., Lewinsohn, P., Rohde, P., Hops, H., & Seeley, J. (1999). Cognitive-behavioral group treatment of adolescent depression: Efficacy of acute treatment and booster sessions. *Journal of the American Academy of Child and Adolescent Psychiatry, 38,* 272–279.

Clarkin, J. F., & Levy, K. N. (2004). The influence of client variables on psychotherapy. In M. J. Lambert (Ed.), *Bergin and Garfield's handbook of psychotherapy and behavior change* (5th ed., pp. 195–226). New York: Wiley.

Cobia, D., & Henderson, D. (2007). *Developing an effective and accountable school counseling program* (2nd ed.). Upper Saddle River, NJ: Prentice Hall.

Cochran, J. L. (1996). Using play and art therapy to help culturally diverse students overcome barriers to school success. *The School Counselor, 43,* 287–298.

Coffee, G., & Ray-Subramanian, C. E. (2009). Goal attainment scaling: A progress-monitoring tool for behavioral interventions. *School Psychology Forum: Research in Practice, 3,* 1–12. Retrieved May 1, 2011, from http://www.nasponline.org/publications/spf/issue3_1/coffee abstract.aspx.

Coleman, V. D., Parmer, T., & Barker, S. A. (1993). Play therapy for multicultural populations: Guidelines for mental health professionals. *International Journal of Play Therapy, 2*(1), 63–74.

Committee for Children. (2010). *Second step.* Retrieved February 6, 2011, from http://www .cfchildren.org/programs/ssp/overview/.

Conduct Problems Prevention Research Group. (1999). Initial impact of the Fast Track prevention trial for conduct problems: I. The high-risk sample. *Journal of Consulting and Clinical Psychology, 67,* 631–647.

Corey, G. (2010). *Theory and practice of group counseling* (7th ed.). Belmont, CA: Brooks/Cole.

Cormier, S., & Hackney, H. (2008). *Counseling strategies and interventions.* Boston: Allyn & Bacon.

Council for Accreditation of Counseling and Related Educational Programs. (2009). *2009 standards.* Retrieved December 8, 2010, from http://www.cacrep.org/doc/2009%20Standards%20 with%20cover.pdf.

Crawley, S. A., Podell, J. L., Beidas, R. S., Braswell, L., & Kendall, P. C. (2010). Cognitive-behavioral therapy with youth. In K. S. Dobson (Ed.), *Handbook of cognitive-behavioral therapies* (pp. 375–410). New York: Guilford Press.

Crick, N. R., Ostrov, J. M., Burr, J. E., Cullerton-Sen, C., Jansen-Yeh, E., & Ralston, P. (2006). A longitudinal study of relational and physical aggression in preschool. *Journal of Applied Developmental Psychology, 27,* 254–268.

Cuijpers, P., van Straten, A., Smit, F., Mihalopoulos, C., & Beekman, A. (2008). Preventing the onset of depressive disorders: A meta-analytic review of psychological interventions. *American Journal of Psychiatry, 165,* 1272–1280.

Curtis, M. J., Castillo, J. M., & Cohen, R. M. (2008). Best practices in systems level change. In A. Thomas & J. Grimes (Eds.), *Best practices in school psychology V* (pp. 887–901). Bethesda, MD: National Association of School Psychologists.

Curtis, M. J., Chesno Grier, J. E., & Hunley, S. A. (2004). The changing face of school psychology: Trends in data and projections for the future. *School Psychology Review, 33,* 49–66.

Daki, J., & Savage, R. S. (2010). Solution-focused brief therapy: Impacts on academic and emotional difficulties. *Journal of Educational Research, 103,* 309–326.

Daunic, A., Smith, S. W., Brank, E. M., & Penfield, R. D. (2006). Classroom-based cognitive-behavioral intervention to prevent aggression: Efficacy and social validity. *Journal of School Psychology, 44,* 123–139.

Davis, T. (2005). *Exploring school counseling: Professional practices and perspectives.* Boston: Lahaska/Houghton Mifflin.

Davis, T. E., & Osborn, C. J. (2000). *The solution-focused school counselor.* Philadelphia, PA: Taylor Francis.

Deegear, J., & Lawson, D. M. (2003). The utility of empirically supported treatments. *Professional Psychology: Research and Practice, 34,* 271–277.

Dehart, G. B., Sroufe, L. A., & Cooper, R. G. (2000). *Child development: Its nature and course* (4th ed.). Boston: McGraw Hill.

Dekraai, M., Sales, B., & Hall, S. (1998). Informed consent, confidentiality, and duty to report laws in the conduct of child therapy. In T. R. Kratochwill & R. J. Morris (Eds.), *The practice of child therapy* (3rd ed., pp. 540–559). Boston: Allyn & Bacon.

de Shazer, S. (1985). *Keys to solution in brief therapy.* New York: Norton.

de Shazer, S. (1987, September-October). Minimal elegance. *The Family Therapy Networker, 11,* 57–59.

DiGiuseppe, R. (2009). An introduction to cognitive behavior therapies. In A. Akin-Little, S. G. Little, M. A. Bray, & T. J. Kehle (Eds.), *Behavior interventions in schools: Evidence-based positive strategies* (pp. 95–110). Washington, DC: American Psychological Association.

DiGiuseppe, R., Linscott, J., & Jilton, R. (1996). Developing the therapeutic alliance in child-adolescent psychotherapy. *Applied and Preventive Psychology, 5,* 85–100.

Dinkmeyer, D., & Carlson, J. (2006). *Consultation: Creating school-based interventions* (3rd ed.). New York: Routledge.

Dinkmeyer, D., & Dinkmeyer, D. (1989). Adlerian psychology. *Adlerian Psychology: A Journal of human behavior, 26*(1), 26–34.

Dinkmeyer, D., & Sperry, L. (2000). *Counseling and psychotherapy: An integrated, individual psychology approach* (3rd. ed.). Upper Saddle River, NJ: Prentice Hall.

DiPerna, J. C., & Elliott, S. N. (2000). *ACES: The Academic Competence Evaluation Scales.* San Antonio, TX: The Psychological Corporation.

Dobson, K. S., & Dozois, D. J. A. (2010). Historical and philosophical bases of the cognitive-behavioral therapies. In K. S. Dobson (Ed.), *Handbook of cognitive-behavioral therapies* (3rd ed., pp. 3–38). New York: Guilford Press.

Dodge, K. A., Lansford, J. E., Burks, V. S., Bates, J. E., Pettit, G. S., Fontaine, R., et al. (2003). Peer rejection and social information-processing factors on the development of aggressive behavior problems in children. *Child Development, 74,* 374–393.

Doll, B., & Cummings, J. (2008). *Transforming school mental health services: Population-based approaches to promoting the competency and wellness of children.* Thousand Oaks, CA: Corwin Press in cooperation with the National Association of School Psychologists.

Doll, B., Zucker, S., & Brehm, K. (2004). *Resilient classrooms: Creating health environments for learning.* New York: Guilford Press.

Donigian, J., & Malnati, R. (1997). *Systemic group therapy: A triadic model.* Pacific Grove, CA: Brooks/Cole.

Donnelly, C., & Carswell, A. (2002). Individualized outcome measures: A review of the literature. *Canadian Journal of Occupational Therapy, 69,* 84–94.

Dougherty, A. M. (2009). *A casebook of psychological consultation and collaboration in school and community settings* (5th ed.). Pacific Grove, CA: Brooks/Cole CENGAGE.

Dreikurs, R. (1957). *Psychology in the classroom.* New York: Harper and Row.

Dreikurs, R. (with Soltz, V.). (1964). *Children: The challenge.* New York: Dutton.

Dweck, C. S. (2002). The development of ability conceptions. In A. Wigfield & J. Eccles (Eds.), *The development of achievement motivation* (pp. 57–88). San Diego, CA: Academic Press.

Eber, L., Sugai, G., Smith, C. R., & Scott, T. M. (2002). Wraparound and positive behavioral interventions and supports in the schools. *Journal of Emotional & Behavioral Disorders, 10,* 171–180.

Elliott, S. N., & Gresham, F. (2008). *Social skills improvement system (SSIS).* San Antonio, TX: Pearson.

Ellis, A. (1979). The theory of rational-emotive therapy. In A. Ellis & J. Whitely (Eds.), *Theoretical and empirical foundations in rational-emotive therapy* (pp. 9–26). Monterey, CA: Brooks/Cole.

Ellis, A. (1994). *Reason and emotion in psychotherapy* (Rev. ed.). New York: Kensington.

Ellis, A. (2005). Rational emotive behavior therapy. In R. Corsini & D. Wedding (Eds.), *Current psychotherapies* (7th ed., pp. 166–201). Belmont, CA: Brooks/Cole.

Ellis, A., & Bernard, M. E. (2006). *Rational emotive behavioral approaches to childhood disorders.* New York: Springer.

Ennett, S. T., Ringwalt, C. L., Thorne, J., Rohrback, L. A., Vincus, A., Simons-Rudolph, A., et al. (2003). A comparison of current practice in school-based substance use prevention programs with meta-analysis findings. *Prevention Science, 4,* 1–14.

Epstein, J. L. (1995). School/family/community partnerships: Caring for the families we share. *Phi Delta Kappan, 76,* 701–712.

Epstein, J. L. (2001). *School, family, and community partnerships: Preparing educators and improving schools.* Boulder, CO: Westview Press.

Epstein, J. L., & Van Voorhis, F. L. (2010). School counselors' roles in developing partnerships with families and communities for student success. *Professional School Counseling, 14,* 1–14.

Erford, B. (2011). Outcome research in group work. In B. Erford (Ed.), *Group work: Process and applications* (pp. 312–322). Upper Saddle River, NJ: Pearson.

Erikson, E. (1963). *Childhood and society.* New York: Norton. (Original work published 1958)

Eysenck, H. J. (1960). *Behavior therapy and the neuroses.* Oxford: Pergamon Press.

Fall, M. (2001). An integrative play therapy approach to working with children. In A. A. Drewes, L. J. Carey, & C. E. Shaefer (Eds.), *School-based play therapy* (pp. 315–328). New York: Wiley.

Fall, M., Balvanz, J., Johnson, L., & Nelson, L. (1999). A play therapy intervention and its relationship to self-efficacy and learning behaviors. *Professional School Counseling, 2,* 194–204.

Fein, R. A., Vossekuil, B., Pollack, W. S., Borum, R., Modzeleski, W., & Reddy, M. (2002). *Threat assessment in schools: A guide to managing threatening situations and creating safe school climates.* Washington, DC: United States Secret Service and United States Department of Education.

Flannery-Schroeder, E. C., & Kendall, P. C. (2000). Group and individual cognitive-behavioral treatments for youth with anxiety disorders: A randomized clinical trial. *Cognitive Therapy Research, 24,* 251–278.

Franklin, C., Biever, J., Moore, K., Clemons, D., & Scamardo, M. (2001). The effectiveness of solution-focused therapy with children in a school setting. *Research on Social Work Practice, 11,* 411–434.

Franklin, C., Moore, K. L., & Hopson, L. (2008). Effectiveness of solution-focused brief therapy in a school setting. *Children and Schools, 30,* 15–26.

Friedberg, R. D., & McClure, J. M. (2002). *Clinical practice of cognitive therapy with children and adolescents: The nuts and bolts.* New York: Guilford Press.

Froebel, F. (1903). *The education of man.* New York: D. Appleton.

Garza, Y., & Bratton, S. C. (2005). School-based child-centered play therapy with Hispanic children: Outcomes and cultural considerations. *International Journal of Play Therapy, 14*(1), 51–79.

Gauvin, M. (2001). The social context of cognitive development. New York: Guilford Press.

Ge, X., Conger, R. D., & Elder, G. H., Jr. (2001). Pubertal transition, stressful life events, and the emergence of gender differences in depressive symptoms during adolescence. *Developmental Psychology, 37,* 404–417.

German, T. P. (1999). Children's causal reasoning: Counterfactual thinking occurs for "negative" outcomes only. *Developmental Science, 2,* 442–447.

Gibson, D. G. (1999). *A monograph: Summary of the research related to the use and efficacy of the Systematic Training for Effective Parenting (STEP) program: 1976–1999.* Circle Pines, MI: American Guidance Services.

Gilligan, C., & Attanucci, J. (1988). Two moral orientations: Gender differences and similarities. *Merrill-Palmer Quarterly, 34,* 223–237.

Gladding, S. T. (2005). *Counseling as an art: The creative arts in counseling* (3rd ed.). Alexandria, VA: American Counseling Association.

Gladding, S. T. (2008). *Group work: A counseling specialty* (5th ed.). Upper Saddle River, NJ: Prentice Hall.

Glass, J. S., & Benshoff, J. M. (1999). PARS: A processing model for beginning group leaders. *Journal for Specialists in Group Work, 24,* 15–26.

Glass, J. S., & Shoffner, M. F. (2001). Adventure-based counseling in schools. *Professional School Counseling, 5,* 42–48.

Glasser, W. (1969). *Schools without failure.* New York: Harper and Row.

Glasser, W. (1983). *The basic concepts of Reality Therapy* (brochure). Los Angeles: Author.

Glasser, W. (1998a). *The Quality School: Managing students without coercion* (Rev. ed.). New York: HarperCollins.

Glasser, W. (1998b). *The Quality School teacher: A companion volume to* The Quality School (Rev. ed.). New York: HarperCollins.

Glasser, W. (2001). *Every student can succeed.* Chatsworth, CA: Author.

Glosoff, H. L., & Pate, R. H. (2002). Privacy and confidentiality in school counseling. *Professional School Counseling, 6,* 20–27.

Gordon, E., & Yowell, C. (1999). Cultural dissonance as a risk factor in the development of students. In E. Gordon (Ed.), *Education and justice: A view from the back of the bus* (pp. 34–51). New York: Teachers College Press.

Greenberg, M. T., & Kusché, C. A. (2006). Building social and emotional competence: The PATHS curriculum. In S. R. Jimerson & M. J. Furlong (Eds.), *Handbook of school violence and school safety: From research to practice* (pp. 395–412). Mahwah, NJ: Erlbaum.

Greenberg, M. T., Weissberg, R. P., O'Brien, M. U., Zins, J. E., Fredericks, L., Resnick, H., et al. (2003). Enhancing school-based prevention and youth development through coordinated social, emotional, and academic learning. *American Psychologist, 58,* 466–474.

Grey, L. (1998). *Alfred Adler, forgotten prophet: A vision for the 21st century.* Westport, CT: Praeger.

Guay, F., Marsh, H. W., & Boivin, M. (2003). Academic self-concept and academic achievement: Developmental perspectives on their causal ordering. *Journal of Educational Psychology, 95,* 124–136.

Halbur, D. A., & Halbur, K. V. (2011). *Developing your theoretical orientation in counseling and psychotherapy* (2nd ed.). Boston: Pearson.

Hall, K. R. (2006). Solving problems together: A psychoeducational group model for victims of bullies. *Journal for Specialists in Group Work, 31,* 201–207.

Hammond, L. C., & Gantt, L. (1998). Using art in counseling: Ethical considerations. *Journal of Counseling and Development, 76,* 271–276.

Hardman, M., Drew, C., Egan, M., & Wolf, B. (1993). *Human exceptionality: Society, school and family.* Boston: Allyn & Bacon.

Harter, S. (2006). The self. In W. Damon & R. M. Lerner (Eds. in Chief) & N. Eisenberg (Vol. Ed.), *Handbook of child psychology: Vol. 3. Social, emotional, and personality development* (6th ed., pp. 505–570). Hoboken, NJ: Wiley.

Havighurst, R. J. (1972). *Developmental tasks and education* (3rd ed.). New York: David McKay.

Hawley, K., & Weisz, J. (2005). Youth versus parent working alliance in usual clinical care: Distinctive associations with retention, satisfaction, and treatment outcome. *Journal of Clinical & Adolescent Psychology, 34,* 117–128.

Heath, M., & Sheen, D. (2005). *School-based crisis intervention: Preparing all personnel to assist.* Practical Intervention in the Schools Series. New York: Guilford Press.

Heine, S. J., Lehman, D. R., Markus, H. R., & Kitayama, S. (1999). Is there a universal need for positive self-regard? *Psychological Review, 106,* 766–794.

Helker, W. P, & Ray, D. C. (2009). Impact of child teacher relationship training on teachers' and aides' use of relationship-building skills and the effects on student classroom behavior. *International Journal of Play Therapy, 18*(2), 70–83.

Herring, R. D., & Runion, K. B. (1994). Counseling ethnic children and youth from an Adlerian perspective. *Journal of Multicultural Counseling and Development, 22,* 215–226.

Hill, C. E., & O'Brien, K. M. (2004). *Helping skills: Facilitating exploration, insight, and action* (2nd ed.). Washington, DC: American Psychological Association.

Hines, P. L., & Fields, T. H. (2002). Pregroup screening issues for school counselors. *Journal for Specialists in Group Work, 27,* 358–376.

Hoag, M. J., & Burlingame, G. M. (1997). Evaluating the effectiveness of child and adolescent group treatment: A meta-analysis review. *Journal of Clinical Child Psychology, 26,* 234–246.

Hoagwood, K., Burns, B. J., & Weisz, J. R. (2002). A profitable conjunction: From science to service in children's mental health. In B. J. Burns & K. Hoagwood (Eds.), *Community treatment for youth: Evidence-based interventions for severe emotional and behavioral disorders* (pp. 1079–1089). New York: Oxford.

Hoagwood, K., & Johnson, J. (2003). School psychology: A public health framework. I. From evidence-based practices to evidence-based policies. *Journal of School Psychology, 41,* 3–21.

Homan, M. S. (2004). *Promoting community change: Making it happen in the real world* (3rd ed.). Pacific Grove, CA: Brooks/Cole.

Homeyer, L. E., & Sweeney, D. S. (1998). *Sandtray: A practical manual.* Royal Oak, MN: Self Esteem Shop.

Honig, A. (2007, Sept.). Play: Ten power boosts for children's early learning. *Young Children, 62*(5), 72–78.

Horner, R. H., Sugai, G., Todd, A. W., & Lewis-Palmer, T. (2005). School-wide positive behavior support. In L. Bambara & L. Kern (Eds.), *Individualized supports for students with problem behaviors: Designing positive behavior plans* (pp. 359–390). New York: Guilford Press.

Horowitz, J. L., & Garber, J. (2006). The prevention of depressive symptoms in children and adolescents: A meta-analytic review. *Journal of Consulting and Clinical Psychology, 74,* 401–415.

Hudley, C., Graham, S., & Taylor, A. (2007). Reducing aggressive behavior and increasing motivation in school: The evolution of an intervention to strengthen school adjustment. *Educational Psychologist, 42,* 251–260.

Hughes, T. L., & Theodore, L. A. (2009). Conceptual frame for selecting individual psychotherapy in the schools. *Psychology in the Schools, 46,* 218–224.

Hulse-Killacky, D., Killacky, J., & Donigian, J. (2001). *Making task groups work in your world.* Upper Saddle River, NJ: Prentice Hall.

Hulse-Killacky, D., Kraus, K. L., & Schumacher, R. A. (1999). Visual conceptualization of meetings: A group work design. *Journal for Specialists in Group Work, 24,* 13–124.

Ishikawa, S., Okajima, I., Matsuoka, H. L., & Sakano, Y. (2007). Cognitive behavioural therapy for anxiety disorder in children and adolescents: A meta-analysis. *Child and Adolescent Mental Health, 12,* 164–172.

Jacobs, E. E., Masson, R. L., & Harvill, R. L. (2009). *Group counseling: Strategies and skills* (6th ed.). Belmont, CA: Thomson Brooks Cole.

Jacobs, H. H., & Johnson, A. (2009). *The curriculum mapping planner: Templates, tools, and resources for effective professional development.* Alexandra, VA: Association for Supervision and Curriculum Development.

Jacobs, J. E., Lanza, S., Osgood, D. W., Eccles, J. S., & Wigfield, A. (2002). Changes in children's self-competence and values: Gender and domain differences across grades one through twelve. *Child Development, 73,* 509–527.

Jaffee, S., & Hyde, J. S. (2000). Gender differences in moral orientation: A meta-analysis. *Psychological Bulletin, 126,* 703–726.

James, R. K. (2008). *Crisis intervention strategies* (6th ed.). Belmont, CA: Thompson Brooks/Cole.

Jarvis, P. S., & Keeley, E. S. (2003). From vocational decision making to career building: Blueprint, real games, and school counseling. *Professional School Counseling, 6,* 244–250.

Jenkins, J. M., & Astington, J. W. (2000). Theory of mind and social behavior: Causal models tested in a longitudinal study. *Merrill-Palmer Quarterly, 46,* 203–220.

Johnson, D. W., & Johnson, F. P. (2009). *Joining together: Group theory and group skills* (10th ed.). Boston: Pearson.

Kahn, B. B. (1999). Art therapy with adolescents: Making it work for school counselors. *Professional School Counseling, 2,* 291–298.

Kahn, B. B. (2000). A model of solution-focused consultation for school counselors. *Professional School Counseling, 3,* 248–254.

Kanel, K. (2007). *A guide to crisis intervention* (3rd ed.). Belmont, CA: Brooks/Cole.

Karver, M., & Caporino, N. (2010). The use of empirically supported strategies for building a therapeutic relationship with an adolescent with optional-defiant disorder. *Cognitive and Behavioral Practice, 17,* 222–232.

Karver, M., Handelsman, J., Fields, S., & Bickman, L. (2006). Meta-analysis of therapeutic relationship variables in youth and family therapy: The evidence for different relationship variables in the child and adolescent treatment outcome literature. *Clinical Psychology Review, 26,* 50–65.

Kazdin, A. E. (1998). *Research design in clinical psychology* (3rd ed.). Boston: Allyn & Bacon.

Kazdin, A. E. (2000). Understanding change: From description to explanation in child and adolescent psychotherapy research. *Journal of School Psychology, 38,* 337–347.

Kees, N. L., & Jacobs, E. (1990). Conducting more effective groups: How to select and process group exercises. *Journal for Specialists in Group Work, 15,* 24–29.

Kellam, S. G., & Langevin, D. J. (2003). A framework for understanding "evidence" in prevention research and programs. *Prevention Science, 4,* 137–153.

Kelly, F. D., & Lee, D. (2007). Adlerian approaches to counseling with children and adolescents. In H. T. Prout & D. T. Brown (Eds.), *Counseling and psychotherapy with children and adolescents: Theory and practice for school and clinical settings* (pp. 131–179). Hoboken, NJ: Wiley.

Kelly, M. S. (2008). *The domains and demands of school social work practice: A guide to working effectively with students, families, and schools.* New York: Oxford University Press.

Kelly, M. S., Berzin, S. C., Frey, A., Alvarez, M., Shaffer, G., & O'Brien, K. (2010). The state of school social work: Findings from the National School Social Work Survey. *School Mental Health, 2,* 132–141.

Kelly, M. S, Kim, J. S., & Franklin, C. (2008). *Solution-focused brief therapy in schools: A 360-degree view of research and practice.* Oxford, NY: Oxford University Press.

Kendall, P. C. (2006). *Child and adolescent therapy: Cognitive-behavioral procedures* (3rd ed.). New York: Guilford Press.

Kendall, P. C., & Chu, B. C. (2000). Retrospective self-reports of therapist flexibility in a manual-based treatment for youths with anxiety disorders. *Journal of Clinical Child Psychology, 29,* 209–220.

Kendall, P. C., & MacDonald, J. P. (1993). Cognition in the psychopathology of youth and implications for treatment. In K. S. Dobson & P. C. Kendall (Eds.), *Psychopathology and cognition* (pp. 387–430). San Diego, CA: Academic Press.

Kendall, P. C., & Southam-Gerow, M. (1996). Long-term follow-up of a cognitive-behavioral therapy for anxiety-disorder youth. *Journal of Consulting and Clinical Psychology, 64,* 724–730.

Kim, J. (2006). The effect of a bullying prevention program on responsibility and victimization of bullied children in Korea. *International Journal of Reality Therapy, 26*(1), 4–8.

Kim, J. S., & Franklin, C. (2009). Solution-focused brief therapy in schools: A review of the outcome literature. *Children and Youth Services Review, 31,* 464–470.

Kingery, J. N., Roblek, T. L., Suveg, C., Grover, R. L., Sherrill, J. T., & Bergman, R. L. (2006). They're not just "little adults": Developmental considerations for implementing cognitive-behavioral therapy with anxious youth. *Journal of Cognitive Psychotherapy: An International Quarterly, 20,* 263–273.

Kiresuk, T., & Sherman, R. (1968). Goal attainment scaling: A general method for evaluating comprehensive community mental health programs. *Community Mental Health, 4,* 443–453.

Kiresuk, T., Smith, A., & Cardillo, J. (1994). *Goal attainment scaling: Applications, theory, and measurement.* Hillsdale, NJ: Erlbaum.

Klein, J. B., Jacobs, R. H., & Reinecke, M. A. (2007). Cognitive-behavioral therapy for adolescent depression: A meta-analytic investigation of changes in effect-size estimates. *Journal of the American Academy of Child & Adolescent Psychiatry, 46,* 1403–1413.

Knotek, S. E., & Sandoval, J. (2003). Current research in consultee-centered consultation. *Journal of Educational and Psychological Consultation, 14,* 243–250.

Koeppen, A. S. (1974). Relaxation training for children. *Elementary School Guidance and Counseling, 9,* 14–26.

Kohlberg, L. (1981). *The philosophy of moral development.* New York: Harper & Row.

Kottman, T. (1995). *Partners in play: An Adlerian approach to play therapy.* Alexandria, VA: American Counseling Association.

Kratochwill, T. R., Albers, C. A., & Shernoff, E. S. (2004). School-based interventions. *Child & Adolescent Psychiatric Clinics of North America, 13,* 885–903.

Kristal, J. (2005). *The temperament perspective: Working with children's behavioral styles.* New York: Paul J. Brookes.

Kubler-Ross, E. (1969). *On death and dying.* New York: Scribner.

LaFountain, R. M., & Garner, N. E. (1998). *A school with solutions: Implementing a solution-focused/Adlerian-based comprehensive school counseling program.* Alexandria, VA: American School Counselor Association.

Landreth, G. L. (2002). *Play therapy: The art of the relationship* (2nd ed.). New York: Brunner-Routledge.

Larson, J. P., & Choi, H. (2010). The effect of university training and educational legislation on the role and function of school psychologists. *Journal of Applied School Psychology, 26,* 97–114.

Lassen, S. R., Steele, M. M., & Sailor, W. (2006). The relationship of school-wide positive behavior support to academic achievement in an urban middle school. *Psychology in the Schools, 43,* 701–712.

Learning Disabilities Association of America. (n.d.). *Types of learning disabilities.* Retrieved May 7, 2011, from http://www.ldanatl.org/aboutld/teachers/understanding/types.asp.

Legum, H. L. (2005, May/June). Finding solutions. *ASCA School Counselor, 41*(5), 33–37.

Levitt, J. J. (2009). Applying art therapy in schools. In R. W. Christner & R. B. Mennuti (Eds.), *School-based mental health: A practitioner's guide to comparative practices* (pp. 327–352). New York: Routledge.

Lew, A., & Bettner, B. L. (1995). *Responsibility in the classroom: A teacher's guide to understanding and motivating students.* Newton Center, MA: Connexions.

Liddle, H. (1982). On the problem of eclecticism: A call for epistemological clarification and human scale theories. *Family Process, 21,* 243–250.

Lieberman, M., Yalom, I., & Miles, M. (1973). *Encounter groups: First facts.* New York: Basic Books.

Littrell, J. M., Malia, J. A., & Vanderwood, M. (1995). Single-session brief counseling in a high school. *Journal of Counseling and Development, 73,* 451–459.

Luthar, S. S., Cicchetti, D., Becker, B. (2000). The construct of resilience: A critical evaluation and guidelines for future work. *Child Development, 71,* 543–562.

Magnuson, S., Black, L., & Norem, K. (2001). Supervising school counselors and interns: Resources for site supervisors. *Journal of Professional Counseling: Practice, Theory, and Research, 22*(2), 4–15.

Magnuson, S., Wilcoxon, S. A., & Norem, K. (2000). Exemplary supervision practices: Retrospective observations of experienced counselors. *Texas Counseling Association Journal, 28*(2), 93–101.

Malchiodi, C. A. (Ed.). (2003). *Handbook of art therapy.* New York: Guilford Press.

Manaster, C. J., & Corsini, R. J. (1982). *Individual psychology: Theory and practice.* Itasca, IL: F. E. Peacock.

Markus, H. R., & Hamedani, M. G. (2007). Sociocultural psychology: The dynamic interdependence among self systems and social systems. In S. Kitayama & D. Cohen (Eds.), *Handbook of cultural psychology* (pp. 3–39). New York: Guilford Press.

Mayer, M. J., & Van Acker, R. (2009). Historical roots, theoretical and applied developments, and critical issues in cognitive-behavior modification. In M. J. Mayer, R. Van Acker, J. E. Lochman, & F. M. Gresham (Eds.), *Cognitive-behavioral interventions for emotional and behavioral disorders: School-based practice* (pp. 3–28). New York: Guilford Press.

McDevitt, T. M., & Ormrod, J. E. (2010). *Child development and education* (4th ed.). Upper Saddle River, NJ: Pearson.

McDougall, D., & Smith, D. (2006). Recent innovations in small-N designs for research and practice in professional school counseling. *Professional School Counseling, 9,* 392–400.

McDougall, J. L., Bardos, A. N., & Meier, S. T. (2010). *Behavior intervention monitoring assessment system (BIMAS).* Toronto, CAN: Multi-Health Systems.

McDowell, B. (1997). The pick-up-sticks game. In H. Kaduson & C. Schaefer (Eds.), *101 favorite play therapy techniques* (pp. 145–149). Northvale, NJ: Jason Aronson.

Meichenbaum, D. (1993). Changing conceptions of cognitive behavior modification: Retrospect and prospect. *Journal of Consulting and Clinical Psychology, 61,* 202–204.

Mennuti, R. B., Christner, R. W., & Freeman, A. (2006). An introduction to a school-based cognitive-behavioral framework. In R. B. Mennuti, A. Freeman, & R. W. Christner (Eds.), *Cognitive-behavioral interventions in educational settings: A handbook for practice* (pp. 3–19). New York: Routledge.

Mennuti, R. B., Christner, R. W., & Weinstein, E. (2009). Integrating perspectives into practice. In R. W. Christner & R. B. Mennuti (Eds.), *School-based mental health: A practitioner's guide to comparative practices* (pp. 407–412). New York: Routledge.

Merchant, N. (2009). Types of diversity-related groups. In C. Salazar (Ed.), *Group work experts share their favorite multicultural activities: A guide to diversity-competent choosing, planning, conducting, and processing* (pp. 13–24). Alexandria, VA: Association for Specialists in Group Work.

Merrell, K. W., & Gueldner, B. A. (2010). *Social and emotional learning in the classroom: Promoting mental health and academic success.* New York: Guilford Press.

Miller, J. G. (1997). A cultural-psychology perspective on intelligence. In R. J. Sternberg & E. L. Grigorenko (Eds.), *Intelligence, heredity, and environment* (pp. 269–302). Cambridge, England: Cambridge University Press.

Minuchin, S. (1974). *Families and family therapy.* Cambridge, MA: Harvard University Press.

Morelli, G. A., & Rothbaum, F. (2007). Situating the child in context: Attachment relationships and self-regulation in different cultures. In S. Kitayama & D. Cohen (Eds.), *Handbook of cultural psychology* (pp. 500–527). New York: Guilford Press.

Mosak, H. H., & Maniacci, M. P. (1993). Adlerian child psychotherapy. In T. R. Kratochwill & R. J. Morris (Eds.), *Handbook of psychotherapy with children and adolescents* (pp. 162–184). Boston: Allyn & Bacon.

Moser, A., & Pilkey, D. (1988). *Don't pop your cork on Mondays: The children's anti-stress book.* Kansas City, MO: Landmark Editions.

Mostert, D. L., Johnson, E., & Mostert, M. P. (1997). The utility of solution-focused, brief counseling in schools: Potential from an initial study. *Professional School Counseling, 1,* 21–24.

Muro, J. J., & Kottman, T. (1995). *Guidance and counseling in the elementary and middle schools: A practical approach.* Madison, WI: Brown & Benchmark.

Murphy, J. J. (2008). *Solution-focused counseling in schools* (2nd ed.). Alexandria, VA: American Counseling Association.

Murphy, J. J., & Duncan, B. L. (2007). *Brief intervention for school problems* (2nd ed.). New York: Guilford Press.

Murphy, V. B., & Christner, R. W. (2006). A cognitive-behavioral case conceptualization approach for working with children and adolescents. In R. B. Mennuti, A. Freeman, & R. W. Christner (Eds.), *Cognitive-behavioral interventions in educational settings: A handbook for practice* (pp. 37–62). New York: Routledge.

Nastasi, B. K. (2004). Meeting the challenges of the future: Integrating public health and public education for mental health promotion. *Journal of Educational and Psychological Consultation, 15*(3–4), 295–312.

National Alliance of Pupil Service Organizations [NAPSO]. (n.d.). *Pupil services in schools.* Retrieved December 12, 2010, from http://www.napso.org/pdf/ProfessionalService Descriptions0809.pdf.

National Association of School Psychologists [NASP]. (2010a). Principles for professional ethics. In *Professional conduct manual.* Retrieved December 13, 2010, from http://www.nasponline.org/standards/professionalcond.pdf.

National Association of School Psychologists [NASP]. (2010b). *Model for comprehensive and integrated school psychological services.* Retrieved November 26, 2010, from http://www.nasponline.org/standards/2010standards/2_PracticeModel.pdf.

National Association of School Psychologists [NASP]. (2010c). *A national tragedy: Helping children cope.* Retrieved December 10, 2010, from http://www.nasponline.org/resources/crisis_safety/terror_general.aspx.

National Association of School Psychologists [NASP]. (2010d). *The PREPaRE curriculum.* Retrieved December 10, 2010, from http://www.nasponline.org/prepare/curriculum.aspx.

National Association of Social Workers [NASW]. (2002). *NASW standards for school social work services.* Retrieved July 13, 2010, from http://www.socialworkers.org/practice/standards/NASW_SSWS.pdf.

National Institute of Mental Health [NIMH]. (2010). *Mental health and mass violence: Evidence-based early psychological intervention for victims/survivors of mass violence* [A workshop to reach consensus on best practices]. Retrieved December 10, 2010, from http://www.nimh.nih.gov/health/publications/massviolence.pdf.

National Organization for Victim Assistance [NOVA]. (2010). *An introduction to crisis intervention protocols.* Retrieved December 10, 2010, from http://www.trynova.org/victiminfo/readings/CrisisIntervention.pdf.

National Organization for Victim Assistance. (n.d.). *Reactions of children and adolescents to trauma.* Retrieved December 10, 2010, from http://www.trynova.org/crisis/katrina/reactions-child.html.

National Research Council and Institute of Medicine (NRC & IOM). (2009). *Preventing mental, emotional, and behavioral disorders among young people: Progress and possibilities.* Committee on the Prevention of Mental Disorders and Substance Abuse Among Children, Youth, and Young Adults: Research Advances and Promising Interventions. M. E. O'Connell, T. Boat, & K. E. Warner, (Eds.), Board on Children, Youth, and Families, Division of Behavioral and Social Sciences and Education. Washington, DC: the National Academies Press.

Neill, T. K., Holloway, E. I., Kaak, H. O. (2006). A systems approach to supervision of child psychotherapy. In T. K. Neill (Ed.), *Helping others help children: Clinical supervision of child psychotherapy* (pp. 7–33). Washington, DC: American Psychological Association.

Nelson, C. A., III, Thomas, K. M., & de Haan, M. (2006). Neural bases of cognitive development. In D. Kuhn, R. Siegler (Vol. Eds.), W. Damon, & R. M. Lerner (Series Eds.), *Handbook of child psychology Vol. 2: Cognition, perception, and language* (6th ed., pp. 3–57). New York: Wiley.

Nelson, M. L. (2002). An assessment-based model for counseling strategy selection. *Journal of Counseling and Development, 80,* 416–421.

Neufeldt, S. A., Iversen, J. N., & Juntunen, C. L. (1995). *Supervision strategies for the first practicum.* Alexandria, VA: American Counseling Association.

Newsome, W. S. (2005). The impact of solution-focused brief therapy with at-risk junior high students. *Children and Schools, 27,* 83–90.

Nikels, H., Mims, G. A., & Mims, M. J. (2007). Allies against hate: A school-diversity sensitivity training experience. *Journal for Specialists in Group Work, 32,* 126–138.

No Child Left Behind (NCLB) Act of 2001, Public Law No. 107–110, § 115, Stat. 1425 (2002).

Norcross, J. C. (2005). A primer on psychotherapy integration. In J. C. Norcross & M. R. Goldfried (Eds.), *Handbook of psychotherapy integration* (2nd ed.). New York: Oxford University Press.

Norem, K., Magnuson, S., Wilcoxon, S. A., & Arbel, O. (2006). Supervisees' contributions to stellar supervision outcomes. *Journal of Professional Counseling: Practice, Theory, and Research, 34,* 33–48.

Norenzayan, A., Choi, I., & Peng, K. (2007). Perception and cognition. In S. Katayama & D. Cohen (Eds.), *Handbook of cultural psychology* (pp. 569–594). New York: Guilford Press.

Nystul, M. S. (2003). *Introduction to counseling: An art and science perspective.* Boston: Allyn & Bacon.

O'Connor, K. J. (2000). *The play therapy primer* (2nd ed.). New York: Wiley.

Odom, S. L., Brantlinger, E., Gersten, R., Horner, R. H., Thompson, B., & Harris, K. R. (2005). Research in special education: Scientific methods and evidence-based practices. *Exceptional Children, 71,* 137–148.

O'Hanlon, W. H., & Weiner-Davis, M. (1989). *In search of solutions: A new direction in psychotherapy.* New York: W. W. Norton.

Ollendick, T. H., & Cerny, J. A. (1981). *Clinical behavior therapy with children.* New York: Plenum Press.

Olweus Bullying Prevention Program. (n.d.). Retrieved May 12, 2011, from http://www.olweus .org/public/index.page.

Ortiz, S. O. (2006). Multicultural issues in working with children and families: Responsive intervention in the educational setting. In R. B. Mennuti, A. Freeman, & R. W. Christner (Eds.), *Cognitive-behavioral interventions in educational settings: A handbook for practice* (pp. 21–36). New York: Routledge.

Orton, G. L. (1997). *Strategies for counseling with children and their parents.* Pacific Grove, CA: Brooks/Cole.

Osborn, D. J. (1999). Solution-focused strategies with "involuntary" clients: Practical applications for school and clinical setting. *Journal of Humanistic Education and Development, 37,* 169–181.

Paisley, P. O., & McMahon, G. (2001). School counseling in the 21st century: Challenges and opportunities. *Professional School Counseling, 5,* 106–115.

Parette, H. P., & Hourcade, J. J. (1995). Disability etiquette and school counselors: A common sense approach toward compliance with the Americans with Disabilities Act. *The School Counselor, 52,* 224–233.

Passaro, P. D., Moon, M., Wiest, D. J., & Wong, E. H. (2004). A model for school psychology practice: Addressing the needs of students with emotional and behavioral challenges through the use of an in-school support room and Reality Therapy. *Adolescence, 39,* 504–517.

Patrikakou, E. N., Weissberg, R. P., Redding, S., & Walberg, H. J. (Eds.). (2005). *School-family partnerships: Fostering children's school success.* New York: Teachers College Press.

Pearson. (2010). *AIMSweb for behavior.* Retrieved May 11, 2011, from http://www.aimsweb .com/behavior/.

Perryman, K., & Doran, J. (2010). Guidelines for incorporating play therapy in schools. In A. A. Drewes & C. E. Schaefer (Eds.), *School-based play therapy* (2nd ed., pp. 61–86). Hoboken, NJ: John Wiley & Sons.

Peterson, J. S. (2003). An argument for proactive attention to affect concerns of gifted adolescents. *The Journal of Secondary Gifted Education, 14,* 62–70.

Petras, H., Kellam, S. G., Brown, C. H., Muthen, B. O., Ialongo, N. S., & Poduska, J. M. (2008). Developmental epidemiological courses leading to antisocial personality disorder and violent and criminal behavior: Effects by young adulthood of a universal preventive intervention in first- and second-grade classrooms. *Drug and Alcohol Dependence, 95*(Suppl.1), 45–59.

Piaget, J. (1962). *Play, dreams, and imitation in childhood.* New York: W. W. Norton.

Piaget, J. (1970). Piaget's theory (G. Gellerier & J. Langer, Trans.). In P. H. Mussen (Ed.), *Manual of child psychology* (Vol. 1, pp. 703–732). New York: Wiley.

Presbury, J. H., Echterling, L. G., & McKee, J. E. (2002). *Ideas and tools for brief counseling.* Upper Saddle River, NJ: Merrill Prentice Hall.

Prochaska, J. O., & Norcross, J. C. (2007). *Systems of psychotherapy: A transtheoretical analysis* (6th ed.). Belmont, CA: Thomson Higher Education.

Prout, H. T. (2007). Counseling and psychotherapy with children and adolescents: Historical developmental, integrative, and effectiveness perspectives. In H. T. Prout & D. T. Brown (Eds.), *Counseling and psychotherapy with children and adolescents: Theory and practice for school and clinic settings* (4th ed., pp. 1–31). New York: John Wiley & Sons.

Prout, H. T., & DeMartino, R. A. (1986). A meta-analysis of school-based studies of counseling and psychotherapy. *Journal of School Psychology, 24,* 285–292.

Prout, S. M., & Prout, H. T. (1998). A meta-analysis of school-based studies of counseling and psychotherapy: An update. *Journal of School Psychology, 36,* 121–136.

Raines, J. (2006). Improving educational and behavioral performance of students with learning disabilities. In C. Franklin, M. B. Harris, & Allen-Meares, P. (Eds.), *The school services sourcebook: A guide for school-based professionals* (pp. 201–212). New York: Oxford.

Rapport, Z. (2007). Defining the 14 habits. *International Journal of Reality Therapy, 26*(2), 26–27.

Ray, D. C. (2010). Challenges and barriers to implementing play therapy in schools. In A. A. Drewes & C. E. Schaefer (Eds.), *School-based play therapy* (2nd ed., pp. 87–106). Hoboken, NJ: John Wiley & Sons.

Reese, R. J., Prout, H. T., Zirkelback, E. A., & Anderson, C. R. (2010). Effectiveness of school-based psychotherapy: A meta-analysis of dissertation research. *Psychology in the Schools, 47,* 1035–1045.

Reinecke, M. A., Dattilio, F. M., & Freeman, A. (Eds.). (2003). *Cognitive therapy with children and adolescents: A casebook for clinical practice* (2nd ed.). New York: Guilford Press.

Reis, S. M., & Colbert, R. (2004). Counseling needs of academically talented students with learning disabilities. *Professional School Counseling, 8,* 156–167.

Reis, S. M., & Renzulli, J. S. (2004). Current research on the social and emotional development of gifted and talented students: Good news and future possibilities. *Psychology in the Schools, 41,* 119–130.

Remley, T. P., & Herlihy, B. (2005). *Ethical, legal, and professional issues in counseling* (2nd ed.). Upper Saddle River, NJ: Merrill.

Remmel, E., & Flavell, J. H. (2004). Recent progress in cognitive developmental research: Implications for clinical practice. In H. Steiner (Ed.), *Handbook of mental health interventions in children and adolescents: An integrated developmental approach* (pp. 73–97). San Francisco: Jossey-Bass.

Reynolds, C. R., & Kamphaus, R. W. (2004). *Behavior assessment system for children, second edition (BASC-2)*. Circle Pines, MN: American Guidance Service.

Riley, S., & Malchiodi, C. A. (2003). Solution-focused and narrative approaches. In C. A. Malchiodi (Ed.), *Handbook of art therapy* (pp. 82–92). New York: Guilford Press.

Robins, R. W., & Trzesniewski, K. H. (2005). Self-esteem across the lifespan. *Current Directions in Psychological Science, 14,* 158–162.

Rogers, C. (1961). *On becoming a person.* Boston: Houghton Mifflin.

Rousseau, J. J. (1955). *Emile.* New York: Dutton. (Original work published 1762)

Rubin, H. (2002). *Collaborative leadership.* Thousand Oaks, CA: Corwin.

Rubin, J. H. (1984). *Child art therapy* (2nd ed.). New York: Van Nostrand Reinhold.

Rutter, M., & Maughan, B. (2002). School effectiveness findings 1979–2002. *Journal of School Psychology, 40,* 451–475.

Sabian, B., & Gilligan, S. (2005, November/December). Self-esteem, social skills, and cooperative play. *ASCA School Counselor, 43*(2), 28–35.

Sailor, W., Dunlap, G., Sugai, G., & Horner, R. (2009). *Handbook of positive behavior support.* New York: Springer.

Salazar, C. (2009). Diversity-competent group leadership: Self-awareness and cultural empathy as a foundation for effective practice. In C. Salazar (Ed.), *Group work experts share their favorite multicultural activities: A guide to diversity-competent choosing, planning, conducting, and processing* (pp. 3–23). Alexandria, VA: Association for Specialist in Group Work.

Salo, M. (2006). Counseling minor clients. In B. Herlihy & G. Corey (Eds.), *ACA ethical standards casebook* (6th ed., pp.201–208). Alexandria, VA: American Counseling Association.

Sangganjanavanich, V. F., & Magnuson, S. (2011). Using sand trays and miniature figures to facilitate career decision making. *The Career Development Quarterly, 59,* 264–273.

Schaefer, C. E. (Ed.). (1993). *The therapeutic powers of play.* Northvale, NJ: Aronson.

Schaefer, C. E., & Drewes, A. A. (2010). The therapeutic powers of play and play therapy. In A. A. Drewes & C. E. Schaefer (Eds.), *School-based play therapy* (2nd ed., pp. 3–16). Hoboken, NJ: John Wiley & Sons.

Schaefer, C. E., & Reid, S. E. (Eds.). (2001). *Game play: Therapeutic use of childhood games* (2nd ed.). New York: John Wiley.

Schaffer, D. (1999). *Developmental psychology* (5th ed.). Pacific Grove, CA: Brooks/Cole.

Schneider, J. (1984). *Stress, loss and grief: Understanding the origins and growth potential.* Baltimore: University Park Press.

School Social Work Association of America. (2009). *Elements of school social work services.* Retrieved May 7, 2011, from https://www.sswaa.org/index.asp?page=123.

Scruggs, T. E. (1992). *Single subject methodology in the study of learning and behavioral disorders: Design, analysis, and synthesis* (7th ed.). Greenwich, CT: JAI.

Scruggs, T. E., & Mastropieri, M. A. (1998). Summarizing single-subject research: Issues and application. *Behavior Modification, 22,* 221–242.

Seligman, L. (2006). *Theories of counseling and psychotherapy: Systems, strategies, and skills* (2nd ed.). Upper Saddle River, NJ: Pearson.

Seligman, M. E. R., & Csikszentmihalyi, M. (2000). Positive psychology: An introduction. *American Psychologist, 55,* 5–14.

Selman, R. L. (2003). *The promotion of social awareness: Powerful lessons from the partnership of developmental theory and classroom practice.* New York: Russell Sage Foundation.

Sharf, R. S. (2004). *Theories of psychotherapy and counseling: Concepts and cases.* Belmont, CA: Wadsworth.

Shechtman, Z., & Pastor, R. (2005). Cognitive-behavioral and humanistic treatment of children with learning disabilities: A comparison of outcomes and process. *Journal of Counseling Psychology, 52,* 322–336.

Sheridan, S. M. (1997). Conceptual and empirical bases of conjoint behavioral consultation. *School Psychology Quarterly, 12,* 119–133.

Shirk, S. R., Kaplinski, H., Gudmundsen, G. (2009). School-based cognitive-behavioral therapy for adolescent depression: A benchmarking study. *Journal of Emotional and Behavioral Disorders, 17,* 106–117.

Shure, M. B. (2001). *I can problem solve (ICPS): An interpersonal cognitive problem-solving program.* Champaign, IL: Research Press.

Sileo, F. J., & Kopala, M. (1993). An A-B-C-D-E worksheet for promoting beneficence when considering ethical values. *Counseling and Values, 37,* 89–95.

Skinner, C. H., Skinner, A. L., & Burton, B. (2009). Applying group-oriented contingencies in the classroom. In A. Akin-Little, S. G. Little, M. A. Bray, & T. J. Kehle (Eds.), *Behavior interventions in schools: Evidence-based positive strategies* (pp. 157–170). Washington, DC: American Psychological Association.

Sklare, G. B. (2005). *Brief counseling that works: A solution-focused approach for school counselors and administrators* (2nd ed.). Thousand Oaks, CA: Corwin.

Smith, E. P., Boutte, G. S., Zigler, F., & Finn-Stevenson, M. (2004). Opportunities for schools to promote resilience in children and youth. In K. I. Maton, C. J. Schellenbach, B. J. Leadbeater, & A. L. Solarz (Eds.), *Investing in children, youth, families, and communities: Strength-based research and policy* (pp. 213–232). Washington, DC: American Psychological Association.

Southam-Gerow, M. A., & Kendall, P. C. (2000). Emotion understanding in youth referred for treatment of anxiety disorders. *Journal of Clinical Child Psychology, 29,* 319–327.

Spivak, G., Platt, J., & Shure, M. (1976). *The social problem solving approach to adjustment.* San Francisco: Jossey-Bass.

Spoth, R., Greenberg, M., Bierman, K., & Redmond, C. (2004). PROSPER community–university partnership model for public education systems: Capacity-building for evidence-based, competence-building prevention. *Prevention Science, 5,* 31–39.

Stark, K. D., Hargrave, J., Sander, J., Custer, G., Schnoebelen, S., Simpson, J., et al. (2006). Treatment of childhood depression: The ACTION treatment program. In P. C. Kendall (Ed.), *Child and adolescent therapy: Cognitive-behavioral procedures* (3rd ed., pp. 169–216). New York: Guilford Press.

Steiner, H. (2004). The scientific basis of mental health interventions in children and adolescents. In H. Steiner (Ed.), *Handbook of mental health interventions in children and adolescents: An integrated developmental approach* (pp. 11–34). San Francisco: Jossey-Bass.

Stoiber, K. C., & Kratochwill, T. R. (2001). *Outcomes PME: Planning, monitoring, evaluating.* San Antonio, TX: The Psychological Corporation.

Stone, C. B., & Dahir, C. A. (2006). *The transformed school counselor.* Boston: Lahaska.

Stone, C. B., & Dahir, C. A. (2011). *School counselor accountability: A MEASURE of student success* (3rd ed.). Boston: Pearson.

Stroul, B. A., & Friedman, R. M. (1996). The system of care concept and philosophy. In B. A. Stroul (Ed.), *Children's mental health: Creating systems of care in a changing society* (pp. 3–21). Baltimore: Paul H. Brookes.

Substance Abuse and Mental Health Services Administration [SAMHSA]. (2007). *Results from the 2006 National Survey on Drug Use and Health: National findings.* Office of Applied Studies, NSDUH Series H-32, DHHS Pub. No. SMA 07-4293. Rockville, MD: U.S. Department of Health and Human Services.

Substance Abuse and Mental Health Services Administration [SAMHSA]. (2008). *Mental health service use among youths aged 12 to 17: 2005 and 2006.* Office of Applied Studies. Rockville, MD: U.S. Department of Health and Human Services.

Sugai, G., & Horner, R. H. (2008). What we know and need to know about preventing problem behaviors in the schools. *Exceptionality, 16,* 67–77.

Sukhodolsky, D., Golub, A., Stone, E., & Orban, L. (2005). Dismantling anger control training for children: A randomized pilot study of social problem solving versus social skills training components. *Behavior Therapy, 36,* 15–23.

Sweeney, D. S., & Homeyer, L. E. (1999). *The handbook of group play therapy.* San Francisco: Jossey-Bass.

Sweeney, T. (1989). *Adlerian counseling: A practical approach for a new decade* (3rd ed.). Muncie, IN: Accelerated Development.

Sweeney, T. (1998). *Adlerian counseling: A practitioner's approach* (4th ed.). Muncie, IN: Accelerated Development.

Thompson, C. L., & Henderson, D. A. (2007). *Counseling children* (7th ed.). Belmont, CA: Thomson.

Thompson, R. A. (2004). *Crisis intervention and crisis management: Strategies that work in schools and communities.* New York: Brunner-Routledge.

Todd, A. W., Campbell, A. L., Meyer, G. G., & Horner, R. L. (2008). The effects of a targeted intervention to reduce problem behaviors. *Journal of Positive Behavioral Interventions, 10,* 46–55.

Travis, F. (1998). Cortical and cognitive development in 4th, 8th and 12th grade students: The contribution of speed of processing and executive functioning to cognitive development. *Biological Psychology, 48,* 37–56.

Tuckman, B. W., & Jensen, M. A. C. (1977). Stages of small group development revisited. *Group and Organizational Studies, 2,* 419–427.

Valentine, J. C., DuBois, D. L., & Cooper, H. (2004). The relation between self-beliefs and academic achievement: A meta-analytic review. *Educational Psychologist, 39,* 111–133.

Vernon, A. (2009). Working with children, adolescents, and their parents: Practical application of developmental theory. In A. Vernon (Ed.), *Counseling children & adolescents* (4th ed., pp. 1–37). Denver, CO: Love.

Vernon, A., & Clemente, R. (2005). *Assessment and intervention with children and adolescents: Developmental and multicultural approaches.* Alexandria, VA: American Counseling Association.

Vygotsky, L. S. (1978). *Mind in society: The development of higher mental processes.* Cambridge, MA: Harvard University Press.

Waldron, H., & Kaminer, Y. (2004). On the learning curve: The emerging evidence supporting cognitive-behavioral therapies for adolescent substance abuse. *Addiction, 99,* 93–105.

Waldron, H., Slesnick, N., Brody, J., Charles, W. T., & Thomas, R. P. (2001). Treatment outcomes for adolescent substance abuse at 4- and 7-month assessments. *Journal of Consulting and Clinical Psychology, 69,* 802–813.

Wampold, B. E. (2001). *The great psychotherapy debate: Models, methods, and findings.* Mahwah, NJ: Erlbaum.

Wampold, B. E. (2010). *The basics of psychotherapy: An introduction to theory and practice.* Washington, DC: American Psychological Association.

Wang, Q., & Li, J. (2003). Chinese children's self-concepts in the domains of learning and social relations. *Psychology in the Schools, 40,* 85–101.

Watkins, C. E., & Guarnaccia, C. A. (1999). The scientific study of Adlerian theory. In R. E. Watts & J. Carlson (Eds.), *Interventions and strategies in counseling and psychotherapy.* Philadelphia: Accelerated Development.

Watson, J. J., & Rees, C. S. (2008). Meta-analysis of randomized, controlled treatment trials for pediatric obsessive-compulsive disorder. *Journal of Child Psychology and Psychiatry, 49,* 489–498.

Watts, R. (2000). Adlerian counseling: A viable approach for contemporary practice. *Texas Counseling Association Journal, 28*(1), 11–23.

Watts, R. (2003). Adlerian therapy as a relationship constructivist approach. *The Family Journal, 11,* 139–147.

Watts, R. E., & Pietrzak, D. (2000). Adlerian "encouragement" and the therapeutic process of solution-focused brief therapy. *Journal of Counseling and Development, 78,* 442–447.

Webb, L., Lemberger, M., & Brigman, G. (2008). Student success skills: A review of a school counselor intervention influenced by individual psychology. *Journal of Individual Psychology, 64,* 339–352.

Webster-Stratton, C., & Herman, K. C. (2010). Disseminating Incredible Years series early-intervention programs: Integrating and sustaining services between school and home. *Psychology in the Schools, 47,* 36–54.

Weiner, I. B. (1992). *Psychological disturbance in adolescence* (3rd ed.). New York: Wiley.

Weiner, I. B., & Bornstein, R. F. (2009). *Principles of psychotherapy: Promoting evidence-based psychodynamic practice.* New York: Wiley.

Weiss, B., Catron, T., Harris, V., & Phung, T. M. (1999). The effectiveness of traditional child psychotherapy. *Journal of Clinical and Consulting Psychology, 67,* 82–94.

Weist, M. D. (2005). Fulfilling the promise of school-based mental health: Moving towards a public health promotion approach. *Journal of Abnormal Child Psychology, 33,* 735–741.

Weisz, J. R., Sandler, I. N., Durlak, J. A., & Anton, S. A. (2005). Promoting and protecting youth mental health through evidence-based prevention and treatment. *American Psychologist, 60,* 628–648.

Weisz, J. R., Weiss, B., Han, S. S., Granger, D. A., & Morton, T. (1995). Effects of psychotherapy with children and adolescents revisited: A meta-analysis of treatment study outcomes. *Psychological Bulletin, 117,* 450–468.

Welfel, E. R. (2006). *Ethics in counseling & psychotherapy: Standards, research, and emerging issues* (3rd ed.). Belmont, CA: Thomson.

Wellman, H. M., & Lagattuta, K. H. (2000). Developing understanding of mind. In S. Baron-Cohen, H. Tager-Flusber, & D. J. Cohen (Eds.), *Understanding other minds: Perspectives from developmental cognitive neuroscience* (2nd ed., pp. 21–49). New York: Oxford University Press.

Wells, A., & Sembi, S. (2004). Metacognitive therapy for PTSD: A preliminary investigation of a new brief treatment. *Journal of Behavior Therapy & Experimental Psychiatry, 35,* 307–318.

Wickers, F. (1988). The misbehavior reaction checklist. *Elementary School Guidance and Counseling, 23*(1), 70–74.

Wicks-Nelson, R., & Israel, A. C. (2003). *Behavior disorders of childhood* (5th ed.). Upper Saddle River, NJ: Prentice Hall.

Wilcoxon, S. A., Norem, K., & Magnuson, S. (2005). Supervisees' contributions to lousy supervision. *Journal of Professional Counseling: Practice, Theory, and Research, 33*(2), 31–49.

Wood, A. (2003). Alfred Adler's treatment as a form of brief therapy. *Journal of Contemporary Psychotherapy, 33,* 287–301.

Worden, J. W. (1991). *Grief counseling and grief therapy: A handbook for the mental health practitioner* (2nd ed.). New York: Springer.

Wubbolding, R. E. (2000). *Reality therapy for the 21st century.* Philadelphia: Brunner-Routledge.

Wubbolding, R. E. (2004). Professional school counselors and reality therapy. In B. Erford (Ed.), *Professional school counseling: A handbook of theories, programs, and practices* (pp. 211–218). Austin, TX: CAPS.

Wubbolding, R. E. (2007). Glasser Quality School. *Group Dynamics, Theory, Research, and Practice, 11,* 253–261.

Wubbolding, R. E. (2009). Applying reality therapy approaches in schools. In. R. W. Christner & R. B. Mennuti (Eds.), *School-based mental health: A practitioner's guide to comparative practices* (pp. 225–250). New York: Routledge.

Wubbolding, R. E. (2011). Reality therapy theory. In D. Capuzzi, & D. R. Gross (Eds.), *Counseling and psychotherapy: Theories and interventions* (5th ed., pp. 263–286). Alexandria, VA: American Counseling Association.

Wubbolding, R. E., Brickell, J., Imhof, L., Kim, R. I., Lojk, L., & Al-Rashidi, B. (2004). Reality therapy: A global perspective. *International Journal for the Advancement of Counselling, 26,* 219–228.

Yarbrough, J. L., & Thompson, C. L. (2002). Using single-participant research to assess counseling approaches on children's off-task behavior. *Professional School Counseling, 5,* 308–314.

Ziffer, J. M., Crawford, E., & Penney-Wietor, J. (2007). The boomerang bunch: A school-based multifamily group approach for students and their families recovering from parental separation and divorce. *Journal for Specialists in Group Work, 32,* 154–164.

Zins, J. E., Weissberg, R. P., Wang, M. C., & Walberg, H. J. (Eds.). (2004). *Building academic success on social and emotional learning: What does the research say?* New York: Teachers College Press.

Index

ABC Model, 268
Academic Competence Evaluation Scales
(ACES), 321
Accommodation, 53
Accountability, 307
academic achievement focus and, 8, 43,
307–308
accountability, definition of, 308–309
case study (AB) design and, 311–312,
312 (figure)
clinical significance, determination of,
315, 318–319
entire student population, services for,
329–330
evidence-based interventions, selection of,
325–326
existing data, utilization of, 323
formal effectiveness measures
and, 309–323
goal attainment scaling and, 319–323,
320 (table), 322 (figure)
intervention-education outcome linkage
and, 326
measurable outcomes and, 21, 43
MEASURE assessment model and, 329

multiple-baseline designs and, 314–315,
316–317 (figure)
percentage of nonoverlapping data and,
315, 318–319, 318 (figure)
premeasures/postmeasures and, 309–310
program effectiveness evaluation and, 328–329
program-level accountability and, 324–330
reversal (ABAB) design and, 312–314,
313 (figure)
school counseling services and, 20–21, 308
school psychology services and, 19, 308
school system needs, appropriate services
and, 329
single-case designs and, 310–315
time allocation considerations and, 326–328,
327 (table)
Achievement motivation, 24
Action stage, 36
Active Parenting programs, 120
Adaptive coping, 130
Adelman, H. S., 326
Adler, A., 102, 104, 117, 118
Adlerian approaches to counseling, 91, 101–102
acting-as-if technique and, 114
Active Parenting programs and, 120
Adler's theory, principles of, 102–106

404

About the Authors

Robyn S. Hess is a professor and chair of the Department of School Psychology at the University of Northern Colorado. She earned her doctorate in school psychology in 1993 and her M.S. in counseling psychology in 1987. Dr. Hess blends her experiences as a counselor, school psychologist, and academician together to provide a scholarly yet practical approach to understanding counseling and mental health promotion within schools. She has published both nationally and internationally in the areas of culturally responsive assessment and intervention strategies, coping and stress in children and adolescents, and school completion among high-risk youth. Her teaching assignments over the last 17 years have included introductory counseling practica and children's mental health. Dr. Hess is a licensed psychologist and school psychologist in the state of Colorado. She is also board certified in the area of school psychology by the American Board of Professional Psychology.

Sandy Magnuson received her master's degree in elementary school counseling at Southwest Missouri State University in 1983. Her doctoral work in counselor education was completed at the University of Alabama. After teaching in counselor education programs in Alabama, Texas, and Colorado, Dr. Magnuson returned to the wonderful world of elementary school counseling at University Schools in Greeley, Colorado. She retired in 2010. During her career as a counselor educator and school counselor, she was committed to active participation in school counseling organizations and her own continuing education and supervision. She also conducted research related to development of counselors across the professional lifespan and supervision of counselors. Dr. Magnuson has authored over 60 articles that have been published in professional journals. She is a licensed professional counselor and licensed school counselor in the state of Colorado as well as an approved supervisor and clinical member of the American Association for Marriage and Family Therapy.

Linda Beeler currently serves as core faculty in the school counseling specialization for the Department of Counselor Education at Capella University. She earned her Ph.D. in counselor education and supervision from the University of Northern Colorado in 2001 and began working in the public schools at that time. She has carved a niche for herself in working with high-needs and at-risk youth and has also been actively involved in crisis intervention work in the schools. An additional area of focus for Dr. Beeler is in the supervision of current school counselors and school counselors-in-training. She holds the approved clinical supervisor credential.

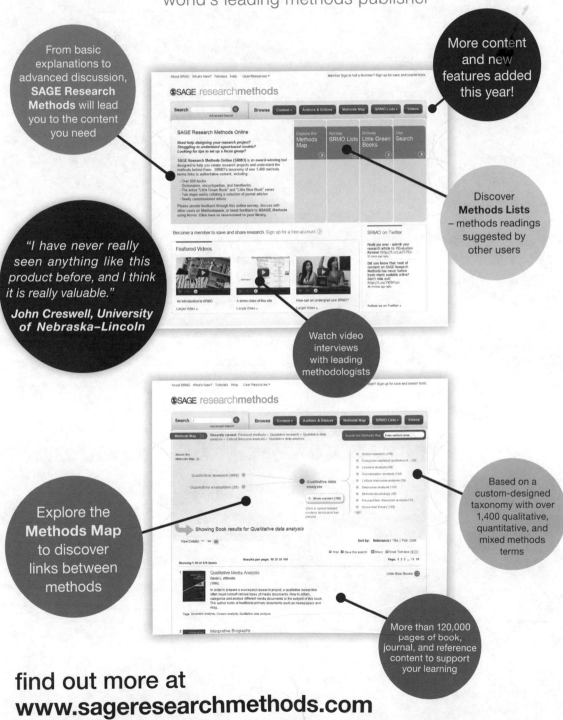